California

A LITERARY CHRONICLE

Edited, with Commentaries, by

W. STORRS LEE

Illustrations by W. Ralph Merrill

FUNK & WAGNALLS

NEW YORK

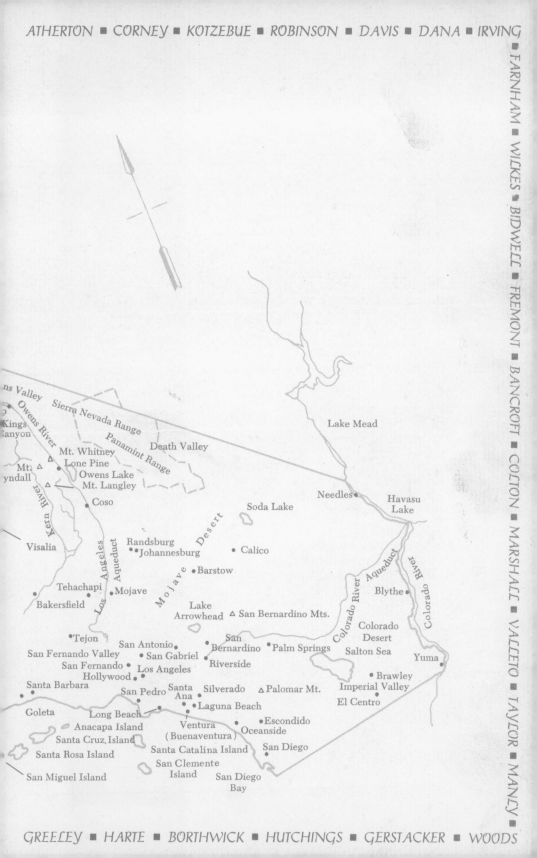

FARNHAM • WILKES • BIDWELL • FREMONT • BANCROFT • COLTON • MARSHALL • VALLEJO • TAYLOR • MANLY

ns Valley
Owens River
Kings
Canyon
Sierra Nevada Range
Panamint Range
Death Valley
Lake Mead
Mt. Whitney
Lone Pine
Owens Lake
Mt. Langley
Mt.
yndall
Coso
Needles
Havasu
Lake
Soda Lake
Kern River
Visalia
Randsburg
Johannesburg
Calico
Mojave Desert
Los Angeles Aqueduct
Barstow
Colorado River Aqueduct
Tehachapi
Mojave
Blythe
Colorado River
Bakersfield
Lake
Arrowhead
△ San Bernardino Mts.
Colorado
Desert
Salton Sea
Yuma
Tejon
San Antonio
San
Bernardino
Palm Springs
San Fernando Valley
San Gabriel
Riverside
Brawley
San Fernando
Los Angeles
Imperial Valley
Hollywood
El Centro
Santa Barbara
Santa
Ana
Silverado
△ Palomar Mt.
San Pedro
Goleta
Long Beach
Laguna Beach
Anacapa Island
Ventura
Escondido
Santa Cruz, Island
(Buenaventura)
Oceanside
Santa Rosa Island
Santa Catalina Island
San Diego
San Miguel Island
San Clemente
Island
San Diego
Bay

CALIFORNIA

A Literary Chronicle

BOOKS BY W. STORRS LEE

Hawaii: A Literary Chronicle
Maine: A Literary Chronicle

The Islands
The Great California Deserts
The Sierra
Canal Across a Continent
God Bless Our Queer Old Dean
The Strength to Move a Mountain
Yankees of Connecticut
Green Mountains of Vermont
Town Father
Stagecoach North
Father Went to College

A Vanishing America (Contributor)
Bread Loaf Anthology (Editor)
Footpath in the Wilderness (Editor)

TO

the Berkeley trio
Gretchen, Eleanor, and Constance,
distinguished educators and authors,
superior hostesses,
indefatigable travelers
and good Samaritans all

Contents

Foreword   xvii

   I. JUAN RODRÍGUEZ CABRILLO   1
       Into the Land of Valleys

  II. SIR FRANCIS DRAKE   9
       New Albion—In the Name of Her Majesty

 III. SEBASTIÁN VIZCAÍNO   16
       Heathens for the Harvest

 IV. EUSEBIO FRANCISCO KINO   21
       Cowboy in Cassocks

  V. JUAN CRESPI   28
       Elusive Monterey

 VI. FRANCISCO PALÓU   34
       No Use to Ring the Bells

VII. JUAN BAUTISTA DE ANZA   41
       Across the Desert in a Snowstorm

VIII.   FRANCISCO PALÓU   48
        Triumphal Entry

 IX.   GEORGE VANCOUVER   53
        From the British Point of View

  X.   RICHARD J. CLEVELAND   61
        The Battle of San Diego

 XI.   GERTRUDE ATHERTON   69
        Suitor from St. Petersburg

XII.   PETER CORNEY   78
        In Quest of Furs

XIII.   OTTO VON KOTZEBUE   85
        The Blessings of Russian Civilization

XIV.   ALFRED ROBINSON   90
        Commerce in the Cloisters

 XV.   WILLIAM HEATH DAVIS   101
        A Million Cattle—More or Less

XVI.   RICHARD HENRY DANA   112
        Into a Christian Country

XVII.   WASHINGTON IRVING   118
        Most Disgraceful Expedition

XVIII. ZENAS LEONARD   123
        A Truly Desperate Situation

 XIX.   THOMAS JEFFERSON FARNHAM   129
        A Bow to Bureaucracy

 XX.   CHARLES WILKES   134
        More Vices Than Virtues

XXI.   JOHN BIDWELL   141
        First American Emigrant Train

XXII. JOHN CHARLES FRÉMONT   149
      Snowbound in the Sierra

XXIII. HUBERT HOWE BANCROFT   158
      The Bear Flag Filibusters

XXIV. WALTER COLTON   163
      Merry-making Magistrate

XXV. JAMES WILSON MARSHALL   172
      Something Shining in a Ditch

XXVI. MARIANO GUADALUPE VALLEJO   177
      At Six Dollars an Ounce

XXVII. BAYARD TAYLOR   184
      Great Day for California

XXVIII. WILLIAM LEWIS MANLY   192
      Good-bye Death Valley

XXIX. DANIEL B. WOODS   200
      We Made Ten Cents Today

XXX. WILLIAM TAYLOR   206
      Preaching Don't Pay Here

XXXI. FRIEDRICH GERSTÄCKER   214
      The Bull Fight at Mission Dolores

XXXII. JAMES M. HUTCHINGS   221
      The Discovery of Yosemite

XXXIII. J. D. BORTHWICK   228
      Tallyho for Hangtown

XXXIV. HARRIS NEWMARK   234
      Pueblo of the Angels

XXXV. BRET HARTE   242
      Tennessee's Partner

XXXVI.   HORACE GREELEY   251
         One of the Finest Drives on Earth

XXXVII. J. ROSS BROWNE   256
         The Inmates of Strawberry Flat

XXXVIII. HELEN HUNT JACKSON   264
         Señora Moreno

XXXIX.   CLARENCE KING   271
         Two Against Mount Tyndall

XL.   ARTEMUS WARD   279
         Here to Amuse People

XLI.   MARK TWAIN   285
         No Better Place to Die Than This

XLII.   Alta California   290
         Stand and Deliver!

XLIII.   OSCAR LEWIS   295
         Over the Hump

XLIV.   SAMUEL BOWLES   305
         Golden Pathway to the Golden Gate

XLV.   AMBROSE BIERCE   310
         Satirist at Large

XLVI.   CHARLES NORDHOFF   314
         Big Trees of the Big River Country

XLVII.   WALT WHITMAN   323
         Song of the Redwood Tree

XLVIII. ISABELLA LUCY BIRD   329
         The Trail to Tahoe

XLIX.   KATE DOUGLAS WIGGIN   337
         Paradise on Earth

L. JOHN MUIR 341
Storms Are Fine Speakers

LI. ROBERT LOUIS STEVENSON 347
The Silence of Silverado

LII. MARY AUSTIN 355
They Steered a Course by the Stars

LIII. JOAQUIN MILLER 362
In San Francisco, and other poems

LIV. ROBERT FROST 368
Once by the Pacific, and A Peck of Gold

LV. LINCOLN STEFFENS 370
The Privileged Vices of Berkeley

LVI. JOHN R. SPEARS 378
Twenty-mule-team Traffic

LVII. RUDYARD KIPLING 388
Three Stories Underground

LVIII. HILDEGARDE HAWTHORNE 392
Hoop-la for L.A.

LIX. HENRY G. TINSLEY 397
The Randsburg Rush

LX. EDWIN MARKHAM 404
A Mendocino Memory, and other poems

LXI. FRANK NORRIS 410
To the Bitter End

LXII. JACK LONDON 418
From Out of the Fog

LXIII. GELETT BURGESS 428
Hyde Street Grip

LXIV.   CHARLES CALDWELL DOBIE   431
        Forty-eight Hours of Red Terror

 LXV.   WILL IRWIN   440
        The City That Was

LXVI.   SINCLAIR LEWIS   446
        New Fountain of Youth

LXVII. E. ROSCOE SHRADER   454
        A Ditch in the Desert

LXVIII. GEORGE STERLING   465
        Exposition Ode

LXIX.   HARRIET MONROE   469
        Morning of Creation

LXX.   UPTON SINCLAIR   472
        This Land of Hope

LXXI.   J. SMEATON CHASE   477
        Palm Springs—by Candlelight

LXXII. ROBINSON JEFFERS   483
        Point Pinos and Point Lobos, and other poems

LXXIII. WILLIAM SAROYAN   486
        A Raisin in Every Pot

LXXIV. JOHN STEINBECK   493
        A Great Sorrow on the Land

LXXV.   DONALD CULROSS PEATTIE   498
        The Smile of Mojave

LXXVI. GEORGE R. STEWART   505
        The Spitcat

LXXVII. MAX MILLER   512
        I Like Hollywood

Contents

LXXVIII. STANTON A. COBLENTZ   519
              Land's End, and other poems

LXXIX.   EUGENE BURDICK   523
              Three Californias

LXXX.   REMI A. NADEAU   530
              American in the Making

          KEY DATES IN CALIFORNIA ANNALS   535

Foreword

The citizenry of every state is inclined toward a little braggadocio on the merits of its productivity, its dimensions, its scenic wonders, its untainted traits of character, its place in history. Bay Staters are not about to permit anyone to forget their Pilgrims, Bunker Hill, or The Hub; for Hoosiers no country holds quite the charm of the Wabash, no corn grows quite as straight and tall as Indiana corn, no poet quite measures up to James Whitcomb Riley; Louisianans boast as ardently of their Mississippi, their Mardi Gras, their Sugar Bowl, and cotton-fields; and nothing anywhere in the United States of America is as big, beautiful and unbeatable as a Texan's conception of his dominion.

Californians, however, are relatively conservative in estimating the glories and triumphs of their state. They can afford to be. In the Golden State it is unnecessary to exaggerate to point up a bigness; proportions speak for themselves. The landscape, history, statistics, and the evaluations of impartial scouts from the country east of the Sierra put things into perspective without complementary aggrandizement.

The spread of Los Angeles, for example, need not be trumped up: a tourist learns for himself how large the megalopolis is merely from speeding on freeways for half a day trying to get beyond reach of the city's tentacles. Peroration on the wealth of the state is superfluous: neon signs of the Bank of America and the presence of two monetary establishments in every boom town block say enough. No one has to enlarge upon the rate of population expansion: on the outskirts of almost any urban center can be found a sprawling development that was not there yesterday. The scale of California's agriculture need not be magnified to impress even a Midwest planter accustomed to mile-long rows: he can see for himself patches of grain in the Central Valley that stretch to the horizon, fields so enormous that they are seeded by airplane, fertilized by airplane, sprayed by airplane, and harvested by Goliath-like contraptions as large as the Lone Star Stater's hyperbole.

Nor does a historical or descriptive recital on California have to be written pretentiously. The drama of reality is sufficiently stirring to discourage overstatement: the Spanish missions, the forty-niners, the gold rush, the Great San Francisco Fire, twenty million orange trees, the Colorado flood that created an inland sea, canneries that gulp peaches and tomatoes by the carload, Hollywood, cities bristling with backyard oil derricks, World War II convoys so long that their mere passage through the Golden Gate took the best part of a day or night, the mothball fleet of Suisun Bay, the high cost of high living in Beverly Hills, the maze of aerial freeways cutting across metropolitan skylines, the budget of the University of California, the state with the greatest concentration of population.

California has always been reconciled to extravagant measure; both bounty and disaster have come in large portion. Even Nature performs there with grandiosity. California's deserts are the driest; its interior valleys the longest, broadest, and most fertile; its river floods the most overwhelming; its mountain snows the deepest; its spring wildflower displays the most dazzling; its giant trees the largest and most ancient; its coastline the ruggedest; its one great natural harbor the most commodious on the continent; and its Sierra Nevada Range the most formidable physical obstruction in midcontinental North America.

Natural spectacle and superlative are so commonplace in the state that they seem to inspire spectacular effort and superlative accomplishment. Californians do things in a big way compulsively. They have never adapted themselves to the halfway measure, never explored the path of moderation. Having set a course, they go all out. Theirs is a land of prodigality, of superabundance, of *excess* and of passion for *progress*. The only halting epoch in California history came during the Mexican occupation, before the Americans usurped the land.

Toward the end of that halting period, in the first half of last century, almost anything could have happened to California. With a little well-directed military assertion at the right time, it might have become a permanent Spanish dependency, an English colony, or a Russian colony. It might even have been turned into a Little Africa, if a movement in the United States Congress to transport thousands of liberated slaves to the West instead of to Liberia had taken hold. It might have become the panhandle of the Mexican Republic, or an independent nation. Certainly as much chance as statesmanship went into bringing that stretch of Pacific frontier into the Union. But once it was linked to the United States, it sprang to life, entered a race as if to make up for the head start of the mother states, gathered momentum, and in little more than a century not only caught up but was setting a pace for the rest of the nation.

California developed into a state of excess—excess in rapidity of growth, excess in production, excess in wealth, excess in readiness to adopt new fads, freedoms, and faiths, new industrial enterprise, new educational experiment. And haste was imperative: Californians had no time to lose. Excess became an addiction and a doctrine, a doctrine so alluring that it drew millions into the fold from every part of the country and converted to the faith more millions who could not transplant themselves physically to the booming commonwealth.

For almost a century a whimsical political aphorism belonged to the state in the diagonally opposite corner of the country: "As goes Maine, so goes the rest of the nation." It became obsolescent there. The aphorism more properly belonged to California, where the original limited purport could be dropped and it could be applied to a national culture and social bearing: "As goes California, so goes the rest of the nation." Whether or not Americans approved of the leadership, they were going the way of California, the way of excess, of explosive growth, expansive motivation, impetuous conviction, immoderate haste.

Inevitably the spirit of excess crept into the creation of California's literature. Everyone who reached the Golden West, from the days of the explorers, trappers, and miners on down to the era of the fruit canners, freeway builders, showmen, and hippies, wanted to talk about it and write about it. At one time or another the state, too, drew most of the literary commentators of the East for a reconnaissance, and they also wrote about it, until California possessed a formidable body of literature.

This volume is a sampling of that accumulation—the story of the state as told by California writers and writers of California. The book is not so much an appraisal of the authors as their appraisal of the state; they speak for California. It is a life scenario or biography of California as revealed by the real recording secretaries of the state's past, the eyewitnesses to major events, participants in the events, or as evaluated by men and women who, with the advantage of hindsight, later reconstructed them.

Unfortunately no volume of reasonable dimensions could contain satisfactory specimens of all the major writers of the state; the roster is far too long. In fact, the final text for this collection was reduced from an original compilation more than twice as long. Favorite writers, accordingly, are missing. Suitability of material to the chronology, as well as literary distinction, had to be taken into consideration in making the selections. Priority was given to primary sources; factual writing was favored over fiction; and in a few instances omissions were necessary because of reprint restrictions.

Contrary to appearance, it is not an anthology in the usual sense. The book has continuity and it is intended to be read in sequential order. Anyone who peruses the selections from beginning to end will get at least a panoramic impression of the emergence of California from disputed Spanish outpost and Mexican province to American frontier, an expanding region of great mineral, agricultural, and industrial wealth, and finally a leader among states, the one with the largest population.

Both the great writers and the less great are given a voice in this collective appraisal of California, each in his preferred literary medium —essay, letter, historical interpretation, journal, poetry, diary, fiction. From the reservoir of buried, forgotten, or long out-of-print material, we have attempted to restore to circulation at least a few selections. Many of the distinguished writers of earlier generations are virtually unknown to the current generation. Through examples of their work we present to student and general reader alike what we hope will be accepted as an invitation to investigate them further and reevaluate their contribution to the literature of the state.

In order to keep the length of the collection within bounds, it was not possible to include all selections in their entirety, but for each author we have endeavored to reprint an extract of sufficient length to demonstrate his flavor, style, and message. Expendable amplifications and material not pertinent to an immediate subject have been excised, and the excision indicated by ellipses, which may represent deletion of a few words from a sentence (. . .), deletion of much longer passages (. . . .), or occasional transposition of topical material. Since most of the selections are taken from the body of a longer piece, ellipsis marks at the beginning and end of a selection are omitted.

Represented in the text are samples of English covering over four centuries, and in that period grammatical usage has been modified so materially that old forms can make for halting reading or even convey unintended meaning. Accordingly, in some of the older documents spelling, punctuation, and obsolete expressions have been modernized; interminable paragraphs have been broken into more digestible nuggets; obscure and outmoded abbreviations have been written out. However, this is a compromise at best; we have made no attempt to dress the selections to grammatical conformity, and where quaintness of spelling or currently unacceptable usage contribute to the character of the composition, they have been retained.

W. S. L.

I

Juan Rodríguez Cabrillo

Three quarters of a century before British Pilgrims were timidly exploring the New England shores on the Atlantic side of the North American continent, Spanish pilgrims on the Pacific side were boldly scouting not only the coast of New Spain but also its deep interior. New Spain included California.

The penetration into California by the Spaniards was a by-product of the conquest of Mexico by Hernándo Cortés in 1521. After the fall of the Aztec empire, the conquistadores fanned out north and south in an effort to enlarge and consolidate their American dominions. From Mexico the military probings extended into Guatemala and El Salvador, as far south as Ecuador and Peru, and north across the Rio Grande, the Gila, and the Colorado rivers. Exploration on land was supported by exploration at sea. The soldiers and sailors accompanying these expeditions were the first white men to set foot on Alta California.

Among the more zealous officers conducting these exploits for Cortés was Juan Rodríguez Cabrillo (d. 1543). After reconnoitering the west coast of South America, in 1541 he helped organize a new maritime expedition to investigate the shores to the north—a fated venture, for he met his end before the mission was half completed.

Late in June 1542, Cabrillo sailed from Navidad, some three hundred miles north of Acapulco, with two small vessels in his charge. Delayed by contrary winds and frequent landings, he did not reach

San Diego Bay until the middle of September. From there he explored superficially the full length of the California coast and made the first contact with coastal Indians.

Harassed by almost continuous gales, cold fog, and mountainous seas, Cabrillo missed a number of important landmarks, including San Francisco Bay, but he did learn the nature of the coast, with its infrequent anchorages; he landed at many Indian villages, sighted and named the Sierra Nevada Range, mapped most of the offshore islands, and took possession of all he saw in the name of the king of Spain. The fact that extensive inland explorations were being conducted simultaneously is evident from the repeated reports of savages that bearded men, clothed and armed like the Spaniards, had been seen in the interior.

Although Cabrillo may have dictated the first part of the log covering his adventures, most of the text was probably composed by his pilot, Bartolomé Ferrelo, who, as a professional navigator, was naturally more interested in recording observations on weather, winds, and seamanship than on the land and its inhabitants. And accuracy was not one of his better traits. Geographical descriptions, like those of the Sierra Nevada, were sometimes utterly fanciful, and recorded positions so erroneous as to confuse generations of later explorers. Then, to add to the confusion, most of the place names fixed by Cabrillo were subsequently ignored and new ones substituted. The log is prosaic and halting; and frequent use of the third-person "they," instead of "we," to designate participants, is distracting; but as the first description of the California coast and its occupants, it is nevertheless a significant document.

Into the Land of Valleys

All the land from the extremity of [Lower] California . . . is sandy like a sea beach. Here [just north of Agua Caliente] begins land of another character, as it is a country of beautiful vegetation and better appearance, like orchards. Sunday on the 17th day of [September, 1542] . . . they found a good port, well enclosed . . . [which] was called San Mateo [San Diego]. It is a good country in appearance. There are large cabins, and herbage like that of Spain, and the land is high and rugged. They saw herds of animals like flocks of sheep, which went together by the hundred or more [probably antelope], which resembled in appearance and movement Peruvian sheep, and with long wool. . . .

They were in this port until Saturday, the 23rd of said month [when] they departed . . . and sailed along the coast. . . . They saw very beautiful valleys and groves, and a country flat and rough . . . and on land great signal smokes. . . . The Thursday following they . . . discovered a port enclosed and very good, to which they gave the name of San Miguel [San Pedro] . . . and after anchoring in it, they went on shore, which had people, three of whom remained, and all the others fled. To these they gave presents; and they said by signs that in the interior had passed people like the Spaniards. They manifested much fear. . . .

The next day in the morning they entered further within the port, which is large, with the boat, and brought away two boys, who understood nothing by signs, and they gave them both shirts and immediately sent them away. And the following day in the morning there came to the ship three large Indians, and by signs they said that there were traveling in the interior men like us with beards, and clothed and armed like those of the ships, and they made signs that they carried crossbows and swords, and made gestures with the right arm as if they were throwing lances, and went running in a posture as if riding on horseback, and made signs that they killed many of the native Indians, and for this they were afraid. This people were well disposed and advanced; they go covered with the skins of animals. . . .

Saturday, the 7th of October, at daybreak they arrived at the islands which they named San Salvador [Santa Cruz] and La Vittoria [Anacapa], and they anchored off one of them and went with the boat on shore . . . and as the boat came near there issued a great quantity of Indians from among the bushes and grass, yelling and dancing and making signs that they should come ashore; and they saw that the women were running away, and from the boats they made signs that they should have no fear, and immediately they assumed confidence and laid down on the ground their bows and arrows, and they launched a good canoe in the water, which held eight or ten Indians, and they came to the ships.

They gave them beads and little presents, with which they were delighted, and they presently went away. The Spaniards afterward went ashore and were very secure, they and the Indian women and all. Here an old Indian made signs to them that on the mainland men were journeying clothed and with beards like the Spaniards. . . .

They held on their voyage along the coast about ten leagues, and there were always many canoes, for all the coast is very populous, and many Indians are continually coming aboard the ships, and they pointed out to us the villages and named them by their names. . . . They said that inland there were many towns, and much maize at three days' distance . . . and also there were many cows [probably bison]. . . .

Wednesday, the 18th . . . they stood off from the shore and discovered two islands [Santa Rosa and San Miguel] . . . ten leagues from the continent; they are called las Islas de San Lucas. . . . They were in these islands until the following Wednesday, because it was very stormy. . . . The one which was more to the windward . . . has a very good port, so that from all the storms of the sea no damage will be suffered by those within its shelter; they called it La Posesion.

This day [and for six more days and nights] they advanced little, as the wind was not favorable . . . beating about from one side to the other with foul winds. . . . Nor did they anchor, for the coast was very bold. They found during this month on this coast the weather as in Spain, from 34° and upward, and with much cold mornings and evenings, and with storms, dark and cloudy weather, and the air heavy. Wednesday at midnight, on the 1st day of November, standing off, a heavy wind from the north northwest struck them, which . . . by the dawn of day freshened so much that they could do no less than seek shelter, and they took shelter under Cabo de Galera, and anchored there and went on shore, and because there was a large town which they call Xexo, and wood did not appear to be very much at hand, they agreed to go to Pueblo de las Sardinas [Goleta], because there water and wood were very near and accessible. . . .

Their houses [are] round and covered very well down to the ground; they go covered with skins of many kinds of animals; they eat acorns and a grain which is as large as maize and is white, of which they make dumplings; it is good food. They say that inland there is much maize and that men like us are traveling there. . . . They have in their villages large public squares, and they have an enclosure like a circle, and around the enclosure they have many blocks of stone fastened in the ground . . . and in the middle of the enclosures they have many sticks of timber driven into the ground like masts, and very thick; and they have many pictures on these same posts, and we believe that they worship them, for when they dance they go dancing around the enclosure. . . .

They proceeded . . . running along the coast, and they found themselves at night off El Cabo de San Martin [Point Sur]. All the coast they passed this day is very bold; . . . there are mountains which rise to the sky and the sea bursts upon them. While sailing near the land it appears as if they would fall upon the ships; they are covered with snow to the summit. They gave them the name of las Sierra Nevadas. . . .

On the 23rd of the month, they approached on a backward course the islands of San Lucas, and one of them named La Posesion [San Miguel]. . . . While wintering in this Isla de Posesion, on the 3rd of January, 1543, departed from this present life Juan Rodríguez Cabrillo, captain of the said ships, from a fall which he had on the same island at the former time when they were there, by which he broke an arm near the shoulder . . . and he charged them much at the time of his death that they should not give up the discovery as far as possible of all that coast. They [re]named the island la Isla de Juan Rodríguez. . . .

The Indians of these islands are very poor. They are fishermen; they eat nothing but fish; they sleep on the ground; all their business and employment is to fish. In each house they say there are fifty souls. They live very swinishly; they go naked. They were in these islands . . . almost two months. . . . The weather was very tempestuous. . . .

The 12th . . . of February . . . they went to Puerto de las Sardinas [Goleta] to take in wood and other things necessary for their voyage, as they were not to be obtained on those islands. Wednesday, the 14th, they departed . . . not dar[ing] to remain longer there on account of the great swell of the sea. . . . After they had proceeded about a hundred leagues, they found the wind more violent and the sea high; and Thursday . . . the 22nd of February they again stood ashore to endeavor to reach Cabo de Pinos [Point Arena]. . . . In the middle of the night the wind suddenly shifted to the south southwest, and they ran to the west northwest. . . .

The 28th . . . toward night the wind freshened and . . . they ran this night [off the extreme northern coast of California] to the west northwest with much difficulty, and Thursday at daybreak the wind shifted to the southwest with great fury, and the seas came from all parts, which harassed them much, and broke over the ships, which, not having decks, if God should not succor them, they could not escape, and not being able to lay by, of necessity they ran aft northeast toward the land; and now, holding themselves for lost, they commended themselves to our Lady of Guadaloupe and made their wills, and ran thus until three o'clock in the afternoon with much fear and labor, for they saw that they were going to be lost, and already saw many signs of the land which was near, as small birds and logs very fresh, which floated from some rivers, although from the dark and cloudy weather the land did not appear.

At this hour the Mother of God succored them with the grace of her Son, and there came a very violent rainstorm from the north, which made them run all that night and the following day until sunset to the south, with the foresails lowered; and because there was a high sea from the south it broke over them each time by the prow, and passed over them as if over a rock, and the wind shifted to the northwest with great fury, so that it made them run until Saturday, the 3rd of March, to the southeast and to the east southeast, with such a high sea that it made them cry out without reserve that if God and His blessed Mother did not miraculously save them, they could not escape.

Saturday at noon the wind moderated and remained at the northwest, for which they gave many thanks to our Lord. They suffered also in provisions, as they had only biscuit, and that damaged. . . . This day in the evening they recognized Cabo de Pinos [Point Arena], and on account of the high sea which prevailed they could do no less than run along the coast on the return course in search of a port. They experienced much cold.

Monday, on the 5th day . . . of March, 1543, . . . they ran into the harbor of the island of San Salvador [Santa Cruz] on the southeast side; and the night before, coming with a violent tempest, with only two small foresails, the other ship disappeared, so that they suspected that the sea had swallowed it up, and they could not discover it any more. . . .

Thursday, the 8th . . . they departed from the island of San Salvador to stand in for the mainland in search of the other ship, and they proceeded to Pueblo de las Canoas [Buenaventura] and did not obtain news of the other ship; and here they took four Indians. The Friday following . . . they proceeded to the island of San Salvador and found no signs of their consort. Sunday, the 11th . . . they came near Puerto de San Miguel [San Pedro]; neither did they find here their consort nor any news of her; here they waited six days, and they took two boys to carry to New Spain for interpreters, and left certain signals in case the other ship should approach. . . .

The following Sunday they arrived off Bahia de San Mateo [San Diego] and found no more signs of the other ship. . . . Friday, on the 23rd . . . they arrived off Isle de Cedros [Cerros Island], and being there the following Monday, the 26th day of the said month, arrived the other ship off Isla de Cedros, at which they rejoiced much and gave many thanks to God; this ship put into La Isla de Juan Rodríguez [San Miguel] by night, passing over some breakers, so that they expected to be lost, and the mariners promised to go in procession naked to her church, and our Lady delivered them.

On Monday, the 2nd day of the month of April, they departed

from Isla de Cedros on their return to New Spain, because they did not have a supply of provisions to renew their attempt to discover the coast. They arrived in el Puerto de Navidad Saturday, the 14th . . . of April. Came as captain of the ships Bartolomé Ferrel, chief pilot of the said ships, in default of Juan Rodríguez Cabrillo, who died in Isla de la Posesion.

From "Voyage of Cabrillo," Appendix to Part I, Volume VII, *Report upon United States Geographical Surveys* (Washington: U.S. Government Printing Office, 1879).

II

Sir Francis Drake

Spain had posted its claim to a lion's share of the New World, but its great European rival, tenant of the British Isles, was not ready to concede the validity of that claim, and England had a champion itching to dispute it with guns, broadswords, and the fine art of piracy.

While William Shakespeare was creating masterpieces in make believe for the English stage, that champion, Sir Francis Drake (1540?–1596), was enacting almost as exciting real life drama on the high seas. During the long Elizabethan era, Drake stood out as the paragon among British warrior-adventurers, the sailor about whom seemed to center the mounting rivalry between England and Spain. His first encounter with these rivals on the Spanish Main had been a signal defeat. He barely escaped with his life, and devoted most of the remainder of it to putting the Spaniards in their places.

In 1572, with two small ships manned by only seventy-four men, Drake successively took the town of Nombre de Dios on the Isthmus of Panama, captured a ship in the harbor of Cartagena, burned Portobelo, crossed and recrossed the Isthmus to capture mule teams portaging tons of pilfered silver. The escapade established his reputation, and five years later he was off on another marauding expedition, with the secret blessings of Queen Elizabeth, to raid Spanish holdings on the Pacific coast of the New World.

Four of his ships were lost or forced to turn back before he completely cleared the Straits of Magellan. On the one remaining ship, the

Golden Hind, he proceeded north, plundered Valparaiso and many smaller settlements, cut loose the shipping at Callao, captured a rich Spanish treasure ship bound for Lima, and eventually returned to England with booty valued at two and a half million pounds.

He visited California on that expedition largely by accident. From the pillaged ports of South America he sailed up the coast in an unsuccessful search for a shortcut across the continent to the Atlantic. Damaged by storms, the *Golden Hind* was in dire need of repair, so Drake put in at the first haven he could find—Drake's Bay, a few miles north of the Golden Gate, though the location of his landing may always remain in dispute. The great admiral—called "General" by his men—was the first Englishman to disembark on California shores, and to spite the Spanish, lost no time in giving the land the Latin name for New England, *Nova Albion,* and in claiming it for his queen.

Though it is probable that one of the scribes accompanying Drake penned the account of the landing, he was the principal in the drama and it remains his story. It is presented here in modern English with contemporary spelling, rather than the Elizabethan English in which it was composed.

New Albion—In the Name of Her Majesty

The fifth day of June [1579], being in 43° toward the pole Arctic, we found the air so cold that our men, being grievously pinched with the same, complained of the extremity thereof, and the further we went the more cold increased upon us. Whereupon we thought it best for that time to seek the land, and did so, finding it not mountainous, but low plain land, and clad and covered over with snow, so that we drew back again without landing till we came within 38° toward the line, in which height it pleased God to send us into a fair and good bay with a good wind to enter the same.

In this bay we anchored, and the people of the country, having their houses close by the water's side, showed themselves unto us, and sent a present to our general. When they came unto us, they greatly wondered at the things that we brought, but our general,

Landing of Sir Francis Drake

according to his natural and accustomed humanity, courteously treated them and liberally bestowed on them necessary things to cover their nakedness, whereupon they supposed us to be gods and would not be persuaded to the contrary. The presents which they sent to our general were feathers and cauls [caps] of network.

The houses were digged round about with earth, and have from the uttermost brimness of the circle, clifts of wood set upon them, joining close together at the top like a spire steeple, which for reason of that closeness are very warm. Their beds are the ground with rushes strewed on it and lying about the house. [They] have a fire in the middle.

The men go naked; the women take bulrushes and comb them after the manner of hemp, and thereof make their loose garments, which, being knit about their middles, hang down about their hips, having also about their shoulders a skin of deer with the hair upon it. These women are very obedient and serviceable to their husbands.

After they were departed from us, they came and visited us the second time and brought with them feathers and bags of tobacco for presents. And when they came to the top of the hill, at the bottom whereof we had pitched our tents, they stayed themselves, where one appointed for the speaker wearied himself with making a long oration, which done, they left their bows upon the hill and came down with their presents.

In the meantime the women remaining on the hill tormented themselves lamentably, tearing their flesh from their cheeks, whereby we perceived that they were about a sacrifice. In the meantime our general with his company went to prayer and to reading of the Scriptures, at which exercise they were attentive and seemed greatly to be affected with it. But when they were come unto us, they restored again unto us those things which before we bestowed upon them.

The news of our being there, being spread through the country, the people that inhabited round about came down, and amongst them the king [chief] himself, a man of goodly stature and comely personage, with many other tall and warlike men, before whose coming were sent two ambassadors to our general to signify that their king was coming, in doing of which message, their speech was continued about half an hour.

This ended, they by signs requested our general to send something by their hand to their king as a token that his coming might be in peace, wherein our general having satisfied them, they returned with glad tidings to their king, who marched to us with a princely majesty, the people crying continually after their manner, and as they drew near unto us, so did they strive to behave themselves in their actions with comeliness.

In the forefront was a man of goodly personage who bore the scepter or mace before the king, whereupon hung two crowns, a less and a bigger, with three chains of a marvelous length. The crowns were of knit work, wrought artificially with feathers of divers colors; the chains were made of a bony substance, and few be the persons among them that are permitted to wear them; and of that number also the persons are stinted, as some ten, some twelve, etc.

Next unto him which bore the scepter was the king himself, with his guard about his person, clad with cony [rabbit] skins and other skins. After them followed the naked common sort of people everyone having his face painted, some with white, some with black, and other colors, and having in their hands one thing or another for a present, not so much as their children, but they also brought their presents.

In the meantime our general gathered his men together and marched within his fenced place, making against their approaching a very warlike show. They being trooped together in their order, and a general salutation being made, there was presently a general silence. Then he that bore the scepter before the king, being informed by another whom they assigned to that office, with a manly and lofty voice proclaimed that which the other spoke to him in secret, continuing half an hour, which ended, and a general *amen*, as it were, given, the king with the whole number of men and women (the children excepted) came down without any weapon, who, descending to the foot of the hill, set themselves in order.

In coming toward our bulwarks and tents, the scepter bearer began a song, observing his measures in a dance, and that with a stately countenance, whom the king with his guard and every degree of persons following, did in like manner sing and dance, saving only the women which danced and kept silence. The general permitted them to enter within our bulwark, where they continued their song and dance a reasonable time.

When they had satisfied themselves, they made signs to our general to sit down, to whom the king and divers others made several orations, or rather supplications, that he would take their province and kingdom into his hand and become their king, making signs that they would resign unto him their right and title to the whole land and become his subjects.

In which to persuade us the better, the king and the rest, with one consent and with great reverence, joyfully singing a song, did set the crown upon his head, enriched his neck with all their chains and offered unto him many other things, honoring him by the name of *Hioh,* adding thereunto, as it seemed, a sign of triumph, which thing our general thought not meet to reject, because he knew not what honor and profit it might be to our country.

Wherefore in the name and to the use of her Majesty, he took the scepter, crown and dignity of the said country into his hands, wishing that the riches and treasure thereof might so conveniently be transported to the enriching of her kingdom at home, as it aboundeth in the same.

The common sort of people, leaving the king and his guard with our general, scattered themselves, together with their sacrifices, among our people, taking a diligent view of every person; and such as pleased their fancy, which were the youngest, they, enclosing them about, offered their sacrifices unto them with lamentable weeping, scratching and tearing the flesh from their faces with their nails, whereof issued abundance of blood.

But we used signs to them of disliking this and stayed their hands from force, and directed them upward to the living God, whom only they ought to worship. They showed unto us their wounds and craved help of them at our hands, whereupon we gave them lotions, plasters and ointments, agreeable to the state of their griefs, beseeching God to cure their diseases.

Every third day they brought their sacrifices unto us, until they understood our meaning, that we had no pleasure in them, yet they would not be long absent from us, but daily frequented our company to the hour of our departure, which departure seemed so grievous unto them that their joy was turned into sorrow. They entreated us that being absent we would remember them and by stealth provided a sacrifice, which we misliked.

Our necessary business being ended, our general with his company traveled up into the country to their villages, where we found herds of deer by a thousand in a company, being most large and fat of body. We found the whole country to be a warren of a strange kind of connies, their bodies in bigness as be the Barbary connies, their heads as the heads of ours, the feet of a want [mole], and the tail of a rat, being of great length; under their chin on either side a bag, into the which she gathereth her meat when she hath filled her belly abroad. The people eat their bodies and make great account of their skins, for the king's coat was made of them.

Our general called this country *Nova Albion,* and that for two causes: the one in respect of the white banks and cliffs which lie toward the sea, and the other because it might have some affinity with our country in name, which sometime was so called. There is no part of earth here to be taken up wherein there is not a reasonable quantity of gold and silver.

At our departure hence our general set up a monument of our being there, as also of her Majesty's right and title to the same, namely a plate nailed upon a fair great post, whereupon was engraved her Majesty's name, the day and year of our arrival there, with the free giving up of the province and people into her Majesty's hands, together with her highness's picture and arms in a piece of sixpence of current English money under the plate, whereunder was also written the name of our general.

It seems that the Spaniards hitherto had never been in this part of the country, neither did ever discover the land by many degrees to the southward of this place.

From *The Principal Navigations, Voyages and Discoveries of the English Nation,* Richard Hakluyt (London: Bishop and Newberie, 1589).

III

Sebastián Vizcaíno

For want of higher worldly authority, nations had adopted the practice of appealing to the Pope for arbitration of international territorial disputes, and in response to a Spanish complaint, His Holiness, long before Drake's filibustering expedition, had made it unequivocally clear that the west coast of North America was a possession of Spain. The audacity of Sir Francis Drake, therefore, in sailing into Spanish waters and affixing an English title to a parcel of Spanish territory, was a grave affront.

Spain reacted by demonstrating renewed interest in the western bounds of the continent. Besides parrying British competition, Spain had two other major incentives: locating way stations for the galleons bringing cargoes of silks, velvets, ivory, and spices back from her expanding colonies in the Philippines; and gratifying the perennial interest of the Spanish Crown in acquiring divine blessings through drawing heathen souls to the Catholic faith—pagan California was an ideal field for the harvest of Christian converts.

On a return voyage from the Orient in 1584, Francisco de Gali discovered the great Japanese current that sped vessels northeastward to the general area of Cape Mendocino. Thereafter the galleons followed that route, though seamen dreaded the last leg down the coast through the fogs, the cold, and the tempests. Safe harbors had to be found on that stretch of coast. On his return from Manila to Acapulco in 1595 Sebastián Cermeno was ordered to make a search for "harbors in which galleons might take refuge." He lost his ship in the endeavor.

Finally in 1602 the merchant navigator Sebastián Vizcaíno (c.1550–c.1629) received orders from the Viceroy of Mexico, Gaspar de Zuniga, Count of Monterey, to discover "the harbors and bays of the coast of the South Sea as far as Cape Mendocino." He sailed from Acapulco on the most important mission yet.

If he was aware that Cabrillo had covered the same itinerary sixty years earlier, he gave no evidence of it. He renamed practically all of the places Cabrillo had previously visited, and this time the names stuck: Monterey, in honor of the Mexican Viceroy; Carmel, for the three Carmelite friars accompanying him; Santa Barbara, for the saint, on whose day—December 4—he anchored there; and a long list of others, including San Diego, which he acclaimed as "the best harbor in all the South Seas." He sailed past the Farallones on January 7, 1603, and on to Drake's Bay, which he reclaimed for Spain and renamed Puerto de los Reyes.

He had much more respect for the Indians of the Channel Islands than Cabrillo had shown, observed the proficiency of their Stone Age craftsmanship, noted their fine earthernware pots and jars, their mortars, pestles, grinding stones, and wheel-shaped stones, which later were to be gathered by the hundreds for display in the museums of the world. For the benefit of the public, Vizcaíno's yeomen prepared a full report of the voyage, but of equal interest is a letter the merchant venturer penned himself to the King of Spain, emphasizing and exaggerating exactly what he knew the monarch would like to hear, and hoping, of course, to be given appropriate rewards for the risks he had taken.

Heathens for the Harvest

In the past year of 1602 . . . I set out on the discovery of the coast of the South Sea with two ships, a *lancha* and a *barcoluengo*, with the requisite sailors and soldiers, armed and provisioned with everything necessary for a year. I sailed from the port of Acapulco . . . on the fifth day of May of said year; and in conformity with the order and instructions I had, I explored very diligently the whole coast, not leaving harbor, bay, island or bight without sounding and delineating it in accordance with the rules of good cosmography and the art of demarcation; for . . . I was accompanied by a cosmographer in whom confidence can be reposed and cunning in the matter of geographical computations, in order that he might put down and note in the most complete manner on map and chart the result of the examination. . . .

Among the ports of greater consideration which I discovered was one in thirty-seven degrees of latitude which I called Monterey. . . . It is all that can be desired for commodiousness and as a station for ships making the voyage to the Philippines. . . . This port is sheltered from all winds, while on the immediate coast there are pines from which masts of any desired size can be obtained, as well as live oaks and white oaks, rosemary, the vine, the rose of Alexandria, a great variety of game, such as rabbits, hares, partridges, and other sorts and species found in Spain . . . and flying birds of kinds differing from those to be found there.

This land has a genial climate, its waters are good, and it is very fertile—judging from the varied and luxuriant growth of trees and plants; for I saw some of the fruits, particularly chestnuts and acorns, which are larger than those in Spain. And it is thickly settled with people whom I found to be of gentle disposition, peaceable and docile, and who can be brought readily within the fold of the holy gospel and into subjection to the crown of Your Majesty.

Their food consists of seeds, which they have in abundance and variety, and of the flesh of game, such as deer, which are larger than cows, and bear, and of neat cattle and bisons and many other animals. The Indians are of good stature and fair complexion, the women being somewhat less in size than the men and of pleasing countenance.

The clothing of the people of the coast lands consists of the skins of the sea wolves abounding there, which they tan and dress better than is done in Castile; they possess also in great quantity flax like that of Castile, hemp and cotton, from which they make fishing lines and nets for rabbits and hares. They have vessels of pine wood, very well made, in which they go to sea with fourteen paddlemen of a side, with great dexterity—even in very stormy weather.

I was informed by them and by many others I met with in great numbers along more than eight hundred leagues of a thickly settled coast, that inland there are great communities, which they invited me to visit with them. They manifested great friendship for us and a desire for intercourse; were well affected toward the image of Our Lady which I showed to them, and very attentive to the sacrifice of the mass. They worship different idols . . . and they are well acquainted with silver and gold, and said that these were found in the interior.

And, as some port or place on this coast is to be occupied, none is so proper for the purpose as this harbor of Monterey. For the reasons given, this port can be made by ships on the return voyage from the Philippines; and if, after putting to sea, a storm be encountered, they need not as formerly run for Japan, where so many have been cast away and so much property lost; and had this port been known previously, Your Majesty would not have been so badly served.

The time of the occurrence of the dry season being known, from this place the interior can be reached and explored, such exploration promising rich returns; and proceeding along the coast, the remainder of it can be examined, for, although I went as far as the forty-second degree of latitude, this being the limit fixed in my instructions, the coast line trends onward to near Japan and the coast of Great China, which are but a short run away, and the same is the case with regard to Tartary and the famous city of Quinsay; and according to the reports I received, there are to be found very numerous peoples akin to those I have referred to—so the door will be opened for the propagation of the faith and the bringing of so many souls to a knowledge of God in order that the seed of the holy gospel may yield a harvest among all these heathen.

Eleven months were spent on the voyage, during which note-worthy hardships were suffered; and notwithstanding the un-happy experience of my men, who were all sick and of whom forty-two died before our return to the port of Acapulco, I again offer to serve Your Majesty in continuing this exploration, as I did on the voyage to California and on many others . . . in which it is shown I have spent the greater part of my fortune and of my health.

Yet the little of these remaining to me, as well as my person, is devoted to your royal service with the constancy, love and fidelity of a loyal vassal and servant of Your Majesty, who, I pray, will order the necessities of my men to be considered, and that they be rewarded with boons from those powerful royal hands. . . . God guard the royal and Catholic person of Your Majesty.

SEBASTIÁN VIZCAÍNO.

Mexico, 23d of May, 1603.

From *Publications of the Historical Society of Southern California*, Vol. II, Part I. Documents from the Sutro Collection. Translated by George Butler Griffin. (Los Angeles: Franklin Printing Company, 1891).

IV

Eusebio Francisco Kino

After the stunning defeat of her "Invincible Armada" in a futile attempt to invade and conquer England, Spain had fewer galleons to expend on missions of exploration. Half her fleet of 130 vessels was destroyed, along with the pick of her armed forces. Spain never recovered from the disaster, and for the next hundred and fifty years no attempt was made to follow up Viscaíno's discoveries.

In that century and a half, much that had been learned about California passed into oblivion. Since Baja California was separated from the mainland by a broad gulf, geographers everywhere assumed that all of California was a vast island, and so represented it on their maps. Spanish administrators in Mexico, accordingly, concluded that any colonization of California would have to be carried out by sea, and that would require a larger fleet than was at their disposal.

It took a humble but learned friar, Eusebio Francisco Kino (1644–1711), a professional "cosmographer" as well as missionary, to correct the geographical error. A native of the Austrian Tyrol, educated in Germany, he was one of the army of scholars who were being recruited from the Catholic countries of Europe to serve as Jesuit priests in heathen lands. Father Kino had hoped to be assigned to the Orient, but instead was sent in 1681 to Mexico, where he was put in charge of northern Sonora and southern Arizona, a sprawling area then known as Pimería Alta, extending north to the Gila River, west to the Gulf of Mexico and the lower Colorado River basin, incorporating many tribes and divisions of the Pima and Yuma Indians. He remained there almost a quarter of a century, using as his headquarters the mission of Nuestra Señora de los Dolores, which he founded.

From that outpost Kino established a chain of missions and rancherías as far north as Nogales and Tucson, in a wilderness that no white man was known to have visited in over a century. "The direct way to the hearts of the Indians," philosophized Kino, "is through their stomachs." He won their confidence and mass loyalty by feeding them, by importing new seed grains and immense herds of cattle, horses, and sheep; wherever he built a chapel, he laid out and stocked an enormous ranch to be operated by his converts. He was a rancher extraordinary, the first American cattle king.

Eventually the radius of his activity reached California, which he had been taught in Europe was a great island. As late as 1698 he referred to it as "the largest island in the world." Then he began to doubt the accuracy of his teachers. Not until he had personally ridden over desert that appeared on his maps as part of the Sea or Gulf of California was he convinced it was not an island.

Little of Kino's work was done in California; he explored only the southern limits and himself demarcated the line between Alta and Baja California; but he befriended Indian tribes, preached to them, and through creating the pattern for huge cattle-producing missions, laid the groundwork for the establishment of a line of coastal missions in California. Excerpts from his diaries, covering trips to the Colorado River area, reveal not only his affection for the Indians and their affection for him, but also his scholarly preoccupation with "cosmology."

Cowboy in Cassocks

On arriving at the great ranchería of the Rio Colorado, more than a thousand persons, assembled together, welcomed us; soon more than two hundred others came, and the following day more than three hundred, who came from the other side of this very large-volumed Rio Colorado . . . swimming across it.

We made them many talks about our holy faith, which were very well received, and they thanked us for them with very tender and loving words and talks, both in the Pima language and in the Yuma. . . . These talks, ours and theirs, lasted almost the whole afternoon and afterward until midnight, with very great pleasure to all. They begged of me to stay with them, if only one or two days, saying that many people were coming from up the river . . . and from down the river . . . but I dared not linger, lest I fail in coming to collect the cattle for California, as I had been charged, and as the branding time was near at hand.

On the seventeenth [of November, 1701] we set out from San Pedro westward for San Dionisio, a great ranchería at the confluence of the Rio Grande de Gila and the very large Rio Colorado; and having crossed the Rio Grande [Gila] on horseback by the only ford which it had in that vicinity, with a following of more than two hundred Yumas and Pimas . . . at nightfall we arrived in safety at San Dionisio, where also they received us with great affection.

On November the eighteenth, having said mass and crossed the Rio Grande again, and taking . . . a road which up to this time we had never traveled or entered, we set out directly by the most level roads toward the Quiquimas of this California Alta, in thirty-three degrees latitude, and rounded the head of the sea, which lay to the south of us, about three hundred Yuma and Pima Indians, mingled, small and great, accompanying us from San Pedro and San Dionisio.

They went in these great numbers on this occasion because, they having told me that the Quiquimas had an abundance of provisions, maize, beans, pumpkins, etc., and they being that year very short of provisions, I said to them that I was now going to the Quiquimas and would barter for and buy and give them provisions, beans, maize, etc., as I did; and all returned well-loaded with all kinds of provisions.

Having traveled about thirteen leagues through very level country, seeing to the eastward the very great sandy beach of the head of the Sea of California, and to the westward the banks of the very large-volumed Rio Colorado near-by, we arrived at sunset at the new ranchería, still of Yumas, which must have been about five hundred souls, and which we named Santa Ysabel. . . . All the people, although they were rather poor, welcomed us with all friendship and affability. . . .

On the nineteenth we set out for the first ranchería, and having arrived at midday we were received with all kindness, with many of their provisions, maize, beans and various kinds of pumpkins, etc., things which in the six days preceding we had not been able to procure. So great was the affection of these natives that with these provisions they came more than two leagues to meet and to welcome us.

While we alighted to receive the food, and to reciprocate with some little gifts and trifles, and to make them a talk on Christian doctrine and on the purposes of our coming, etc., the only Spanish servant who came in our company, on seeing so great a number of so many new people was so terrified that, without noticing it until a quarter of an hour after mounting our horses again, fled from us to the rear through fright, leaving us very disconsolate and very apprehensive lest he should go to give some false ill news that some great disaster had happened to us; and although immediately I dispatched in his pursuit the two best boys in the party, who came on the best mounts, they could not overtake him. . . .

In this first ranchería of these Quiquimas, with the messages and little gifts which we had sent them during the months preceding, they received us with much friendship, asking us that we should remain some days with them. We remained that day and half of the day following. . . . Through the interpreters, whom we brought in our following, we made them some talks on our holy faith, which were well received by the natives. Very many people were present from all the surrounding country, and to their principal chiefs we gave justices' staves, and to the principal one of all the nation we gave a captain's staff. We made a decent little house or bower in a pleasant field of maize, which they had just gathered, for here begin very fertile lands, well cultivated, and very good pasturage.

The natives greatly wondered at many of our things, for they had never seen nor heard of them. They wondered much at the

vestment in which mass is said, and at its curious sort of embroidery representing spring, and its skillfully woven flowers of different beautiful colors; and they would ask us to keep it on so that
those who continually came to visit us might have the pleasure of
seeing it.

Also it was a matter of much astonishment to them to see our
pack animals and mounts, for they had never seen horses or mules
or heard of them. And when the Yumas and Pimas who came with
us said to them that our horses could run faster than the most
fleet-footed natives, they did not believe it, and it was necessary
to put it to the test. Thereupon a cowboy from Nuestra Señora de
los Dolores saddled a horse and seven or eight of the most fleet-
footed Quiquima runners set out, and although the cowboy at
first purposely let them get a little ahead, and they were very
gleeful thereat, he afterward left them far behind and very much
astonished and amazed.

This afternoon the Coanopa nation came also, from the north
and from the northwest, with many provisions, maize, beans,
pumpkins and various other gifts, greatly desiring our trade, our
friendship and our holy faith, as a result of the message which
these days and months past they had received.

On the twentieth we set out from San Feliz, continuing our
course to the southwest, down the river . . . more than five
hundred souls accompanying us. . . . After a five leagues' journey we arrived at the crossing, where the two banks were
crowded with people. All of them at once brought us abundant
provisions and they made us a decent little house on this side; for
we determined to cross the river the following day, God willing.

The people on the other bank and from the west swam across
to this one on the east, bringing us their provisions in their
baskets, which were so large that each would hold a *fanega* or
more of maize or beans. And they made them float on the water of
the quiet, gentle river, after the fashion of and in imitation of
little canoes. All these Quiquima natives showed themselves most
affectionate toward us, in particular their most friendly captain. . . .

On November the twenty-first . . . having in the morning carried some long and dry timbers from the little wood very near by, the same captain of the Quiquimas greatly aiding us personally therein, and lashing them together very securely and making a good raft with some ropes . . . we crossed in it this very large-volumed Rio Colorado, . . . the captain of the Quiquima nation aiding them in keeping the raft afloat.

In order that I might not wet my feet, I accepted the large basket in which they wished me to cross, and placing it and fastening it upon the raft, I seated myself in it and crossed very comfortably and very pleasantly, without the least risk, taking with me only my breviary, some trifles, and a blanket in which to sleep, and afterward some branches of broom weed which I wrapped up in my bandana to serve me as a pillow.

As we crossed the river many more people came to us and there were dances and entertainments after their fashion. I preached to them through an interpreter, here and on the road, and in the afternoon, when, after about three leagues' journey, we arrived at the house of the captain of the nation. In all parts the word of God and the Christian doctrine were well received.

All the road was full of small but very continuous rancherías, with very many people, very affable, very well featured, and somewhat whiter than the rest of the Indians. All this road was through a veritable champaign of most fertile lands, of most beautiful cornfields very well cultivated with abundant crops of maize, beans and pumpkins, and with very large drying places for the drying of pumpkins, for this kind lasts them afterward all the year.

When, two hours before sunset, we arrived at the ranchería and house of the captain, the captain of the neighboring Cutgana nation came also to see us, with a great following of people from the north and from the west, and with various gifts . . . and saying that the Sea of California ended a day's journey farther to the south than where we were, this very large-volumed Rio Colorado and two others emptying at its head, I asked them also about everything farther on, particularly toward the west and south, and by what way a road could be found to go at the proper time to trade. . . .

We left, partially established, some general peace agreements among the Yumas, Pimas, Quiquimas, Cutganes, Hogiopas and other nations, in order that all in their time might be very friendly and good Christians. I slept in a little house which they had made me, and almost all night they kept talking among themselves in regard to their very earnest desire to embrace our friendship and our holy faith.

Having left a variety of good advice for these natives . . . I determined to turn back for my district of Nuestra Señora de los Dolores . . . because now, thanks to our Lord, already this much-disputed but now very certain land route to California had been discovered.

In case there should be some incredulous persons or someone ignorant of it, the continuity of these lands with California would be rendered certain and proved . . . because in four other journeys inland which I made, traveling fifty leagues to the northwest of the said hill of Santa Clara, which is near to and to the eastward of the arm and head of the Sea of California, and afterward in going ten leagues more to the westward, along the Rio Grande to where it unites with the Colorado River, and from this confluence forty leagues more to the southwest, along the same Colorado River to its mouth, no Sea of California has been found or seen, for it does not rise higher than barely to the latitude of thirty-two degrees.

Hence it is plainly to be inferred that Drake, besides many other modern cosmographers, in their various printed maps, with notable discredit to cosmography, deceive themselves as well as others by extending this sea or arm or strait of the Sea of California from thirty-two to forty-six degrees, making it thereby an island, and the largest in the world, whereas it is not an island but a peninsula.

From *Kino's Historical Memoir of Pimeria Alta*, Vol. I. Father Eusebio Francisco Kino, S.J., translated and edited by Herbert Eugene Bolton (Berkeley and Los Angeles: University of California Press, 1948).

V

Juan Crespi

For almost three-quarters of a century after Kino had blazed an overland route from Mexico to Alta California, there was virtually no Spanish traffic over it: Mexican administrators were preoccupied with colonization efforts south of the Rio Grande. But interest in California revived in the 1760s with the appointment of an alert new colonial governor, José de Galvez, who was quick to acknowledge that control over California and the northern regions of Sonora was likely to be forever lost unless they were occupied: if Spain failed to take action, some other nation would—England, for example, whose empire now included Canada; France, which was expanding aggressively in the Pacific; or Russia, which was already sending expeditions from Kamchatka down the North American coast.

Almost simultaneous to Galvez' appointment, the Jesuits were expelled from all Spanish colonies, largely for their resistance to royal supremacy. The Franciscans took their place, and immediately Galvez and his viceroy enlisted the services of the Father-President of the new order, Junípero Serra, a veteran of close to twenty years in Mexican missionary fields, to work out a three-fold plan of colonization for California: religious, civil, and military, involving the establishment of missions, presidios, and pueblos as integral parts of each settlement. Since the native Indians had first to be subjected, civilized, and Christianized, initial activity would be focused on missions. In Alta California they would set up at least three—at San Diego, at Monterey, and at some intermediate point—but the key mission would be planted at Monterey, and that started at once.

The first "Sacred Expedition" set out from Villacatá in 1769—a group of 225 men organized in four divisions under the general command of the experienced Spanish explorer, Gaspar de Portolá. Two divisions traveled by land, two by sea. All reached San Diego safely, though the overlanders suffered fifty-two days of misery on the march, "in danger every instant" from Indian attacks, from food shortages and, according to complaints of the padres, from inexcusable mismanagement of the military guard.

After pausing for two months at San Diego, the overlanders resumed their march to Monterey, anticipating no difficulty in locating that port, which had been so glowingly described by earlier explorers. Accompanying the expedition was Father Juan Crespi (1721–1782), who had been laboring in Mexico since 1749 and was now designated to head one of the new California missions. In chatty letters to his brothers superior, he described the discomforts of the prilgrimage and the elusiveness of Monterey.

Elusive Monterey

[*February 6, 1770*]

Now I will tell your Reverence how on the 14th of July of last year, '69, we left this port of San Diego, traveling by land with faces toward the north, to go in search of the much-praised port of Monterey. . . . We always kept close to the shore . . . until we entered the first regular town of the Channel of Santa Bárbara. . . .

This channel . . . is very well settled, with towns composed of large huts roofed with thatch and with a very great number of peaceful and friendly Indians. There are at least nine or ten towns. All have canoes, very well made. Six villages had as many as fifteen canoes each, which they use for fishing. . . . All these towns welcomed us with much rejoicing and entertained us well, bringing us a fine supply of fish, in particular fresh tunny, of which they made great piles for us. We had to tell them we could not take so much because it would be wasted, for if we had wished to use all the pack animals, without doubt it would have loaded them down. All these people are very wide awake and active, and have no fault except that of being very nimble with their fingers. There may well be ten thousand souls along the channel. . . .

I will recount to you as briefly as possible the remainder of our journey. The time that we spent going and coming was six months and eight days. We did not find Monterey in all that distance that we passed over; and I do not know whether it exists or not. . . . Seeing that Monterey did not appear, it was decided, with great eagerness . . . to continue until it was found. And at 37° and 49′, according to my reckoning . . . we found ourselves in front of a very large inlet or bay. . . . We do not doubt that it was the port of San Francisco. . . .

This is not an estuary proper, but a large arm of the sea, which enters the land for at least ten leagues. At the narrowest point it must be about three leagues, and at the widest expanse it must be not under four. In a word, it is a very large and fine harbor, such that not only all the navy of our Most Catholic Majesty but those of all Europe could take shelter in it. . . . Therefore, if the ships do not find the port of Monterey after a time, a thing I doubt completely since it was sought by so many eyes and with so much care, inasmuch as the whole undertaking depended on it, we have in place of it this fine bay of San Francisco in which to set up the standard of the Holy Cross and from which to convert to our holy Catholic Faith the numerous friendly and kindly Indians who inhabit the land round about this estuary. . . .

I counted twelve rivers from San Diego to San Francisco, including those at this port of San Francisco. Towns and missions could be established between San Diego and San Francisco at any distances desired, as three, four, or six leagues, or whatever you like, since there is land to spare for it everywhere. . . . All this land is populated with a large number of Indians who are very gentle, generous and well-formed. The most savage natives that we have found are those of San Diego and a circle in the same neighborhood. All the others are very good, peaceable and gentle. . . .

I have already pointed out that there are many villages round about the estuary of the port of San Francisco. When we were there several groups came out inviting us to come to their villages, promising that they would give us food. Since we were out of our way, it was not possible to accept lest we should lose time, but . . . some of them who urged very strongly that we go to their villages, seeing that we offered excuses, went off on the run, and soon we saw a string of them descending from the mountain. There must have been at least sixty, some very much burdened. . . . They had four very large baskets, two almost full of some very thick atoles, which were similar to blanc-mange, and the two others also nearly full of pinoles. Without doubt each one of the baskets would hold half a bushel of the seeds, which I tasted and found very good. They distributed them all to the members of the expedition.

On the 11th of November we started on the return from San Francisco to this port. For seven days we had very hot sunshine, but at the same time the cold at nightfall was insupportable. . . . We reached the Point of Pines the 28th of November to explore the Sierra de Santa Lucía again, and to see if the port of Monterey had been hidden in some corner, but we did not find it.

[June 11, 1770]

I am sending you this letter to tell your Reverence and all the Discretory the joyful news that we have taken formal, solemn and legal possession of this most famous port of San Carlos de Monterey. On the 3rd of this month of June, day so notable, Feast of Espíritu Santo, the reverend Father President said the first Mass. . . . The ceremony was concluded with the *Te Deum*, with a salute by all the soldiers, answered from the harbor by the packet boat *El Príncipe*, which must have been about four hundred yards from us. The Mass was sung on the very edge of the beach of this harbor under a live oak. . . . Let thanks be given to His Divine Majesty for the achievement of what has cost so many steps and toils. . . .

While we were in San Diego, the packet boat *El Príncipe* . . .

was seen in the vicinity of that harbor in the afternoon of the 19th of March. . . . On the 24th of the same month it dropped anchor there. As soon as it arrived it was decided to make a second journey by land, the vessel going by sea, confident now that we should find this harbor.

On the 16th of April . . . the vessel sailed for the north. . . . The next day, the 17th, in the afternoon, we of the land expedition set forth. . . . On the 24th of May, Ascension Day, we arrived at this harbor with perfect ease, without the least mishap or sickness, thank God, having spent in the journey thirty-eight days. As soon as we arrived, the very same day, before we dismounted, about half a league before reaching the Point of Pines and the beach where we had halted on the first journey, we wished to see a cross which they said they had set up when we started back last December. We were consumed with curiosity to see this cross and the beach, which we had not seen or been on, except those who had explored that place. . . .

We found the cross all surrounded by arrows and darts with plumes stuck in the ground; a dart with a string of sardines, still nearly fresh; another dart with a piece of meat hanging on it; and at the foot of the cross a little pile of mussels, all put there by the heathen in token of peace. . . . And now, as soon as they saw us, they all came out unarmed, just as though they had dealt with us all their lives.

Satisfied with having seen the cross, we returned to the beach and went down to it. There we began to see thousands of sea lions, which looked like a pavement. About a hundred yards from land we saw two whales together, the sea being very quiet as though calmed with oil, or like a very quiet lake. At the same time we noticed that the very large bay which begins at the Point of Pines was enclosed by the land, the two points coming together and forming a large O.

Seeing this, all three of us broke forth in the same breath, saying that this doubtless was the harbor of Monterey, which according to the histories is northeast of the Point of Pines. I took out the compass . . . and exactly in the north-northwest is the place where it opens. We were all greatly pleased to see that the cross was placed on the very harbor, whereas we were told by those who had explored it that there were no signs of the harbor. . . .

On the 31st of May, in the afternoon, a week after our arrival, the bark was seen very close to the Point of Pines, and soldiers went to signal to it that we were already here. It saluted us . . . and then came in to the very spot where the cross was, entering like Pedro into his own house, guided by the very same anchorage and signs given by the histories. The same night it anchored in six fathoms, and the captain of the bark sent a messenger to us to say that he was now in Monterey. . . .

This spot where we are encamped and which has been cleared for the establishment of the presidio and mission is in front of the bark, in a plain about two or three gunshots from the beach. . . . We will remain here alone as long as God may be pleased to have us.

Condensed from letters of Fray Juan Crespi to Fray Francisco Palóu and Fray Juan Andres published in *Fray Juan Crespi, Missionary Explorer on the Pacific Coast, 1769–1774,* translated and edited by Herbert Eugene Bolton (Berkeley: University of California Press, 1927).

VI

Francisco Palóu

The main conclusion reached by the leaders of the "Sacred Expedition" was that three missionary establishments in Alta California would not be nearly enough. They would have to plant a long succession of settlements all the way from San Diego to San Francisco in order to influence even a minority of the Indian population. The Franciscans seemed only to be overjoyed at the challenge so suddenly imposed.

Starting a mission colony in unbroken wilderness—a community complete with formal church or chapel in the European tradition, quarters for padres and servants, barracks for military guards, suitable fortifications, storehouses, stables, schools, a trading center, and dormitories for a throng of hoped-for converts—normally would have called for the requisition of mountains of building supplies and equipment, a monumental amount of planning, and inexhaustible faith in the Almighty. The Catholic Fathers did it largely on faith—faith, a string of burros, materials they found in the wilderness, their own brawn, and the borrowed brawn of natives to whom they brought the promise of salvation. Moreover, their notion of a mission was not merely a cluster of buildings. It was also a vast plantation and a ranch of many thousands of acres, in accordance with the example set years before by Father Kino.

The most gifted organizer of that line of missions along the West Coast was Father Junípero Serra, who had personally accompanied

Gaspar de Portolá in the second division of the 1769 overland expedition. In popular conception Serra's great triumph was the founding of the missionary outpost at San Francisco, but if ever the Venerable Father stooped to judge the comparative rank of the many stations he created, first place in all likelihood would go to San Carlos at Carmel, where he took up permanent residence, or to San Antonio, high in the Santa Lucia mountains, where he witnessed the largest ingathering of native converts, for Father Junípero judged his own worldly accomplishment solely in terms of the number of souls brought into the Catholic fold.

Though each mission had its own individual problems of organization, the simple story of the founding of San Antonio is representative; an abiding faith was the cornerstone of all. The narrative of the pioneer party that established San Antonio was related by Serra's lifelong companion and biographer, Father Francisco Palóu (1723–1789). Both were born on the Mediterranean island of Majorca. Together they crossed the Atlantic from Spain in 1749; together they took up residence briefly in Mexico City, whence they radiated out into country villages, accompanied exploration expeditions to the north, and eventually set out for one of the outermost frontiers of civilization—Alta California.

Father Junípero stands forth as the greatest of the eighteenth-century Catholic missionaries in California, and Palóu shared that greatness. His biography of Serra ranks as a masterpiece of Spanish-American literature.

No Use to Ring the Bells

That ardent zeal for the conversion of the gentiles which ever burned in the heart of our Venerable Father Junípero gave him no rest nor permitted him to delay in putting into operation the means necessary for the carrying out of his plans. As soon as he had finished the exploration of the Carmel River and had set to work there the men employed in the cutting of timber, he returned immediately to Monterey in order to prepare for his trip to the Santa Lucia Mountains, and soon after set out with the Fathers destined to serve as the founders of the Mission of San Antonio.

They took with them all the necessary equipment for that new Mission as well as the guard of soldiers necessary for their protection. They traveled twenty-five leagues toward the southeast from Monterey, in the direction of these mountains, and when they had arrived at the base of them, they found there a large canyon which was called *Los Robles,* as it was thickly covered with oak trees, and there they set up the camp.

Having examined the contour of the land and found a wide and sightly plain in the canyon near to a river (to which they immediately gave the name of San Antonio), it seemed to them to be the proper place for the building of the Mission because there was a good head of water in the river even in the month of July, which was the time of the greatest drought, and also because the waters could be conducted without difficulty for the irrigation of the land.

As all had agreed upon the choice of the place for the Mission, the Venerable Father ordered that the mules should be unloaded and the bells hung up from the branch of a tree, and as soon as everything was in readiness the Servant of God began to ring them, shouting at the same time as if he were beside himself, "Hear, oh Gentiles, come, oh come to the Holy Church! Come, oh come and receive the Faith of Jesus Christ!"

The Reverend Father Fr. Miguel Pieras, one of the two Missionaries, and the one designated to act as the President of the Mission, after watching him awhile said: "Why do you weary yourself unnecessarily, as this is not the place where the church is to stand, nor is there anywhere within hearing in these regions a single pagan soul? It is of no use to ring the bells." To this the Father answered: "In this way, Father, let me give expansion to my heart, as I would that this bell might be heard in all the world . . . or at least I would that the bell might be heard by all the pagan people who live in this sierra."

They then set up a large cross which, after it had been blessed, they venerated. A little shelter of branches was also made, and underneath was placed the table for the altar and here the Venerable Father celebrated the first Mass in honor of San Antonio, the Patron Saint of this Mission, on the 14th of July of the year 1771. . . .

A single Indian who had been attracted by the ringing of the bell, or by the strangeness of the people there gathered, happened to draw near at the time that the Mass was being celebrated and so was a witness to the act of the Divine Sacrifice. This the Venerable Priest discovered as he turned from the altar in order to preach the sermon after the reading of the Gospel, and with his heart overflowing with joy he expressed himself in his sermon in the following manner: "I trust in God and in the favor of San Antonio that this Mission will come to be a great settlement of many Christians because we see here what has not been seen in any of the other Missions founded hitherto, that at the very first Mass the first fruits of paganism have been present, and he will surely not fail to communicate to his fellows what he has here seen."

This is indeed what took place. . . . As soon as the Mass was over, he began to manifest his affection with little gifts to the gentile, in order to attract by these means the rest; and this he accomplished that very day, for as soon as the word spread, many of them, moved by curiosity, began to come in.

Having attempted to make them understand by signs (in the absence of an interpreter) that the friars had come to settle and live in this region, they showed their great appreciation of the same by continuing to make their visits with little gifts of pinions and acorns, which they brought with them and from which, as well as from other wild grains, they make their meals and porridge which they use for food, and which they harvest in great abundance. The Venerable Father reciprocated by giving them in return for their gifts, strings of beads of glass of different colors, as well as some of our food made from corn and beans, and which immediately pleased the palate of these pagan people.

They immediately began the construction of the wooden houses which were to serve for the dwelling house of the Fathers with their servants, the barracks for the soldiers and the church for divine worship, surrounding all these buildings with a stockade for defense so that the squad of six soldiers and corporal could act as guard.

Within a short time the Fathers had attracted the attention of the Indians, who became singularly attached to them because of the love and affection with which they treated them, and immediately they began to show their entire trust in the Fathers by bringing to them their grains as soon as they had harvested them, saying that they might eat what they pleased of them and that the rest they could keep for the winter season.

This the Missionaries did with great satisfaction, wondering that the gentiles should have such confidence in them from the very first, and also wondering how much greater that trust might be when, after being converted to baptism, they might come to look upon them as their real Fathers. In this good opinion our Venerable Father Junípero freely shared as he saw these demonstrations of regard, and it was in this hope that he left the Missionaries of this Mission of San Antonio in order to return to Monterey, after remaining a fortnight with them.

Following the instructions of the Venerable President, the new Missionaries gave themselves up with the greatest consecration to the learning of the language of these barbarians, making use of the small boys in order to obtain from them the names of things and to explain to them that their object in coming to this land was to direct their souls toward heaven. This result they obtained at the sacrifice of great diligence, and when they had begun to teach them the doctrine and to baptize, the Mission had been founded only two years, and at that time when I visited it there were one hundred and fifty-eight new Christians. . . .

This Mission of San Antonio, as I have already said, is situated in the center of the Sierra of Santa Lucia about eight leagues from the coast of the Pacific Ocean, but which can only be reached by a very hilly and stony road . . . and is twenty-five leagues from the port of Monterey. The hills are covered with very large pine trees, which produce a great abundance of pinions (very similar to those of Spain). These the Indians eat, although on account of their heating nature they cause some sickness.

There is an abundance also of large live oaks and other oak trees which furnish the Indians with several varieties of acorns. These they dry in the sun and store for use, making from them porridge and meal, and for which they also use some plants and vegetables, which the country produces in great abundance. No less is the supply of rabbits and squirrels, the latter being quite as savory as hares. The soil is very fertile and supplies abundant harvests of wheat, corn, beans and other cereals brought out from Spain, and with which the inhabitants now have supplied themselves.

During the summer time the climate is extremely hot, but in the winter time it is extremely cold, on account of the severe frosts which are felt there. The stream which never ceases to flow during the year, and which is close to the Mission houses, is often frozen over to such a degree that the water is sometimes frozen solid until the sun shines again and melts the ice. For this same reason there have been serious losses in the early part of the season, especially if the corn and beans are planted too early.

So very severe was the frost that fell on Easter Sunday in the year 1780 that a great part of the wheat fields, which had already begun to ear and was in blossom, was dried up like the dried stalks seen in the month of August. This misfortune brought great despair to the Indians but affected the Fathers even more seriously when they considered what drawbacks would follow the lack of provisions at the Mission, as it would be necessary for the young converts to go out into the hills in search of wild grains for food, as they did when they were pagans.

But the Fathers, feeling a revival of their faith and trusting in the patronage of San Antonio, invited all the new Christians to join them in nine days of prayer. They all attended the services with great punctuality and devotion; and just before the period of prayer began, the Fathers ordered that the frozen fields be irrigated, although they appeared to be entirely dry.

Within a few days they noticed that the wheat began to sprout up from the roots, and by the time the Novena was over the field was green. They continued to irrigate it and it grew with such rapidity that within the fifty days, at the time of the feast of the Holy Spirit, the grain was as tall as it had been before, with fine large ears, and they were able to see it ripen at the usual time of harvest and to gather the largest crop which they had ever seen from the same amount of land. When the Fathers and the Indians recognized their deep obligation for so very special a prodigy as the Lord our God had deigned to work in their favor . . . they all rendered to him the most sincere thanks.

This incident and many others . . . have contributed a great deal toward the confirming of the faith of the converts and to the bringing in of the gentiles, so that it has happened that the number of Christians in that Mission exceed those of any other, as the number of them just before the death of the Venerable Father Junípero amounted to 1,084 neophytes. Thus we see how his hope was fulfilled, when on the first day of the founding he put his trust in God and in the patronage of San Antonio and declared that there would be there some day a great settlement filled with many Christians.

So God granted to his Servant Fr. Junípero the privilege of seeing during his own lifetime his desires brought to fruition, and after his most exemplary death, the number of Christians continued to increase daily.

From *The Life and Apostolic Labors of the Venerable Father Junípero Serra,* Francisco Palóu, translated by C. Scott Williams, edited by George Wharton James (Pasadena: G. W. James, 1913). Copyright 1913 by Edith E. Farnsworth.

VII

Juan Bautista de Anza

Until 1775 Spanish advocates of colonization in the upper reaches of New Spain had concerned themselves principally with establishing footholds along the California coast, befriending or subduing the Indians, and drawing them into the mission folds. Friars, civil servants, and soldiery had comprised most of the pioneering expeditions. Beginning in 1775, however, the emphasis shifted to permanent emigration by Mexican settlers. Placed in charge of the first emigration party was one of Mexico's most dynamic and gallant soldier-explorers, Juan Bautista de Anza (1735–1788), who had been sent north in 1774 to scout a suitable route over which a large body of settlers might travel all the way to San Francisco in more safety and comfort than had previous expeditions.

Anza found no such safe, easy route; he was forced to conclude that there was none. For a large company crossing the desert, particularly, first consideration had to be given to sources of water and to cattle forage without regard for rough terrain or hostile Indians. In a circuit covering almost five thousand miles, Anza had plotted the most feasible trail—up the Magdalena and Santa Cruz valleys of Mexico, across Arizona from Tucson to the Gila and Colorado rivers, through the outskirts of what is now the Imperial Valley and the Anza-Borrego Desert, along the western foothills of the San Jacinto Mountains to Santa Ana and San Gabriel, then north by way of Santa Barbara and Monterey.

Even Anza acknowledged that it would be a wearying, hazardous journey. Nevertheless, on October 23, 1775, he set out from the northern Mexican village of Tubac over that route on one of the great migratory marches of history—a notable American event, robbed of its notoriety by other epoch-making events occurring simultaneously in New England, where Boston was under British siege and Yankee rebels were still smarting from the battles of Lexington, Concord, and Bunker Hill.

In Anza's entourage was a company of 240 men, women, and children, including 136 colonists; forty soldiers and officers with their families; Church Fathers Pedro Font and Francisco Garcés; Lieutenant Joachín Morago; five interpreters of Indian languages; assorted servants and cowboys herding a three-mile-long train of 165 pack mules, 340 saddle animals, and over 300 beef and milch cattle that would provide sustenance en route and stock for a settlement at San Francisco.

Three months later, after a journey of 1,600 miles, they reached Monterey with more prospective colonists than had started, for on the way there had been half a dozen births and only one fatality—a remarkable record of survival considering the ordeals endured in transit. At Monterey, Anza left the main body and forged ahead with a small company to the Bay of San Francisco, leaving to his lieutenant the task of later leading the emigrants to the Golden Gate. "First to open a route across the Sierras and first to lead a colony overland to the North Pacific shores," summarized Anza's historian, Dr. Herbert Bolton, "he was the forerunner of MacKenzie, Thompson, Lewis and Clark, Smith, Frémont, the forty-niners, and all the eager-eyed throng who since have yielded to the urge of Westward Ho. His monument is the Imperial City which stands beside the Golden Gate."

But it was not an easy triumph. The most trying part of the trek came in the middle of December when the expedition, separated into three divisions and stretched out for many miles, was approaching the east flank of what is now known as the Anza-Borrego Desert State Park; and cattle and pack animals, on which survival depended, were dying in alarming numbers from exposure and fatigue. The animals, as well as the people, had come from a tropical country and never seen snow or experienced severe cold. Heat and drought had been expected in the desert north of the Colorado River, but nature went on a rampage that winter and bore down with Arctic gales and blizzards instead of heat and sandstorms. In his diary Anza described the loss of cattle as an irreparable disaster, but despite the disaster and human suffering, the colonists reached Monterey, and later San Francisco, in safety and with animals to spare.

Across the Desert in a Snowstorm

December 14.—As soon as day began to dawn it commenced to snow, with fierce and extremely cold wind, which continued the entire day, and for this reason it was not possible to march. . . . At twelve o'clock the cattle arrived. . . . In bringing them we lost ten head, which became tired out. These animals, notwithstanding that they had not been watered for four days, needed so little in this present season that even when they were taken to the verge of the water, most of them preferred to eat rather than drink. . . . At eleven o'clock at night it stopped snowing, but the mountains and plains continued to be so covered with snow that it looked like daylight, and there now followed a very severe freeze, as a consequence of which this was a night of extreme hardship.

December 15.—At daybreak it was very windy, and the snow which had fallen the day and the night before was very hard from the freezing which had preceded, as a result of which six of our cattle and one mule died. At a quarter past twelve the second division began to arrive. . . . The people were crippled by the storm, which overtook them between Santa Rosa and here. In spite of all their efforts to reach here yesterday, they were unable to do so, and on the way several persons were frozen, one of them so badly that in order to save his life, it was necessary to bundle him up for two hours between four fires. As a result of these inclemencies, five saddle animals died in their division. . . .

December 16.—I remained in this place awaiting the third division. This morning four of our cattle died from injuries and cold because of the severe freezing weather. At eleven o'clock they informed me that when they were looking for some saddle animals which had disappeared from sight, they found that they were being driven off by four of the heathen who had come to see us. . . .

December 17.—Since the third division did not appear yesterday, at seven o'clock in the morning I sent two soldiers to meet it with twenty saddle animals, in order that they may have new mounts to replace those which may be tired out or made useless because of the cold. At half past three in the afternoon the third division arrived at this place, in command of Alférez Don Joseph Moraga. His forces were in worse condition than the two earlier divisions because the storm of snow and cold caught them in a more exposed position, and as a result several persons were frozen to the point of being in danger of death. From the same cause six saddle animals were left by the wayside and four others died.

In attending to this division, providing fire for them, and in other services for their relief, this officer so exposed himself that he contracted very severe pains in his ears, and although these have been cured, the weather is so bad that he has been left totally deaf in both ears.

Today two more of our cattle have died as a result of injury and cold. In the midst of these misfortunes, which have been caused us by the snowstorm, with the loss of the animals which have died, it almost seems to have been designed for the benefit of the health of our people, for whereas nine days ago we counted more than fifteen invalids, three of them dangerously ill, today there are less than five of the first class and none of the second. Their sudden recovery . . . is attributed partly to the many watermelons which were eaten at the lake of Santa Olaya [near the Colorado River crossing]. . . .

December 18.—Notwithstanding the care which we have tried to observe with the cattle, it has not been possible to keep down the mortality, both from cold and from injuries. This morning two of them were found dead and five others, it is thought, will not be able to go forward from this place. We have made such use of them as has been possible, making of them jerked beef and salting it well, but even so it is unpalatable because of its scent, color and taste.

At half past one in the afternoon we raised our camp in order to

Anza Expedition crossing the desert

set out and shorten the next journey. . . . Over level country we
traveled about three and a half leagues in as many hours, until we
came to the first pasturage and firewood that was found in a wide
valley [Borrego Valley], where a halt was made for the night. All
the sierras which we have seen today in all directions have
appeared covered with snow, except those along the line of our
route. . . .

December 19.—At nine o'clock in the morning we raised our
train and began the march toward the west . . . over sandy
country with bad footing. In this direction we traveled four
leagues . . . to the site of San Gregorio. . . . After nightfall the
cattle arrived, and although they had taken all day to accomplish
the journey, this was not sufficient to prevent the loss of four
head. The same thing happened with three mounts, for these
animals, like the rest, have become so scrawny and lean that they
have no resemblance to those which started on the journey. . . .
On leaving this place we begin crossing the range which runs
from the Peninsula of California, which gives the appearance of
having fair openings through which to go out to the port and
mission of San Diego. . . .

December 20.—This morning it was so frigid and the night
before was so extremely cold that three saddle animals and five
head of cattle were frozen to death, and the weather was so hard
on our people that almost none of them slept, for they spent the
night occupied in feeding the fires in order to withstand it. At
seven o'clock I was informed that . . . on account of the thirst
which the cattle of necessity felt, many of them had escaped in
the darkness of the night from the men who were watching them.
I therefore ordered three soldiers to go with a sergeant and a
vaquero to look for them, and that the rest should proceed on the
next journey. . . .

Having traveled along the valley four leagues . . . we halted
in the same valley, where plentiful running water, as well as some
pasturage was found. . . . At seven o'clock at night the cattle
which had set out ahead of us from San Gregorio arrived at the
camp, eleven of them having died because they were completely

worn out. For the same reason five saddle animals were left at a watering place less than a league from where we halted. . . .

December 22.—We remained in this place because the sergeant and the cattle which he was to bring did not put in an appearance during the whole day. At half past four in the afternoon the sergeant arrived with the distressing news that all the cattle . . . [were] found dead. . . . No effort whatever has been spared to prevent any kind of misfortune, although in spite of this, I have had the disaster here set forth, which has been to me as distressing as it is irreparable.

Condensed from *Anza's California Expeditions,* Volume III, translated and edited by Herbert Eugene Bolton (Berkeley: University of California Press, 1930).

VIII

Francisco Palóu

For four months the Mexican emigrant train, which Anza led as far as Monterey, remained there awaiting the arrival of their supply ship, the *San Carlos,* in accordance with the original plan for the expedition. Its tardy appearance in June 1776 was the signal for Lieutenant Moraga, now the commander of the party, to proceed on the last leg of the journey.

Fray Francisco Palóu who could well stand as literary spokesman for the group, as well as spiritual guide, sketched the uneventful circumstances of the final days of march and the actual founding of San Francisco, an event as significant in the West as the landing of the Pilgrims in the East a century and a half earlier—though the qualms shown by the British Pilgrims in establishing their colony on Cape Cod could hardly be compared with the fortitude, the efficiency and spirit of optimism with which the Spanish-Mexicans went about the business on San Francisco Bay.

Triumphal Entry

On the 17th day of June, 1776, about two in the afternoon, the company of soldiers and families from Sonora [Mexico] set out from Monterey. It was composed of its commander, Lieutenant

Don José Joaquín Moraga, a sergeant, two corporals and ten soldiers, all with their wives and families except the commander, who had left his in Sonora. In addition there were seven families of settlers, rationed and provisioned by the king; other persons attached to the soldiers and their families; five servant boys, muleteers and vaqueros, who conducted about two hundred of the king's cattle and some belonging to individuals, and the mule train, which carried the provisions and utensils necessary for the road.

All of the foregoing belonged to the new presidio. And for whatever concerned the first mission that was to be founded, we two ministers, Father Fray Pedro Benito Cambón and I, went with two servants who conducted the loads, and three unmarried Indian neophytes, two of them from Old California and the other from the mission of Carmelo, who drove the cattle for the mission, numbering eighty-six head, which were incorporated with those for the presidio. . . . The day's marches were short, in order not to fatigue the little children and the women, especially those who were pregnant, and for this reason it was even necessary to make several stops.

On the whole way there was not a single mishap, thanks to God. We were well received by all the heathen whom we met on the road, who were surprised to see so many people of both sexes and all ages, for up to that time they had not seen more than some few soldiers, on the occasions when they went to make the explorations. And they were astonished at the cattle, which they had never seen before.

On the 27th of June the expedition arrived in the neighborhood of the harbor, and the commander ordered the camp halted on the bank of the lagoon called by Señor Anza "Nuestra Señora de los Dolores," which is in sight of the bay of Los Llorones [Mission Bay] and the beach of the bay or arm of the sea which runs to the southeast, with the intention of waiting here for the bark in order to select the spot for the founding of the fort and presidio, and in the meantime to explore the land.

On the following day he ordered a shelter of branches built to serve as a chapel in which to celebrate the holy sacrifice of Mass.

In it the first Mass was said on the 29th, the feast of the great holy apostles, San Pedro and San Pablo, and we continued to celebrate in it every day until the camp was moved to the site which it occupies near the landing place, when the ground and the convenience of water permitted it.

As soon as the expedition halted, the heathen of the surrounding villages came to the camp, attracted by the novelty of seeing such neighbors in their country. They came to visit us frequently, bringing their rude gifts of mussels and wild seeds, which were always reciprocated with beads and some of our food, to which they soon took a liking, except the milk, which they refused to taste.

These natives are well formed, many of them being bearded, bald and rather homely, for they have a habit of pulling out the hair of their eyebrows by the roots, which makes them ugly. They are poor, and have no houses except little enclosures made of brush to shelter them somewhat from the heavy winds which prevail and are extremely annoying. The men go totally naked, though here and there one covers his shoulders with a sort of little cape of beaver skins and pelican feathers. The women cover themselves only with plaited tules, for very few skins of animals are seen among them.

For an entire month the expedition remained in that camp, which was composed of field tents, waiting for the bark. Meanwhile soldiers, citizens and servants employed themselves in cutting logs in order to have this much done when the bark should arrive. The lieutenant busied himself in exploring the land in the vicinity, where he found some springs of water, lagoons, pastures and good sites for all kinds of stock.

Near the white cliff [Fort Point] he found two springs of water sufficient for the use of the presidio, and not far from them he found a good plain which is in view of the harbor and entrance, and also of its interior. As soon as he saw the spot the lieutenant decided that it was suitable for the presidio, but he delayed moving the people there, as he was waiting day by day for the arrival of the packet.

Seeing that it did not appear for a whole month . . . the lieutenant decided to move to that spot, so that the soldiers might begin to build their huts for shelter, since it was nearer at hand for making a beginning of the houses. This he did on the 26th of July, setting to work immediately to construct some tule huts. The first was the one that was to serve as a chapel, and in it I said Mass on the 28th of the same month. . . .

[On the 18th of August, the *San Carlos,* which had been driven far off course by contrary winds] successfully entered the harbor, and about two o'clock in the afternoon it anchored not very far from the spot where the soldiers were lodged. . . . As soon as the bark was made fast, the commander, pilots and Father Nocedal went ashore. When they saw the site of the camp, they were all of the opinion that it was a very suitable place for the fort and presidio, and they thought the same of the site of the Laguna de los Dolores for the mission. In view of the opinion of the captain of the bark and the pilots, work was begun on the buildings of the houses and the presidio.

A square measuring ninety-two varas each way was marked out for it, with divisions for church, royal offices, warehouses, guard houses, and houses for soldier settlers, a map of the plan being formed and drawn by the first pilot. And so that the work might be done as speedily as possible, the commander [of the *San Carlos*] designated a squad of sailors and the two carpenters to join the servants of the royal presidio in making a good warehouse in which to keep the provisions, a house for the commanding officer of the presidio, and a chapel for celebrating the holy sacrifice of the Mass, while the soldiers were making their own houses for their families.

The work of the presidio being now under way, Captain Don Fernando Quirós [of the *San Carlos*] came to the site of the mission, accompanied by the chaplain, a pilot, the surgeon and six soldiers, to aid in building a church or chapel in which to celebrate Mass and a room to live in. With this assistance the buildings were begun, and everything progressed so well that by the middle of September the soldiers had their houses already

made of logs, all with flat roofs; the lieutenant had his government house; and a warehouse of the same material was finished
large enough to store all the provisions brought by the bark.

It was then decided that the formal act of possession should
take place, the day appointed for it being that on which our
Mother Church celebrates the impression of the stigmata of Our
Seraphic Father San Francisco, that is, the 17th of September, a
most appropriate day, since he is the patron of the harbor, the
new presidio and the mission. And for taking formal possession of
the mission, the 4th of October was designated, which is the day
dedicated to Our Seraphic Father San Francisco.

The commander of the packet, his two pilots and the greater
part of the crew were present at the ceremony of taking formal
possession . . . and with the people from the presidio, troops as
well as citizens, they made up a goodly number of Spaniards. . . .

A solemn Mass was sung by the ministers, and when it was
concluded, the gentlemen performed the ceremony of taking
formal possession. This finished, all entered the chapel and sang
the *Te Deum Laudamus*, accompanied by peals of bells and
repeated salvos of cannon, muskets and guns, the bark responding
with its swivel guns, whose roar and the sound of the bells
doubtless terrified the heathen, for they did not allow themselves
to be seen for many days.

The ceremony concluded, the commander [Moraga] of the
presidio invited to it all the people, conducting himself with all
the splendor that the place permitted, and supplying with his
true kindness what elsewhere would have been lacking, for which
all the people were grateful, expressing their gratitude in the joy
and happiness which all felt that day.

From *Anza's California Expeditions*, Volume III, translated and edited by
Herbert Eugene Bolton (Berkeley: University of California Press, 1930).

IX

George Vancouver

Regardless of what the Spaniards called Alta California, the British persisted in giving it the name New Albion. With the American Revolution discreditably concluded for them and New England on the Atlantic Coast lost, it behooved the British Admiralty to reassert their claim to the "New England" of the Pacific Coast. Just as the Revolutionary War was starting, Captain Cook was scouring the northwest shores in a futile search for a shortcut to the Atlantic and England; and a decade after the war, one of Cook's most versatile officers, George Vancouver (1758–1798), was back in the same waters with orders to carry on from where Cook left off.

Over a period of three years, from 1792 to 1794, Vancouver made the most thorough survey of the coast yet undertaken by an Englishman. Essentially he was a sleuth for the Admiralty, and the Spanish officials in the California ports soon recognized him as such. On his arrival in 1792 he was received hospitably, given free shore privileges, and even presented with a cargo of cattle to transport to Hawaii—the first ever seen by the Sandwich Islanders. But on a return visit the following year he found his welcome worn thin, new officials in charge, and all ports closed to foreigners. Though he pleaded with San Francisco authorities, insisting that his voyage was "for the general use and benefit of mankind," "for the good of the world in general, rather than for the advantage of any particular sovereign," he was denied shore privileges in a way he considered "ungracious and degrading."

At some of the coastal missions, however, he was welcomed cordially, treated as a fellow scholar and scientist, allowed to study the padres' maps, given frank and effusive answers to his questions, and conducted about the countryside, so that he was able to gather most of the information he sought. A century ahead of his time, he was probably the inadvertent discoverer of California oil, when he sailed into a vast oil slick on Santa Monica Bay and noted that "the surface of the sea, which was perfectly smooth and tranquil, was covered with a thick slimy substance," resembling "dissolved tar" and smelling strongly of "burning tar or some such substance"; it covered the ocean, he claimed, "in all directions within the limits of our view," but he was content to let it stand as one of the unexplained phenomena of the New World.

Though impressed with the possibilities for future commercial development of California, he was most unimpressed with what the Spaniards were doing. He thought the missions "in a horrid state of uncleanliness, and laziness seemed to pervade the whole." Among the Indians domiciled there he saw "scarcely any sign in their general deportment of their being at all benefited or of having added one single ray of comfort to their general condition." For a peaceful man working for the "benefit of mankind," he seemed unduly curious about military defenses and was always counting soldiers. Whether or not he was primarily a scientific observer or a secret agent, he succeeded in preparing an illuminating intelligence report for the British Crown.

From the British Point of View

The profound secrecy which the Spanish nation has so strictly observed with regard to their territories and settlements in this hemisphere naturally excites in the strongest manner a curiosity and a desire to be informed of the state, condition and progress of the several establishments provided in these distant regions for the purpose of converting its native inhabitants to Christianity and civilization. . . .

The new settlements . . . are placed under four distinct jurisdictions [San Francisco, Monterey, Santa Barbara, and San

Diego], of which Monterey is the principal, and the established residence as well of the governor. . . . In each of the divisions is fixed one military post only, called the Presidio, governed by a lieutenant, who has under him an ensign, with sergeants, corporals, etc. And although the jurisdiction of the governor extends over the whole province, yet the respective commanders of the several Presidios are invested with great authority in the ordinary matters relative to their civil and military jurisdiction; but they seem to have very little influence or concern in anything that appertains to the missions. . . .

The pueblos differ materially from either the missions or the Presidios, and may be better expressed by the name of villages, being unsupported by any other protection than that of the persons who are resident in them. These are principally old Spanish or Creole soldiers who, having served their respective turns of duty in the missions or in the Presidios, become entitled to exemption from any further military services and have permission either to return to their native country or to pass the remainder of their lives in these villages.

Most of these soldiers are married and have families, and when the retirement of the pueblos is preferred, grants of land with some necessary articles are given them to commence their new occupation of husbandry, as a reward for their former services and as an incitement to a life of industry. . . . Fertile spots are always chosen for planting these colonies, by cultivating which, they are soon enabled to raise corn and cattle sufficient not only for their own support but for the supply of the wants of the missions and Presidios in their neighborhood.

Being trained to arms, they early instruct the rising generation and bring them up to the obedience of military authority, under the laws of which they themselves continue to be governed. There is no superior person or officer residing amongst them for the purpose of officiating as governor or as chief magistrate, but the pueblos are occasionally visited by the ensign of the Presidio, within whose particular jurisdiction they are situated. This officer is authorized to take cognizance of and in a certain degree to redress such grievances or complaints as may be brought before him, or to represent them, together with any crimes or misdemeanors, to his commanding officer. . . .

These pueblos generally consist of about thirty or forty old soldiers with their families, who may be considered a sort of militia of the country, and as assisting in the increase of its population, which, as far as it respects the Spaniards, is yet in a very humble state. The mode originally adopted and since constantly pursued in settling this country is by no means calculated to produce any great increase of white inhabitants.

The Spaniards in their missions and Presidios, being the two principal distinctions of Spanish inhabitants, lead a confined and, in most respects, a very indolent life, the religious part of the society within a cloister, the military in barracks. The last mentioned order do nothing, in the strictest sense of the expression, for they neither till, sow nor reap, but wholly depend upon the labor of the inhabitants of the missions and pueblos for their subsistence and the common necessities of life.

To reconcile this inactivity whilst they remain on duty in the Presidio with the meritorious exertions that the same description of people are seen to make in the pueblos is certainly a very difficult task; and the contradiction would have remained very prejudicial to their character had I not been informed that to support the consequence of the soldier in the eyes of the natives and to ensure him their respect, it had been deemed highly improper that he should be subjected to any laborious employment. This circumstance alone is sufficient to account for the habitual indolence and want of industry in the military part of these societies.

The introduction of Christianity amongst the natives, the cultivation of their minds and making them disciples of the Romish Church [are] wholly intrusted to the religious of the respective orders; none of those Indians is suffered to be employed in the Presidios but such as are particularly recommended, to whom the officers who give them employ are obliged to pay a certain daily sum of money, according to the service received, whilst at the same time the fathers have hundreds at their command, who when employed by them are rewarded with the produce resulting from the labors of such of their own society as are engaged in agriculture, in manufacturing their woolen garments or in gardening.

These are the payments by which the wages of the carpenter, the smith, the mason and other mechanics are satisfied, and as they have few persons of these trades amongst themselves, the whole of such business is performed by the Indians under the immediate instruction and inspection of the Reverend Fathers, who by these means alone have erected all their fabrics and edifices. . . . These benevolent fathers are the corporeal as well as spiritual physicians of all the Indian tribes in the neighborhood of the missions, and they exercise the arts both of surgery and medicine with great success, especially the latter, for the credit of which they may be indebted to the unimpaired constitutions of their patients and the natural healthfulness of the climate. . . .

The number of the natives at this period who were said to have embraced the Roman Catholic persuasion under the discipline of the Franciscan and Dominican orders of missionaries in New Albion and throughout the peninsula of California amounted to about twenty thousand, and they are estimated at an eighth or tenth of the whole native population. . . .

Their progress toward civilization seems to have been remarkably slow, and it is not very likely to become more rapid until the impolicy of excluding foreign visitors shall be laid aside, and an amicable commercial intercourse substituted. . . . The Spanish monarchy . . . retains this extent of country under its authority by a force that, had we not been eyewitnesses of its insignificance in many instances, we should hardly have given credit to the possibility of so small a body of men keeping in awe and under subjection the natives of this country, without resorting to harsh or unjustifiable measures.

The number of their forces between port San Francisco and San Diego, including both establishments, and occupying an extent in one line of upward of 420 nautical miles, does not amount to three hundred, officers included. . . . These are all that are employed for the protection of the missions. . . . Some

[are] guarded by five, whilst others have eight, ten or twelve soldiers for their protection, in those situations where the Indians are more numerous and likely to prove troublesome. . . .

The garrison of Monterey generally, I believe, consists of a company of fifty or eighty men, and that of San Francisco thirty-six men only. These soldiers are all very expert horsemen and, so far as their numbers extend, are well qualified to support themselves against any domestic insurrection, but are totally incapable of making any resistance against a foreign invasion.

The number of vessels that have lately visited the coast of Northwest America in new commercial pursuits have been instrumental in awakening the attention of the Spaniards, and they have recently made some efforts to show an appearance of defense. On our last visit to San Francisco eleven dismounted brass cannon, nine-pounders, with a large quantity of shot of two different sizes were lying on the beach. . . . At Monterey . . . is now erected a sorry kind of barbet battery, consisting chiefly of a few logs of wood irregularly placed, behind which the cannon, about eleven in number, are opposed to the anchorage, with very little protection in the front and on the rear and flanks entirely open and exposed. . . .

Such is the condition of this country as it respects its internal security and external defense. But why such an extent of territory should have been thus subjugated, and after all the expense and labor that has been bestowed upon its colonization turned to no account whatever, is a mystery in the science of state policy not easily to be explained.

The natives are not, nor can they be, rendered tributary, because they possess no tribute to offer, nor do these territories, though greatly favored by nature, contain . . . large towns or cities whose inhabitants could in any respect add to the affluence, grandeur or dignity of the monarch who upholds them. If these establishments are intended as a barrier against foreign intruders, the object in view has been greatly mistaken, and the most ready means have been adopted to allure other powers by the defenseless state of what the Spaniards consider as their fortresses and strongholds.

Should the ambition of any civilized nation tempt it to seize on these unsupported posts, they could not make the least resistance, and must inevitably fall to a force barely sufficient for garrisoning and securing the country. . . . By the formation of establishments so wide from each other, and so unprotected in themselves, the original design of settling the country seems to have been completely set aside and, instead of strengthening the barrier to their valuable possessions in New Spain, they have thrown irresistible temptations in the way of strangers to trespass over their boundary.

From their dominions in New Spain they have stocked this frontier country with such an abundance of cattle of all descriptions that it is no longer in their power, even were they so inclined, to effect their extermination. They have also pointed out many fertile spots, some of which are very extensive, where they have introduced the most valuable vegetable productions, not only necessary to the sustenance, but ministering to many of the luxuries of civilized society. . . . All these circumstances are valuable considerations to new masters, from whose power, if properly employed, the Spaniards would have no alternative but that of submissively yielding.

That such an event should take place appears by no means to be very improbable, should the commerce of Northwest America be further extended. The advantages that have already been derived and are likely still to accrue in the prosecution of a well-conducted trade between this coast and China, India, Japan and other places may on some future day, under a judicious and well-regulated establishment, become an object of serious and important consideration to any nation that shall be inclined to reap the advantages. . . .

Exploring these shores any further . . . might possibly have excited additional jealousy in the breast of the Spanish acting governor. Under these considerations I was compelled, though with infinite reluctance, to abandon this interesting pursuit and to determine on making the best of our way to the Sandwich Islands, where I could firmly rely on the sincerity of Kamehameha and the professions of the rest of our *rude uncivilized* friends in those islands for a hearty welcome, a kind reception and every service and accommodation in their humble power to afford, without any of the inhospitable restrictions we must have been under from the then *civilized* governor at Monterey.

From *A Voyage of Discovery to the Pacific Ocean and Round the World,* Volume IV, George Vancouver (London: Stockdale, 1801).

X

Richard J. Cleveland

Exactly ten years after Vancouver had observed that the fortifications of California ports were more theatrical than redoubtable and that port officials were more uncivil than the "savages" of Hawaii, a mariner of less conspicuous gentility visited the same coast and drew similar conclusions. He was thirty-year-old Captain Richard J. Cleveland (1773–1860), a Yankee from Salem, Massachusetts, one of the vanguard of traders who were soon to appear in scores, all looking for cargoes of cowhides in response to Vancouver's report that there were more cattle in California than could ever be exterminated.

Cleveland had been sailing the seven seas since he was fourteen; at nineteen he was commander of his own vessel, which he navigated to Calcutta; and before visiting California a decade later, he had become familiar with the major ports of five continents and could boast that he had suffered on the high seas not only "the ordinary perils of hurricanes and storms, of rocks and shoals," but also "the greater ones of the cupidity and villainy of man." In turn he had experienced captivity, robbery, imprisonment, occasional ruin—and immoderate success as a trader, which he attributed to the fact that he had never lighted a cigar nor taken a drop of spirituous liquor in his life; somewhat inconsistently, however, he did accept the axiom of the day that "drinking grog and chewing tobacco were two essential and indispensable requisites for making a good seaman."

Besides temperance, Captain Cleveland was also endowed with a

[61]

spirit of humanitarianism, a sense of honor and a sense of humor. It was his gift of humanitarianism that led him to transport to horseless Hawaii the first Mexican broncos, in the same way that Vancouver had introduced cattle there; and it was his sense of honor and humor, rather than any natural belligerence, that led him to make war in San Diego harbor, after being thwarted in his attempt to secure the cargo he wanted, in a port now closed to foreign trade.

The Battle of San Diego

We stood to the eastward under easy sail all night [of March 16, 1803] and found ourselves early in the morning abreast of the port of San Diego. A brisk northerly wind prevented our gaining the anchorage till the afternoon, when having passed near the battery without being hailed, we came to anchor about a mile within it. The next day the Commandant, Don Manuel Rodriguez, with an escort of twelve dragoons came down abreast of the ship and requested that the boat might be sent for him.

This being done immediately, he crowded the boat with his escort and probably regretted the necessity of leaving his horses on shore. We had been told at San Blas that Don Manuel was an exceedingly vain and pompous man, and, indeed, we found him so, for such a ridiculous display of a "little brief authority" and pompous parade I never before witnessed. His dress and every movement evinced the most arrant coxcomb.

Having saluted us on coming over the ship's side, he waited before proceeding aft until his escort were drawn up in two lines, with hats off in one hand and drawn swords in the other, and then passed between them to the companionway. After the ordinary inquiries of whence we came, whither bound and the object of our visit, he called to the officer of the escort and desired him to make a minute of the articles required.

With these he said he would supply us the next day, on receiving which he should expect we would not delay a moment in leaving the port. He counted our men and, perceiving us to be only fifteen all told, expressed astonishment at the presumption of undertaking so long and dangerous a navigation with so few men. He forbade our going to the town, which is distant about three miles, but gave us leave to go on shore in the neighborhood of the vessel. He took leave with characteristic pomp, leaving on board five of his escort, as he said, to see that we carried on no contraband trade.

In the afternoon we made an excursion on shore, and having rambled toward the battery which commands the entry of the port, without meeting with any person to prevent our entering it, we availed ourselves of the opportunity to ascertain its strength and state. We found eight brass nine-pounders mounted on carriages, which appeared to be in good order, and a plentiful supply of ball, but there was no appearance of their having been used for a long time. As the examination of a battery belonging to a people—the most jealous and suspicious on earth—was a delicate business, we did not remain long within its precincts and, having had an agreeable excursion, returned on board at sunset.

In the evening we made acquaintance with our guard, the sergeant of which appeared to be an intelligent young man. He informed us that only a few days past, the ship *Alexander* of Boston, Captain Brown, had been there, that he had succeeded in purchasing from the soldiers and people several hundred skins, that information of it had been given to the Commandant, who, without first demanding their surrender, boarded the ship with an armed force, made a search and took away all the skins they could find, together with some merchandise.

These skins, the guard said, were now in possession of the Commandant, which, with what he had of his own, probably exceeded a thousand. These we made every effort to obtain from him and, though there is no doubt that he would have been as well pleased to sell as we should have been to purchase them—if the transaction had been practicable without being known to the people—yet as this was out of the question and they were all spies on each other, he dared not indulge his desire of selling them to us. . . .

It was evident now that the object for which we came here was unattainable. Having on the 21st of March received the supplies we had asked, the Commandant again visited us in the same pompous style to receive his pay. On leaving us he made known his expectation that we would leave the port next morning, wished us a pleasant voyage, and we parted on the most friendly terms.

We had been offered a number of skins in small parcels in the course of the day, to be delivered to us after dark, and determined to purchase as many as we could that night. Accordingly, between eight and nine o'clock, the time agreed on, both boats were dispatched to different parts of the harbor, one of which returned in proper time with several skins. But the other, in which was the mate and two men, did not return that night.

That some disaster had occurred to prevent their return was presumable, but to attempt ascertaining the cause in the night would have been incurring too great a risk. We watched the approach of morning with a view to seize and act upon any contingency that circumstances might present, before the moving of the people.

The first discovery after dawn was that of our boat lying on the beach abreast of our vessel with apparently no person in her. On seeing this, I went immediately to the boat, and when there, perceived a group of men at a short distance, among whom ours were discernible. Being without arms, an attempt to rescue them would have been imprudent. I therefore returned on board, taking with me the other boat.

It was now very evident that not a moment was to be lost in deciding on the course to be pursued. The choice presented us was that of submission, indignant treatment and plunder or resistance and hazarding the consequences. There was not the least hesitation . . . in adopting the latter alternative. As a preliminary step the guard on board were disarmed and made to go below; then I went with four men, each with a brace of loaded pistols, to the rescue of those on shore.

On landing we ran up to the guard and, presenting our pistols, ordered them instantly to release our men from their ligatures, for they had been tied hand and foot and had been lying on the ground all night. This order was readily complied with by the three soldiers who had been guarding them, and to prevent mischief we took away their arms, dipped them in the water and left them on the beach. The mate reported that they were arrested immediately on landing by a party of horsemen with the Commandant in person at their head, whence we concluded that he had sent the soldier with whom we made the agreement for the skins, expressly to decoy us that he might have an excuse to plunder us.

Arriving on board, we perceived our men to be so indignant at the treatment of their shipmates as to be ready for the fight, even had the odds been greater against us. We had, however, a disagreeable and very hazardous task to perform, a failure in which would be attended with ruin to us, besides subjecting us to the humiliating treatment of an incensed petty tyrant.

Our position at anchor was about a mile from the fort. . . . It was necessary to pass within musket shot of this fort. With a strong wind the quick passage of the vessel would render the danger trifling, but unfortunately we had now but the last expiring breath of the land breeze, sufficient only to give the ship steerage way, and an hour would elapse before we could presume on passing the fort. But no other alternative was left us that did not present a more dreaded aspect.

While making our preparations we perceived that all was bustle and animation on shore. Both horse and foot were flocking to the fort. Our six three-pounders, which were all brought on the side of the ship bearing on the fort, and our fifteen men was all our force with which to resist a battery of three nine-pounders and at least a hundred men.

As soon as our sails were loosed and we began to heave up the anchor, a gun without shot was discharged from the battery and the Spanish flag hoisted. Perceiving no effect from this, they fired a shot ahead. By this time our anchor was up, all sail was set and we were gradually approaching the fort. In the hope of preventing their firing, we caused the guard in their uniforms to stand along in the most exposed and conspicuous station, but it had no effect, not even when so near the fort that they must have been heard imploring them to desist firing and seen to fall with their faces to the deck at every renewed discharge of the cannon.

We had been subjected to a cannonade of three quarters of an hour, without returning a shot, and fortunately with injury only to our rigging and sails. When arrived abreast the fort, several shot struck our hull, one between wind and water which was temporarily stopped by a wad of oakum. We now opened our fire and at the first broadside saw numbers, probably of those who came to see the fun, scampering away up the hill at the back of the fort.

Our second broadside seemed to have caused the complete abandonment of their guns as none was fired afterward; nor could we see any person in the fort, excepting a soldier who stood upon the ramparts waving his hat as if to desire us to desist firing.

Having passed out of the reach of their cannon, the poor guards who had been left on board saw themselves completely in our power without the chance of rescue, and probably calculated on such treatment as they knew would have been our lot if equally in the power of their Commandant. Their exhibition of fear was really ludicrous, for while we were tying up their firearms so as to prevent their using them, and getting the boat ready to send them harmlessly on shore, they were all the time tremblingly imploring for mercy. Nor could they be made to believe, until they were actually on shore, that we intended to do them no harm. When landed, and their arms handed to them, they embraced each other, crossed themselves and fell on their knees in prayer. As our boat was leaving them they rose up and cried at the utmost stretch of their voices, "Vivan, vivan los Americanos."

Having plugged up the hole made by the shot near the water, we steered southward for the bay of St. Quentins [in Baja California] and arrived there on the 24th. . . . We were visited by the padres of the missions of San Vincente, San Domingo, San Rosario and San Fernando, who came on horses with a retinue of Indian domestics, making quite a formidable train. . . . They formed together a jolly set of fellows. Their object seemed to be principally recreation, though they brought a few sea otters' skins, which they bartered with us for European manufactures.

They pitched their tents on the beach abreast the vessel and having provided themselves with an abundant supply of provisions and the requisite cooking utensils, they became quite domiciliated. Never was there an equal number of men more disposed to promote harmony and good fellowship, and we dined together alternately on shore and on board during the week that they remained with us.

As for several days after their arrival they did not mention the affair of San Diego, we supposed they might not have heard of it, yet . . . it would have been strange if news of an event so novel and extraordinary should not have reached them. After the acquaintance had been promoted, however, by a few days of such familiar intercourse, we were asked by the eldest of the padres if we had not been to San Diego. With the peculiarity attributed to New Englanders, our answer was evasive and the question put, "Why?" He then . . . related our transactions so precisely as they occurred that we acknowledged ourselves to have been the actors. He said that the account of the affair was transmitted by letter from the corporal who commanded in the battery to his senior officer at Loretto, and that the letter was left unsealed that it might be read at the several missions on its way, and to be sealed at the last mission before arriving at Loretto.

While the corporal in his letter was severe in his strictures on the conduct of the Commandant in first enticing us into this difficulty and then taking care not to enter the fort until he ascertained that we were out of reach of cannon shot, he was profuse in his eulogies of us. Our forbearance so long before returning their fire, our humanity and generosity to the guards under such provocation and our ceasing to fire when they did were considered by the corporal as acts of magnanimity which should recommend us to the kindness and hospitality of all good Spaniards.

The padres had been friendly before this acknowledgment, but they seemed afterward to vie with each other on who should show us the greatest kindness, offering to procure us supplies in any quantity and assuring us of meeting a hospitable reception at any of the missions we might visit in California. . . .

Having, with ill-judged economy, coppered our vessel only to light-water mark, we perceived that the worm had already made dreadful ravages in our wooden sheathing and that it was necessary to lay her ashore to cleanse and boot-top the bottom. The port being well adapted to such purpose, it was accomplished without difficulty. In the performance of this business, of repairing the injury sustained in our sails and rigging by the cannon shot, in the recreation of fishing and fowling and in taking a plan of the port, the time was filled up until the fortnight agreed on had elapsed. . . .

Although there was nothing now to cause us another day's detention, yet the padres were so urgent for our remaining another week, alleging that they had brought provisions with that expectation, that we could not resist their importunate persuasions. . . . These good padres, though very amiable, were very ignorant on all subjects excepting that of their profession, and so intolerant and bigoted as frequently to express astonishment that men so humane and intelligent should be blind to the truth and beauty of Catholicism.

In remarking, however, on the apparent amiability of these people, I ought to except the padre of San Vincente who, it must be acknowledged, had no just pretension to such character after boasting as he did that he had rendered God service by killing many of the Indians who obstinately refused to be converted.

They expressed great disgust with the character and conduct of Don Manuel Rodriguez, called him a poltroon and said he would be broken—not so much for having fired on a ship of friendly power as for undertaking what he was unable to accomplish, thereby exposing the weakness of the place and subjecting the royal flag to insult. It is indeed doubtful whether the éclat caused in Europe by the Battle of Copenhagen was greater than that of the battle of San Diego in California.

The week we had engaged to pass with the padres having expired, on the 3rd of May we then, with reciprocal friendly salutations and cordial exchange of good wishes for prosperity and happiness, bade them farewell and put to sea.

From *In the Forecastle or Twenty-five Years a Sailor*, Richard J. Cleveland (New York: Hurst and Co., c. 1843).

XI

Gertrude Atherton

To the list of nations that had already entered bids for California real estate and commerce, Russia in 1806 began insisting, with ever-increasing perseverance, that her name be added. The Russian bid was one of urgency, even desperation; she had to have California produce to stave off hunger in her fur colonies on the coast of Alaska. The Muscovite fur companies had a formidable obstacle to maintenance and expansion of their operations for the simple reason that both their food supplies and the pelts they collected had to be freighted thousands of miles across Siberia, as well as the Pacific. They were too far from home base, so far that at times Sitka and its outposts were on the verge of starvation.

What the fur traders—the *promyshlenniki*—urgently needed were the grains, fruits, vegetables, and meats that California could so conveniently provide. And it was in search of such supplies that hungry—and ambitious—Baron Nicholas Resanov sailed into San Francisco Bay in 1806. The implications of that visit were weighed by Gertrude Atherton (1857–1948), a native of San Francisco and a pioneer in the field of the California historical novel, who for fifty years contributed voluminously to the literature of the state.

According to Miss Atherton's interpretation of the facts, California might well have turned into a Soviet puppet state, and the whole Pacific Coast developed into a region "swarming with muzhiks and their overlords, big, blond and prolific," if the romance between

Resanov and the young daughter of the San Francisco commandant in 1806 had ended differently.

Suitor from St. Petersburg

When His Excellency, Nicolai Petrovich Resanov, one of the ten barons of Russia, Privy Councilor and High Chamberlain of His Imperial Majesty Alexander I, first ambassador to the court of Japan, chief partner of the great Shelekov-Golikhov Fur Company of Russian America, circumnavigator of the globe, sailed in the bark *Juno* (bought from a Boston skipper) through what was then awkwardly known as the Mouth of the Gulf of Farallones, on that fateful morning of 1806, he was in no romantic mood.

Suffering from malnutrition himself, and further depleted by a recent attack of malarial fever, he was even more concerned for his workmen at Sitka, ravaged with scurvy, their teeth loose or missing, after too long a diet of dried fish, sea dogs, fat of whales. They could no longer eat the tough flesh of those animals whose furry hides were making a fortune for the company in St. Petersburg and Moscow. He had bought the tempting cargo of the *Juno* and embarked for California with the purpose of trading it for farinaceous foods, vegetables and fruits.

He also had another purpose, as yet confided to no one. There was little he did not know of that beautiful and fertile department of New Spain and it was his definite intention to annex it to Russia. All in good time. A few agricultural emigrants at first, who would pay handsomely for superfluous acres of those immense ranchos; then, ever-increasing numbers, including many of his own class, ten thousand at least. Spain was weak and Russia too strong to defy.

During his brief visit to the Presidio of San Francisco, which lay on the right of the "Mouth," he had glorious visions of the great sweep of valley before the Mission Dolores, that rugged mass of hills and ravines down on the southeastern shore of the Bay where one of its long arms turned abruptly to the right, those graceful islands in the central waters—all, all, to be magnificent with palaces large and small; towers, battlements, spires, gilded domes, cupolas spherical or helmet-shaped; cathedrals, museums, institutions, government buildings; the architecture, as in Russia, Byzantine, Romanesque, baroque, or the classical columns beloved of Catherine the Great. And every island should be a fortress with guns pointing toward those narrow straits that separated the Pacific Ocean from the grand sweep of inland waters whose like in his travels as circumnavigator he had never seen.

And himself plenipotentiary, overlord. California was 3,000 leagues from Russia and these thousands of fertile acres, that city more imposing than Moscow or St. Petersburg, would virtually be his own.

But alas!

Doña Concha Argüello y Moreaga, daughter of Don José Argüello, Comandante of the Presidio of San Francisco, *La Favorita* of all California, was the most beautiful girl he had ever seen, and he had visited all the capitals of Europe. She had the white skin of her Castilian ancestors, her immense black eyes were trimmed with lashes so long they swept her cheeks, her delicate profile was faintly Roman, and her mouth, although childish, betrayed infinite possibilities. Her tall swaying figure above tiny arched feet was the essence of youth budding into maturity. In her masses of black hair she wore either a Castilian rose or a tall Spanish comb. Although only fifteen she was an accomplished coquette; she managed her numerous adorers with infinite skill, prided herself on her knowledge of men—and believed that babies were left under a rosebush by the Blessed Virgin.

More potent than her beauty, she had a subtle magnetic charm, a unique personality that further bedazzled her suitors, even while it filled them with vague misgivings. She was tired of them all, of their melting eyes, their fervid and flowery protestations, their nightly warbling beneath her grating. She longed for some personage from the City of Mexico to visit this rim of the world and rescue her; take her to Europe, above all to Madrid, give her a place in the great world of which she had read. But only old men came from the capital of New Spain, and it so happened that this distinguished Russian was the first man of the great world she had ever met.

But with Rezanov and Concha it was not that classic adventure, love at first sight, immortal as their romance was to be. He was too hungry. Until he sat down to dinner in the house of the Comandante he had not enjoyed a square meal for three years. Moreover, his mind was preoccupied with the mission upon whose success or failure hundreds of lives and his own future depended. Nevertheless, he made up his mind instantly to marry this daughter of the most important man in California; such an alliance would smooth the way to his ultimate goal.

And *La Favorita?* She too made up her mind, and with no maidenly hesitation—nor doubts. She would marry this *grand seigneur* from the north, and she too was inspired by ambition, not love. She saw herself, the wife of a great noble, at the court of Alexander, Czar of all Russias, perhaps at that of the almost mythical Napoleon Bonaparte, whose like had not appeared on earth since Julius Caesar. And perhaps even at the court of Spain, the land of her noble ancestors!

Rezanov was forty or more. Although a commanding figure he was by no means a romantic one with his emaciated face, his cold blue eyes (which, however, could light and flash), his severe green uniform, so different from the silks and lace ruffles of her *caballeros,* whose long hair was confined by a ribbon, while this man's pale locks were short and not even powdered, as was the custom in Europe—Concha, unlike other girls of her race, had read many books. But he was of imposing height and physique; he had an air of elegant repose, and was far more interesting to talk to than any man in the length and breadth of California.

Although Rezanov was treated with warm hospitality by the Californians, who liked and admired him, his mission would have failed but for Concha. A recent law had been passed by the Viceroy of New Spain abolishing trade with all foreigners. The Boston skippers came no more with cloth, silks, satins, laces, fans, dainty slippers, to say nothing of more practical wares, and although the hold of the *Juno* was abundantly supplied, the Governor was obdurate.

The girls, the women, even the *caballeros*, besought him in vain. The padres of the Mission Dolores, ecstatic over Rezanov's presents of cloth of gold for the church, and heavy brown cloth to replace their threadbare habits, when their eloquence produced no effect, wrote to the Viceroy, setting forth the pressing needs of both Presidio and Mission, subtly insinuating that it might be wise to win the friendship of that formidable settlement in the north, whose need was so great. But letters took long to travel from California to the City of Mexico.

It was Concha who advised him to tempt the padres and win their allegiance, and when hope was ebbing it was she who conceived the brilliant idea of selling the cargo to the Governor, and, as Spanish money was forbidden to leave the country, returning the gold immediately in payment for a cargo of corn, vegetables and dried fruits. No law would be violated, no conscience racked.

And meanwhile? Great hampers of food were sent to the *Juno* every morning. Rezanov dined with the Comandante or one of the officers daily. His strength was restored, his appearance vastly improved. There were picnics (*meriendas*) on the islands, which, during long walks with Concha, he investigated thoroughly. They crossed the Bay in the *Juno* and climbed Mount Tamalpais, from whose crest he had a fine view of the surrounding country with its forests of redwoods, pines and oak trees, its ranchos with their herds of cattle and abundant harvests. On the eastern side of the Bay was the lofty range of the Contra Costa Mountains, and beyond, he was told, were more fertile valleys, bounded, thirty miles away, by the Sierra Nevada Mountains, a still mightier range. A principality! A kingdom! An empire!

The young people on these excursions were chaperoned by amiable young matrons, and he had many long conversations with Concha. At first it was her intelligence that interested him, although had she been plain she might have interested him less. Moreover, she had a bewildering variety of moods; she was companionable and sympathetic; those great black eyes, that could sparkle with coquetry or flash with anger, grew dim with tears when he dwelt upon the plight of his miserable *promyshlenniki*.

But when he became aware that he was falling in love—he who had loved so many women in his youth, but for years had been too occupied with great affairs to regard them as aught but a sex created for the pleasure and convenience of man—he was incredulous. He, a man of forty-two, a long-disillusioned man-of-the-world, to fall in love with a girl of fifteen, however beautiful and alluring, to thrill at her touch, at the magnet in her blood, the music of her deep warm voice! His head swam as he watched her dance *la jota* or *el son* in the *sala* at night, when she looked like a floating wraith from another sphere. The *caballeros* applauded and shouted, flung gold and silver, their jeweled chains at her feet (to be returned discreetly by her brother Santiago next day), but he sat silent and enthralled, every nerve quivering.

The time came when he deluded himself no longer. Concha Argüello was the love of his life, and he was consumed not only with the passion of youth but with that of a man for his mate.

But should he ever be able to see her alone?

One morning after a sleepless night he sprang out of bed before dawn, plunged for a moment into the Bay, dressed himself hurriedly, and started for a long walk. He was in a towering bad humor, but his insomnia had not been caused by love alone; the weeks were passing and the hold of the *Juno* was still empty, for Concha had not yet revealed her cunning plan. Nor was there a hint from those cursed Spaniards that they would grant his request.

Failure grinned and jabbered at him. His men would starve; his future was black. As he strode through the sand dunes he hated them all. As for love, he anathematized himself for a fool. If he were to win Concha, and she had given him no sign of anything but sweet friendliness, would that compensate for the death of ambition, of power, of the brilliant future he had planned? And what could he offer her? He, a ruined man?

He left the sand dunes and entered that mass of hills and ravines down by the eastern shore. But he gave not a glance to those slopes and crests which his fancy had set with palaces and cathedrals, shining domes and lofty spires, all glittering in the crystal air and sun flood. Vain dreamer that he was!

He climbed to the top of the promontory where the Bay turned to the south, his body tired, but his brain still seething, and stood glaring at the sun rising over Monte Diablo, the loftiest peak of the Contra Costa Range. Suddenly he whirled about. A familiar voice floated up from the ravine below: *"Señor, señor."* He looked down. Concha was forcing a mustang up the side of the ravine. Half-believing, he stumbled down the uneven slope. She reined in and told him hurriedly that, unable to sleep, she had been out in the garden and had seen him striding along the shore. No one else was awake. She had saddled her horse and followed to tell him of the solution of his difficulties she had conceived during a sleepless night. And then all barriers crashed down and there followed a love scene that has no place in a biography.

The opposition by parents, priests and Governor to the marriage of a Catholic maid with a heretic was even more determined than to a mere matter of trade. But Concha and Rezanov were equally determined, and after long hours of discussion and protestations, often violent, the would-be masters of the couple's fate conceived a subtle plan. They would buy the cargo of Rezanov with their own money, promise a constant exchange of goods in the same fashion and consent to the marriage—if he would leave at once and personally obtain the consent of the Holy Father in Rome, and of the King of Spain in Madrid; a journey that would take two years at least. Meanwhile Concha would forget him and marry a *caballero*.

Rezanov, although appalled, was forced to consent. Two years! His only consolation was that he was permitted to see Concha alone occasionally, and he knew that her love was as deathless as his own. It was a lovely morning in May when he sailed with a bursting hold, and looked his last on Concha as she stood alone on a cliff, the breeze lifting her unbound hair and swirling it, a black cloud, about her tense form.

And so California moved smoothly on to her appointed destiny. Had Rezanov and Concha been permitted to marry at once, they would have lingered at Sitka for a time, then proceeded by slow stages over the vast wastes of Siberia in comfortable sleds, resting at the different outposts. At St. Petersburg he would have presented his bride at court, witnessed her triumphs with adoring pride, confided his plans (although not their ultimates) to the Czar, who would have eagerly welcomed the prospect of that fertile addition to his empire. Emigration would have begun at once. In due course they would have returned to California and he would have outwitted the Spaniards and accomplished his purpose.

Or if Concha had already been married when he arrived in California, or had been paying a long visit to Monterey or Santa Barbara, and his good friend Luis Argüello had conceived this plan to sell and buy, he would still have traveled by slow stages across those terrible wastes, mindful of his damaged constitution, have taken a luxurious rest in his palace in St. Petersburg, and then proceeded to carry out his plans.

In Sitka he had a brief attack of malaria. Persuading himself that he had fully recovered, at the end of ten days he sailed on the *Juno* to Okhotsk, where a caravan with forty horses for relays awaited him.

The first stage of the journey from Okhotsk to Yakutsk, some 650 miles, would have been a rigorous journey for a young man in robust health. The road led over the Stanovoi Mountains in a southwesterly direction to the Maya River, along the latter's wavering course to Aldan, then south beside the Lena. He galloped far ahead of the caravan, splashing through bogs and streams, fording rivers without ferries, sleeping at night in forests whose bitter cold penetrated his abundant furs. On the eighth day the rains began; they descended in torrents and without intermission.

In a rapid, swollen torrent his horse lost its footing and fell. He was soaked to the skin and they did not reach a hut where a fire could be made until nine hours later. It was then that the germs of malaria stirred more vigorously than in Sitka. He rode on in a burning fever. On the following day his servant Jon and one of the Cossack guards caught him as he fell from his horse, unconscious. He was doctored from the medicine chest, and Jon used the lancet while Rezanov slept. The fever ebbed and Rezanov insisted upon continuing the journey although he felt heavy with intolerable lassitude.

When he reached Yakutsk he went to bed in the house of the agent of his company, and this time his fever and convalescence lasted for eight weeks. Despite the stern warnings of the doctor and the supplications of his friends, he started off again, although this time by sledge. The journey of 1,500 miles to Irkutsk, in the open air and with no effort on his part so invigorated him that he mounted his horse and galloped again, although forced at times to return to the sledge.

Then came a long stretch of country so frozen that sledges were left behind, and Rezanov was forced to travel in a telega, a conveyance little larger than an armchair and even lighter. It was drawn by two horses that galloped up-and-downhill with no change of gait and over a road so rough that the little vehicle seemed to be propelled by a succession of earthquakes.

At Irkutsk, once more consumed by fever, he lay in the home of the Governor where he had the best of nursing and medical care, and if he had remained in that luxurious city for six months he would undoubtedly have lived for many years longer. But he resumed his terrible journey, for he was a man of indomitable will and little patience. On March 8, 1807, he succumbed in Krasnoyarsk, and Concha Argüello became the first nun in California.

From *My San Francisco,* Gertrude Atherton (New York: Bobbs-Merrill, 1946).

XII

Peter Corney

From Moscow to Madrid, from Peking to Paris, from Quebec to the Carolinas, the fashion was for furs—luxury furs for hats, wraps, muffs, robes, blankets, and upholstery. The demand was insatiable, and it was this demand that first brought the West Coast into mercantile prominence. Great Pacific explorers like Cook and Vancouver won their laurels as "natural philosophers" in fields of maritime geography and scientific navigation, yet even these "philosophers" were not above mixing business with science, taking on cargoes of furs wherever they were obtainable, and trading for tidy profits on the side. In fact, they were the ones who discovered that fortunes could be made in shipping pelts from the Northwest to the Orient.

By the first decade of the 1800s the fur trade between the opposite coasts of the Pacific had developed into an enormous commerce. The Russians, most eager of furriers, were extending their interests to the very outskirts of the California missions, and in 1809 started erecting temporary or seasonal shelters in the Bodega Bay area. They employed Aleutian hunters, and most of their catch was shipped to Russia. The Europeans and Yankees had a more complicated system. Their general procedure was to establish supply bases anywhere from the Columbia River region to Alaska, coax the Indians and Eskimos into swapping fifty-dollar pelts for a cheap piece of hardware or a few cents' worth of beads and baubles, transport the cargo to Canton or Shanghai, exchange it at handsome profit for silks, ivories, and oriental splendors, then rush the Chinese goods to an Atlantic port to make a final killing.

There were innumerable variations in the pattern—bonus trading in South American ports, extra profit to be made in freighting provisions and assorted wares to Pacific outposts, catering to whalers, sandalwood barter in the Sandwich Islands, trafficking with other remote island chains—but taking on a shipload of furs on some leg of the voyage inevitably brought the most munificent rewards.

Though the bulk of the furs was found farther to the north, California ports were not overlooked when customs officials could be bribed to disregard trade restrictions. To the beans and beef taken aboard at mission outlets, hides were gradually added, until there was a booming commerce in cattle, horse, and elk skins, in seal and sea otter furs, and quantities of beaver pelts from the mountain rivers.

For almost a quarter of a century during the height of this commerce, Peter Corney (d. 1836) periodically roved up and down the West Coast as seaman, supercargo, master, trader, spy, and buccaneer. He crossed the Pacific on trading expeditions more times than he could count; sired a family in Honolulu; worked for half a dozen agencies including John Jacob Astor's Northwest Company and Hudson's Bay Company; and in 1821 prepared a report on his experiences for the London *Literary Gazette*.

The report had the flavor of a personal log or diary; it was inconsistently sketchy or overdetailed, but it did re-create an unsurpassed picture of the day-to-day itinerary of a fur coaster working out of the Columbia River basin, trying to make it worthwhile for the Mexicans at Monterey and the Russians at Bodega to trade with him.

In Quest of Furs

In November [1814, at the Columbia River settlements] we finished a cargo of furs for China and an assortment of goods for the Spanish Maine, and having completed our wood and water, and taken on board plenty of spare spars, we at length cleared the dangerous bar and stood off to the southward toward Monterey.

On the 23rd of November made the coast of California, saw the harbor of Sir Francis Drake and the port of San Francisco, passed the Farlone rocks about one mile from them, at daybreak saw the north point of Monterey Bay, . . . came to in the bay, . . . weighed and turned into the anchorage . . . about a quarter of a mile from the fort.

I went on shore to report the ship and was kindly received by the Spaniards, who had all their force (about fifty horsemen) drawn up on the beach to receive me. I asked the governor if he would answer a salute; he complied and I went on board and saluted with eleven guns, which was returned. Captain Robson and the gentlemen then went on shore and sent off some fresh beef and vegetables for the crew.

Mr. McDougal [manager of the Columbia River trading station] informed the governor that he wished to remain at Monterey to collect provisions for the North West Company's establishment on the Columbia River. The governor could not grant him permission without receiving an order from the viceroy of Mexico; accordingly a courier was dispatched to Mexico with letters to state our wishes to him.

In the meantime, we had fresh beef and vegetables sent off daily. The people [crew] had liberty to walk and ride about the town, the Spanish men and women often coming on board. On Friday, the 16th of December, we received a final answer from Mexico to the following purport, viz., that they could not allow any gentleman to remain in the country; we might land the goods we had brought to barter, and the governor was to see to the collecting of provisions for us against our return to Canton; but the cooper was allowed to remain (as a great favor) to superintend the curing of the beef.

With these terms we were obliged to comply. We accordingly landed the goods, consisting of bale goods, iron, sugar, tobacco, rum, etc. On the 17th eight of our men deserted, and though we tried all means we possibly could devise to bring them back, we failed in that object. On the 21st of December we sailed from Monterey toward Bodago [Bodega], a Russian establishment on New Albion . . . which we reached in due time.

On the 24th we saw a large storehouse on shore. . . . We landed, and found ourselves *above* an Indian village, for here they live underground, and we could hear their voices beneath

us. Several old women and children made their appearance; we
gave them some beads, and by signs inquired where the Russians
were. They pointed to the men round the fire, to whom we accordingly went up, and found them killing rabbits.

Their mode of hunting them is to fire the grass for a considerable distance and kill the rabbits as they are endeavoring to
escape from the flame. The natives on this part of the coast
appear to be a very harmless race. We inquired for the Russians
and they pointed toward the northward. We then left them and
on passing the village some of our party had the curiosity to
venture into their subterraneous abodes, but were obliged to
make a hasty retreat, pursued by swarms of fleas and an intolerable stench from the mass of filth.

We re-embarked and made all sail to the northward, and at 4
P.M. were visited by some Russians in bodarkees. They brought
with them a present of fresh pork and vegetables, and one of them
piloted us to the settlement, where we anchored . . . about one
mile from the shore. Mr. McDougal then went on shore to ask
permission to remain until the schooner arrived from Canton,
which was refused. . . . He returned on board, and at daylight
we weighed and made sail for the Sandwich Islands. . . .

The *Columbia* [a year later] took another trip to Monterey,
where we recovered our people who deserted when we were last
here. . . . We found the cooper had not been idle; he had cured
plenty of beef and collected flour, beans, corn, tallow, peas, etc.,
the farmers bringing in these provisions daily. On our arrival a
guard was posted at the landing place to prevent smuggling, all
trade except through the governor being prohibited. The Spaniards were not allowed to come on board as formerly, neither
were our people allowed so much liberty on shore.

The town of Monterey . . . consists of about fifty houses of
one story, built in a square, surrounded by a stone wall about
eighteen feet high. On the south side of the square stands the
church; on the west, the governor's house; on the east side, the
lieutenant-governor's house and king's stores; on the north side is
the grand and principal entrance, gaol and guard house, and in

the middle are two field pieces, six-pounders. . . . The governor and a few others are old Spaniards; the remaining inhabitants are Creoles of the country. They keep the Indians under great subjection, making them work very hard, chained two and two. The whole population of Monterey does not exceed 400 souls. . . .

The country is well wooded with pine and oak, but badly watered. There are many bears, wolves, foxes, deer, beavers, etc., and in the winter the ducks and geese are very plentiful. The bullocks are sold at four dollars each, and the sheep at one. Two ships touch here annually for tallow and to bring supplies for the establishments on California. . . .

On the 24th [of July, 1817] . . . we made sail for Port Trinidad and hauled into a small bay. . . . We had scarcely time to moor before we were surrounded with canoes. We triced our boarding nets up and shut all our ports but one, at which the natives entered, keeping all the canoes on the starboard side; and, as the Indians came on board, we took their bows and daggers from them, at which they seemed much displeased. . . . We gave them some bread and molasses, of which they ate heartily. We then commenced trading and got a few land furs, which they brought off, for pieces of iron hoop cut into six-inch lengths. They also brought us plenty of red deer and berries. In the afternoon some women made their appearance. The people offered them blankets and axes, but nothing could tempt them to come on board. This is the only place on the coast where we could not induce the females to visit the ship.

It appears that these natives have not had much communication with Europeans, as they do not know the use of firearms, nor have they any iron among them. Their daggers are made of a sort of flintstone, and they are clothed in dressed leather apparel, prettily ornamented with shells. The women wear a very finely dressed leather petticoat, which reaches halfway down the leg, and a square garment of the same thrown loosely over the shoulders. Their tongues and chins are tattooed; the former is quite black, the latter in stripes. Whether this is considered a mark of beauty or not, I cannot tell, but the women here are in general very handsome and well made.

We saw a cross on shore, fixed there by the Spaniards many years ago, when there was a Spanish launch driven on shore, and the Indians massacred the whole crew. The different tribes in this bay are always at war with each other; they never met on board, and if the tribe which was on board trading saw another tribe approaching, they immediately went on shore to protect their wives and property. They all seem to be brave, warlike people. Their canoes are by far the safest I ever saw on the coast, being from sixteen to twenty feet long, and from six to eight feet broad, square at both ends and flat bottomed. . . .

After having bought all the furs here, on the 24th of July we weighed anchor and after encountering considerable difficulties, owing to the bad weather, succeeded in getting out. This was fortunate, as, had we gone on shore (there not being the least shelter in this part of the bay), the Indians were ready to receive and massacre us, for they are without exception the most savage tribes on all the coast. . . .

We immediately made all sail from the coast. Next day, July 26, we saw Cape Mendocino, north about four leagues, found our bowsprit sprung, and determined to run to Bodago Bay and fish it. Stood along shore accordingly and on the 28th got off the settlement, fired a gun, and several bodarkees came off, bringing with them some fresh pork and vegetables. We here moored and fished our bowsprit.

Captain Jennings then went to the settlement in the whaleboat to try to dispose of his cargo to the Russians, but returned to the ship in two days without having effected his purpose. While we lay here the Russians sent us some fresh provision and vegetables; the natives also visited us in their canoes, which are nothing more than several large bundles of rushes lashed together. They seem to be the poorest tribe in these parts, although the country is by far the finest. The climate is so pure and the grounds so good that the Russians grow two crops per year.

The Russian establishment on the coast of New Albion is . . .

about four leagues to the northward of this fine bay and harbor called Bodago, where they have a large store. Here their ships generally call and sometimes winter, there being no shelter for ships off the establishment. The reason for their having it so far from the harbor is the scarcity of timber, which is very necessary in the forming of a settlement, and where they now are the country is covered with fine oak, ash and pine timber fit for ship building. They had on the stocks, and nearly fit for launching, a fine brig of 150 tons, built of good oak. They get excellent hemp on the coast of California and make good rope.

This settlement consists of about 100 houses and huts, with a small fort on the point, and about 500 inhabitants, Russians and Kodiacks. The land is in the highest state of cultivation, growing excellent wheat, potatoes, hemp and all kinds of vegetables. . . . I have seen radishes that weighed from one pound to 28 pounds, and much thicker than a stout man's thigh, and quite good all through without being the least spongy.

They have a large stock of cattle, sheep and pigs, and seem to be in the most flourishing condition under the direction of Governor Kutzkoff [Kuskov]. Hence hunters are sent down the coast of California for the purpose of taking the sea otter, which are very plentiful along the coast. The colony also sends a vessel to Norfolk Sound once a year with the furs collected, and with wheat and hemp. Norfolk Sound is the principal depot; from thence the furs are sent to Kamschatka.

On the 18th of August, 1817, we completed our work here [Bodega], weighed anchor and stood away for the Farlone rocks.

From *Voyages in the Northern Pacific,* Peter Corney (Honolulu: Thrum, 1896).

XIII

Otto von Kotzebue

If anything, Peter Corney underestimated the extent of influence and activity of the Russians in California. He did not realize that they were literally ravaging the coast of its most prized wild life.

From a temporary encampment set up at Bodega Bay in 1809 they had shipped out at the end of the season 2,350 sea-otter pelts. Two years later they established a ranch near Jenner and a warehouse at Russian Gulch, and following a shortened period of hunting, returned to Sitka with a catch of 1,160 pelts. Then in 1812 a crew of ninety-five Russians and forty Aleuts built permanent headquarters at a small harbor thirty miles north of Bodega Bay, erected log cabins, storage sheds, and blockhouses, and encircled the whole with a stockade, which shortly acquired the name of Fort Ross—a corruption of "Rus."

The Russians kept coming. To all appearances they were in California with the intention of remaining forever. During the next decade and a half thousands upon thousands of sea otters and seals were slaughtered and the pelts stored at the fort for shipment to Asia and Europe. The coast between Cape Mendocino and Monterey was such a prolific and profitable source of furs that in 1821 the Czar boldly issued a ukase closing the Pacific Coast north of San Francisco to all fur trade ships not flying the Russian colors.

But the hunters had not counted on the depletion of their quarry. By 1830 the California sea otter was rapidly becoming extinct. The colonists at Fort Ross turned to agricultural pursuits, without notable success. They held out until 1839, when Saint Petersburg finally ordered the tenants to sell out and abandon the fort.

In 1824, just before the Russian fortunes in California began to turn, Fort Ross was visited by the great Russian explorer and naval officer, Otto von Kotzebue (1787–1846), Captain of the Imperial Navy, thrice circumnavigator of the globe and discoverer of many Pacific islands. Kotzebue was honestly impressed with what he found at Fort Ross, but in writing about it he was inclined to go overboard in glorifying the accomplishments of his countrymen.

The Blessings of Russian Civilization

From the summit of a high hill we at length to our great joy perceived beneath us the fortress of Ross, to which we descended by a tolerably convenient road. We spurred our tired horses and excited no small astonishment as we passed through the gate at a gallop. M. Von Schmidt, the governor of the establishment, received us in the kindest manner, fired some guns to greet our arrival on Russian-American ground and conducted us into his commodious and orderly mansion, built in the European fashion with thick beams. . . .

The fortress is a quadrangle, palisaded with tall, thick beams and defended by two towers which mount fifteen guns. The garrison consisted on my arrival of a hundred and thirty men, of whom a small number only were Russians, the rest Aleutians.

The Spaniards lived at first on the best terms with the new settlers and provided them with oxen, cows, horses and sheep; but when in process of time they began to remark that, notwithstanding the inferiority of soil and climate, the Russian establishment became more flourishing than theirs, envy and apprehension of future danger took possession of their minds. They then required that the settlement should be abandoned—asserted that their rights of dominion extended northward quite to the Icy Sea, and threatened to support their claims by force of arms.

The founder and then commander of the fortress of Ross, a man of penetration and one not easily frightened, gave a very decided answer. He had, he said, at the command of his superiors, settled in this region, which had not previously been in the possession of any other power, and over which, consequently, none had a right but the natives; that these latter had freely consented to his occupation of the land, and therefore that he would yield to no such unfounded pretension as that now advanced by the Spaniards, but should always be ready to resist force by force.

Perceiving that the Russians would not comply with their absurd requisitions, and considering that they were likely to be worsted in an appeal to arms, the Spaniards quietly gave up all further thought of hostilities and entered again into friendly communications with our people, since which the greatest unity has subsisted between the two nations.

The Spaniards often find Ross very serviceable to them. For instance, there is no such thing as a smith in all California; consequently the making and repairing of all manner of iron implements here is a great accommodation to them, and affords lucrative employment to the Russians. The dragoons who accompanied us had brought a number of old gunlocks to be repaired.

In order that the Russians might not extend their dominion to the northern shore of the Bay of San Francisco, the Spaniards immediately founded the missions of San Gabriel and San Francisco Solano. It is a great pity that we were not beforehand with them. The advantages of possessing this beautiful bay are incalculable, especially as we have no harbor but the bad one of Bodega or Port Romanzow.

The inhabitants of Ross live in the greatest concord with the Indians, who repair in considerable numbers to the fortress and work as day laborers for wages. At night they usually remain outside the palisades. They willingly give their daughters in marriage to Russians and Aleutians; and from these unions, ties of relationship have arisen which strengthen the good understanding betweeen them.

The inhabitants of Ross have often penetrated singly far into the interior when engaged in the pursuit of deer or other game, and have passed whole nights among different Indian tribes, without ever having experienced any inconvenience. This the

Spaniards dare not venture upon. The more striking the contrast between the two nations in their treatment of the savages, the more ardently must every friend to humanity rejoice on entering the Russian territory.

The Greek Church does not make converts by force. Free from fanaticism, she preaches only toleration and love. She does not even admit of persuasion, but trusts wholly to conviction for proselytes, who, when once they enter her communion, will always find her a loving mother. How different has been the conduct both of Catholic priests and Protestant missionaries!

The climate of Ross is mild. Reaumur's thermometer seldom falls to the freezing point; yet gardens cannot flourish on account of the frequent fogs. Some versts [verst = .6 mile] farther inland beyond the injurious influence of the fog, plants of the warmest climates prosper surprisingly. Cucumbers of fifty pounds' weight, gourds of sixty-five, and other fruits in proportion are produced in them. Potatoes yield a hundred or two hundred fold, and as they will produce two crops in a year, are an effectual security against famine.

The fortress is surrounded by wheat and barley fields which, on account of the fogs, are less productive than those of Santa Clara, but which still supply sufficient corn for the inhabitants of Ross. The Aleutians find their abode here so agreeable that, although very unwilling to leave their islands, they are seldom inclined to return to them.

The Spaniards should take a lesson in husbandry from M. Von Schmidt, who has brought it to an admirable degree of perfection. Implements equal to the best we have in Europe are made here under his direction. Our Spanish companions were struck with admiration at what he had done; but what astonished them most was the effect of a windmill; they had never before seen a machine so ingenious and so well adapted to its purpose.

Ross is blessed with an abundance of the finest wood for building. The sea provides it with the most delicious fish; the land with an inexhaustible quantity of the best kinds of game; and, notwithstanding the want of a good harbor, the northern settlements might easily find in this a beautiful magazine for the supply of all their wants. Two ships had already run in here from Stapel.

The Indians of Ross are so much like those of the missions that they may well be supposed to belong to the same race, however different their language. They appear indeed by no means so stupid, and are much more cheerful and contented than at the missions, where a deep melancholy always clouds their faces, and their eyes are constantly fixed upon the ground; but this difference is only the natural result of the different treatment they experience.

They have no permanent residence, but wander about naked and, when not employed by the Russians as day laborers, follow no occupation but the chase. They are not difficult in the choice of their food, but consume the most disgusting things, not excepting all kinds of worms and insects, with good appetite, only avoiding poisonous snakes.

For the winter they lay up a provision of acorns and wild rye. The latter grows here very abundantly. When it is ripe, they burn the straw away from it, and thus roast the corn, which is then raked together, mixed with acorns, and eaten without any further preparation. The Indians here have invented several games of chance; they are passionately fond of gaming, and often play away everything they possess. Should the blessing of civilization ever be extended to the rude inhabitants of these regions, the merit will be due to the Russian establishments, certainly not to the Spanish missions.

From *A Voyage Round the World in the Years 1823 to 1826,* Vol. II, Otto von Kotzebue (London: Colburn and Bentley, 1830).

XIV

Alfred Robinson

Kotzebue had an exaggerated idea of the blessings of civilization his country was bringing to North America, but the intrusion of the Russians was not altogether detrimental to the advancement of California, despite their reduction of fur seals and sea otter almost to the point of extinction. The competition they offered kept the Spanish-Mexicans on their mettle, and they were responsible at least in part for challenging bureaucratic officials at Monterey to adopt a more reasonable attitude toward foreign commerce and for challenging the Church fathers to extend the line of missions to the north.

Instead of the three missions originally planned for Alta California, seven times that number were eventually established, the twenty-first, San Francisco Solano, in 1823. Although these continued for a few years to be the most influential educational, commercial, and doctrinal agencies in the province, they fell into rapid decline after the Mexican break with Spain in the early 1820s, when California became first a province in the short-lived Empire of Mexico and then an outpost in the Republic of Mexico.

The last period when the missions could be seen in full operation, still radiating some of their former glory, was in the late 1820's, and those were the years in which a proper Bostonian, Alfred Robinson (1806–1895), visited them one by one and sized them up in candor and good humor. Professionally Robinson was a West Coast agent for the illustrious Bay State firm of Bryant, Sturgis and Company, general merchants, importers, dealers in furs and leather goods; avocationally he was a talented artist, raconteur, and writer.

As the representative of Bryant, Sturgis, Robinson had the responsibility, with the assistance of his servant-companion Deppe, to assemble cargoes of hides at mission landings for his ships to load. Half of his job, therefore, was to befriend the mission Fathers and persuade them to reserve their supply of hides for the Bryant, Sturgis trade. He was a remarkably successful operator. His usual procedure was to race on horseback from one mission to the next—on fine steeds supplied gratuitously by the padres—while his ship followed a parallel course at sea. The hides were usually stacked on shore ready for shipment by the time the vessel put in at a prearranged anchorage.

Robinson, only twenty-three at the time of his arrival in 1829, had a rare opportunity to assess mission organization. He discovered that a presiding Father held almost dictatorial authority over a mission, and its prosperity and rapport were inevitably a reflection of the character of the chief administrator. There were, accordingly, tidy, paternalistic, thriving missions, while others were slovenly, ill-managed, almost destitute. Robinson portrayed their color, romance, and relative affluence as a man of commerce saw them, but he did not look very closely behind scenes to observe that the Indians were virtual slaves, restless, unhappy, rebellious, and inarticulate—not subject to sale, but subject to pursuit, capture, severe punishment, and impoundage, if they escaped. He did not sense that the whole system was nearing its end, nor did he foresee that a more republican Mexican government was about to release them from bondage, restore at least token lands to them, and secularize the Church domains.

Commerce in the Cloisters

San Gabriel

It was Saturday evening, and as we approached the buildings of the Mission, the chapel bells tolled the hour for prayer. Hundreds of Indians were kneeling upon the ground and, as the tolling ceased, they slowly rose to retire, and a merry peal announced the coming of the Sabbath.

The director of San Gabriel was Father José Sanches, who for many years had controlled the establishment, which, through his management, had advanced to its present flourishing condition. Possessing a kind, generous and lively disposition, he had acquired in consequence a multitude of friends who constantly flocked around him, whilst through his liberality the needy wanderer, of whatever nation or creed, found a home and protection in the Mission.

In the morning at six o'clock we went to the church, where the priest had already commenced the service of the mass. The imposing ceremony, glittering ornaments and illuminated walls were well adapted to captivate the simple mind of the Indian, and I could not but admire the apparent devotion of the multitude, who seemed absorbed heart and soul in the scene before them.

The solemn music of the mass was well selected, and the Indian voices accorded harmoniously with the flutes and violins that accompanied them. On retiring from the church, the musicians stationed themselves at a private door of the building, whence issued the reverend father, whom they escorted with music to his quarters. There they remained for a half-hour, performing waltzes and marches until some trifling present was distributed among them, when they retired to their homes.

As is usual on all their *dias de fiesta,* the remaining part of the Sabbath is devoted to amusements, and the Indian generally resorts to gambling, in which he indulges to the most criminal excess, frequently losing all he possesses in the world—his clothes, beads, baubles of all kinds, and even his wife and children! We saw them thus engaged, scattered in groups about the Mission, while at a little distance quite an exciting horse race was going on, the Indians betting as wildly on their favorite animals as upon the games of chance which found so many devotees.

There are several extensive gardens attached to this Mission, where may be found oranges, citrons, limes, apples, pears, peaches, pomegranates, figs and grapes in abundance. From the latter they make yearly from four to six hundred barrels of wine and two hundred of brandy, the sale of which produces an income of more than twelve thousand dollars. The storehouses

Mission Dolores

and granaries are kept well supplied, and the corridor in the square is usually heaped up with piles of hides and tallow. Besides the resources of the vineyard, the Mission derives considerable revenue from the sale of grain; and the weekly slaughter of cattle produces a sufficient sum for clothing and supporting the Indians.

The two ranchos of San Bernardino and Santa Anita are included in the possessions of the Mission; the former of these has been assigned by the padres for the sole purpose of domesticating cattle, and is located some leagues distant in a secluded valley among the mountains; the latter is for cultivation and is one of the fairy spots to be met with so often in California.

On the declivity of a hill is erected a *molino* or gristmill, surrounded with fruit trees and flowers. A beautiful lake lies calm and unruffled in front, and all around fresh streams are gushing from the earth and scattering their waters in every direction. It would be a magnificent spot for a summer retreat, and much reminded me of many of the beautiful locations to be met with in the vicinity of Boston.

The Mission of San Gabriel was founded in the year 1771 and its population, including the two ranchos before mentioned, now numbered from twelve to fifteen hundred. It was thought at one time to possess from eighty to over a hundred thousand head of cattle, besides horses, mules and sheep and countless numbers which run at large. No advantage is derived from them beyond the value of their hides and tallow, and thus thousands of dollars are yearly left to perish in the field.

San Juan Bautista

This Mission was founded in the year 1797 and had in 1831 a population of about twelve hundred civilized Indians. It is conveniently located in the center of the valley, with an abundance of rich land and large stocks of cattle. Padre Filipe Arroyo was the missionary, whose infirm state of health kept him confined closely to his chamber. For amusement, when tired of study, he called in the children of the place and set them to dancing and playing their games. In his eccentric taste he has given them the names of all the renowned personages of antiquity, and Ciceros, Platos and Alexanders were to be found in abundance.

A peculiar regard for us procured from the old gentleman a sleeping apartment adjoining his own, not usually bestowed upon travelers. When we retired, however, we were surprised to find no sheets upon the bed, but instead coarse blankets. Shut out from any means of access to the other parts of the building, except through the room of the Padre, it was impossible to remedy the deficiency.

Our light was extinguished, and soon Deppe's nasal organs announced how deep was his repose; but I lay restless and uneasy. I could not sleep. The blankets pricked my flesh; the room was warm; and at times it would seem as if a thousand needles penetrated my legs and sides. Can it be the blankets, thought I, or are they filled with fleas; and, if so, how is it that Deppe sleeps so sound? The more I reasoned, the more horrible became my situation, and I feared I was to become a martyr to never-ending tortures.

They were fleas, indeed! and it appeared to me as if they came in armies to glut their appetites with human blood! It was terrifying! for I thought they would surely suck me dry before morning, and I jumped with horror from the bed to the floor. But it was like jumping out of the frying pan into the fire, for the floor was of tile, and the crevices their place of abode. I felt them jump upon my legs and feet and, reaching down my hand, I swept them off by the dozens.

The bed was least exposed on this account, so back I got, when a sudden twitch of Deppe's frame, and an extra snore or snort revealed his similar fate. Rolling about from side to side, he could suffer no longer in silence, but cried out, "Carramba! what de devil is in de bed?"

"Fleas!" said I, "Ha! ha! fleas! and they will devour us before morning!"

Thus the whole tedious night was passed in scratching and complaining till morning broke, when, worn out with fatigue and loss of sleep, we finally closed our eyes and slept till roused to chocolate. As we passed the old friar on our way to the breakfast room, his friendly inquiries were incessant: *"Buenos dias! como pasaron vmds. la noche?"* To which I would have frankly replied, but politeness forbade, and a shrug of the shoulders brought forth a feeble and laconic answer, *"Bien! gracias!"*

The whole country is infested with fleas, and it is a rare thing to find a house without them, so·that the natives have become accustomed to their bite and think nothing of it.

San Fernando

San Fernando was founded in the year 1797, and at this time was governed by the Reverend Father Francisco Ybarra, a short, thick, ugly-looking old man, whose looks did not belie his character. In his own opinion no one knew so much as himself; nothing was so good as that which he possessed; and being at the head of the establishment no one ever presumed to call his sentiments into question.

The niggardly administration of this place, compared with the liberality and profusion of the other missions we had visited, presented a complete contrast; and the meanness and unpopularity of our host had gained for him the nickname of "Cochino" or "Hog."

At supper I was amused at the economy displayed in the arrangement of his table, which seemed perfectly in accordance with the narrowness of his mind. A door hinged at the bottom, which served to close a recess in the wall used as a cupboard, was let down upon the occasion and on this was placed our repast. The dimensions were only sufficient to admit of four persons comfortably seated, and when that number was larger, to accommodate them all, recourse was had to a dirty-looking bench which stood in one corner of the apartment.

Distrustful of everyone who wished to purchase his tallow or hides, he had accumulated an immense amount in his storehouses, where many of the latter had been destroyed by the length of time they had remained deposited. The tallow had been laid down in large, arched stone vats of sufficient capacity to contain several cargoes.

In the morning we left [without hides or tallow]. . . .

Santa Clara and San Jose

It was three o'clock when we arrived at this Mission [Santa Clara]. . . . Father José Viader was director of the establishment, a good old man whose heart and soul were in proportion to his immense figure. . . . Like the other missions in the neighborhood of San Francisco, its resources are immense from the annual production of grain; and possessing large stocks of cattle, it was enabled to make liberal *matanzas,* of which the abundant proceeds were usually heaped up under the corridor in the square of the main building. A large garden of choice fruit trees adorned its right, whilst another of greater magnitude occupied a space in front. The hills of San Jose were visible beyond, and betwixt the trees that covered the plain we obtained a distant view of the town of that name. . . .

[Since it was a] festival eve at San Jose, many of the Indians were starting off in numbers, and ere the sun had set, hundreds were upon the road for San Jose. Father Viader was to go in the morning before breakfast, and it being but a short ride, we concluded to remain and accompany him.

The morning presented the same lively scene of people going to the feast, and at an early hour the Padre's carriage was brought to the door. It was a singular contrivance, invented by himself and built by the Indian mechanics under his direction—a narrow body of sufficient width for one person only, hung on a pair of low wheels, and the whole frame was covered with brown cotton. The seat, well stuffed with lambs' wool, served to compensate for the absence of springs; and the harness, which he had made from green hide twisted into rope, though not very ornamental, was sufficiently strong and answered every purpose.

All being in readiness, Padre Viader got into his carriage. We mounted our horses and off we started in grand equestrian order. The carriage was drawn by a fine black mule, astride of which sat a little Indian boy who assisted in guiding the animal in connection with a more experienced Indian who, mounted on a fiery steed, led the mule with a *reata* fastened about his neck.

On each side were two vaqueros with lassos fixed to the axle-tree, by which they facilitated the movement of the carriage over the road and essentially aided the mule in ascending steep places. Three or four of the priest's pages attended him also, and in the rear followed a number of alcaldes of the Mission. All were attired for the occasion, and from their hats were flowing red and blue ribbons, which like pennons fluttered in the wind.

A quick movement brought us to a view of the Mission from a neighboring rising ground, from whence we saw the gathering multitude; and as we approached nearer, the bells of the church rang a merry peal in honor of the priest, which continued until the two missionary brothers were fast locked in an embrace, when the ringing ceased and we retired within. It is a prevailing custom at every town or mission in the country to give this demonstration of respect to the holy friar, and not infrequently many of the inhabitants go out to meet him and escort him to his quarters. This respectful observance to a priest rather provoked the jealousy of one of the Mexican governors, who in a circular to this holy brotherhood ordered that the bells should be rung whenever he approached their missions. . . .

The Mission of San Jose was founded in 1797 and had at this time a population of about two thousand Indians. It possesses some of the best lands in the country for agricultural purposes, from which is obtained an immense quantity of grain. It frequently supplies the Russian Company, who yearly send three or four large ships for stores for their northern settlements.

In the rear of the establishment is a large reservoir of excellent water, which is carried through pipes to the gardens and other parts of the Mission. In front of the church is a very neat fountain, and also conveniences for washing and bathing. In point of beauty, the buildings here were very inferior to those of the southern missions. Durability and convenience alone seem to have been consulted in their construction, and they mostly presented a very ordinary appearance. . . .

The padre was . . . Father Narciso Duran, a venerable old man who had spent the most valuable part of his life in incessant labor to promote the advancement of his holy religion. Generous, kind and benevolent, the natives not only revered him as their spiritual father and friend, but seemed almost to adore him. He was universally beloved, and the neighboring village bore testimony to his charitable heart, while many a transient traveler blessed him and thanked God that such a man existed among them. . . .

Mass was soon commenced and Padre Viader . . . ascended the pulpit and delivered an explanatory sermon relative to the celebration of the day. The music was well executed, for it had been practiced daily for more than two months under the particular supervision of Father Narciso Duran. The number of musicians was about thirty; the instruments performed upon were violins, flutes, trumpets and drums, and so acute was the ear of the priest that he could detect a wrong note instantly and chide the erring performer. . . .

After mass was concluded we passed out of the church to the priest's apartment through a shower of rockets, which were fired off incessantly in every direction. Dinner was served early to give us time to witness the performances of the Indians, and . . . a very lengthy table had been prepared so as to accommodate all. An abundance of good things appeared and disappeared, till at length the cloth was removed, cigars were smoked, and the good old friars retired to enjoy their siesta, whilst we repaired to the front corridor to behold the fun.

At a signal from their "capitan" or chief, several Indians presented themselves at a corner of one of the streets . . . and gradually approached us. They were dressed with feathers and painted with red and black paint, looking like so many demons. There were several women amongst them. Soon they formed a circle and commenced what they called *dancing*, which was one of the most ludicrous specimens of grotesque performance I had ever seen.

It did not appear to me that they had any change of figure whatever, but, fixed to one spot, they beat time with their feet to the singing of half a dozen persons who were seated upon the ground. When these had performed their part, they retired to an encampment beyond the building and another party appeared, painted and adorned rather differently from the former, whose mode of dancing also was quite dissimilar.

They retired after a while and arrangements were made for a bear fight. Whilst these amusements were going on, the Padres had risen and we were called to chocolate, but the enthusiasm of the Indians hardly gave us time to finish, when we heard them crying, *"Aqui traen el oso!"* He was soon ready, though almost dead from confinement, and the bull made but a few plunges ere he laid him stiff upon the ground.

This part of the amusement concluded, Deppe and I walked to the encampment where the Indians were dancing in groups. . . . Around the large space which they occupied were little booths displaying a variety of ornaments, seeds and fruits. All was hilarity and good feeling, for the prudence of Father Narciso had forbidden the sale of liquor. At sundown the bells were rung, rockets were let off, guns were fired, and long after supper at a late hour of the night, we could hear from our beds the continued shouts of the multitude.

From *Life in California*, Alfred Robinson (New York: Wiley and Putnam, 1846.)

XV

William Heath Davis

A few ranches in California were almost as old as the missions. The earliest were started on land grants parceled out to Mexican and Spanish families of consequence or to retired officers, for military and political favors rendered. The ranches were of secondary economic and social importance until the missions began to decline. Then they expanded very rapidly, until they dominated the commerce in hides, horses, tallow, and general farm produce, formerly controlled by the missions.

William Heath Davis (1821–1909), son of a prominent shipowner, was a witness to that changeover. He migrated to California, not from the East, but from Honolulu. A remarkably self-reliant lad, he made his first appearance on the coast at the age of nine, and five years later started full-time employment at Monterey and then at Yerba Buena. Before he was out of his teens, he was carrying the responsibilities of supercargo on trips up and down the coast and to the Sandwich Islands; and at twenty-two graduated to the proprietorship of his own merchandising establishment in San Francisco. He helped build that run-down mission-presidio village into a metropolis, and grew in influence and affluence with the city, as one of its foremost merchants and shipowners.

In his various capacities as clerk, trader, supercargo, merchant, and shipper, Davis became acquainted with all classes of Californians from half-breed Indians to arrogant alcaldes. From waiting on them over

the counter, counseling them on their personal affairs, attending their
fiestas, fandangos, and funerals, he came to know them as intimately
as any white immigrant. Then, to celebrate his sixtieth year as resident
of California, he wrote a book on his observations and experience, and
topped that with another on the seventy-fifth year of his residency.

The volumes are a treasury of Western lore, particularly on the
"pastoral" period when the ranches were coming into prominence.
Davis lived with the ranchers; participated in rodeos when they were a
functional part of ranch employment—not an entertainment; knew San
Joaquin Valley when it was populated with thousands of wild horses;
dined many a time on a ranch breakfast of spit-turned beefsteak,
onions, eggs, beans, tortillas, and pea coffee. He could write of details
as only a participant would know them, but his memoirs had shortcomings: they were disjointed, rambling, and repetitious. A few of
Davis' reminiscences on ranch life of the 1830s are here assembled
topically.

A Million Cattle—More or Less

The houses of the rancheros were usually built upon entirely
open ground, devoid of trees, generally elevated, overlooking a
wide stretch of the country round, in order that they might look
out to a distance on all sides, and see what was going on, and
notice if any intruders were about the rancho for the purpose of
stealing cattle or horses, in which way they were occasionally
annoyed by the Indians, or perhaps by some vicious countrymen;
and the house was placed where there was a spring of running
water.

These houses stood out bare and plain, with no adornment of
trees, shrubbery or flowers, and there were no structures, except
the kitchens, attached to the main buildings. Even in towns it was
a rare thing to see flowers or shrubbery about the houses of the
Californians. I have often inquired of the rancheros, on seeing a
beautiful and shaded spot, why they did not select it for their
residence, and they would always answer, it was too near the
forest—they having in view always security against the Indians.
. . .

The people lived in adobe houses, and the houses had tile roofs; they were comfortable and roomy, warm in the winter and cool in the summer. Their furniture was generally plain, mostly imported from Boston in the ships that came to the coast to trade. Generally the houses had floors, but without carpets in the early days. Some of the humble people had no floors to their houses, but the ground became perfectly hard and firm as if cemented.

The women were exceedingly clean and neat in their houses and persons and in all their domestic arrangements. One of their peculiarities was the excellence and neatness of their beds and bedding, which were often elegant in appearance, highly and tastefully ornamented, the coverlids and pillow cases being sometimes of satin and trimmed with beautiful and costly lace. The women were plainly and becomingly attired, but were not such devotees of fashion as at the present day, and did not indulge in jewelry to excess.

Their tables were frugally furnished, the food clean and inviting, consisting mainly of good beef broiled on an iron rod, or steaks with onions, also mutton, chicken, eggs. . . . The bread was *tortillas;* sometimes it was made with yeast. Beans were a staple dish. . . . Their meat stews were excellent when not too highly seasoned with red pepper. The people were sober, sometimes using California wine, but not to excess. They were not given to strong drink, and it was a rare occurrence to see an intoxicated Californian. The men were good husbands generally, and women good wives, both faithful in their domestic relations. The California women, married or unmarried, of all classes, were the most virtuous I have ever seen. There were exceptions, but they were exceedingly rare. The single men were not so much so, associating to some extent with Indian women, although the married men were generally excellent husbands and kind fathers.
. . .

Californians were early risers. The ranchero would frequently receive a cup of coffee or chocolate in bed, from the hands of a servant, and on getting up immediately order one of the vaqueros to bring him a certain horse. . . . He then mounted and rode off about the rancho, attended by a vaquero, coming back to breakfast between eight and nine o'clock. This breakfast was a solid meal, consisting of *carne asada* (meat broiled on a spit), beef-steak with rich gravy or with onions, eggs, beans, *tortillas,* sometimes bread and coffee, the latter often made of peas.

After breakfast the ranchero would call for his horse again, usually selecting a different one, not because the first was fatigued, but as a mattter of fancy or pride, and ride off again around the farm or to visit the neighbors. He was gone till twelve or one o'clock, when he returned for dinner, which was similar to breakfast, after which he again departed, returning about dusk in the evening for supper, this being mainly a repetition of the two former meals. Although there was so little variety in their food from one day to another, everything was cooked so well and so neatly and made so inviting, the matron of the house giving her personal attention to everything, that the meals were always relished.

When the rancheros thus rode about . . . the more wealthy of them were generally dressed in a good deal of style, with short breeches extending to the knee, *botas* (leggings) below, made of fine soft deer skin . . . vests with filagree buttons of gold or silver, . . . a kind of jacket of good length, most generally of dark blue cloth also adorned with filigree buttons. Over that was the long *serape* or *poncho,* made in Mexico and imported from there. . . .

Although the cattle belonging to the various ranchos were wild, yet they were under training to some extent, and were kept in subjection by constant rodeos. At stated times, say, two or three times a week at first, the cattle on a particular ranch were driven in by the vaqueros from all parts thereof to a spot known as the rodeo ground, and kept there for a few hours, when they were allowed to disperse.

Shortly they were collected again, once a week perhaps, and then less seldom, until after considerable training, being always driven to the same place, they came to know it. Then, whenever the herd was wanted, all that was necessary for the vaqueros to do was, say twenty-five or thirty of them, to ride out into the hills and valleys and call the cattle, shouting and screaming to them, when the animals would immediately run to the accustomed spot; presently the whole herd belonging to the ranch finding their way there.

At times, cattle strayed from one ranch to another and got into the wrong herd. Whenever a rodeo was to be held, the neighbors of the ranchero were given notice and attended at the time and place designated. If any of these cattle were found in the band, they were picked out, separated and driven back to the rancho where they belonged. As the cattle were all branded, and each rancho had earmarks, this was not difficult. . . .

When a rodeo took place, six or eight *cabestros,* or tame cattle, were brought together in a stand, or *parada,* about one hundred yards or more from the rodeo. . . . The vaqueros rode quietly in among them in pairs, and two of them, seeing one they wanted to remove, gently approached the animal, one on each side, and without making any disturbance, edged him along to one side of the rodeo ground opposite to where the *parada* stood. When they got just to the edge, they gave him a sudden start by shouting *"hora"* (now), and off he went at full speed, followed by them. Seeing the *parada* a little distance off, the wild steer or cow generally made for that, or was guided by the vaqueros. . . . Two or three hundred cattle belonging to a neighboring ranch would be taken from a rodeo. . . .

The work of separating the cattle, while a necessity, was really more of an amusement than a labor, and I have frequently participated in it for sport. On such occasions many persons from the different ranchos came, as at a cattle fair, to exchange greetings and talk over affairs. . . . Rodeos were held at marking and slaughtering times. . . . The marking season always commenced about the first of February . . . and ended about the middle of May; . . . the killing commenced about the first of July and continued until the first of October—for the hides and tallow. About 200 pounds of the best part of the bullock was preserved by drying, for future consumption, the balance of the animal being left to go to waste; it was consumed by the buzzards and wild beasts. . . .

It was usual to slaughter from fifty to one hundred at a time, generally steers three years old and upward, the cows being kept for breeding purposes. The fattest would be selected for slaughter, and about two days would be occupied in killing fifty cattle, trying out the tallow, stretching the hides and curing the small portion of meat that was preserved. The occasion was called the *matanza*. . . .

About fifty were driven into a corral near the *matanza* ground; a vaquero then went in on horseback and lassoed a creature by the horns. . . . The animal was brought out of the corral and, another vaquero coming up, the animal when it reached the spot where it was wanted, was lassoed by one or both hind legs, and at that moment the horse by a sudden movement jerked the animal to one side or the other, and it was thrown instantly to the ground.

The man who had him by the head then backed his horse, or the horse, understanding the business perfectly, backed himself until the whole reata was straightened out; and the horse of the vaquero who had the creature by the hind legs did the same, and the two lines were drawn taut. The man at the tail end, then dismounting, tied the fore legs of the animal together with an extra piece of rope and the hind legs also, drawing all the feet together in a bunch and tying them. . . . After the steer was thus tied and powerless to rise, the reatas were taken from him entirely and the man on foot stuck a knife in his neck. When he was dead, the two took off the skin in a short time, not over half an hour, so expert were they at the business. . . .

In securing the tallow, the *manteca,* or fat lying nearest the hide of the bullock, was taken off carefully, and tried out apart from the interior fat, or *sebo.* The latter constituted the tallow for shipment; about seventy-five to one hundred pounds being obtained from each creature. The former, of which forty or fifty pounds were obtained, was more carefully and nicely prepared, and was saved for domestic use in cooking, being preferred to hog's lard. . . . Whenever there was more of the *manteca* than was needed for a family, the Russians were eager purchasers for shipment and for their own use. . . .

The tallow was tried in large pots brought by the American

whale ships—such as are used to try out blubber, and was then run into bags made of hides, each containing twenty to forty arrobas. (An arroba is twenty-five pounds.) . . . *Manteca* was sold for $2 per arroba, and the *sebo* at $1.50. . . . From 1826 to 1848 the actual number of hides exported approximated one million and a quarter; . . . during the above period I place the product of tallow for export at two arrobas for each animal killed, which for one million and a quarter would give 62,500,000 pounds. . . .

When cattle were slaughtered, bears came to the place at night to feast on the meat that was left after the hides and tallow were taken, and the rancheros with vaqueros would go there for the purpose of lassoing them. . . . This was one of the greatest sports, highly exciting and dangerous, but the bear always got the worst of it. One would lasso a bear by the neck and another lasso the same beast by the hindfoot, and then, pulling in different directions, the poor bear was soon strained and strangled to death. Sometimes half a dozen or more would be taken in a single night. . . .

At the ranchos very little use was made of milch cows for milk, butter or cheese. I have frequently drunk my tea or coffee without milk on a ranch containing from 3,600 to 8,000 head of cattle. But in the spring of the year when the grass was green, the wives of the rancheros made from the milk *asaderas,* a fresh cheese in small flat cakes, which had to be eaten the day it was made. . . .

The Californians cut up a great many hides for the use of the ranchos. Strips of the skins were used for reatas and in building corrals, also for covering wagons and for many other purposes. Many of the rancheros tanned their own leather. . . . Some of the sons of the rancheros were shoemakers and made shoes for home use. The soles of the shoes were made from the leather and tanned deer skin was used for the uppers. The hides were also used to cover the trees of the saddles. Large quantities of tallow were used by the rancheros for candles and soap. . . .

The supercargoes of the vessels that were trading on the coast, of course, had occasion to visit all the settlements in the interior or along the coast to conduct their business with the people. . . .

The rancheros would attend them with their loads of hides and tallow to pay their indebtedness incurred on a former trip, or to make purchases by exchanging them for goods. . . .

They would convey their hides and tallow in large wagons of very primitive fashion. The body of the vehicle was set on the axles, having no spring, but with four wheels sawed out of a tree four feet in diameter, and about a foot thick, a solid block or section with a hole in the middle for the axle. Sticks were set up perpendicularly along the sides and covered with hides stretched across them, thus enclosing the body of the wagon. . . . The wagons were drawn by oxen.

Families sometimes took long journeys in these wagons fitted up with more style, the sides being lined with calico or sheeting, or even light silk, with mattresses on the floor of the wagon. With cooking and eating arrangements, they went along comfortably, camping by a spring and sleeping in the wagon, traveling days at a time.

A large number of horses was needed on each rancho for herding stock, as they were used up very fast. They were numerous and cheap, and the owners placed no restraint upon the vaqueros, who rode without a particle of regard for the horses. . . . When the horses became disabled or too poor for use, they were generally given away to the poorer people of the country, or to Indians. . . . Civilized Indians from the Missions were scattered about the country and many were to be found on the different ranchos. They were of peaceful disposition, were employed as vaqueros and helped the rancheros at the planting season and at harvest time. . . .

The California horses were originally from Arabian stock, imported from Spain by the Padres at the time of the first establishment of the Missions. They had multiplied here extensively. At first it was very fine stock, but it became degenerated by breeding in, generation after generation for over a hundred years. No attention was given by the rancheros to the production of good stock, either cattle or horses. . . .

The horses were never stabled. They were broken for the saddle only and were used almost wholly for herding cattle. They were divided up into *caponeras,* or small bodies of about twenty-five, each *caponera* having a bell mare. . . . And so accustomed were they to their leaders that the different little bands never mixed. . . . On a rancho with 8000 head of cattle there would be, say, twelve *caponeras.* The vaqueros were continually breaking in young colts three years old and upwards to replace those already beyond service. . . .

There were large bands of wild horses in the Valley of the San Joaquin, which at that time was entirely unsettled. At times a few mares and perhaps a young stallion would stray away from a rancho and get out of reach, until in the course of time there were collected in that valley immense herds, thousands and tens of thousands of horses, entirely wild and untamed, living and breeding by themselves, finding there plenty of good feed to sustain them.

Frequently during the summer time, young men, the sons of rancheros, would go in companies of eight or ten or twelve to the valley on their best and fleetest steeds to capture a number of these wild horses and bring them to the ranchos. On reaching the place where a large band was collected, the saddles being removed, the horses were ridden bareback, a piece of reata being tied loosely around the body of each horse just behind the forelegs, and the rider, having no saddle or stirrups, slipped his knees under the rope, one end of the lasso being tied to the rope also.

Thus prepared, they rode toward the wild horses, who, on seeing them approach, would take alarm and rush off at great speed, the riders following. Sometimes the chase lasted for miles before they came up with the horses. On getting near enough, each horseman selected his victim, pursued him, and at the right moment cast a lasso, which never failed to encircle the neck of the horse; then bringing his own horse to a stand, there was a wild struggle, the rider holding his horse firm, and the captured horse pulling and straining on the rope until he became so choked and exhausted that he was compelled to succumb. . . .

It was a very hazardous sport, and required the greatest nerve and the best horsemanship. If the rider found himself in the midst of a band of wild horses, there was danger that he and his horse might be overridden and trampled to death. This sometimes occurred.

When fifty or sixty of the wild horses were thus captured, they were taken to the ranchos, corralled at night and herded in the daytime until they became sufficiently subdued to be introduced among the horses of the ranch. This was great diversion for the young men, and at the same time it added to their stock the best animals of the wild herds. . . .

[Visitors] were supplied with fresh horses whenever they required them, free of charge, by the Fathers or the rancheros. These horses were furnished as a matter of course. . . . When a traveler reached another stopping place he was provided with a fresh horse, and such a thing as continuing the journey on the horse he rode the day before was not to be thought of, so polite and courteous were these generous Californians.

The traveler had no further care or thought in regard to the horse he had been using, but left him where he happened to be, and the Padre or ranchero would undertake to send him back, or if this was not convenient, it was no matter, as the owner would never ask any questions. It would have been considered impoliteness for the guest to express any concern about the horse or what was to become of him. . . .

In my long intercourse with these people, extending over many years, I never knew an instance of incivility of any kind. They were always ready to reply to a question, and answered in the politest manner, even the humblest of them; in passing along the road, the poorest vaquero would salute you politely. If you wanted any little favor of him, like delivering a message to another rancho or anything of that sort, he was ready to oblige, and did it with an air of courtesy and grace and freedom of manner that was very pleasing. They showed everywhere and always this spirit of accommodation, both men and women. . . .

The merchants sold to the rancheros and other Californians whatever goods they wanted, to any reasonable amount, and gave them credit from one killing season to another. . . . [No] note or other written obligation was required of them. I never knew a case of dishonesty on their part. . . . They always kept their business engagements, paid their bills promptly at the proper time in hides and tallow, which were the currency of the country, and sometimes, though seldom, in money. They regarded their verbal promise as binding and sacred. They were too proud to condescend to do anything mean or disgraceful. . . .

The native Californians were about the happiest and most contented people I ever saw, as also were the early foreigners who settled among them and intermarried with them, adopted their habits and customs, and became, as it were, a part of themselves.

From *Sixty Years in California*, William Heath Davis (San Francisco: A. J. Leary, 1889).

XVI

Richard Henry Dana

Mission patrons and ranchers alike, while concentrating on cattle raising, had singularly neglected production of other everyday necessities such as refined clothing, furniture, household utensils, hardware, and variations in foods and beverages. The natives could get along on a minimum diet and minimum accessories, but people who had inherited European tastes and standards were more demanding, and as trade restrictions were gradually eased, Californios became increasingly dependent upon that phenomenon in the world of commerce, the Yankee peddler.

This hawker on wheels, who had originally started out in New England as a door-to-door dispenser of everything from tea and tinware to clocks and calicoes, over the years had extended his territory down the Atlantic seaboard, into the Deep South, out to the Midwest, and even to the Canadian provinces; then he had exchanged his wagon for a ship and continued the peddlery around the globe. In transit he had discovered California as an outlet, where señors and señoritas, rancheros and carabineros, padres and presidio officials all fell hard for his line.

Their favorite drummer for almost a decade was the Boston firm of Bryant, Sturgis, for whom Alfred Robinson served as resident agent and hide collector. At least twice a year one of the company's floating country stores beat up or down the California coast, putting in for quick sales at every port or anchorage. Late in the winter of 1835 a typical Bryant, Sturgis emporium, the brig *Pilgrim,* sailed into Monterey Bay with Richard Henry Dana (1815–1882) aboard as seaman-peddler. Later Dana was to become one of America's most distinguished writers, maritime lawyers, and political reformers, but in 1835, at the age of twenty, he was playing hooky from Harvard, where during his sophomore year he had contracted an ailment that, according to prescription of the day, could best be cured by a long ocean voyage.

The Harvardian also had a chip on his shoulder. As a forerunner of the American muckraker, he wanted to evaluate for himself the tales he had heard about the brutal treatment inflicted upon seamen of the merchant marine. Practically all that the public knew of life on board a trading vessel had been told by officers—by "a gentleman with his gloves on," as Dana put it; he intended to present the seaman's point of view, to expose himself to all the hardships of the forecastle, and then to expose the officers.

Dana gathered some appalling details. After witnessing the flogging of a fellow deckhand he vowed, "If God should ever give me the means, I would do something to redress the grievances and relieve the sufferings of that poor class of beings." *Two Years Before the Mast,* published in 1840, was the God-given means. Almost immediately it was accepted as an American classic, not only for Dana's revelations of "the life of a common sailor at sea as it really is," but also for his vivid descriptions of places and people he saw at ports of call, including the account of Yankee peddlers in action at Monterey.

Into a Christian Country

It was a fine Saturday afternoon when we came to anchor [at Monterey], the sun about an hour high, and everything looking pleasantly. . . . As it was now the rainy season, everything was as green as nature could make it—the grass, the leaves and all; the birds were singing in the woods, and great numbers of wild fowl were flying over our heads. . . . The town lay directly before us, making a very pretty appearance. . . . The red tiles, too, on the roofs, contrasted well with the white plastered sides, and with the extreme greenness of the lawn upon which the houses—about an hundred in number—were dotted about here and there irregularly. . . .

The Mexican flag was flying from the little square Presidio, and the drums and trumpets of the soldiers, who were on parade, sounded over the water and gave life to the scene. Everyone was delighted with the appearance of things. We felt as though we had got into a Christian (which in the sailor's vocabulary means *civilized*) country. . . . We landed the agent and passengers, and found several persons waiting for them on the beach, among whom were some who, though dressed in the costume of the country, spoke English; and who, we afterward learned, were English and Americans who had married and settled in the country. . . .

The next day we were "turned-to" early, and began taking off the hatches, overhauling the cargo, and getting everything ready for inspection. At eight the officers of the customs, five in number, came on board and began overhauling the cargo, manifest, etc. The Mexican revenue laws are very strict, and require the whole cargo to be landed, examined, and taken on board again; but our agent, Mr. R[obinson] had succeeded in compounding with them for the last two vessels, and saving the trouble of taking the cargo ashore. . . .

Among the Spaniards there is no working class (the Indians being slaves and doing all the hard work); and every rich man looks like a grandee, and every poor scamp like a broken-down gentleman. I have often seen a man with a fine figure and courteous manners dressed in broadcloth and velvet, with a noble horse completely covered with trappings, without a *real* in his pockets, and absolutely suffering for something to eat.

The next day the cargo having been entered in due form, we began trading. The trade room was fitted up in the steerage, and furnished out with the lighter goods, and with specimens of the rest of the cargo; and M——, a young man who came out from Boston with us, before the mast, was taken out of the forecastle, and made supercargo's clerk. He was well qualified for the business, having been clerk in a counting house in Boston. . . .

For a week or ten days all was life on board. The people came off to look and to buy—men, women and children; and we were continually going in the boats, carrying goods and passengers—for they have no boats of their own. Everything must dress itself and come aboard and see the new vessel, if it were only to buy a paper of new pins. The agent and his clerk managed the sales, while we were busy in the hold or in the boats.

Our cargo was an assorted one; that is, it consisted of everything under the sun. We had spirits of all kinds (sold by the cask), teas, coffee, sugars, spices, raisins, molasses, hardware, crockeryware, tinware, cutlery, clothing of all kinds, boots and shoes from Lynn, calicoes and cottons from Lowell, crapes, silks; also shawls, scarfs, necklaces, jewelry and combs for the ladies; furniture; and in fact everything that can be imagined, from Chinese fireworks to English cartwheels—of which we had a dozen pairs with their iron rims on.

The Californians are an idle, thriftless people, and can make nothing for themselves. The country abounds in grapes, yet they buy bad wine made in Boston and brought round by us, at an immense price, and retail it among themselves at a *real* (12½ cents) by a small wine-glass. Their hides, too, which they value at two dollars in money, they give for something which costs seventy-five cents in Boston; and buy shoes (as like as not made of their own hides) which have been carried twice round Cape Horn) at three and four dollars, and "chicken-skin" boots at fifteen dollars apiece.

Things sell on an average at an advance of nearly three hundred per cent upon the Boston prices. This is partly owing to the heavy duties which the government, in their wisdom, with the intent no doubt of keeping the silver in the country, has laid upon imports. These duties, and the enormous expenses of so long a voyage, keep all merchants but those of heavy capital from engaging in the trade. Nearly two-thirds of all the articles imported into the country from round Cape Horn, for the last six years, have been by the single house of Bryant, Sturgis & Co., to whom our vessel belonged and who have a permanent agent on the coast.

This kind of business was new to us, and we liked it very well for a few days, though we were hard at work every minute from daylight to dark, and sometimes later. By being thus continually engaged in transporting passengers with their goods to and fro, we gained considerable knowledge of the character, dress and language of the people. . . .

Generally speaking, each person's caste is decided by the quality of the blood, which shows itself too plainly to be concealed at first sight. Yet the least drop of Spanish blood, if it be only of quadroon or octoroon, is sufficient to raise them from the rank of slaves and entitle them to a suit of clothes—boots, hat, cloak, spurs, long knife, and all complete, though coarse and dirty as may be—and to call themselves Españolos, and to hold property, if they can get any.

The fondness for dress among the women is excessive, and is often the ruin of many of them. A present of a fine mantle, or of a necklace or pair of earrings, gains the favor of the greater part of them. Nothing is more common than to see a woman living in a house of only two rooms, and the ground for a floor, dressed in spangled satin shoes, silk gown, high comb, and gilt if not gold earrings and necklace. They used to spend whole days on board our vessel examining the fine clothes and ornaments, and frequently made purchases at a rate which would have made a sempstress or waiting maid in Boston open her eyes.

Next to the love of dress, I was most struck with the fineness of the voices and beauty of the intonations of both sexes. Every common ruffian-looking fellow, with a slouched hat, blanket coat, dirty underdress and soiled leather leggins, appeared to me to be speaking elegant Spanish. It was a pleasure simply to listen to the sound of the language, before I could attach any meaning to it.

They have a good deal of the Creole drawl, but it is varied with an occasional extreme rapidity of utterance, in which they seem to skip from consonant to consonant, until, lighting upon a broad, open vowel, they rest upon that to restore the balance of sound. The women carry this peculiarity of speaking to a much greater extreme than the men, who have more evenness and stateliness of utterance. A common bullock driver on horseback delivering a message seemed to speak like an ambassador at an audience. In fact, they sometimes appeared to me to be a people on whom a curse had fallen, and stripped them of everything but their pride, their manners and their voices.

Another thing that surprised me was the quantity of silver that was in circulation. I certainly never saw so much silver at one time in my life, as during the week we were at Monterey. The truth is that they have no credit system, no banks, and no way of investing money but in cattle. They have no circulating medium but silver and hides—which the sailors call "California bank notes." Everything they buy they must pay for in one or the other of these things. The hides they bring down dried and doubled in clumsy ox-carts or upon mules' backs, and the money they carry tied up in a handkerchief—fifty, eighty, or an hundred dollars and half dollars. . . .

In Monterey there are a number of English and Americans . . . who have married Californians, became united to the Catholic church, and acquired considerable property. Having more industry, frugality and enterprise than the natives, they soon get nearly all the trade into their hands. They usually keep shops, in which they retail the goods purchased in larger quantities from our vessels, and also send a good deal into the interior, taking hides in pay, which they again barter with our vessels. In every town on the coast there are foreigners engaged in this kind of trade, while I recollect but two shops kept by natives. . . .

Monterey, as far as my observation goes, is decidedly the pleasantest and most civilized-looking place in California. . . . Nothing but the character of the people prevents Monterey from becoming a great town.

Condensed from *Two Years Before the Mast*, Richard Henry Dana, Jr. (Boston and New York: Houghton, Mifflin and Company, 1895).

XVII

Washington Irving

On November 27, 1826, a straggling line of fourteen ragged, shaggy-bearded, half-starved, half-demented woodsmen from the East stumbled into the precincts of Mission San Gabriel on the outskirts of Los Angeles pueblo. The Indians, who saw them first, were struck dumb; the holy Fathers, to whom they were quickly led, were incredulous. The fourteen might as well have descended from Mars. The only Americanos previously seen at the missions had come in ships; these, by stages, mostly on foot, had accomplished the impossible—crossed the continent. They were Rocky Mountain trappers, far out of bounds. After meeting with a series of disasters while exploring the lower Colorado basin for furs, they had learned from friendly Indians that the nearest source of white man's supplies was San Gabriel, and in what amounted to a death march they had barely made it there. Their leader was the noted trapper and frontiersman Jedediah Smith.

The padres nursed the outlanders back to health, reoutfitted them, and sent them on their way back to St. Louis, but the mission hosts were soon to learn that Smith and his uncouth company were only the forerunners of long retinues of Eastern trappers who were about to invade California.

Stories about these venturesome overlanders were not long in reaching the East, and suddenly the most popular subject in journals and newspapers of the Atlantic states was the "Wild West." Even the literary idol of the decade, Washington Irving (1783–1859), who had written so charmingly and romantically of the Catskills, the Hudson River, Spain, and the Prairies, began looking around for material on the Great American West that he could write about without actually making the journey to California.

He found it one night right in New York at the dinner table of John Jacob Astor, where the patriarch of the American fur trade introduced him to Captain Benjamin Bonneville. The Captain had recently returned from a privately financed expedition to the Green River country of Utah and Wyoming, with a company of over a hundred. As a fur trader he had proved an utter failure, and was little more successful as an explorer, but under him had been an adventurer of real spirit, Joseph Reddeford Walker, whom he had given the assignment of reconnoitering the shores of the Great Salt Lake for furs.

In a futile search for fur-bearing animals in that expanse of desert, Walker and his party had exhausted their supplies, and on realizing they could never make it back to camp without replenishment, they had headed west for food, water—and furs. They crossed the Sierra in a nip-and-tuck battle with the elements, discovered Yosemite and the Big Trees, struggled on to Monterey where the trespassers were granted short-term asylum, then recrossed the Sierra by a new pass, and en route back to Salt Lake cheated death in a frightful ordeal in the desert.

Walker's exploits were by far the most exciting episode in the whole Bonneville expedition, but the arrogant Captain did not see it that way. According to Bonneville, Walker had disobeyed orders, gone off on a wild junket, tried to steal the show, and was entirely responsible for the commercial failure of the expedition. He passed on his version, with the built-in bias, to Irving, along with assorted diaries, maps, and notes. The literary giant gullibly accepted them as untainted fact and from them wrote a résumé of Walker's California trek into his *Adventures of Captain Bonneville*.

Most Disgraceful Expedition

The trappers continued down Ogden's River [the Humboldt] until they ascertained that it lost itself in a great swampy lake, to which there was no apparent discharge. They then struck directly westward across the great chain of Californian mountains intervening between these interior plains and the shores of the Pacific.

For three and twenty days they were entangled among these mountains, the peaks and ridges of which are in many places covered with perpetual snow. Their passes and defiles present the wildest scenery, partaking of the sublime rather than the beautiful, and abounding with frightful precipices.

The sufferings of the travelers among these savage mountains were extreme. For a part of the time they were nearly starved; at length they made their way through them and came down upon the plains of New California, a fertile region extending along the coast, with magnificent forests, verdant savannas and prairies that look like stately parks. Here they found deer and other game in abundance and indemnified themselves for past famine. They now turned toward the south, and passing numerous small bands of natives posted upon various streams, arrived at the Spanish village and post of Monterey. . . .

The wandering band of trappers were well received at Monterey. The inhabitants were desirous of retaining them among them and offered extravagant wages to such as were acquainted with any mechanic art. When they went into·the country, too, they were kindly treated by the priests at the missions, who are always hospitable to strangers, whatever may be their rank or religion. They had no lack of provisions, being permitted to kill as many as they pleased of the vast herds of cattle that graze the country, on condition merely of rendering the hides to the owners.

They attended bull fights and horse races, forgot all the purposes of their expedition, squandered away freely the property that did not belong to them, and, in a word, revelled in a perfect fool's paradise. What especially delighted them was the equestrian skill of the Californians. The vast number and the cheapness of the horses in this country makes everyone a cavalier. The Mexicans and halfbreeds of California spend the greater part of their time in the saddle. They are fearless riders, and their daring feats upon unbroken colts and wild horses astonished our trappers, though accustomed to the bold riders of the prairies. . . .

The California horsemen seldom ride without the lasso, that is to say, a long coil of cord with a slip noose, with which they are expert almost to a miracle. The lasso, now almost entirely confined to Spanish America, is said to be of great antiquity, and to have come originally from the East. It was used, we are told, by a postoral people of Persian descent, of whom eight thousand accompanied the army of Xerxes.

By the Spanish Americans it is used for a variety of purposes, and among others, for hauling wood. Without dismounting, they cast the noose round a log and thus drag it to their houses. The vaqueros, or Indian cattle drivers, have also learned the use of the lasso from the Spaniards, and employ it to catch the half-wild cattle by throwing it round their horns. The lasso is also of great use in furnishing the public with a favorite, though barbarous, sport: the combat between a bear and a wild bull. . . . Beside this diversion, the travelers were likewise regaled with bull fights in the genuine style of Old Spain, the Californians being considered the best bull fighters in the Mexican dominions.

After a considerable sojourn at Monterey, spent in these very edifying but not very profitable amusements, the leader of this vagabond party set out with his comrades on his return journey. Instead of retracing their steps through the mountains, they passed round their southern extremity and, crossing a range of low hills, found themselves in the sandy plains south of Ogden's River, in traversing which they again suffered grievously for want of water.

In the course of their journey they encountered a party of Mexicans in pursuit of a gang of natives who had been stealing horses. The savages of this part of California are represented as extremely poor and armed only with stone-pointed arrows. . . . As they find it difficult with their blunt shafts to kill the wild game of the mountains, they occasionally supply themselves with food by entrapping the Spanish horses. Driving them stealthily into fastnesses and ravines, they slaughter them without difficulty and dry their flesh for provisions. . . .

The Mexicans are continually on the alert to intercept these marauders, but the Indians are apt to outwit them and force them to make long and wild expeditions in pursuit of their stolen horses. Two of the Mexican party just mentioned joined the band of trappers and proved themselves worthy companions. In the course of their journey [they passed] through the country frequented by the poor Root Diggers. . . . The trappers still considered them in the light of danger and the Mexicans, very probably, charged them with the sin of horse stealing. We have no other mode of accounting for the infamous barbarities of which, according to their own story, they were guilty: hunting the poor Indians like wild beasts and killing them without mercy. The Mexicans excelled at this savage sport, chasing their unfortunate victims at full speed, noosing them round the neck with their lassos and then dragging them to death.

Such are the scanty details of this most disgraceful expedition; at least such are all that Captain Bonneville had the patience to collect, for he was so deeply grieved by the failure of his plans and so indignant at the atrocities related to him that he turned with disgust and horror from the narrators. Had he exerted a little of the Lynch law of the wilderness and hanged these dexterous horsemen in their own lassos, it would have been a well-merited and salutary act of retributive justice.

The failure of this expedition was a blow to his pride and a still greater blow to his purse. The Great Salt Lake still remained unexplored; at the same time the means which had been furnished so liberally to fit out this favorite expedition had all been squandered at Monterey, and the peltries also which had been collected on the way. . . .

The horror and indignation felt by Captain Bonneville at the excesses of the Californian adventurers were not participated by his men; on the contrary, the events of that expedition were favorite themes in the camp. The heroes of Monterey bore the palm in all the gossipings among the hunters. Their glowing descriptions of Spanish bear baits and bull fights especially were listened to with intense delight, and had another expedition to California been proposed, the difficulty would have been to restrain a general eagerness to volunteer.

From *The Adventures of Captain Bonneville, U.S.A., in the Rocky Mountains and the Far West,* Washington Irving (New York: G. P. Putnam, 1849).

XVIII

Zenas Leonard

Washington Irving's third-hand account of Walker's historic march to the coast was a masterpiece of understatement, misinformation, and Bonneville-dictated acrimony. By pushing west rather than attempting the return to Bonneville's rendezvous, Joseph Reddeford Walker had saved half the expedition from almost certain doom in the salt flats. He was the real hero of the expedition. Instead of going off on an escapade as the captain would have had it, they had endured the tortures of perdition in crossing the desert, worse agonies in conquering the Sierra, and in California they were seldom sure from one day to the next whether they would survive the machinations of hostile Indians and suspicious Spaniards.

But their greatest trial came after all these adversities, after they had won friends in Monterey and at the missions, replenished their supplies, found a new, shorter pass over the Sierra, and were traveling north on the eastern flank of the range, trying to intercept the trail they had blazed on their way west.

That crisis was narrated by Captain Walker's company clerk, an experienced trapper from Pennsylvania, Zenas Leonard (1809–1857), who made no pretense of being an author, but who proved that he could write far more sensitively and authoritatively of California than the professional Washington Irving. "We felt," he wrote on reaching the Pacific, "as if all our previous hardships and privations would be adequately compensated if we could be spared to return in safety to

the homes of our kindred, and have it to say that we had stood upon
the extreme end of the Great West."

Leonard was spared; he survived another desert ordeal and eventually returned to Clearfield, Pennsylvania, where his parents, who had
not heard from him in almost six years, greeted him "as from the
dead." His *Adventures* served as eloquent rebuttal to the travesty of
Washington Irving.

A *Truly Desperate Situation*

Our direct course after reaching the eastern base of this mountain
[the Sierra Nevada Range] would have been a northeast direction, but we were apprehensive of perishing for water in crossing
this extensive desert—which would doubtless be the fate of any
traveler who would undertake it, when it is recollected that it
extends from the base of the Rocky Mountains to this mountain, a
distance of several hundred miles. This being the case, we were
obliged to pass along the base of the mountain in a northern
direction until we would arrive at the point where we ascended
the mountain when going to the coast, and then follow the same
trail east toward the Rocky Mountains or Great Salt Lake. . . .

Traveling along the mountain foot, crossing one stream after
another, was anything but pleasant. Day after day we traveled in
the hope each day of arriving at the desired point when we would
strike off in a homeward direction. Every now and then some of
the company would see a high peak or promontory which he
would think was seen by the company on a former occasion, but
when we would draw near to it, our pleasing anticipations would
be turned into despondency; and at one time about the middle of
May our Captain was so certain that he could see a point in the
distance which he distinctly marked as a guide on our former
tramp that he ordered the men to prepare for leaving the mountain. This also proved to be the result of imagination only.

The next morning our Captain, thinking the desert not very
wide at this point, decided on striking across in a northeastern
direction, which would shorten our route considerably, if we

could only be so successful as to surmount the difficulties of traveling through loose sand, without water. . . . Everything necessary for our dry tramp being in readiness, we started across the plain, which was done with a willing heart by almost every man, as we were all anxious to get home and had been traveling many days without getting any nearer.

The traveling in the plain, after passing the termination of the streams, we found to be extremely laborious. The sand lays quite loose, and as the wind would blow whilst driving our horses and cattle ahead of us, the sand would be raised up in such clouds that we could scarcely see them, which was very painful to our eyes. The first night in the plain we encamped at a large hole or well dug deep in the ground, which we supposed to be the work of Indians, and in which we found a small portion of stagnant water, but not enough to slake the thirst of our numerous herd.

The next morning we resumed our toilsome march at an early hour, finding our stock suffering greatly from the want of water. This day we traveled with as much speed as possible, with the hope of finding water whereat to encamp. But at length night arrived and the fatigues of the day obliged us to encamp without water, wood or grass. The day had been excessively warm, except when the wind would blow, and in the afternoon two of our dogs died for want of water. On examination, we found that the feet of many of our dumb brutes were completely crippled by the sand.

Our situation at present seemed very critical. A dull, gloomy aspect appeared to darken the countenance of every member of the company. We were now completely surrounded with the most aggravating perplexities, having traveled two long days' journey into the plain and no idea how far yet to its termination, and from the manifestations of many of our most valuable stock, we were well convinced they could not endure these hardships much longer.

To add to the vexation of our present difficulties, a violent altercation took place between the men as to whether we would proceed in our present direction or turn back to the mountain. A majority of the men were in favor of the latter, but Captain Walker, who never done anything by halves, with a few others, were of the opinion that we were half way across, and could as easily proceed as return.

On all such disputes on all former occasions the majority decided on what steps would be taken, but when our Captain was in the minority, and being beloved by the whole company, and being a man also who was seldom mistaken in anything he undertook, the men were very reluctant in going contrary to his will. The dispute created much confusion in our ranks; but fortunately about midnight the Captain yielded to the wishes of his men and, as it was cool and more pleasant traveling than in the day time, we started back toward the mountain, intending to follow the same trail, in order to come to the hole at which we encamped on the first night in the plain.

Previous to starting, we took the hides off our dead cattle and made a kind of moccasin for such of our beasts as were lame, which we found to be of great advantage, as it effectively shielded their feet from the scouring effects of the sand. Nothing happened through the night, and we moved carelessly along our trail, as we thought. But our feelings cannot be described at daylight when no signs of our former tracks could be discovered.

Men were despatched in every direction on search, but all returned without any tidings with which to comfort our desponding company. The compass told which direction we should go, but otherwise we were completely bewildered. Our horses, cattle and dogs were almost exhausted this morning. The pitiful lamentations of our dogs were sufficient to melt the hardest heart. The dumb brutes suffered more for water than food, and these dogs, when death threatened to seize them, would approach the men, look them right in the face with the countenance of a distracted person, and if no help could be afforded, would commence a piteous and lamentable howl, drop down and expire.

When the day became warm we slackened our pace and moved slowly forward, but without any hope of meeting with any water at least for a day longer. When night came we halted for a short time in order to collect the men and animals together, which were scattered in every direction for a mile in width, lest we should get separated at night, as we intended to travel on without ceasing until we would find water or arrive at the mountain.

When our forces collected together, we presented a really forlorn spectacle. At no time, either while crossing the Rocky or California mountains, did our situation appear so desperate. We had to keep our dumb brutes constantly moving about on their feet, for if they would once lay down it would be impossible to get them up again, and we would then be compelled to leave them.

Nor were the men in a much better condition. It is true, we had food, but our thirst far exceeded any description. At last it became so intense that whenever one of our cattle or horses would die, the men would immediately catch the blood and greedily swallow it down.

When our men had collected together and rested their wearied limbs a little, our journey was resumed, finding that the cattle and horses traveled much better at night than in daylight. We advanced rapidly this evening without any interruption until about midnight, when our horses became unmanageable and, contrary to our utmost exertions, would go in a more northern direction than we desired.

After several ineffectual attempts to check them, we thought perhaps it would be well enough to follow wherever they would lead. We had not followed our horses far until we discovered to our indescribable joy that the instinct of our horses was far more extensive and more valuable than all the foresight of the men, as we unawares came suddenly upon a beautiful stream of fresh water.

We now had the greatest trouble to keep our beasts from killing themselves drinking water—in which we succeeded only in part, and were thus occupied until daylight, when we counted our force for the purpose of ascertaining how much loss we sustained by undertaking to cross the desert, and found that we had lost sixty-four horses, ten cows and fifteen dogs.

In order to get something to eat for our stock, and also to keep them from drinking too much water, we left this stream which had afforded such delight, before either the men or beasts had time to repose their wearied limbs. After traveling a few miles this morning we had the good luck to come across tolerable pasture and plenty of wood and water. Here we determined on staying until the next morning for the purpose of resting our wearied stock. . . .

The next morning after finding the pasture, our herd having rested and satisfied their hunger pretty well, we resumed our journey along the edge of the plain, traveled as fast as their weakened state would admit of, still finding pasture sufficient for their subsistence, until, after several days' constant traveling, we fortunately came to our long-sought-for passage to the west.

This was hailed with greater manifestations of joy by the company than any circumstance that had occurred for some time, as it gave us to know where we were and also to know when we might expect to arrive in a plentiful country of game. Here we again layed by a day for the purpose of resting and making preparations to follow our old trail toward the Great Salt Lake.

From *Narrative of the Adventures of Zenas Leonard* (Cleveland: Burrows Brothers, 1904).

XIX

Thomas Jefferson Farnham

According to the efficient Americanos, all government officials in Alta California per se were ineffectual, siesta-minded, conniving, lickpenny bureaucrats. Even Governor Juan Bautista Alvarado, a ball of fire by Mexican standards, fell into that category, as lawyer-annalist Thomas Jefferson Farnham (1804–1848), one of America's most popular spokesmen on the West, saw him. But Farnham was prejudiced. Alvarado was the governor who with the assistance of some seventy-five rebels—mostly foreigners—had ousted his predecessor in one of the frequent California coups, and had no sooner taken the official chair than he leaped out of it to arrest all seventy-five of the other valiant members of his junta, reasoning that if they could so easily elevate him to office, they could as easily depose him.

The rebels were languishing behind the bars of the Monterey jail when Farnham arrived at the capital in 1840. He hailed from republican Maine and freedom-loving Illinois and did not consider the governor's action fair play. For a few days Farnham entertained rebellious ideas of blasting the prisoners out of their confinement; then he decided it would be less perilous and perhaps more effective to vent his spleen in words. He left no doubt on what he thought of autocratic Spanish officials.

A Bow to Bureaucracy

The first duty on setting foot in California is to report oneself to the governor and obtain from him a written permission to remain in the country. This I proceeded to do. Mr. Larkin [an American merchant in Monterey and later the U. S. Consul] was obliging enough to accompany me to the governor's residence.

We found before it a small number of men, who were usually complimented with the cognomen of "guard." They consisted of five half-breed Indians and what passed for a white corporal, lounging about the door in the manner of grog-shop savants. Their outer man is worth a description. They wore raw bull's-hide sandals on their feet, leathern breeches, blankets about their shoulders, and anything or everything upon their heads.

Of arms they had nothing which deserved the name. One made pretensions with an old musket without lock; and his four comrades were equally heroic, with kindred pieces so deeply rusted that the absence of locks would have been an unimportant item in estimating their value.

We passed this valorous body, ascended a flight of stairs, and entered the presence of Governor Juan Baptiste Alvarado, a well-formed, full-blooded Californian Spaniard, five feet eleven inches in height, with coal-black curly hair, deep black eyes, fiercely black eyebrows, high cheek bones, an aquiline nose, fine white teeth, brown complexion and the clearly marked mien of a pompous coward, clad in the broadcloth and whiskers of a gentleman.

When we entered he was sitting behind a kind of writing desk at the farther end of the room. He rose as we entered and received us with the characteristic urbanity of a Spanish body without a soul; waved us to chairs when he would have seen us tumbling from the balcony; smiled graciously at us with one corner of his mouth, while he cursed us with the other; seated himself, laid up his arms and hands on the upper shelf of his abdomen and asked if the ship had anchored.

El Goubernador had sundry reasons for making this inquiry

concerning the *Don Quixote*. The chief one, however, was that he
and his officers, like all their predecessors, had been in the habit
of looking upon the arrival of a ship in the port of Monterey as a
discharge of debts and a license for new levies on their credit. Let
it not be supposed that I believe a Californian Spaniard is ever so
far false to his nature as to wish his debts paid while his credit
will supply his wants. My investigations into the character of his
progenitors, both Indian and Spanish, will always preserve me
from such an error.

Nor would I have it believed that the transplanted chivalry of
the Andalusians does not absolutely boil and bubble at the bare
thought of not being able to plunder from the rest of mankind a
gentleman's living. Any such impeachment of the sagacity and
scrupulousness of these men would be a wrong against which my
sense of justice would most vehemently protest. In plain words,
then, at the time the *Don Quixote* came into the bay, Alvarado
and his officers were deeply in debt, and distressed only to select
means of paying them, accordant with Californian honor. The
arrival of a ship in port furnished just these means. The manner in
which it did so may be unworthy of speculation.

El Alta California is a department of the Mexican Republic,
and by law the moneys collected for port dues and duties belong
to the revenue of the central government. But as the right to life,
property and the pursuit of happiness is, among the Californian
Spaniards, construed to authorize both individuals and States to
defraud, plunder and murder, if they find it safe and lucrative to
do so, the freemen, or rather the Governor of California and his
subalterns, were in the habit of commuting a large portion of the
port dues and duties for certain sums of money and quantities of
goods for their own personal use. Their capacity for this kind of
plundering formed in part the basis of their credit with foreign
merchants and traders, from whom they obtained their supplies.

Hence the anxieties of Sa Excellentissimo about the bark. If she
had come to anchor, there must necessarily be a small chance for
robbery in the tonnage dues; and if richly laden with goods
subject to duties, she could be quite a mine, which he already
dreamed himself plundering with golden success. As soon as we

could turn his attention from these hopes of gain, Mr. Larkin informed him of my wishes, and with much deference suggested the humanity of transferring me from idleness on shipboard to the enjoyment of Castilian industry ashore: to wit, lounging, grinning, sleeping and smoking rolls· of paper tinctured with "the weed."

Sa Excellentissimo found it difficult to comprehend the necessity of the request inasmuch as the bark might come to anchor for my quiet and health, in which case I would be permitted, as seamen were, to be on shore during her stay in port. But being informed that there were no goods on board the bark, that it was not intended to bring her to anchor, and that consequently neither bribes nor Mexican tribute would be paid to Don Juan Baptiste Alvarado, El Goubernador del Alta California, he frankly confessed that he saw no necessity, indicated by his interest, why I should ever have existed, and still less made any of my pleasures dependent on him or his Alta California.

This I esteemed, as in chivalry I was bound to do, an exhibition of the great elevation of character as well as an indication of the height from which Sa Excellentissimo had descended to reach my case. Therefore, I bowed assent to the majesty of such philanthropic and truly civilized opinions. What man in Castilian presence could do otherwise? But a doubt still hung over the eyebrows of the don. He looked at my height, six feet Green Mountain measure; at my wardrobe, consisting of a Hudson Bay Company's frockcoat of blue, a speckled vest from London, pants of English extraction, boots from the lapstones of Lynn; and, shrugging his shoulders like a grizzly bear in an effort to be a gentleman, said we could go to the alcalde; then with most sovereign emphasis bowed us out of his presence.

The alcalde was at home, or rather in his adobie den, for there is neither a home nor the semblance of it in all the Spanish world. He was taking his siesta, or midday nap, on a bull's hide in the corner of his apartment. The dog which had barked us into his presence, had awakened him, so that when we entered the room he was rolling his burly form towards a chair.

After being well-seated, and having with some difficulty

brought his eyes to bear upon us, he was pleased to remark that the weather was fine and that various other things existed in a definite state, as that his dog was very fat, the bean crop gave good promise, the Hawaiian Islands were ten leagues from Monterey, the Californians were very brave men, and that the *Don Quixote* had not come to anchor! To each of these announcements I gave an unqualified assent.

Having ascertained by these means that I was well-instructed in beasts, beans, men and geography, he immediately took me into favor, expressed great surprise that my friend should have thought that he could refuse my request, and assured me that it would give him infinite pleasure to write me a permission of residence. Here it is. When the reader is informed that it was an impromptu production, he will be able to estimate in a faint degree, indeed, the intelligence and genius of the Californians. Only one hour and a quarter were consumed in bringing it forth!

> Mr. Thomas J. Farnham pasagero en la barca Americana Don Quixote habiendama manifesta do el pasporte de su consul y queriendo quidar en tierra a (vertarblesse) en su salud le doy el presente bolito de des en barco en el puerta de Monterey!
> A 18 de Abril de 1840.
>
> *Antonio Ma. Orio.*

A permission this to remain on shore as long as might be necessary for the restoration of my health! Having received it with many demonstrations of regard, we took our leave of the illustrious dignitary under a running salute from his dog and repaired to el casa del goubernador (the governor's house). The dog accompanied us.

From *Life, Adventures and Travels in California,* Thomas Jefferson Farnham (New York: Sheldon, Lampert and Blakeman, 1855).

XX

Charles Wilkes

Farnham sensed that California's affairs were in a deplorable state in 1840: what Lieutenant Charles Wilkes (1798–1877) of the United States Navy found the following year was close to chaos—political revolution compounded by racial, religious, and regional revolutions. The whole coast was demoralized.

In 1837 the last of the missions had been secularized, and the liberated Indians nominally granted half the great estates held in the name of the Catholic Church. But the emancipation had been carried out in too great haste, without plan or preparation. In effect, the Indians had been turned out of their mission quarters and suddenly left to provide for themselves. They went away in bitter resentment, frequently with the intention of joining hostile tribes whom they would lead back on rampages of looting and destruction.

Indians who obtained lands and cattle from a dismembered mission, to which they were entitled, rarely appreciated their value, sold off their possessions to persuasive rancheros, and quickly squandered the little cash they received. Many neophytes chose to remain at least in the vicinity of their old confines, but they no longer found the Fathers so hospitable or paternalistic, for the benevolent, long-suffering erudite European padres had been recalled, and were replaced by lesser men of the cloth, who often were not above conniving with local politicos.

The great landowners now were the proprietors of vast ranches or haciendas, and had commonly obtained their county-sized estates very cheaply through political favoritism. They held the law unto themselves, and this concentration of land ownership and authority among a favored few was leading into a tangle of feuds and jealousies.

Relations between Mexico and the United States, too, were deteriorating. It was increasingly evident that Uncle Sam coveted California, and in 1835 he had showed his hand by offering to buy it. Seven years later war between Mexico and the United States seemed so inevitable that when Commodore Thomas Catesby Jones, USN, put in at Monterey, he assumed that the two countries were at war, seized the capital, and raised the Stars and Stripes. It took him two days to discover that he had jumped the gun; then he merely lowered the flag, apologized, and departed.

Jones's two-day occupation of Monterey occurred a year after Wilkes's visit, but it was quite in line with the turmoil that already reigned there. Lieutenant Wilkes headed the most ambitious American navigation mission yet undertaken by the Navy; he commanded a squadron of six ships commissioned for "The United States Exploring Expedition." California was just one of the scores of foreign lands he was to visit on his four-year, round-the-world cruise, and he could look upon it with global perspective: compared to older, more settled countries, it was unattractive, backward, deranged.

After giving it a cursory survey, he conceded that it might possess possibilities for development if it were to unite with Oregon; under different political auspices, the two areas might even "control the destinies of the Pacific." But that was far off. Northern California had possibilities; southern California he dismissed as a barren waste. The San Francisco Bay area was the principal asset of this foreign province, but in 1841 Wilkes had little to say in favor even of that.

More Vices Than Virtues

Although I was prepared for anarchy and confusion, I was surprised when I found a total absence of all government in California, and even its forms and ceremonies thrown aside.

After passing through the entrance [to San Francisco Bay], we were scarcely able to distinguish the Presidio; and had it not been for its solitary flag staff, we could not have ascertained its situation. From this staff no flag floated; the building was deserted, the walls had fallen to decay, the guns were dismounted, and everything around it lay in quiet. We were not even saluted by the stentorian lungs of some soldier, so customary in Spanish places, even after all political power as well as military and civil rule has fled. . . .

As soon as the ship anchored, an officer was despatched on shore to call upon the authorities; but none of any description was to be found. The only magistrate, an alcalde, was absent. The frequency of revolutions in this country had caused a great change. . . .

I afterward learned that the Presidio was still a garrison in name, and that it had not been wholly abandoned; but the remnant of the troops stationed there consisted of no more than an officer and one soldier. I was not able to learn the rank of the former, as he was absent and appeared, at least among the foreigners, to be little known.

At Yerba Buena there was a similar absence of all authority. The only officer was the alcalde, who dwells at the mission of - Nostra Señora de los Dolores, some three miles off. He was full of self-importance, making up for what he wanted in the eyes of others by a high estimate of his own dignity. I could find no one who could furnish me with his name. . . . Some excuse may be offered for his inattention to his duties, as I understand that he had just been united in wedlock to a lady of one of the distinguished families of the country; and after such an event in California much gaiety and rejoicing usually follow, until the hilarity at times becomes so uproarious as to end in fighting and bloodshed. . . .

Yerba Buena is the usual, though by no means the best anchorage. The town is not calculated to produce a favorable impression on a stranger. Its buildings may be counted, and consist of a large frame building occupied by the agent of the Hudson Bay Company; a store kept by Mr. Spears, an American; a billiard room and bar; a poop cabin of a ship occupied as a dwelling by Captain Hinckley; a blacksmith's shop and some outbuildings. These, though few in number, are also far between.

With these I must not forget to enumerate an old dilapidated adobe building which has a conspicuous position on the top of the hill overlooking the anchorage. When to this we add a sterile soil and hills of bare rock, it will be seen that Yerba Buena and the country around it are anything but beautiful. This description holds good when the tide is high, but at low water it has for a foreground an extensive mud flat, which does not add to the beauty of the view. . . .

At the time of our visit the country altogether presented rather a singular appearance, owing, as I afterward observed, to the withered vegetation and the ripened wild oats of the country. Instead of a lively green hue, it had generally a tint of a light straw color, showing an extreme want of moisture. The drought had continued for eleven months; the cattle were dying in the fields; and the first view of California was not calculated to make a favorable impression either of its beauty or fertility.

I found it difficult to obtain accurate information in relation to Upper California. The country, at the time of our visit, and for several years previous, had been in a state of revolution; and as is often the case under similar circumstances, was involved in an-archy and confusion, without laws or security of person and property. It is undergoing such frequent changes that it is diffi-cult to understand or to describe them.

With California is associated the idea of a fine climate and a rich and productive soil. This, at least, was the idea with which I entered its far-famed port; but I soon found, from the reports of the officers, after the trial they had had of it during the months of August and September, that their experience altogether contra-dicted the received opinion upon the first-mentioned point. Many of them compared its climate to that of Orange Harbor at Cape Horn, with its cold blustering winds and cloudy skies. This kind of weather prevails during the greater part of the year, and the comparison is literally true in relation to one part of California— the seacoast. There is, perhaps, no other country where there is such a diversity of features, soil and climate as California. The surface exhibits the varieties of lofty ranges of mountains, con-fined valleys and extensive plains. . . .

Upper California may boast of one of the finest, if not the very best, harbor in the world—that of San Francisco, as before described. Few are more extensive or could be as readily defended as it; while the combined fleets of all the naval powers of Europe might moor in it. This is, however, the only really good harbor which this country possesses, for the others, so-called, may be frequented only during the fine seasons, being nothing more than roadsteads, affording little safety and but few supplies to vessels. Among these bays are that of Monterey, the capital of Upper California, and that of Santa Barbara and San Pedro. . . . They are, however, but seldom used, there being comparatively little trade upon all this coast, for the hides and tallow that formerly abounded and made the business profitable for vessels are no longer to be procured.

The destruction of the missions, and the onerous laws, duties and prohibitions have nearly destroyed the little traffic that once existed, and it is now all transferred to the bay of San Francisco. There a few hulks may be seen lying, furnished with every needful article. These keep up an illicit intercourse by the connivance of the officers of the customs, by whose cupidity the revenue laws are openly infringed, and what of right belongs to the government goes to enrich the governor and his officers. . . . Foreigners, however, contrive to evade this by keeping their vessels at anchor, and selling a large portion of their cargoes from on board. Great partiality is shown to those of them who have a full understanding with his excellency the governor; and from what I was given to understand, if this be not secured, the traders are liable to exactions and vexations without number.

The enormous duties, often amounting to eighty per cent ad valorem, cause much dissatisfaction on the part of the consumers. The whole amount raised is about $200,000 per annum, which is found barely sufficient to pay the salaries of the officers and defray the costs of the government feasts, which are frequent and usually cost $1000 each. These emoluments are shared among the heads of departments at Monterey, whilst the soldiers are often for months without their pay, and are made to take it in whatever currency it may suit the government to give.

Besides the above duties, there is a municipal tax on many things. Thus a dollar is demanded on every gallon of spirits imported; fifty cents on each beaver or otter skin and on other articles in the same ratio. Next come the church tithes, which are enormous. I heard of a farmer who was made to pay $190 as the tithe on his produce, although he lives far removed from either church or priest.

All these things are bringing the government into great disrepute, and the governor is every day becoming more and more unpopular—so much so that his orders have not been complied with, and have been treated with contempt, particularly when he desires to recruit his forces. A short time before our arrival he sent a list to a pueblo of the young men to be drafted as soldiers; when it was received, they in a body refused to go and sent back the disrespectful and defying message that he might come and take them.

Nothing can be in a worse state than the lower offices, such as the alcaldes, etc. They are now held by ignorant men who have no ideas of justice, which is generally administered according to the alcalde's individual notions, as his feelings may be enlisted, or the standing of the parties. To recover a debt by legal means is considered as beyond a possibility, and creditors must wait until the debtor is disposed to pay.

Fortunately, and to the honor of the country, a just claim is rarely or never denied; and until lately the word of a Californian was sufficient to insure the payment of claims to him. But such has been the moral degradation to which the people have fallen since the missions have been robbed by the authorities, and the old priests driven out, that no reliance can be placed now upon their promises, and all those who have of late trusted them complain that engagements are not regarded and that it is next to impossible to obtain any returns for goods that have been delivered. . . .

It was at first believed that the revolution which took place in November 1836 would result in much immediate good to those who effected it, but such has not been the case. Foreigners unquestionably performed a large part in planning and carrying the change out, yet none has suffered so much by it as they. . . . There has been an exaggeration in the computation of the number of whites, or *gente de razon*. These have been usually estimated at five thousand, but from the best information, I could not satisfy myself that they number more than three thousand souls. . . . In the whole of Upper California at the date of our visit the entire population was about fifteen thousand souls, and this estimate cannot be far from the truth. . . .

Although the Californians are comparatively few in number, yet they have a distinctive character. Descended from the old Spaniards, they are unfortunately found to have all their vices, without a proper share of their virtues. . . . The situation in Upper California will cause its separation from Mexico before many years. The country between it and Mexico can never be anything but a barren waste.

From *Narrative of the United States Exploring Expedition,* Volume V, Charles Wilkes (Philadelphia: Lea and Blanchard, 1845).

XXI

John Bidwell

Easterners with an itch to migrate West were inclined to believe what they wanted to believe among all the contradictory information that was being circulated about California. A single glowing report on this wonderland of opportunity and sunshine was enough to discount all the derogatory accounts of Mexican anarchy, Spanish duplicity, blood-thirsty Indians, drought, disaster, and the high cost of living. Already it was fairly common knowledge that an unknown Swiss fellow by the name of John Augustus Sutter had arrived in California and with no trouble at all had carved out a principality for himself on the Sacramento River. No good American was going to be outdone by an outlander from the Alps.

So argued twenty-year-old John Bidwell (1819–1900), a frontier schoolmaster who had already hacked his way in long stages from New York to the Missouri settlements. And when a neighbor one day dropped in to tell him about a letter that a chance acquaintance had received from a "Dr. Marsh" of California, picturing the Sacramento country as the most attractive farm land on earth, with a great many details to prove it, Bidwell was conclusively persuaded it was the place for him; he was going to California; he would find Dr. Marsh. It became an obsession.

Though trappers had blazed many a trail westward, Bidwell knew very well there was still no reliable, mapped route from Missouri to the West Coast. He would find one. The schoolmaster was a respected,

convincing, creditable talker, and soon had half his community thinking his way. The more he talked, the surer his listeners were that they
too wanted nothing more than to go to California. The contagion
spread to a dozen families, to fifty, a hundred. In no time he had
created the Western Emigration Society with over five hundred
members.

He gave up schoolteaching to organize the Society and actually
prepare for the road. A departure date was set. Every family, he
insisted, would have to be self-sufficient; each must provide its own
horses, mules or oxen, wagons, and provisions. But as the day for
setting out drew near, the faint-hearted faced up to realities and
membership in the Western Emigration Society rapidly declined. The
number that finally took to the road in the spring of 1841 was exactly
sixty-nine. However, just as they were getting under way, they were
joined by three Catholic missionaries and their retinue, bound for the
Flathead Indian territory beyond the northern Rockies. The addition
was providential, for the padres knew at least the first part of the
way.

The general route was to the future site of Kansas City, along the
Platte River to Fort Laramie, across the Green River, to Soda Springs,
Salt Lake, and across the Great Basin to the Humboldt River and the
Sierra. Hostile Indians, shortage of supplies, disagreements within the
company, and encounters with wildlife provided suspense, terror, and
adventure for every mile of the journey. Still they made amazing
progress.

And then came the grand climax when they were confronted by the
formidable Sierra Nevada Range. By that time tempers were short and
supplies were shorter; they were travel-weary; horses and oxen were
on their last legs, and alas, dissenters began accusing Bidwell of
leading them on a wild goose chase; after all, what did he know about
California? who was this Doctor Marsh he intended to find? what
made him think the doctor might help them? did he know anything
about Marsh? No. At the very moment when cooperation was most
called for, the company broke in two, and one contingent under the
leadership of impetuous Captain Bartleson, who felt that the others
were not moving fast enough, went on ahead, declaring: "If you can
keep up with us, all right; if you cannot, you may go to hell."

And it *was* hell as they plodded through Humboldt Sink, crossed the
Carson River and camped almost in a state of starvation at the base of

the Sierra. Schoolteacher Bidwell, who was destined to establish at Chico a more productive empire than Sutter's, to become a brigadier general, congressman, and nominee for the presidency of the United States, told their story.

First American Emigrant Train

We were now camped on the Walker River at the very eastern base of the Sierra Nevadas, and had only two oxen left. We sent men ahead to see if it would be possible to scale the mountains, while we killed the better of the two oxen and dried the meat in preparation for the ascent. The men returned toward evening and reported that they thought it would be possible to ascend the mountains, though very difficult.

We had eaten our supper and were ready for the climb in the morning. Looking back on the plains, we saw something coming, which we decided to be Indians. They traveled very slowly, and it was difficult to understand their movements. To make a long story short, it was the eight men who had left us nine days before [the Bartleson party]. They had gone farther south than we, and had come to a lake, probably Carson Lake, and there found Indians, who supplied them plentifully with fish and pine nuts . . . and had got something akin to cholera morbus.

We ran out to meet them and shook hands, and put our frying pans on and gave them the best supper we could. Captain Bartleson, who when he started from Missouri was a portly man, was reduced to half his former girth. He said: "Boys, if ever I get back to Missouri, I will never leave that country. I would gladly eat out of the troughs with my hogs." . . .

We ascended the mountain on the north side of Walker River to the summit, and then struck a stream running west, which proved to be the extreme source of the Stanislaus River. We followed it down for several days and finally came to where a branch ran into it, each forming a canyon. The main river flowed in a precipitous gorge, in places apparently a mile deep, and the gorge that came into it was but little less formidable.

At night we found ourselves on the extreme point of the promontory between the two, very tired, and with neither grass nor
water. We had to stay there that night. Early the next morning
two men went down to see if it would be possible to get down
through the smaller canyon. I was one of them; Jimmy Johns was
the other. . . . A party also went back to see how far we should
have to go around before we could pass over the tributary
canyon.

The understanding was that when we went down the canyon, if
it was practicable to get through, we were to fire a gun so that all
could follow, but if not, we were not to fire, even if we saw game.
When Jimmy and I got down about three-quarters of a mile, I
came to the conclusion that it was impossible to get through and
said to him, "Jimmy, we might as well go back; we can't go here."

"Yes, we can," said he, and insisting that we could, he pulled
out a pistol and fired. It was an old dragoon pistol and reverber-
ated like a cannon.

I hurried back to tell the company not to come down, but before
I reached them the captain and his party had started. I explained,
and warned them that they could not get down; but they went on
as far as they could go and then were obliged to stay all day and
all night to rest the animals, and had to go among the rocks and
pick a little grass for them, and go down to the stream through a
terrible place in the canyon and bring water up in cups and camp
kettles, and some of the men in their boots, to pour down the
animals' throats in order to keep them from perishing. Finally,
four of them pulling and four pushing a mule, they managed to
get them up one by one, and then carried all the things up again
on their backs—not an easy job for exhausted men.

In some way, nobody knows how, Jimmy got through that
canyon and into the Sacramento Valley. He had a horse with
him—an Indian horse that was bought in the Rocky Mountains,
and which could come as near to climbing a tree as any horse I
ever knew. . . .

We went on, traveling as near west as we could. When we
killed our last ox, we shot and ate crows or anything we could kill,
and one man shot a wildcat. We could eat anything. One day in

Emigrant train

the morning I went ahead, on foot of course, to see if I could kill
something, it being understood that the company would keep on
as near west as possible and find a practicable road. I followed an
Indian trail down into the canyon, meeting many Indians on the
way up. They did not molest me, but I did not quite like their
looks.

I went about ten miles down the canyon, and then began to
think it time to strike north to intersect the trail of the company
going west. A most difficult time I had scaling the precipice. Once
I threw my gun ahead of me, being unable to hold it and climb,
and then was in despair lest I could not get up where it was, but
finally I did barely manage to do so, and make my way north. As
the darkness came on, I was obliged to look down and feel with
my feet, lest I should pass over the trail of the party without
seeing it.

Just at dark I came to an immense fallen tree and tried to go
around the top, but the place was too brushy, so I went around
the butt, which seemed to me to be about twenty or twenty-five
feet above my head. This I suppose to have been one of the fallen
trees in the Calaveras Grove of *sequoia gigantea* or mammoth
trees. . . .

Of course, sleep was impossible, for I had neither blanket nor
coat, and burned or froze alternately as I turned from one side to
the other before the small fire which I had built, until morning,
when I started eastward to intersect the trail, thinking the company had turned north. But I traveled until noon and found no
trail; then striking south I came to the camp which I had left the
previous morning.

The party had gone, but not where they said they would go, for
they had taken the same trail I followed into the canyon, and had
gone up the south side, which they had found so steep that many
of the poor animals could not climb it and had to be left. When I
arrived, the Indians were there cutting the horses to pieces and
carrying off the meat. My situation, alone among strange Indians
killing our poor horses, was by no means comfortable.

Afterward we found that these Indians were always at war
with the Californians. They were known as the Horse Thief Indians, and lived chiefly on horse flesh; they had been in the habit

of raiding the ranches even to the very coast, driving away horses by the hundreds into the mountains to eat.

That night I overtook the party in camp. A day or two later we came to a place where there was a great quantity of horse bones, and we did not know what it meant; we thought that an army must have perished there. They were, of course, horses that the Indians had driven in and slaughtered. A few nights later, fearing depredations, we concluded to stand guard—all but one man who would not. So we let his two horses roam where they pleased. In the morning they could not be found. A few miles away we came to a village; the Indians had fled, but we found the horses killed and some of the meat roasting on a fire.

We were now on the edge of the San Joaquin Valley, but we did not even know that we were in California. We could see a range of mountains lying to the west—the Coast Range—but we could see no valley. The evening of the day we started down into the valley we were very tired, and when night came our party was strung along for three or four miles, and every man slept where darkness overtook him. He would take off his saddle for a pillow and turn his horse or mule loose, if he had one. His animal would be too poor to walk away, and in the morning he would find him, usually within fifty feet.

The jaded horses nearly perished with hunger and fatigue. When we overtook the foremost of the party the next morning, we found they had come to a pond of water, and one of them had killed a fat coyote. When I came up, it was all eaten except the lights and the windpipe, on which I made my breakfast.

From that camp we saw timber to the north of us, evidently bordering a stream running west. It turned out to be the stream that we had followed down in the mountains—the Stanislaus River. As soon as we came in sight of the bottom land of the stream we saw an abundance of antelopes and sandhill cranes. We killed two of each the first evening. Wild grapes also abounded. The next day we killed fifteen deer and antelopes, jerked the meat and got ready to go on—all except the captain's mess of seven or eight, who decided to stay there and lay in meat enough to last them into California.

We were really almost down to tidewater and did not know it.

Some thought it was five hundred miles yet to California. But all thought we had to cross at least that range of mountains in sight to the west before entering the promised land, and how many beyond no man could tell. Nearly all thought it best to press on lest snows might overtake us in the mountains before us, as they had already nearly done on the mountains behind us—the Sierra Nevadas.

It was now about the first of November. Our party set forth bearing northwest, aiming for a seeming gap north of a high mountain in the chain to the west of us. That mountain was found to be Mount Diablo. At night the Indians attacked the captain's camp and stole all their animals, which were the best of the company, and the next day the men had to overtake us with just what they could carry in their hands.

The next day, judging from the timber we saw, we concluded there was a river to the west. So two men went ahead to see if they could find a trail or a crossing. The timber proved to be along what is now known as the San Joaquin River. We sent two men on ahead to spy out the country. At night one of them returned, saying they came across an Indian on horseback without a saddle, who wore a cloth jacket but no other clothing.

From what they could understand, the Indian knew Mr. Marsh and had offered to guide us to his place. He plainly said "Marsh," and of course we supposed it was the Dr. Marsh who had written the letter to a friend in Jackson County, Missouri, and so it proved. One man went with the Indian to Marsh's ranch and the other came back to tell us what he had done, with the suggestion that we should go and cross the river (San Joaquin) at the place to which the trail was leading.

In that way we found ourselves two days later at Dr. Marsh's ranch, and there we learned that we were really in California and our journey at an end. After six months we had now arrived at the first settlement in California, November 4, 1841.

From "The First Emigrant Train to California," John Bidwell, *Century Magazine*, November 1890.

XXII

John Charles Frémont

Charles Wilkes had made at least a superficial survey of the Pacific Coast for the federal government, but a large third of the continental expanse from the coast to the Rocky Mountains was still uncharted. So shrouded in mystery was that stretch of wilderness that no one knew, for example, the bounds of a magnificent body of water, Mary's Lake, reported to lie somewhere just east of the Sierra Nevada, or the course of the great Buenaventura River, which ran, some said, from the Rocky Mountains to the Bay of San Francisco. The close call of the first emigration party en route to California and the ever-mounting popular interest in westward expansion pointed up the urgent need for an adequate survey of that territory.

At last in 1843 John Charles Frémont (1813–1890), a restless explorer from Georgia, who, like Sutter and Bidwell, was to become a major landholder and political figure in California annals, was commissioned by the federal government to solve some of the mystery of the geographical hiatus and "give a connected survey of the interior of our continent." In May 1843 he assembled a party of thirty-nine—mostly rough-hewn Creoles and Frenchmen—in Kansas and set out on this important expedition. They were joined later by famed "Kit" Carson.

Proceeding northward from the headwaters of the Arkansas River, they located a new pass over the Rockies, crossed the Great Basin, explored the Northwest as far as Fort Vancouver, and then with new

guides and provisions and 104 fresh horses and mules, pointed south
to explore the region of Mary's Lake, hoping to descend the Buenaventura River to the coast. But where the lake was supposed to be they
found nothing but desert, and in place of a broad river exit to the sea
that they had counted on, only the unbroken barrier of the Sierra.

Their plight was far more desperate than that of the Bidwell party,
for the month was January rather than October. With provisions
almost exhausted, burdened with cumbersone scientific equipment and
a bulky collection of minerals and plants gathered on the thousands of
miles they had traveled, with the pack train reduced to sixty-seven
emaciated beasts and his own company reduced to two dozen men,
Frémont faced the necessity of scaling the Sierra in midwinter: their
only chance of survival, he concluded, was in crossing the range to
Sutter's Fort.

Against the counsel of Indians, who warned that the crossing was
utterly impossible, they headed into the mountains in the thick of a
late January blizzard, floundering in drifts of snow from five to twenty
feet deep. Indian guides deserted; spent horses plummeted over cliffs,
with irreplacable supplies still lashed to their backs; the way was
strewn with abandoned effects. To make paths the horses could
ascend, they found it necessary to beat trails in the snow with heavy
hand mauls. They transferred the baggage to crude improvised
sledges, and modeled for themselves snowshoes similar to those worn
by the Indians.

At night they were obliged usually to camp in the open in subzero
temperatures. By February 4 they had gained considerable altitude,
snows were getting deeper, frostbite was taking its toll on the men
and the expedition seemed doomed—but every night by the light of a
magnificent bonfire, Frémont forced himself to scribble in his diary the
major events of the day.

Snowbound in the Sierra

I went ahead early with two or three men, each with a lead horse
to break the road. We were obliged to abandon the hollow entirely and work along the mountainside, which was very steep,
and the snow covered with an icy crust. We cut a footing as we
advanced and trampled a road through for the animals, but occa-

sionally one plunged outside the trail and slid along the field to the bottom a hundred yards below. . . .

Toward a pass which the guide indicated, we attempted in the afternoon to force a road, but after a laborious plunging through two or three hundred yards our best horses gave out, entirely refusing to make any further effort, and for a time we were brought to a stand. The guide informed us that we were entering the deep snow and here began the difficulties of the mountain; and to him and to almost all, our enterprise seemed hopeless. . . . The camp had been occupied all the day in endeavoring to ascend the hill, but only the best horses had succeeded, the animals generally not having sufficient strength to bring themselves up without the packs, and all the line of road . . . was strewed with camp stoves and equipage, and horses floundering in snow. I therefore immediately encamped on . . . a small spot of level ground, protected on one side by the mountain and on the other sheltered by a little ridge of rock. . . .

Tonight [*February 4*] we had no shelter, but we made a large fire around the trunk of one of the huge pines, and covering the snow with small boughs on which we spread our blankets, soon made ourselves comfortable. The night was very bright and clear, though the thermometer was only at 10°. A strong wind which sprang up at sundown made it intensely cold, and this was one of the bitterest nights during the journey.

Two Indians joined our party here; and one of them, an old man, immediately began to harangue us, saying that ourselves and animals would perish in the snow, and that if we would go back he would show us another and a better way across the mountain. He spoke in a very loud voice and there was a singular repetition of phrases and arrangement of words which rendered his speech striking and not unmusical. . . . "Rock upon rock— rock upon rock—snow upon snow," said he; "even if you get over the snow, you will not be able to get down from the mountain." He made us the sign of precipices and showed us how the feet of the horses would slip and throw them off from the narrow trails that led along their sides.

Our Chinook, who comprehended even more readily than ourselves and believed our situation hopeless, covered his head with his blanket and began to weep and lament. "I wanted to see the whites," said he; "I came away from my own people to see the whites, and I wouldn't care to die among them, but here"—and he looked around into the cold night and gloomy forest and, drawing his blanket over his head, began again to lament. Seated around the tree, the fire illuminating the rocks and the tall bolls of the pines round about, and the old Indian haranguing, we presented a group of very serious faces.

February 5th. The night had been too cold to sleep, and we were up very early. Our guide was standing by the fire with all his finery on; and seeing him shiver in the cold, I threw on his shoulders one of my blankets. We missed him a few minutes afterward, and never saw him again. . . .

February 6th. . . . I set out today with a reconnoitering party on snowshoes. We marched all in single file, trampling the snow as heavily as we could. Crossing the open basin in a march of about ten miles, we reached the top of one of the peaks, to the left of the pass indicated by our guide. Far below us, dimmed by the distance, was a large snowless valley, bounded on the western side, at the distance of about a hundred miles, by a low range of mountains, which Carson recognized with delight as the mountains bordering the coast.

"There," said he, "is the little mountain—it is fifteen years since I saw it, but I am just as sure as if I had seen it yesterday." Between us, then, and this low coast range was the valley of the Sacramento, and no one who had not accompanied us through the incidents of our life for the last few months could realize the delight with which at last we looked down upon it. At a distance of apparently thirty miles beyond us were distinguished spots of prairie; and the dark line which could be traced with the glass was imagined to be the course of the river; but we were evidently at a great height above the valley, and between us and the plains extended miles of snowy fields and broken ridges of pine-covered mountains.

It was late in the day when we turned toward the camp, and it grew rapidly cold as it drew toward night. One of the men became fatigued and his feet began to freeze. . . . After a day's march of twenty miles we straggled into the camp one after another at nightfall, the greater number excessively fatigued, only two of the party having ever traveled on snowshoes before.

All our energies are now directed to getting our animals across the snow; and it was supposed that after all the baggage had been drawn with the sleighs over the trail we had made, it would be sufficiently hard to bear our animals. At several places between the point and the ridge we had discovered some grassy spots where the wind and sun had dispersed the snow from the sides of the hills, and these were to form resting places to support the animals for a night in their passage across. On our way across we had set on fire several broken stumps and dried trees to melt holes in the snow for the camps. . . .

February 7th. With one party drawing sleighs loaded with baggage, I advanced today about four miles along the trail, and encamped at the first grassy spot where we expected to bring our horses. . . .

February 8th. The night has been extremely cold, but perfectly still and beautifully clear. Before the sun appeared this morning the thermometer was 3° below zero. . . . Our provisions are getting fearfully scant. Sleighs arrived with baggage about ten o'clock, and leaving a portion of it here, we continued on for a mile and a half and encamped at the foot of a long hill. . . . Two other sleighs arrived in the afternoon, and the men being fatigued I gave them all tea and sugar. Snow clouds began to rise in the south southwest and, apprehensive of a storm which would destroy our road, I sent the people back . . . with directions to send for the animals in the morning. . . . Elevation of the camp, by the boiling point, is 7,920 feet.

February 9th. During the night the weather changed, the wind rising to a gale, and commencing to snow before daylight; before morning the trail was covered. We remained quiet in camp all day. . . . We suffer much from the want of salt; and all the men are becoming weak from insufficient food.

February 10th. . . . Continuing on with three sleighs carrying a part of the baggage, we had the satisfaction to encamp within two and a half miles of the head of the hollow and at the foot of the last mountain range. . . . The elevation of the camp . . . is 8,050 feet . . . and still we are not done ascending. . . . Putting on our snowshoes, we spent the afternoon in exploring the road ahead. The glare of the snow, combined with great fatigue, had rendered many of the people nearly blind, but we were fortunate in having some black silk handkerchiefs which, worn as veils, very much relieved the eye.

February 11th. High wind continued and our trail this morning was nearly invisible. . . . Our situation became tiresome and dreary, requiring a strong exercise of patience and resolution, [because of] the utter failure . . . to get our mules and horses over the snow. . . . They had broken through and were plunging about or lying half buried in snow. . . .

February 12th. We made mauls and worked hard at our end of the road all day. . . .

February 13th. We continued to labor on the road. . . . The meat train did not arrive this evening, and I gave Godey leave to kill our little dog Tlamath, which he prepared in Indian fashion, scorching off the hair and washing the skin with soap and snow, and then cutting it up into pieces, which were laid on the snow. . . . We had tonight an extraordinary dinner—pea soup, mule, and dog.

February 14th. The dividing ridge of the Sierra is in sight from this encampment. . . . I ascended today the highest peak to the right, from which we had a beautiful view of a mountain lake at our feet, about fifteen miles in length [Tahoe]. . . .

February 16th. . . . I started on a reconnoitering expedition beyond the mountain. We traveled along the crests of narrow ridges, extending down from the mountain in the direction of the valley. . . . We encamped on the headwater of a little creek, where at last the water found its way to the Pacific. The night was clear and very long. . . . I was now perfectly satisfied that we had struck the stream on which Mr. Sutter lived; and turning about, made a hard push and reached the camp at dark. Here we had the pleasure to find all the remaining animals, 57 in number, safely arrived at the grassy hill near the camp. . . .

On the 19th the people were occupied in making a road and bringing up the baggage, and on the afternoon of the next day, *February 20, 1844*, we encamped with the animals and all the materiel of the camp on the summit of the Pass . . . 9,338 feet above the sea. . . .

February 21st. We now considered ourselves victorious over the mountain; having only the descent before us and the valley under our eyes, we felt strong hope that we should force our way down. But this was a case in which the descent was *not* facile. . . . We had hard and doubtful labor yet before us, as the snow appeared to be heavier. . . . Ascending a height, we traced out the best line we could discover for the next day's march . . . and we saw a shining line of water directing its course toward another, a broader and larger sheet. We knew that these could be no other than the Sacramento and the Bay of San Francisco. . . . Tonight a mule was killed for food. . . .

February 22nd. . . . The delay of making a road occasioned much labor and loss of time . . . in a desperate push over a snowfield ten to fifteen feet deep. . . . Encamped on a ridge after a march of three miles. . . . Tonight we killed another mule—now our only resource from starvation. . . .

February 23rd. This was our most difficult day; we were forced off the ridges by the quantity of snow among the timber and obliged to take to the mountainsides . . . but these were steep and slippery with snow and ice, and the tough evergreens of the mountain impeded our way, tore our skins and exhausted our patience. . . . Axes and mauls were necessary today to make a way through the snow. Going ahead with Carson to reconnoiter the road, we reached in the afternoon the river which made the outlet of the lake. Carson sprang over, clear across a place where the stream was compressed among rocks, but the parfleche sole of my moccasin glanced from the icy rock and precipitated me into the river. It was some seconds before I could recover myself in the current and Carson thinking me hurt, jumped in after me, and we both had an icy bath. . . . Making a large fire on the bank, after we had partially dried ourselves, we went back to meet the

camp. . . . Many of the men looked badly, and some this evening were giving out.

February 24th. . . . We continued down the south face of the
mountain; our road leading over dry ground, we were able to
avoid the snow almost entirely. . . . The summer green of the
beautiful foliage, with the singing birds and the sweet summer
wind, which was whirling about the dry oak leaves, nearly intoxicated us with delight, and we hurried on, filled with excitement,
to escape entirely from the horrid region of inhospitable snow to
the perpetual spring of the Sacramento. When we had traveled
about ten miles, the valley opened a little to an oak and pine
bottom. . . . Here we made our encampment. . . . We had descended to an elevation of 3,864 feet. . . . Another horse was
killed tonight for food.

February 25th. Believing that the difficulties of the road were
passed . . . I started ahead this morning with a party of eight
. . . to proceed as rapidly as possible to the house of Mr. Sutter
and return to meet the party with a supply of provisions and fresh
animals. . . . We made twelve miles and encamped at some old
Indian huts, apparently a fishing place. . . . ·

February 26th. We continued to follow the stream, the mountains on either hand increasing in height as we descended and
shutting up the river narrowly in precipices, along which we had
great difficulty to get out horses. . . . Here we saw on the lower
hills the first flowers in bloom. . . .

February 27th. We succeeded in fording the stream and . . .
encamped on the hill slope. . . . We had with us a large kettle,
and a mule being killed here, his head was boiled in it for several
hours and made a passable soup for famished people. . . .

February 28th. . . . Traveling here was good except in crossing the ravines, which were narrow, steep and frequent. . . .
Every hour we had been expecting to see open out before us the
valley which from the mountain above seemed almost at our
feet. . . .

March 6th. We continued on our road through the same sur-
passingly beautiful country. . . . Our horses had now become so
strong that they were able to carry us, and we traveled rapidly—

over four miles an hour. . . . In a few hours we reached a large fork, the northern branch of the river. Together they formed a beautiful stream . . . which we took to be the Sacramento. . . . We made an acorn meal at noon and hurried on, the valley being gay with flowers and some of the banks being absolutely golden with the California poppy. . . .

Shortly afterward we gave a shout at the appearance on a little bluff of a neatly-built adobe house with glass windows. We rode up, but to our disappointment found only Indians. . . . We now pressed on more eagerly than ever . . . and came unexpectedly into a large Indian village, where the people looked clean and wore cotton shirts and various other articles of dress. They immediately crowded around us. . . . Then a well-dressed Indian came up and made his salutations in very well-spoken Spanish. In answer to our inquiries, he informed us that we were upon the River of the Americans and that it joined the Sacramento River about ten miles below. Never did a name sound more sweetly! We felt ourselves among our countrymen, for the name of *American* in these distant parts is applied to the citizens of the United States.

To our eager inquiries he answered, "I am a vaquero in the service of Captain Sutter and the people of this rancheria work for him." . . . He went on to say that Captain Sutter was a very rich man and always glad to see his country people. We asked for his house. He answered that it was just over the hill before us, and offered, if we would wait a moment to take his horse and conduct us to it.

We readily accepted this civil offer, . . . forded the river and in a few miles were met a short distance from the fort by Captain Sutter himself. He gave us a most frank and cordial reception, conducted us immediately to his residence, and under his hospitable roof we had a night of rest, enjoyment and refreshment which none but ourselves could appreciate.

From *Exploring Expedition of the Rocky Mountains, Oregon and California,* John C. Frémont (Buffalo: Derby, Orton and Mulligan, 1853).

XXIII

Hubert Howe Bancroft

Despite his brush with fate in the Sierra snows, Frémont issued such a reassuring report on California, upon his return to the East, that he set off a new wave of enthusiasm for western migration, and was back there himself the following year as guest of the United States consul at Monterey, where he was also graciously entertained by Governor José Castro. But when the governor learned a few days later that Frémont had left behind him back in the hills two detachments of soldiers, temper replaced graciousness and Frémont was peremptorily ordered to leave the country.

Instead of following instructions, however, Frémont withdrew to the crest of a little hill near Salinas, fortified it, and defiantly raised the American flag—the first open act of hostility in the Yankee conquest of California. Obviously he could not hold the hill for long against even the local carabineros, and at the first opportunity he hauled down the flag and retreated to Sutter's Fort at New Helvetia. It was from that fort that the Bear Flag Revolt of June 14, 1846 was launched on Sonoma, though not one of its participants knew at the time that Mexico and the United States had officially been at war for a month, and would never have guessed that the Stars and Stripes would be flying over Monterey three weeks later.

The Bear Flag Revolt was to go down in California lore as a courageous act of heroism, but to historian Hubert Howe Bancroft (1832–1918) it fell far short of that: it was nothing but a "filibustering scheme" contrived by "reckless, daring, unprincipled men with nothing to lose," an illegitimate military occupation "ill-timed, ill-advised and extraordinary in all its phases." And Bancroft's convictions could not be taken lightly, though he himself missed witnessing the revolt by six years.

He arrived at San Francisco in 1852 as a booksalesman for a Buffalo firm, and from that modest start advanced rapidly to the proprietorship of his own shop, conducting the largest book and stationery business west of Chicago. He branched out into printing and publishing, specialized in collecting rare books on Pacific Coast history for the trade and for himself, and then opened his "history-factory," in which he employed six regular ghost writers and as many as six hundred part-time researchers in the production of his thirty-nine-volume *Works of Hubert Howe Bancroft.* Judicious critics acclaimed this compilation of West Coast history as "the greatest feat of historiography since Thucydides," but he often wrote—or edited—as though he had a grudge to settle, and he had a grudge against Frémont and his Bear Flag revolutionaries.

The Bear Flag Filibusters

In narratives of the time, and later, it was customary to magnify the exploit of June 14th by speaking of Sonoma as a Californian stronghold, a fort, a garrisoned town, taken by surprise, or even by a "gallant charge" without shedding of blood, so skillfully was the movement planned.

There was, however, no garrison at Sonoma. The soldiers formerly in service there had been discharged some years before. . . . Some of the citizens even were absent from the town, and there was no thought of even posting a sentinel. It is true, there remained as relics of the old military regime nine small cannon, a few of them still mounted, and over 200 muskets in the *cuartel,* with a small quantity of ammunition.

All was technically public property, though in reality belonging to Colonel Vallejo [Sonoma's Mexican founder and landlord], who had not seen fit to deliver it to the general on his late visit. Two men residing there held commissions in the Mexican army;

otherwise a more peaceful burg than this stronghold of the
Frontera del Norte on that Sunday morning it would be difficult
to find.

At daybreak Vallejo was aroused by a noise and, on looking out,
saw that his house was surrounded by armed men. This state of
things was sufficiently alarming in itself, and all the more so by
reason of the uncouth and even ferocious aspect of the strangers.
. . . "Almost the whole party was dressed in leather hunting
shirts, many of them very greasy; taking the whole party together, they were about as rough a looking set of men as one
could hope to imagine. It is not to be wondered at that anyone
would feel some dread in falling into their hands." And Vallejo
himself declares that there was by no means such a uniformity of
dress as a greasy hunting shirt for each man would imply.

Vallejo's wife was even more alarmed than her husband, whom
she begged to escape by a back door, but who, deeming such a
course undignified as well as impracticable, hastily dressed, ordered the front door opened, and met the intruders as they entered his *sala*, demanding who was their chief and what their
business. Not much progress in explanation was made at first,
though it soon became apparent that the colonel, while he was to
consider himself a prisoner, was not in danger of any personal
violence. . . .

Early in the ensuing negotiations between prisoners and filibusters it became apparent that the latter had neither acknowledged leader nor regular plan of operations beyond the seizure of
government property and of the officers. Some were acting . . .
merely with a view to obtain arms, animals and hostages—to
bring about hostilities and at the same time to deprive the foe of
his resources; others believed themselves to have undertaken a
revolution in which steps to be immediately taken were a formal
declaration of independence and the election of officers. . . .

All seemed to agree, however, that they were acting under
Frémont's orders, and this to the prisoners was the most assuring
feature in the case. Vallejo had for some time favored the annexa-
tion of California to the United States. He had expected and often
predicted a movement to that end. There is no foundation for the
suspicion that the taking of Sonoma and his own capture were

planned by himself, in collusion with the filibuster chiefs, with a view to evade responsibility; yet it is certain that he had little if any objection to an enforced arrest by officers of the United States as a means of escaping from the delicacy of his position as a Mexican officer.

Accordingly, being assured that the insurgents were acting under Frémont, he submitted to arrest, gave up keys to public property and entered upon negotiations with a view to obtain guaranties of protection for non-combatants. The guaranties sought were then drawn up in writing and signed by the respective parties. . . .

I do not . . . deem it at all likely that the leaders drank more than it was customary to drink in a Californian's parlor, or more than they could carry; but that some of the rough characters in the company became intoxicated, we may well believe. At any rate, disagreement ensued; the men refused entirely to ratify the capitulation made by their former leaders, insisting that the prisoners must be sent to the Sacramento; some of them were inclined to be insubordinate and eager for plunder; while the lawless spirits were restrained from committing outrages. . . .

The revolutionists immediately took possession of all public property, as well as such horses and other private property as they needed, at the same time locking up all citizens that could be found. . . . Vallejo, though not encouraged at seeing that the leaders were not permitted by their followers to keep their promises, was not very much displeased at being sent to New Helvetia . . . and he had no reason to doubt that on meeting Frémont he and his companions would at once be released on parole. . . .

For four or five days it does not appear that there was any increase in the insurgent garrison; but during that time several weighty matters of state were disposed of by these *soi-disant* founders of a republic. . . . The need of a banner was naturally one of the first suggested. The insurgents had no right to unfurl the stars and stripes, as many of them would doubtless have preferred to do; yet any flag devised by Americans must needs have at least a star and a stripe; and the appropriateness of a lone star could not fail to suggest itself to men familiar with the history of Texas, and the similarity of condition between that country and what they hoped to make of California.

A simple copy would not, however, suffice, and an additional emblem was required. Somebody proposed the grizzly bear, an animal then common in those regions, and whose reputation for "strength and unyielding resistance" could be attested by every one of those resolute hunters from personal experience. For materials they took what they could find: that is, a piece of common unbleached cotton cloth, the *manta* of the Mexicans, somewhat less than a yard in width and five feet long, and some strips of red flannel about four inches wide.

The flannel, the stripe of the flag, made of the requisite length by piecing, was sewn to the bottom of the cotton. In the upper left-hand corner of the white field was outlined in ink and filled in with red paint an irregular five-pointed star, fifteen inches in its greatest diameter. Just to the right of the star, and facing it, was painted in like manner what was intended for a bear, statant, though it has been pronounced more like a hog by experts who cared little for the feelings of the last-named animal. Under the two emblems was rudely lettered in black ink CALIFORNIA REPUB-LIC. Such was the famous Bear Flag, which has given a name to the revolution, and which caused the insurgents to be known to the natives as Osos. . . .

Some of the leaders looked forward to official prominence in an independent Californian republic; others looked further . . . to future profitable negotiations with the United States; while others looked upon the movement as but the beginning of war in favor of the United States, from the government and people of which nation they expected great honor, and in which war they hoped to secure a more prominent position than if they waited for the naval forces to begin hostilities. They were all mere filibusters, and were entitled to none of the sympathy or honor which the world accords to revolutionists who struggle against oppression.

From *The Works of Hubert Howe Bancroft*, Volume XXII (History of California, Volume V) (San Francisco: History Company, 1886).

XXIV

Walter Colton

By American standards of civic peace and social order, California was in chaos; by Latin American standards, which took for granted a certain amount of perennial insurrection and riot, the situation was by no means so grim. Californios could take their revolutions in stride, and between scuffles attend mass, digest four square meals a day, celebrate all the saints' days, gallop about the countryside in wild exuberance, whoop it up at bullfights, bear baits, rodeos, fandangos, and fiestas. They could be as carefree one day as they could be politically argumentative or bellicose the next.

It was this paradox that a new American consular agent, Walter Colton (1797–1851), the most beloved Yankee ever to hold office in Mexican California, found at Monterey upon his arrival there in 1846 just after the Mexican government had forbidden all further immigration of Americans to California, the year that brought the Bear Flag Revolt, the declaration of California's independence, the invasion of Colonel Steven W. Kearney's army, and war between Mexico and the United States. Colton's was not an enviable assignment.

The new appointee was a Protestant minister from Vermont, who had cast his lot with the United States Navy as a chaplain and then had been given shore duty closely allied to the State Department. No one could have presented credentials that, at face value, would have been less likely to represent a foreigner who would be very warmly respected in Monterey, yet within two months after his arrival he had so ingratiated himself with the citizenry that he was *elected* alcalde of Monterey by popular vote—while continuing his other official responsibilities. "The election is undoubtedly the highest compliment which they can confer," Colton acknowledged, "but this token of confidence brings with it a great deal of labor and responsibility. It devolves upon me duties similar to those of mayor of one of our cities, without any of those judicial aids which he enjoys. It involves every breach of peace, every case of crime, every business obligation and every disputed land title within a space of three hundred miles. From every other alcalde's court in this jurisdiction there is an appeal to this, and none from this to any higher tribunal. . . . There is not a judge on any bench in England or the United States whose power is so absolute as that of the alcalde of Monterey."

For three years he carried those responsibilities with uncommon wisdom, tact, and originality, and on the side preached a sermon—a Protestant sermon in a Catholic land—every Sabbath; started the first newspaper in California; superintended construction of a trim stone capitol—which he referred to as a "town hall"; and when he could break away from the queue of seekers of justice and judgment, he sandwiched in horseback excursions, accepted endless invitations to fandangos, fiestas, and bullfights, and jotted in his journal descriptions of the California way of life that seldom hinted of the contention other authors were featuring.

Merry-making Magistrate

There are no people that I have ever been among who enjoy life so thoroughly as the Californians. Their habits are simple; their wants few; nature rolls almost everything spontaneously into their lap. Their cattle, horses and sheep roam at large—not a blade of grass is cut, and none is required. The harvest waves wherever the plow and harrow have been; and the grain which the wind scatters this year serves as seed for the next.

The slight labor required is more a diversion than a toil; and even this is shared by the Indian. They attach no value to money, except as it administers to their pleasures. A fortune, without the facilities of enjoying it, is with them no object of emulation or

envy. Their happiness flows from a fount that has very little connection with their outward circumstances.

There is hardly a shanty among them which does not contain
more true contentment, more genuine gladness of the heart, than
you will meet within the most princely palace. Their hospitality
knows no bounds; they are always glad to see you, come when
you may; take a pleasure in entertaining you while you remain;
and only regret that your business calls you away.

If you are sick, there is nothing which sympathy and care can
devise or perform which is not done for you. No sister ever hung
over the throbbing brain or fluttering pulse of a brother with
more tenderness and fidelity. This is as true of the lady whose
hand has only figured her embroidery or swept her guitar, as of
the cottage girl wringing from her laundry the foam of the mountain stream; and all this from the *heart!* If I must be cast in
sickness or destitution on the care of the stranger, let it be in
California; but let it be before American avarice has hardened the
heart and made a god of gold.

The Californians breakfast at eight, dine at twelve, take tea at
four, supper at eight, and then go to bed—unless there is a
fandango. The supper is the most substantial meal of the three,
and would visit anybody but a Californian with a nightmare. But
their constant exercise in the open air, and on horseback, gives
them the digestion of the ostrich.

The only meat consumed here to any extent is beef. It is beef
for breakfast, beef for dinner and beef for supper. A pig is quite a
rarity; and as for chickens, they are reserved for the sick. The
woods are full of partridges and hare; the streams and lagoons are
covered with ducks and wild geese; and the harbor abounds with
the most delicious fish. But no Californian will angle or hunt
while he has a horse or saddle left.

And as for the Indians, but very few of them have any hunting
gear beyond the bow and arrow; with these they can kill the deer
and elk, but a partridge and hare are too shy and too quick. They
spear a large salmon which frequents Carmel River, three miles
distant, and bring it in to market. This fish is often three feet long,

extremely fat, and of a flavor that takes from Lent half the merit of its abstinence. Spearing them is high sport for the Indian. . . .

Wild geese prevail here in the greatest abundance. . . . They fly in squadrons which for the moment shut out the sun; a chance shot will often bring two or three to the ground. The boys will often lasso them in the air. This is done by fastening two lead balls, several yards from each other, to a long line, which is whirled into the air to a great height. In its descent the balls fall on opposite sides of the neck of some luckless goose, and down he comes into the hands of the urchin hunter; sometimes a pair are brought down.

A Californian is most at home in his saddle; there he has some claims to originality, if not in character, then in costume. His hat with its conical crown and broad rim throws back the sun's rays from its dark glazed surface. It is fastened on by a band which passes under his chin and rests on a red handkerchief, which turbans his head, from beneath which his black locks flow out upon the wind.

The collar of his linen rolls over that of his blue spencer, which is open under the chin, is fitted closely to his waist and often ornamented with double rows of buttons and silk braid. His trousers, which are fastened around his loins with a red sash, are open to the knee, to which his buckskin leggins ascend over his white cotton drawers. His buckskin shoes are armed with heavy spurs, which have a shaft some ten inches long, at the end of which is a roller which bristles out into six points, three inches long, against which steel plates rattle with a quick, sharp sound.

His feet rest in stirrups of wood carved from the solid oak, and are extremely strong and heavy. His saddle rises high fore and aft, and is broadly skirted with leather, which is stamped into figures, through the interstices of which red and green silk flash out with gay effect. The reins of his bridle are thick and narrow and the headstall is profusely ornamented with silver plate.

His horse, with his long flowing mane, arching neck, broad chest, full flanks and slender legs, is full of fire. He seldom trots, and will gallop all day without seeming to be weary. On his back is the Californian's home. Leave him this home and you may have the rest of the world.

An Indian galloped to my door this morning, having in lead a splendid pied horse, richly caparisoned, and with an invitation from a ranchero forty miles distant that I should come and spend a few days with him at his country seat; so I placed the office in the hands of Don Davido, well competent to its duties, and . . . started for the mansion of my old friend from the mountains of Spain, now in the winter of age, but with a heart warm as a sunbeam.

The town with its white dwellings soon vanished behind the pine and evergreen oak which crown the hills. . . . The little lakes, navelled in the breaks of the forest, flashed on the eye; the water fowl in clouds took wing; the quail whirled into the bushes; and the deer bounded off to their woodland retreats. A grizzly bear with a storm of darkness in his face stood his ground and never even blinked at the crack of our pistols.

We were now on the bank of the Salinas, through which we dashed, allowing our horses a taste of its yellow waters, then up the opposite bank and away over the broad plain, which stretches in vernal beauty beyond. Our horses required no spur, were in fine condition, high spirits, never broke their gallop, and swept ahead like a fawn to its covert. Mine belonged to the daughter of the Don, to whose hearth we were bound, and had often rattled about among these hills beneath his fair owner, whose equestrian graces and achievements might throw a fresh enchantment on the chase that had gathered to its rivalries the beauty and bravery of Old England.

Another mountain stream—a dash through its foaming tide, and away again through a broad ravine, which bent its ample track to the steep hills. . . . Where the forests broke, the wild oats waved like golden lakes, and mirrored the passing cloud, while the swaying pines rolled out their music on the wind like a dirge of ocean. And now another luxuriant plain where cattle and horses and sheep gambolled and grazed by thousands; and on the opposite side the white mansion of our host, crowning the headland and glimmering through the waving shade like the columns which consecrate Colonna.

Here we alighted without weariness to ourselves or our spirited animals, though we had swept through the forty miles in three hours and a half. The señorita who had sent me her horse vaulted into the saddle which I had just relinquished and, patting the noble fellow whom she called Leopaldo, induced him to exhibit a variety of his cunning evolutions. . . .

It was a festive eve at the Don's; youth and beauty were there; and as the sable hues of night sunk on silent tree and tower, the harp and guitar woke into melodious action. The hour was late when the waltz and song resigned their votaries to the calmer claims of slumber. My apartment betrayed the rural diversions of some fairy, one whose floral trophies threw their fragrance from every variety of vase. The air was loaded with perfume, and could hardly be relieved by the visits of the night wind through the lifted window. My dreams ran on tulips and roses.

Morn blazed again in the east; the soaring lark sung from its cloud; the guests were up; glad voices were heard in the hall; light forms glanced through the corridors, and a *buenos dios* rolled in sweet accents from lips circled with smiles. Coffee and tortillas went round, mingled with salutations and those first fresh thoughts which spring from the heart like early birds from the tree. . . .

The horses of the Don were now driven to the door—a sprightly band—vying in their hues with the flowers that sprinkled the meadows, and the guests were invited to make their selection. My choice fell, of course, on Leopaldo, who had brought me from Monterey. But his fair owner would want him— no, he was delivered to me, as the señorita took another quite as full of fire.

The ladies were now tossed into their saddles, and the gentlemen, belted and spurred, vaulted into theirs. We all struck at once into a hand gallop and swept over the broad plain which stretches from the acropolis of the Don to the broken line of a mountain range. Here we spurred into a broad shadowy ravine, overhung with toppling crags. . . . "A coyote!" shouted those in the van, and started in chase; but this prairie wolf had his den near at hand and soon vanished from sight. Another, and a third, but the chasm yielded its instant refuge. A fourth was started, who gave us longer pursuit, but he soon doubled from sight around the bold bluff into a jungle.

Here the horse of Señorita S—— dashed ahead of the whole *caballada* with his dilated eye fastened on a noble buck, and swept up the sloping side of the ravine to gain the ridge and cut off his escape in that direction, while the whole troop spurred hot and fast upon his retreat below. We were now in for a chase, brief though it might be. The buck seemed confused, and no wonder, with such a shouting bevy at his heels, and with the señoritas streaming along the ridge and dashing over chasm and cliff. . . . But the proud buck was not to be captured in this way. . . .

We here wheeled into another mountain gorge, which opened into a long irregular vista of savage wildness. A gallop of two or three miles brought us to a spot where the rocky barriers retreated on either hand, shaping out a bowl, in the center of which stood a cluster of oaks. On the lower limb of one . . . a dark object was described, half lost in the leaves. "A bear, a bear!" shouted our leader and dashed up to the tree, which was instantly surrounded by the whole troop.

"Give us pistols," exclaimed the señoritas as bravely in for the sport as the rest. Click, crack! and a storm of balls went through the treetop. Down came old bruin with one bound into the midst, full of wrath and revenge. The horses instinctively wheeled into a circle, and as bruin sprung for a death grapple, the lasso of our *baccaros*, thrown with unerring aim, brought him up all standing.

He now turned upon the horse of his new assailant, but that sagacious animal evaded each plunge and seemed to play in transport about his antagonist. The pistols were out again, and a fresh volley fell thick as hail around the bear. In the smoke and confusion no one could tell where his next spring might be; but the horse of the *baccaro* knew his duty and kept the lasso taut.

Bruin was wounded but resolute and undaunted. The fire

rolled from his red eyes like a flash of lightning out of a forked cloud. . . . The pistols were reloaded, and señoritas and caballeros all dashed up for another shower of fire and lead. As the smoke cleared, bruin was found with the lasso slack, a sure evidence that the horse who managed it knew his antagonist was dead.

This was sport enough for one day. We galloped on through the defile, which wound round a mountain spur till it struck a precipitous stream. . . . Following the ravine, . . . we debouched at length upon the plain, crowned with the hospitable mansion of our host. The feats of the morning astonished even the old Don, who offered his favorite roan to the one whose bullet had killed the bear. The meed was challenged by each and all, but no one could make good and exclusive claim. . . .

Dinner was announced; then came the siesta, followed by the soft twilight, with the harp, guitar and song, which melted away into sweet sleep. In the morning . . . we waved our adieu and returned to Monterey.

I have never been in a community that rivals Monterey in its spirit of hospitality and generous regard. Such is the welcome to the privileges of the private hearth that a public hotel has never been able to maintain itself. You are not expected to wait for a particular invitation, but to come without the slightest ceremony, make yourself entirely at home, and tarry as long as it suits your inclination, be it for a day or for a month. . . .

If a stranger, you are not expected to bring a formal letter of introduction. No one here thinks any the better of a man who carries the credentials of his character and standing in his pocket. A word or an allusion to recognized persons or places is sufficient. If you turn out to be different from what your first impressions and fair speech promised, still you meet with no frowning looks, no impatience for your departure. You still enjoy in full that charity which suffereth long and is kind. . . .

And when you finally depart, it will not be without a benison, not perhaps that you are worthy of it, but you belong to the great human family where faults often spring from misfortune and the force of untoward circumstances. Generous, forbearing people of Monterey! there is more true hospitality in one throb of your heart than circulates for years through the courts and capitals of kings.

From *Three Years in California,* Walter Colton (New York: A. S. Barnes, 1850).

XXV

James Wilson Marshall

Inevitably someone else would have discovered that the subsoil of inland California was layered with gold if James Wilson Marshall (1810–1885) had not. Since Marshall happened to be the man, the mantle of fame was draped over his shoulders, and symbolically, at least, he was required to carry the onus for instigating the most abrupt transformation ever suffered by any region in the United States. He brought the gold rush, changed the Westward-ho movement into a stampede, upset the whole pattern of Californian—and American—history.

Marshall wore the mantle uncomfortably. To his dying day he was harrowed by the notoriety he accidentally brought upon himself. While others made fortunes from his discovery, he was everlastingly plagued and all but pauperized. During the gold rush years he was tenaciously followed everywhere he went, and knew no peace. Superstitious gold scavengers regarded him as a sort of wizard who possessed occult knowledge of the hidden sources of all the precious metal, who could at will direct them to the most remunerative diggings. He brought some of the harassment upon himself by sending petitioners to far-off gullies just to get rid of them, and sometimes they did find gold where he sent them. Repeatedly his life was threatened by those who failed to locate wealth in places he had designated, and threatened as often by men to whom he forthrightly declined to give spurious counsel.

Except in self-defense, he made no pretense of being a mineralogist. He called himself a millwright; actually he was a wagonmaker and general mechanic, who had hailed originally from New Jersey. On a circuitous journey across the continent he had lived briefly in Indiana, Illinois, Missouri, and Oregon, finally taking up residence at New Helvetia, where John Sutter had put him to work making spinning wheels for the Indian squaws employed there as blanketweavers. Then he was given the job of redesigning a crude mule-powered gristmill, and later placed in charge of constructing a much-needed sawmill.

It was the last assignment that led to the momentous discovery. Marshall was no more a writer than a wizard. Years after the great event, an artist, Charles B. Gillespie, encountered him on the site of his discovery and it was to Gillespie that he recited the story of finding the golden nuggets that dazzled the world.

Something Shining in a Ditch

In May, 1847, with my rifle, blanket and a few crackers to eat with the venison—for the deer then was awful plenty—I ascended the American River, according to Mr. Sutter's wish, as he wanted to find a good site for a sawmill, where he could have plenty of timber and where wagons would be able to ascend and descend the river hills. Many fellows had been out before me, but they could not find any place to suit; so when I left I told Mr. Sutter I would go along the river to the very head and find the place, if such a place existed anywhere upon the river or any of its forks.

I traveled along the river the whole way. Many places would suit very well for the erection of the mill, with plenty of timber everywhere, but then nothing but a mule could climb the hills; and when I would find a spot where the hills were not steep, there was no timber to be had; and so it was until I had been out several days and reached this place, which at first sight looked like the exact spot we were hunting.

I passed a couple of days examining the hills, and found a place where wagons could ascend and descend with all ease. On my return to the fort I went out through the country examining the canyons and gulches, and picking out the easiest places for crossing them with loaded wagons. You may be sure Mr. Sutter was pleased when I reported my success.

We entered into partnership; I was to build the mill, and he was to find provisions, teams, tools, and to pay a portion of the men's wages. I believe I was at the time the only millwright in the whole country. In August, everything being ready, we freighted two wagons with tools and provisions, and, accompanied by six men, I left the fort, and after a good deal of difficulty reached this place one beautiful afternoon and formed our camp on yon little rise of ground right above the town [Coloma].

Our first business was to put up log houses, as we intended remaining here all winter. This was done in less than no time, for my men were great with the ax. We then cut timber and fell to work hewing it for the framework of the mill. The Indians gathered about us in great numbers. I employed about forty of them to assist us with the dam, which we put up in a kind of way in about four weeks.

In digging the foundation of the mill we cut some distance into the soft granite. We opened the foreboy and then I left for the fort, giving orders to Mr. Weimar to have a ditch cut through the bar in the rear of the mill, and after quitting work in the evening to raise the gate and let the water run all night, as it would assist us very much in deepening and widening the mill race.

I returned in a few days and found everything favorable, all the men being at work in the ditch. When the channel was opened it was my custom every evening to raise the gate and let the water wash out as much sand and gravel through the night as possible; and in the morning, while the men were getting breakfast, I would walk down, and, shutting off the water, look along the race and see what was to be done, so that I might tell Mr. Weimar, who had charge of the Indians, at what particular point to set them to work for the day. As I was the only millwright present, all my time was employed upon the frame work and machinery.

One morning in January [January 24, 1848], it was a clear, cold morning; I shall never forget that morning. As I was taking my usual walk along the race, after shutting off the water, my eye was caught by a glimpse of something shining in the bottom of the ditch. There was about a foot of water running there. I reached my hand down and picked it up; it made my heart thump for I felt certain it was gold. The piece was about half the size and of the shape of a pea. Then I saw another piece in the water. After taking it out, I sat down and began to think right hard. I thought it was gold, and yet it did not seem to be of the right color; all the gold coin I had seen was of a reddish tinge; this looked more like brass.

I recalled to mind all the metals I had ever seen or heard of, but I could find none that resembled this. Suddenly the idea flashed across my mind that it might be iron pyrites. I trembled to think of it! This question could soon be determined. Putting one of the pieces on hard river stone, I took another and commenced hammering it. It was soft and didn't break; it therefore must be gold, but largely mixed with some other metal, very likely silver; for pure gold, I thought, would certainly have a brighter color.

When I returned to our cabin for breakfast, I showed the two pieces to my men. They were all a good deal excited, and had they not thought that the gold only existed in small quantities they would have abandoned everything and left me to finish the job alone. However, to satisfy them, I told them that as soon as we had the mill finished we would devote a week or two to gold hunting and see what we could make out of it.

While we were working in the race after this discovery, we always kept a sharp lookout, and in the course of three or four days we had picked up about three ounces—our work still progressing as lively as ever, for none of us imagined at that time that the whole country was sowed with gold.

About a week's time after the discovery I had to take another trip to the fort; and to gain what information I could respecting the real value of the metal, took all we had collected with me and showed it to Mr. Sutter, who at once declared it was gold, but thought with me it was greatly mixed with some other metal.

It puzzled us a great deal to hit upon the means of telling the exact quantity contained in the alloy; however, we at last stumbled on an old American cyclopedia where we saw the specific gravity of all the metals, and rules given to find the quantity of each in a given bulk. After hunting over the whole fort and borrowing from some of the men, we got three dollars and a half in silver, and with a small pair of scales we soon cyphered it out that there was no silver nor copper in the gold, but that it was entirely pure.

This fact being ascertained, we thought it our best policy to keep it as quiet as possible till we should have finished our mill, but there was a great number of disbanded Mormon soldiers in and about the fort, and when they came to hear of it, why, it just spread like wildfire, and soon the whole country was in a bustle. I had scarcely arrived at the mill again when several persons appeared with pans, shovels and hoes, and those that had not iron picks had wooden ones, all anxious to fall to work and dig up our mill; but this we would not permit.

As fast as one party disappeared another would arrive, and sometimes I had the greatest kind of trouble to get rid of them. I sent them off in different directions, telling them about such and such places, where I was certain there was plenty of gold if they would only take the trouble of looking for it. At that time I never imagined the gold was so abundant. I told them to go to such and such places, because it appeared that they would dig nowhere but in such places as I pointed out, and I believe such was their confidence in me that they would have dug on the very top of yon mountain if I had told them to do so.

So there, stranger, is the entire history of the gold discovery in California—a discovery that hasn't as yet been of much benefit to me.

From "California—Marshall's Own Account of the Gold Discovery" (as related to Charles B. Gillespie), *Century Magazine*, February 1891.

XXVI

Mariano Guadalupe Vallejo

The Californians had first pickings in the gold fields. They looked upon the scramble for the yellow nuggets as *their* rush, completely oblivious at first of the reaction in the outside world. Beyond the ill-defined borders of California, news traveled fast, but people traveled slowly. The real invasion did not begin for more than a year after James Marshall picked up the suspicious-looking specimens in the wash of his millrace. But during the twelve months that the local inhabitants ran the show, California was transformed. In days there took place a massive shift in population from the coast to the Sierra. Old towns were deserted and new towns or tent cities, with the most bizarre assortment of names ever to litter a map, sprang up faster than they could be counted:

> Boneyard Meadow, Hangman's Bridge,
> Picture Gallery, Jawbone Ridge,
> Nigger Slide, Sonora, Baker,
> Poker Flat, Couts, Hell's Half Acre,
> Henpeck City, Hottentot,
> Grizzly Gulch, Gwin, Wyandotte,
> Hawkeye, Red Dog, Calaveras,
> Shirttail Canyon, San Andreas,
> Cuteye Fosters, Cherokee,
> Shotgun, Hell's Hills, Trinity,

Slaughter Bar, Louisiana,
Montezuma, Lancha Plana,
Pine Knot Village, Red Cloud Mine,
Brandy City, Porcupine,
New Chicago, You Bet, Sattley,
Dog Town, Shaver Crossing, Mattley,
Gold Hill, Fiddletown, North Branch,
Rough and Ready, Quartz, Burnt Ranch,
Yankee Jim's, Condemned, Mount Bullion,
Rawhide, Devil's Nose, Slumgullion,
Priest, Exchequer, Hazel Green,
Penon Blanco, Hawk Ravine,
Groundhog's Glory, Gold Run Wonder,
Bedbug, Bumpass, Bogus Thunder,
Whiskey Flat, Volcanoville,
Wood's Dry Diggings, Jackass Hill.

Mariano Gaudalupe Vallejo (1807–1890), last of the military governors of Mexican California, holder of enormous estates stretching from Pablo Bay to the mountains, namesake of the town of Vallejo and founder of Sonoma, saw the tumult as could no ordinary seeker of quick wealth. To him it was despoilment, pillage, a disinheritance. Though a hard-fisted militarist, he was also a man of refinement and sensitivity, with a finē feeling for justice and Spanish civility. With bitterness, yet with admirable restraint, the worthy general gave his impressions as the melee swirled about Sonoma.

At Six Dollars an Ounce

Gold in the mines! This cry, resounding throughout the length and breadth of California, created a veritable revolution, social and financial. The farmer left his plough in the furrow, the schoolmaster abandoned his books and blackboards, the sailor deserted his ship, the barber flung down his razor and the tailor his shears. Even the lover relinquished the hand of his sweetheart to clutch the pick and shovel and rush forth in search of the longed-for metal.

Some of the adventurers left Monterey mounted on fine horses.

The gold diggers

Speeding along the roads at twenty miles a day, they were not long in reaching their destination. Others, with an eye to the future, set out in oxcarts loaded with provisions; they spent more time on the road, but on reaching the goal of their desires found themselves in far better circumstances than those who had preceded them, since their carts served them as bedrooms, dining rooms, reception halls and kitchens. As rains fell frequently at the mines, it was not only a comfort but a necessity to have places in which to take refuge from the storms.

Shortly after the discovery of the gold diggings, San Diego, Los Angeles, Monterey, Branciforte [Santa Cruz] and San José lost the greater part of their population, for everyone who could dispose of his property left his home and took the road to the mines or "placers," as they called the spots where the coveted metal could be gathered by the handful.

The few wooden houses which existed in the country were torn apart and loaded into small coasting vessels and sent to Sacramento, whence the lumber went forward to the mines by oxcart. Picks, shovels, sheets of tinplate, nails, rubber boots and medicines . . . sold at fabulous prices. But it must be remembered that as many of the miners were producing more than two hundred pesos in a day of twelve hours, they were not minded to resent the inflated prices which they were forced to pay for tools, medicines and food.

At this time, when the populous cities of the southern part of the state were deserted by their inhabitants, the frontier town of Sonoma, an essentially agricultural community, which up to that time had figured only as an outpost against the raids of the heathen savages, rose to the first rank among the cities of Alta California.

All the caravans from Monterey and other parts of the state, and even those which arrived from the state of Sonora, broke their journey at Sonoma, where they rested the wearied animals, repaired harness and wagons, shod their saddle horses and bought fresh provisions before resuming their march. On the other hand, the miners who had met with good fortune in the diggings came, for the most part, to Sonoma to dispose of their gold, to buy new clothing and to make other necessary preparations for their return to the mines.

In December, 1848, and during all of the year 1849, gold in dust or flakes was so abundant in Sonoma that it was difficult to obtain six dollars an ounce in exchange for coined money. This low rate was attributed in part to the large amount of gold brought in by the Indians. . . .

At the diggings the food consisted of the flesh of wild animals, of ship biscuit or bread made by the miners, onions, potatoes, dried beans, salt pork, and from time to time, of salmon. This fish abounded in the Sacramento River, and at that time could be caught with astonishing ease. The fishermen loaded great carts with salmon and, traveling day and night, brought them still fresh to the mining camps, where they sold them for twenty *reales* [$2.50] a pound.

As a rule, a four-horse wagon carried to the mines a ton of salmon, which produced for its owner, when he had sold it to the miners, about $5,000.00. When it is taken into consideration that the round trip could be made in eight days, and sometimes in even shorter time, it can be seen that the earnings of the fishermen were on a level with those of the miners, without the exposure to the calamitous and unpleasant experiences peculiar to the life of the gold diggers.

When the rainy season drew near, the miners who had been fortunate came down from the diggings to spend the winter in Sacramento, which, by reason of its proximity to San Francisco, offered a thousand comforts which one would have sought in vain in the towns of the interior. There were undoubtedly many cases of miners, owners of rich placers, who feared to lose their claims if they abandoned them during the winter, and so remained in the diggings during the rainy season.

Some of these men lost their lives, buried under the snow, some were drowned in the rivers and some were devoured by wild beasts. Misfortunes of this sort were very frequent in the district behind Downieville, where in the winter the snow lies to a depth of eight, ten or twelve feet, and wild animals are abundant.

In the winter Sacramento was always crowded, since it was

there that the gamblers assembled in droves to fleece the unwary. Gaming tables were set up everywhere; faro, monte, rouge et noire and lasquinet were the favorite games. The amounts waged on a single card were very great, and there were times when they reached five or six hundred ounces of gold.

To attract many persons to their gambling halls, the proprietors engaged musicians and singers to whom they paid high wages. I remember that one such family, composed of four persons, was paid a hundred dollars a day, in addition to lodging, meals, liquor and laundry. Anyone had the right to enter the houses of play and demand liquor and cigars without payment, since the astute proprietors knew that the fumes of tobacco and liquor were powerful auxiliaries in upsetting the judgment of those who came to risk their money. Of course, the bankers cheated continually and those who laid their money on the green cloth rarely won.

. . . Many Californians, drawn by the novelty of the spectacle (for gambling in public was not permitted under Mexican rule, although in private the common people played until they lost the clothes off their backs) and deluded into believing that they could easily enrich themselves by guessing the cards, lost in half an hour cattle and ranches that had been owned for half a century, perhaps, by their ancestors. Blinded by the passion for the game, they did not awaken to the truth of the situation until it was already too late to remedy.

Disputes frequently arose among those who played, and these disputes developed into blows, shootings or stabbings. The police never interfered until hostilities were concluded, and the judges, in fear of their lives, refrained from punishing the guilty if they belonged to the great society of Hounds.

This society, at the beginning of 1849, ruled San Francisco and, by means of its ramifications, dominated all California. The Society of Hounds had been founded under the name of "Society for Mutual Aid" but it was in reality nothing but an organization of soulless wretches whose only object was pillage, robbery and banditry; naturally, human life had no value in the eyes of these malefactors.

The Californians living in San Francisco and its environs, and the Europeans of Latin race furnished most of the victims of the Hounds; but when the supply of "foreigners" began to run low, the Hounds were not above robbing their countrymen, the North Americans. . . .

Malefactors who fell into the hands of the miners seldom escaped with their lives. As at that time there were no laws, everyone did justice for himself, either alone or with the aid of his friends and neighbors. It is well known that '48 and '49 were terrible times for bandits, as the industrious miners hanged them as fast as they caught them, without distinction of sex. A woman was hanged in Downieville, and in Placerville (alias Hangtown) also they hanged a young woman who had caused human blood to flow. . . .

When gold was discovered, the flag of stars already waved over Alta California. No longer were we ruled by the Mexican laws, under whose shadow some had advanced while others fell back, but under which no one had perished of hunger, and only two individuals had been by law deprived of their lives, a very common event during the early years of the North American domination in California.

The language now spoken in our country, the laws which govern us, the faces which we encounter daily, are those of the masters of the land, and, of course, antagonistic to our interests and rights, but what does that matter to the conqueror? He wishes his own well-being and not ours!—a thing that I consider only natural in individuals, but which I condemn in a government which has promised to respect and make respected our rights, and to treat us as its own sons. But what does it avail us to complain. The thing has happened and there is no remedy.

. . . I ask, what has the state government done for the Californians since the victory over Mexico? Have they kept the promises with which they deluded us? I do not ask for miracles; I am not and never have been exacting; I do not demand gold, a pleasing gift only to abject peoples. But I ask and I have a right to ask for an answer.

From *The Course of Empire*, Compiled by Valeska Bari from manuscript in the Bancroft Collection (New York: Coward-McCann, 1931).

XXVII

Bayard Taylor

California history was being made faster than it could be appraised and recorded, and the aggressive Americans who were helping to make that history seemed no more capable of chocking things into place, bringing order and stability, than the Mexicans had been. In January 1847 the Pacific commander of the United States Navy had appointed John C. Frémont the first American governor of California; in February he was removed by the head of the army in the West—to be court-martialed and dismissed from service. That example certainly represented no improvement over past administration. Then less than two weeks before the Treaty of Guadalupe Hidalgo had ended the War with Mexico, everything was thrown into further confusion by the discovery of gold.

Little help came from Washington. Congress inconsiderately adjourned in 1849 without making provision for any kind of civil government in California. Such local laws as existed under Mexican rule, therefore, continued more or less in force, along with a military government stripped of its wartime authority. Lacking any effective form of higher control, the miners took the law into their own hands and set up their own rules of conduct.

Then it was proposed that a convention be called to draft a state constitution with the vague hope of its approval by Congress when it next met—so that California might skip entirely the usual territorial status. At a loss for any better solution, the governor promptly issued a proclamation, recommending that all established communities elect delegates to such a convention. A few mining settlements were too disorganized or too preoccupied with their diggings to bother, but most communities readily complied. Elections were held in August and, with typical Western impetuosity, the appointed representatives assembled at Monterey on September 1st and got down to business.

Bayard Taylor (1825–1878) was on hand—a few days late—to report what went on for the New York *Tribune*. Editor Horace Greeley had sent him out to cover the gold rush, but that could wait while he made a scoop of the convention. Taylor was a first-class roving reporter and traveloguist who had gravitated to journalism after facing up to the fact that neither the poetry nor novels he preferred to write were going to rank as classics.

The constitutional convention was a momentous event in the history of California, but Taylor managed to describe it—not inappropriately—as though he were covering the regional get-together of a fraternal order. One of the great decisions a handful of amateur politicians had to make concerned just how large a chunk of the continent they dared stake out for their state: it might be a relatively narrow belt of coastal terrain; it might stretch inland to the crests of the Sierra; or it might incorporate an enormous expanse extending far into the Great Basin. They chose to compromise.

Great Day for California

The building in which the Convention met [at Monterey] in September 1849, to draft a State Constitution was probably the only one in California suited to the purpose. It is a handsome, two-story edifice of yellow sandstone situated on a gentle slope above the town. It is named "Colton Hall," on account of its having been built by Don Walter Colton, former Alcalde of Monterey, from the proceeds of a sale of city lots . . . and will last for centuries in that mild climate.

The upper story, in which the Convention sat, formed a single hall about sixty feet in length by twenty-five in breadth. A railing running across the middle divided the members from the spectators. The former were seated at four long tables, the President

occupying a rostrum at the further end, over which were suspended two American flags and an extraordinary picture of Washington, evidently the work of a native artist.

The appearance of the whole body was exceedingly dignified
and intellectual, and parliamentary decorum was strictly observed. A door in the center of the hall opened on a square
balcony, supported by four pillars, where some of the members,
weary with debate, came frequently to enjoy the mild September
afternoon, whose hues lay so softly on the blue waters of the
bay.

The Declaration of Rights, which was the first subject before
the Convention, occasioned little discussion. Its sections, being
general in character and of a liberal republican cast, were nearly
all adopted by unanimous vote. The clause prohibiting slavery
was met by no word of dissent; it was the universal sentiment of
the Convention. . . . The election of judges by the people—the
right of married women to property—the establishment of a
liberal system of education—and other reforms of late introduced
into the State Governments east of the Rocky Mountains were all
transplanted to the new soil of the Pacific Coast. . . .

The Articles of the Constitution relating to the Executive,
Judicial and Legislative Departments occupied several days, but
the debates were dry and uninteresting. . . . The Chair occasionally made a bungling decision, whereupon two of the members, who had previously served in State Assemblies, would aver
that in the whole course of their legislative experience they had
never heard of such a thing. Now and then a scene occurred
which was amusing enough. A section being before the Convention declaring that every citizen arrested for a criminal offense
would be tried by a jury of his peers, a member unfamiliar with
such technical terms moved to strike out the word "peers." "I
don't like the word 'peers,'" said he; "it ain't republican; I'd like
to know what we want with *peers* in this country—we're not a
monarchy, and we've got no House of Parliament. I vote for no
such law."

The boundary question, however, . . . assumed a character of
real interest and importance. The great point of dispute on this
question was the eastern limit of the State. . . . Grounds taken

by the party desiring the whole territory [extending much farther
east than the present boundary] were that the Convention had no
right to assume another boundary than that originally belonging
to California; that the measure would extend the advantages and
protecting power of law over a vast inland territory which would
otherwise remain destitute of such protection for many years to
come; that, finally, it would settle the question of slavery for a
much greater extent of territory, and in a quiet and peaceful
manner.

The opposition party—that which advocates the Sierra Nevada
as the boundary line—contended that the Constitution had no
right to include the Mormon settlers in the Great Salt Lake
country in a state whose Constitution they had no share in forming, and that nearly the whole of the country east of the Sierra
Nevada was little better than a desert.

After a hot discussion, which lasted a whole day . . . the
report of the Boundary Committee (including all the territory as
far as New Mexico) was adopted. The opposition party, defeated
after they were sure of success, showed their chagrin rather
noisily. At the announcement of the vote, a dozen members
jumped up, speaking and shouting in the most confused and dis-
orderly manner. Some rushed out of the room; others moved an
adjournment; others again protested they would sign no constitution embodying such a provision. In the midst of this tumult the
house adjourned. . . .

When [a final compromise] came to be designated on the map,
most of the members were better satisfied than they had anticipated. They had a State with eight hundred miles of seacoast and
an average of two hundred and fifty miles in breadth, including
both sides of the Sierra Nevada and some of the best rivers of the
Great Basin. . . .

One of the subjects that came up about this time was the
design of the Great Seal for the State. There were plenty of ideas
in the heads of the members, but few draughtsmen, and of the
eight or ten designs presented, some were ludicrous enough. The
choice finally fell upon one drawn by Major Garnett, which was,
in reality, the best offered.

The principal figure is Minerva, with her spear and Gorgon

shield, typical of the manner in which California was born full-grown into the Confederacy. At her feet crouches a grizzly bear, certainly no very appropriate supporter for the Gorgon shield. The wheat sheaf and vine before him illustrate the principal agricultural products of the country, and are in good keeping—for Ceres sat beside Minerva in the councils of the gods. Near at hand is a miner with his implements, in the distance the Bay of San Francisco, and still further the Sierra Nevada, over which appears the single word: "Eureka!"

The discussion on the subject was most amusing. None of the designs seemed at first to tally with the taste of the Convention, as each district was anxious to be particularly represented. The Sacramento members wanted the gold mines; the San Francisco members wanted the harbor and shipping; the Sonoma members thought no seal could be lawful without some reminder of their noted "bear flag"; while the Los Angeles and San Diego members were clamorous for the rights of their vines, olives and wild horses—so that, no doubt, the seal they chose was the most satisfactory of all. . . .

The Convention yesterday [October 12] gave token of bringing its labors to a close; the morning session was short and devoted only to the passing of various miscellaneous provisions, after which an adjournment was made . . . on account of the ball given by the Convention to the citizens of Monterey. The members, by a contribution of $25 each, raised the sum of $1,100 to provide for the entertainment which was got up in return for that given by the citizens about four weeks since.

The hall was cleared of the forum and tables, and decorated with young pines from the forest. At each end were the American colors, tastefully disposed across the boughs. Three chandeliers, neither of bronze nor cut glass, but neat and brilliant withal, poured their light on the festivities. At eight o'clock—the fashionable ball hour in Monterey—the guests began to assemble, and in an hour afterward the hall was crowded with nearly all the Californian and American residents.

There were sixty or seventy ladies present, and an equal number of gentlemen, in addition to the members of the Convention.

The dark-eyed daughters of Monterey, Los Angeles and Santa Barbara mingled in pleasing contrast with the fairer bloom of the trans-Nevadian belles. The variety of feature and complexion was fully equaled by the variety of dress. In the whirl of the waltz, a plain, dark, nunlike robe would be followed by one of pink satin and gauze; next, perhaps, a bodice of scarlet velvet with gold buttons, and then rich-figured brocade, such as one sees on the stately dames of Titian.

The dresses of the gentlemen showed considerable variety, but were much less picturesque. A complete ball dress was a happiness attained only by the fortunate few. White kids could not be had in Monterey for love or money, and as much as $50 was paid by one gentleman for a pair of patent-leather boots. Scarcely a single dress that was seen belonged entirely to its wearer and, I thought, if the clothes had power to leap severally back to their respective owners, some persons would have been in a state of utter destitution.

For my part, I was indebted for pantaloons and vest to obliging friends. The only specimen of the former article which I could get belonged to an officer whose weight was considerably more than two hundred, but I managed to accommodate them to my proportions by a liberal use of pins. . . . The appearance of the company was genteel and respectable. . . .

The band consisted of two violins and two guitars, whose music made up in spirit what it lacked in skill. They played, as it seemed to me, but three pieces alternately, for waltz, contradance and quadrille. The latter dance was evidently an unfamiliar one, for once or twice the music ceased in the middle of the figure. Each tune ended with a funny little squeak, something like a whistle of the octave flute in *Robert le Diable*. . . .

At twelve o'clock supper was announced. The courtroom in the lower story had been fitted up for the purpose and, as it was not large enough to admit all the guests, the ladies were first conducted thither and waited upon by a select committee. The refreshments consisted of turkey, roast pig, beef, tongue and pâtés, with wines and liquors of various sorts, and coffee. A large supply had been provided, but after everybody was served, there was not much remaining. The ladies began to leave about two o'clock, but when I came away an hour later, the dance was still going on with spirit.

The members met this morning at the usual hour to perform the last duty that remained to them—that of signing the Constitution. They were all in the happiest humor, and the morning was so bright and balmy that no one seemed disposed to call an organization. . . . The members took their seats around the sides of the hall, which still retained the pine trees and banners left from last night's decorations. The windows and doors were open and a delightful breeze came in from the bay, whose blue waters sparkled in the distance. The view from the balcony in front was bright and inspiring. The town below—the shipping in the harbor —the pine-covered hills behind—were mellowed by the blue October haze, but there was no cloud in the sky, and I could plainly see on the northern horizon the mountains of Santa Cruz. . . .

Lieutenant Hamilton, who is now engaged in engrossing the Constitution upon parchment . . . had written day and night to have it ready, and was still working upon it, though with a lame and swollen hand. The sheet for the signers' names was ready, and the Convention decided to adjourn for half an hour and then meet for the purpose of signing. . . .

About one o'clock the Convention met again; few of the members, indeed, had left the hall. . . . They proceeded to affix their names to the completed Constitution. At this moment a signal was given; the American colors ran up the flagstaff in front of the Government buildings and streamed out on the air. A second afterward the first gun boomed from the fort, and its stirring echoes came back from one hill after another, till they were lost in the distance.

All the native enthusiasm of Captain Sutter's Swiss blood was aroused; he was the old soldier again. He sprang from his seat and, waving his hand around his head as if swinging a sword, exclaimed: "Gentlemen, this is the happiest day of my life. It makes me glad to hear those cannon; they remind me of the time I was a soldier. Yes, I am glad to hear them—this is a great day for California!" Then, recollecting himself, he sat down, the tears streaming from his eyes.

The members with one accord gave three tumultuous cheers, which were heard from one end of the town to the other. As the signing went on, gun followed gun from the fort, the echoes reverberating grandly around the bay, till finally as the loud ring of the *thirty-first* was heard, there was a shout: "That's for California!" and everyone joined in giving three times three for the new star added to our Confederation.

From *Eldorado, or Adventures in the Path of Empire*, Bayard Taylor (New York: G. P. Putnam, 1850).

XXVIII

William Lewis Manly

Members of the new commonwealth were soon to learn that their gold rush was anything but a local affair. The rallying cry, "On to the diggings!" was heard around the world; it set in motion an invading army of fifty thousand. During midsummer 1849, an almost unbroken line of emigrants stretched from the Missouri River to the Sierra Nevada heights; between April and the end of the year 700 ships, crowded to the holds with human cargo, sailed through the Golden Gate—more ships than there were frame shelters in all of San Francisco. Among the invaders were peoples as diverse as Frenchmen and Australians, Chinese and Chileans, but the great majority were Yankees, Yorkers, Southerners, Hoosiers, Midwesterners, who traveled around the Horn; by the hazardous shortcut through Panama jungles; across the Plains and over the Rockies in covered wagons, in oxcarts, on horseback, afoot, exposed to brutal suffering every mile of the way.

None suffered more than the stragglers who thronged into the Salt Lake settlement too late in the summer of 1849 to risk the Sierra crossing before winter. For weeks they stalled there, harassed by fears and ignorance of what lay ahead, frustrated by conflicting advice. The impasse was resolved the first of November by an experienced Mormon guide who volunteered to pilot the accumulated multitude over a southern route to San Joaquin Valley at the cut rate of $10 a wagon. Quickly 107 families signed up to form the San Joaquin Company— facetiously dubbed "The Sand-Walking Company." But no sooner had they started than dissension took over. Convinced that the guide was leading them on an unnecessarily circuitous detour, they broke up into separate companies, which later divided and subdivided as disagreements over itineraries multiplied.

They squabbled and brawled among themselves, stole from each other, battled friendly Indians. People starved, died of thirst, disappeared in desert wastes. Scarcely half of them survived. The climax for one remnant of the Sand-Walking Company came just at Christmastime when thirty wagons rolled into the depths of then undiscovered, unnamed Death Valley, where they were trapped, unable to find a way out, hopelessly lost. Again they divided; a group known as the "Jayhawkers," for example, abandoned their wagons and marched off, to almost certain death, with what they could carry on their backs.

Seven half-starved families, all with young children, still remained on speaking terms, and they finally reached the sensible conclusion that the only way out of their plight was to send scouts ahead to find a route out of the desert, and if possible to bring back fresh provisions. A hardy Tennessean, John Rogers, and a professional trapper from Vermont, William Lewis Manly (b. 1820), were chosen. Manly had been confident all along that at any time he could strike out on his own, reach civilization, and save himself, but at Salt Lake he had attached himself to the Bennett family, traveled with them, accepted their faith in him, and decided, come what may, he would have to share their fate.

Instead of the few days that the Bennett and Arcane families thought the scouts should take for reconnoitering an exit to some California settlement, the absence stretched to almost a month; but in a harrowing ordeal Manly and Rogers did succeed in crossing the mountains and the Mojave Desert, in finding a ranch on the edge of San Fernando Valley where they were able to secure provisions and fresh pack animals; then, true to their pledge, they plodded back over the long trail to Death Valley—though as they approached the famished encampment, they feared that their friends had long since starved, been killed by the Indians, or had lost faith and decided not to wait.

Good-bye Death Valley

About noon we came in sight of the wagons, still a long way off, but in the clear air we could make them out and tell what they were, without being able to see anything more. Half a mile was the distance between us and the camp before we could see very plainly, as they were in a little depression. We could see the covers had been taken off, and this was an ominous sort of circumstance to us, for we feared the depredations of the Indians. . . . They had shot our oxen before we left and they must have slain them and the people too, this time, we thought.

We surely left seven wagons. Now we could see only four and nowhere the sign of an ox. They must have gone ahead with a small train and left these four standing after dismantling them. No signs of life were anywhere about, and the thought of our hard struggles between life and death to go out and return, with the fruitless results that now seemed apparent, was almost more than human heart could bear. . . . If ever two men were troubled, Rogers and I surely passed through the furnace.

We kept as low and as much out of sight as possible, trusting very much to the little mule that was ahead, for we felt sure she would detect danger in the air sooner than we. . . . One hundred yards now to the wagons and still no sign of life, no positive sign of death, though we looked carefully for both. We feared that perhaps there were Indians in ambush, and with nervous, irregular breathing we counseled what to do.

Finally Rogers suggested that he had two charges in his shotgun and I seven in the Colt rifle, that I fire one of mine and await results before we ventured any nearer, and if there were any of the red devils there we could kill some of them before they got to us. . . . I fired the shot. Still as death and not a movement for a moment, and then as if by magic a man came out from under the wagon and stood up looking all around, for he did not see us. Then he threw up his arms high over his head and shouted, "The boys have come! The boys have come!" Then other bare heads appeared, and Mr. Bennett and wife and Mr. Arcane came toward us as fast as ever they could. The great suspense was over. Our hearts were first in our mouths, then the blood all went away and left us almost fainting as we stood and tried to step. . . .

Bennett and Arcane caught us in their arms and embraced us with all their strength, and Mrs. Bennett when she came fell down on her knees and clung to me like a maniac in the great emotion that came to her, and not a word was spoken. If they had been strong enough they would have carried us to camp upon their shoulders. . . . There was too much feeling for words; convulsive weeping would choke the voice.

All were a little calmer soon, and Bennett soon found voice to say, "I know you have found some place, for you have a mule." Mrs. Bennett through her tears looked staringly at us, as she could hardly believe our coming back was a reality, and then exclaimed: "Good boys! O, you have saved us all! God bless you forever! Such boys should never die!" . . . Hope had almost died within them, and now when the first bright ray came, it almost turned reason from its throne. . . .

We told them it must be two hundred and fifty miles yet to any part of California where we could live. Then came the question, "Can we take our wagons?" "You will have to walk," was our answer, for no wagons could go over that unbroken road that we had traveled. As rapidly and carefully as we could, we told them of our journey and the long distance between the water holes; that we had lost no time and yet had been twenty-six days on the road; that for a long distance the country was about as dry and desolate as the region we had crossed east of the camp. . . .

We inquired after the others whom we had left in camp when we went away, and we were told all they knew about them. Hardly were we gone before they began to talk about the state of affairs which existed. They said that as they had nothing to live on but their oxen, it would be certain death to wait here and eat them up, and that it would be much better to move on a little every day and get nearer and nearer the goal before the food failed. . . . The general opinion of all but Mr. Bennett and Mr. Arcane and their families was . . . that, "If those boys ever get out of this cussed hole, they are damned fools if they ever come back to help anybody." . . . Bennett implored them to stay, as he was sure we would come back, and if the most of them deserted him he would be exposed to the danger of the Indians . . . but the most seemed to think that to stay was to die, and it would be better to die trying to escape than to sit idly down to perish . . . so they packed their oxen and left in separate parties. . . .

We told them of the great snow mountains we had seen all to the north of our road, and how deep the snow appeared to be, and how far west it extended. We told them of the black and desolate ranges and buttes to the south, and of the great dry plains in the same direction. We told them of the Jayhawkers' trail, . . . of the discouraged ones who gave us their names to send back to friends, of the hawk and crow diet, of my lameness, of the final coming out into a beautiful valley, in the midst of fat cattle and green meadows, and the trouble to get the help arranged on account of our not knowing the language to tell the people what we needed. . . . It was midnight before we could get them all satisfied with their knowledge of our experience. . . .

They said they had about given up our coming back a week before, and had set about getting ready to try to move on themselves. . . . They had taken off the covers of the wagons to make them into harness for the oxen, so that they could be used as pack animals. The strong cloth had been cut into narrow strips and well made into breast straps and breeching. . . .

When Mrs. Bennett was ready to show me what to do with the cloth harness, we took a seat under the wagon, the only shady place, and began work. . . . She told me of their sufferings while we were gone, and said she often dreamed she saw us suffering fearfully for water and lack of food and could only picture to herself their own fate, that they must leave the children by the trail side, dead, and one by one drop out themselves in the same way. She said she dreamed often of her old home where bread was plentiful, and then to awake to find her husband and children starving was a severe trial indeed, and the contrast was terrible. . . . I talked to her as encouragingly as I could, but she did not cheer up much and sobbed and wept over her work most of the time. It was not possible to encourage her much, as the outlook seemed so dark. . . .

In a council of the whole party, we now talked over the matter of the way which seemed most promising. If we went by the Jayhawkers' trail, there was a week of solid travel to get over the range and back south again as far as a point directly opposite our camp, and this had taken us only three days to come over. . . . Bennett said he thought we could get the cattle over without killing them, and that . . . this was the best trail to take. Arcane was quite of the same opinion, the saving of a week of hard and tiresome travel being in each case the deciding reason.

They then explained to me what they had decided on doing if we had not come back. They had selected two oxen for the women to ride, one to carry water, and one to carry the four children. . . . Bennett had one old bridle ox called Old Crump, which had been selected to carry the children, because he was slow and steady. "How in the world do you expect to keep the children on?" said I. "Well," said Bennett, with a sort of comical air—about the first relief from the sad line of thought that had possessed us all—"we have taken two strong hickory shirts, turned the sleeves inside, sewed up the neck, then sewed the two shirts together by the tail; when these are placed on the ox they will make two pockets for the youngest children, and we think the two others will be able to cling to his back with the help of a band around the body of the ox. . . ." He thought this plan would operate first rate.

From a piece of hide yet remaining, John and I made ourselves some new moccasins and were all ready to try the trip over our old trail for the third time—and the last—we hoped. . . . We had to leave everything here that we could get along without. No clothing except that on our backs. Only a camp kettle in which to make soup, a tin cup for each one, and some knives and spoons which each happened to have . . . and we decided to carry a shovel along. . . .

The loads of the oxen consisted of blankets and bedding and a small, light tent of their sheeting about four by six feet in size.

We rose early and worked hard till about the middle of the fore-
noon getting all things ready. They had been in a state of
masterly inactivity so long in this one camp that they were anxious to leave it forever. . . . This was our last and only chance.
We must succeed or perish. . . .

Mrs. Arcane was from a city, and had fondly conveyed thus far
some articles of finery, of considerable value and much prized.
She could not be persuaded to leave them here to deck the red-
man's wife, and have her go flirting over the mountains with
them. As they had little weight, she concluded she would wear
them and perhaps thus preserve them. So she got out her best hat
and trimmed it up with extra ribbons, leaving some with quite
long ends to stream out behind. . . .

Mrs. Arcane also dressed up her little boy Charley in his best
suit of clothes, for she thought they might as well wear them out
as to throw them away. She made one think of a fairy in gay and
flying apparel. In the same way all selected their best and most
serviceable garments, for it was not considered prudent to carry
any load, and poor clothes were good enough to leave for Indians.
We set it down as a principle that we must save ourselves all we
could, for it would be a closely contested struggle between death
and us at the very best, and we wanted to get all the advantage
for ourselves that we could. . . .

High overhead was the sun, and very warm indeed on that day
in the early part of February, 1850, when the two children were
put on Old Crump. . . . The two small children were placed in
the pockets on each side, face outward, so they could stand or sit
as they should choose. George and Melissa were placed on top
and given hold of the strap to steady them in their place. I now
led Mrs. Bennett's ox and Mr. Bennett helped his wife to mount
the animal. . . . Mrs. Arcane in her ribbons was now helped to
her seat on the back of Old Brigham and she carefully adjusted
herself to position, and arranged her dress and ornaments to
suit. . . .

Rogers led the march with his ox; Bennett and I started the
others along, and Arcane followed with Old Crump and his
children. . . . I have no doubt we were the first to cross the

valley in this location, a visible sink hole in the desert. . . . The range next east of us across the low valley was barren as a naked, single rock. There were peaks of various heights and colors: yellow, blue, fiery red, and nearly black. It looked as if it might sometime have been the center of a mammoth furnace. . . . Just as we were ready to leave . . . we took off our hats, and then overlooking the scene of so much trial, suffering and death, spoke the thought uppermost, saying, "Good-bye, Death Valley!" . . . Ever after this in speaking of this long and narrow valley over which we had crossed into its nearly central part, and on the edge of which the lone camp was made for so many days, it was called Death Valley.

[March 5, 1850, San Fernando Valley] We were out of the dreadful sands and shadows of Death Valley, its exhausting phantoms, its salt columns, bitter lakes, and wild, dreary, sunken desolation. If the waves of the sea could flow in and cover its barren nakedness . . . it would be, indeed, a blessing, for in it there is naught of good, comfort or satisfaction. Ever in the minds of those who braved its heat and sands was the thought of a horrid charnel house, a corner of the earth so dreary that it requires an exercise of strongest faith to believe that the great Creator ever smiled upon it as a portion of his work and pronounced it "very good."

We had crossed the great North American continent, from a land of plenty, over great barren hills and plains, to another mild and beautiful region, where, though still in winter months, we were basking in the warmth and luxuriance of early summer. We thought not of the gold we had come to win.

Condensed from *Death Valley in '49*, William Lewis Manly (San Jose: Pacific Tree and Vine Company, 1894).

XXIX

Daniel B. Woods

On the agonizing journeys of the forty-niners across the continent or around the Horn, California was looked forward to as a land flowing with milk and honey as well as gold—an Arcadia, an Eden, a fruitful country that would bring quick termination to all trials and troubles. But upon arrival at the gold fields many discovered that their real troubles were just beginning, and most that the Sierra wilderness brought little more than a continuation of their tribulations. All the romantic dreams faded rapidly in the dull routine of drudgery and backbreaking labor; it was a frustrating existence, enlivened only by the gambler's spirit and those rare moments when pay dirt appeared. Some six hundred million dollars' worth of gold was unearthed in California during the peak years of the rush, but that wealth had to be distributed among a vast number of miners, and the greater share went to relatively few lucky ones.

The take of Daniel B. Woods, a young Philadelphia pedagogue who abandoned his classroom to join a "Californy" company, was about average, and his experiences were not out of line with those of his fellow diggers. He soon learned that gold hunting was 98 percent drudgery; he went hungry; he suffered all the common discouragements; he succumbed to the illnesses that harassed the mining camps and at one point was so near death that he marked off the spot where he wished to be buried. A good Samaritan, who happened to come along with the medicine he needed, saved his life, and with larger dreams than ever Woods helped organize a company to dam the Tuolumne River, divert its flow, and wash its bed for gold. That project failed when unseasonable rains flooded the Tuolumne, swept out smaller up-river dams, and rushed down to destroy his labors. At the end of sixteen months he tallied his accounts to find that he had cleared an average of $7.28 a day and was ready to return to less demanding employment as teacher in civilized Philadelphia.

We Made Ten Cents Today

On the afternoon of the second day after our arrival [in San Francisco on June 25th, 1849] we set sail up the Bay, arriving at Sacramento City two days later. The present of this "city" is under canvas and the future on paper. Everything is new except the ground, the trees and the stars, beneath a canopy of which we slept.

Quarreling and cheating form the employments, drinking and gambling the amusements, making the largest pile of gold the only ambition of the inhabitants. As each one steps his foot on shore he seems to have entered a magic circle in which he is under the influence of new impulses. The city is every day newly filled, then emptied but to be filled again. The crowd ever presses on, elated with hope, excited by expectations, which it would be impossible to define or realize.

Salmon Falls, South Fork of the American River—July 4. Here we are, at length, in the gold diggings. Seated around us upon the ground beneath a large oak, are a group of wild Indians from the tribe called "Diggers." They have brought us in some salmon, one of which weighs twenty-nine pounds. These they spear with great dexterity and exchange for provisions or clothing and ornaments of bright colors.

We are surrounded on all sides by high, steep mountains, over which are scattered the evergreen and white oak, and which are inhabited by the wolf and bear. We have spent the day in "prospecting," a term which designates a very important part of the business of mining. In order to find the gold, the ground must be prospected. A spot is first selected, in the choice of which science has little and chance everything to do. The stones and loose upper soil, as also the subsoil almost down to the primitive rock, are removed. Upon or near this rock most of the gold is found, and it is the object of every mining operation to reach this rock, however great the labor, even though it lies forty, eighty, or one hundred feet beneath the surface.

If, when this strata rock is attained, it is found to present a smooth surface, it may as well be abandoned at once; if seamed with crevices running at right angles with the river, the prospect of the miner is favorable. Some of the dirt is then put into a pan, taken to the water and washed out with great care.

The miner stoops down by the stream and, dipping a quantity of water into the pan with the dirt, stirs it about with his hands, washing and throwing out the large pebbles, till the dirt is thoroughly wet. More water is then taken into the pan, the whole mass well stirred and shaken, and the top gravel thrown off with the fingers, while the gold, being heavier, sinks deeper into the pan. It is then shaken about, more water being continually added and thrown off with a sideway motion, which carries with it the dirt at the top, while the gold settles yet lower down.

When the dirt is nearly washed out, great care is requisite to prevent the lighter scales of gold from being washed out with the sand. At length a ridge of gold scales, mixed with a little sand, remains in the pan, from the quantity of which some estimate may be formed of the richness of the place.

If there are five to eight grains, it is considered that it will pay. If less, the miner digs deeper or opens a new hole, until he finds a place affording a good prospect. When this is done, he sets his cradle by the side of the stream and proceeds to wash all the dirt. Thus have we employed the whole of this day, digging one hole after another, washing out many test pans, hoping at every new attempt to find that which would reward our toil—and we have made ten cents each.

July 6th. We have today removed to the opposite side of the river. This, with pitching our tent, had occupied most of the day. Still, we made $4.00 each. For several hours I have been seated by the river side rocking a heavy cradle filled with dirt and stones. The working of the cradle requires from three to five persons, according to the character of the diggings. If there is much of the auriferous dirt and it is easily obtained, three are sufficient; but if there is little soil and this found in crevices so as to be obtained only by 'digging out with a knife, five or more can be employed in keeping the cradle in operation.

One of these gives his whole attention to working the cradle, another takes the dirt to be washed in pans or buckets from the hole to the cradle, while one or more others fill the buckets.

The cradle, so called from its general resemblance to that article of furniture, is placed at the edge of the water so that the person rocking it may at the same time dip up water. The dirt is gradually washed out, the mud being carried off in the stream. Cleats are nailed across the bottom of the cradle, over which the loose dirt passes with the water and behind which the gold settles. Twenty-five buckets of dirt are usually washed through, the residue being then drawn off through holes at the bottom of the cradle, and "panned" out or washed in the same manner as in prospecting.

While this is being done by one of the company, the others commonly spend the ten minutes' interval in resting themselves. Seated upon the rocks about their companion, they watch the ridge of gold as it dimples brightly up amid the black sand. At length, the washing completed, the pan passes from one to another while each one gives his opinion as to the quantity.

The holes in the bottom of the cradle are then stopped up, more dirt is thrown into the hopper and again the grating, scraping sounds are heard, which are peculiar to the rocking of the cradle—which years hence will accompany our dreams of the mines.

July 7th. This morning witnessed an instance of that remarkable success in mining which rarely occurs but which, when it does occur, turns the heads of so many. . . . Two Irishmen followed the lead of the Jordan brothers, who in a few weeks made $3,000 and are now on their way home. They commenced at the edge of the bar and were so lucky as to find the vein which the

Jordans had found. This vein is about seven inches wide, ten feet below the surface of the bank, and is imbedded in a stratum of hard clay.

Before breakfast this morning these two Irishmen, who never before owned a savings in their lives, took out $422. We were working within three yards of them and I have been compelled to contrast our own small operations with their brilliant success.

July 9th. Today we made $20 each. One of the conclusions at which we are rapidly arriving is that the chances of our making a fortune in the gold mines are about the same as those in favor of our drawing a prize in a lottery. No kind of work is so uncertain. A miner may happen upon a good location in his very first attempt and in a few days make hundreds or thousands, while the experienced miners about him may do nothing.

An instance of this kind happened recently when two men who had been some time in the mines started a dispute as to a small space between their claims. As they could not amicably settle the dispute, they agreed to leave it to a newcomer who happened by and had not yet done an hour's work in the mines. He measured off ten feet—the amount allowed by custom to each of the claimants, taking for his trouble the narrow strip of land between them. In a few hours the larger claims belonging to the older miners were abandoned as useless, while the newcomer discovered a deposit which yielded him $7,435.

July 10th. We made $3.00 each today. This life of hardships and exposure has affected my health. Our diet consists of hardtack; flour we eat half cooked, and salt pork, with occasionally a salmon which we purchase from the Indians. Vegetables are not to be procured. Our feet are wet all day, while a hot sun shines down upon our heads and the very air parches the skin like the hot air of an oven. Our drinking water comes down to us thoroughly impregnated with the mineral substances washed through the thousand cradles above us.

After our days of labor, exhausted and faint, we retire—if this word may be applied to the simple act of lying down in our clothes, robbing our feet of their boots to make a pillow of them, and wrapping our blankets about us on a bed of pine boughs, or on the ground beneath the clear, bright stars of the night. Near morning there is always a change in the temperature and several blankets become necessary.

The feet and the hands of a novice in this business become blistered and lame, and the limbs are stiff. Besides all these causes of sickness, the anxieties and cares which wear away the lives of so many men who leave their families to come to this land of gold, contribute in no small degree to the same result.

San Francisco, November, 1850. . . . One could not pass through the city without being impressed with the sentiment which seems to describe the whole thing: "Enterprise run mad." Each one of the vast throng hastens on, busy in his own plans and pursuits. A mysterious, but all-pervading and powerful attraction emanating from this wonderful point has been felt in the remotest parts of the earth. Civilized, semi-barbarous and savage—American, European, Asiatic and African—feel it. The missionary and the gambler, the praying and the profane man have all felt it. Drawn from the pulpit, the farm, the forum, the bench, they all rush—giddy, mazed—into this one vortex. Happy the few who escape unharmed.

From *Sixteen Months at the Gold Diggings,* Daniel B. Woods (New York: Harper and Brothers, 1851).

XXX

William Taylor

California's new state government made room for new religions to replace the fading Catholic influence, and although the great majority of immigrants could not have cared less about a choice of churches, or any church at all, back East Protestant congregations were fairly bursting with zeal to make them care. A great missionary movement was already reaching out to every un-Christian corner of the globe, and California, of course, had to be added to the itinerary. Baptists, Methodists, Episcopalians, and Congregationalists simultaneously entered the competition to get there first—before the disesteemed Mormons overran the area.

William Taylor (1821–1902), of the Methodist Episcopal sect, was one of the forerunners, a dynamo of energy and evangelical fervor. He arrived in San Francisco Bay on September 21, 1849, too late in the afternoon to be ferried ashore to assemble a congregation that day, but the first question popped to the first gentleman to board his ship was "whether or not there were any ministers of the gospel or churches in the place." "Yes," was the reply, "we have one preacher, but preaching don't pay here, so he quit preaching and went to gambling. There is but one church in town, and that has been converted into a jail."

Upon landing the following day, the Reverend Taylor set out immediately to verify that report. "Everywhere I went," he vouched, "I made diligent inquiry whether or not there were any Methodists in the city, but everywhere learned that no such creatures lived in the place."

He was shocked at the godlessness, the devotion to gambling and drinking, the profanity, the total disregard for keeping of the Sabbath. He was equally shocked at the mobility of San Francisco, a tent city of twenty thousand. With a touch of sacerdotal humor he claimed that he "felt oppressed with the fear that under the influence of the gold attractions of the mountains, these tents might all be struck some morning and the city suddenly leave its moorings for parts unknown."

He finally did locate in an out-of-the-way spot the semblance of a church, a square of high board fence roofed with bolts of blue cotton cloth. But, alas, it was Baptist. The Baptists had stolen the march on him. He was not interested in assembling a congregation in any such concealed hideaway. Immediately he announced that he would call a service in the very heart of sinful San Francisco, on the Plaza, the center of the gambling district.

Preaching Don't Pay Here

I announced that I would preach at three P.M. on the Plaza. It was a startling announcement . . . for nearly all the gamblers in the city were located round the Plaza in the best houses the city afforded. An idea of the prestige of the gambling fraternity and the magnificence of their saloons may be obtained from the . . . interior of the El Dorado, a large gambling house at the northeast corner of the Plaza. The tables, loaded with gold and silver, you cannot see for the multitude; but in the rear end of the saloon you see, elevated on a stage, a band of the best musicians the country could furnish, sending forth their melody in such sweetness and variety. . . . Alas! it is but the song of the siren.

On the right may be seen the beautifully ornamented bar with splendid mirrors in the rear, around which many a jolly circle of hopeful young prodigals drank to each other's health the deadly draught. Such places were crowded, especially on Sunday, with men of all nations, the most daring and reckless perhaps in the world; and such was their dominant influence that when they shot a man dead, as they frequently did, there were no arrests, and nothing said but that "C.B. was killed last night in the Parker

House." . . . If the gamblers should regard my attempt to preach on the Plaza, thrilling every one of their saloons with the echoes of the unwelcome Gospel, as an interference with their business, and shoot me down, there would be no redress. It would simply be said, "The gamblers killed a Methodist preacher."

At the appointed time I was on the Plaza . . . and appropriated a carpenter's workbench . . . as a pulpit. At that moment Clarkson Dye, thinking I might need some protection against the rays of the burning sun, went across to Brown's Hotel and asked for the loan of an umbrella to hold over the preacher. He was met with the reply: "I won't let my umbrella be used for such a purpose, but if I had some rotten eggs, I'd give them to him." He had to pay nine dollars per dozen for eggs, and couldn't afford to throw them at the preacher.

Taking my stand on the workbench, I sang, "Hear the Royal Proclamation." . . . By the time the song ended, I was surrounded by about one thousand men. Restless hundreds, always ready for the cry, "A whale! A whale!" or any other wonder under the sun, came running from every direction, and the gambling houses were almost vacated. I had crossed the Rubicon, and now came the tug of war. Said I, "Gentlemen, . . . there is no true American but will observe order under the preaching of God's word anywhere, and maintain it if need be. We shall have order, gentlemen.

"Your favorite rule in arithmetic is the rule of 'loss and gain.' In your tedious voyage around the Horn, or your wearisome journey over the plains, or your hurried passage across the Isthmus, and during the few months of your sojourn in California, you have been figuring under this rule: losses and gains have constituted the theme of your thoughts and calculations. Now I wish most respectfully to submit to you a question under your favorite rule. I want you to employ all the mathematical power and skill you can command, and patiently work out the mighty problem. The question may be found in the 26th verse of the 16th chapter of our Lord's Gospel of St. Matthew. Shall I announce it? 'What is a man profited if he shall gain the whole world and lose his own soul?' "

Every man present was a "true American" for that hour. Perfect order was observed, and profound attention given to every sentence of the sermon that followed. That was our first assault upon the enemy in the open field in San Francisco, and the commencement of a seven years' campaign. . . . I preached that evening to a crowded house, and four men presented themselves at the altar as seekers of salvation. I preached every night during that week, and three persons professed to experience religion—the first revival meeting in California. The little society was greatly refreshed, and especially encouraged by the fact that God could and did convert sinners in that land of gold and crime. . . .

In a preaching tour I made through the mines . . . I traveled nearly a week without the privilege of any Christian association, and I longed for the opportunity of shaking a Christian's hand. . . . On entering a mining town I inquired in the hotel at which I put up whether there were any professors of religion in the town. "Yes," answered the landlord, "there is one. Mr. T., our blacksmith, is a good Christian man." . . . So at my earliest convenience I hastened to see Brother T. He received me very cordially and introduced me to his family. . . . As soon as I took my seat I inquired of Brother T. how he was prospering in religious life.

"Well," replied he, ". . . I support my family by blacksmithing, and the miners have most of their work done on Sunday; and, to tell the truth, I have worked in my shop here every Sunday except two for five years. . . ."

"O," I thought, "shades of the fathers! if this is the best man in these mountains, the Lord pity the worst."

I traveled nearly a week before I found another Christian. He was an old ship master, a good old Methodist from Boston. I invited him to go to Long Bar on the north fork of the Feather River to hear me preach the following Sunday.

At the appointed hour, Sunday morning, I had a large audience to preach to under the shade of an ancient pine. The sound of the Gospel had never echoed through those hills before. Looking over my audience I discovered my old captain and felt glad to think that I had at least one praying heart, who could sympathize with my mission and my message of mercy. After meeting I asked the old captain to take a walk with me "up into the mountains to pray." I felt that I needed the warming influence of a little prayer meeting, and I supposed he did too.

Finding a suitable place, I sang a few verses and prayed; I then sang again, and thinking I had got the good brother pretty warm, and that he in turn would contribute to the fire of my own heart, I called on him to lead in prayer. But I couldn't get a grunt out of him. Thought I, "Poor old Captain, he is dried up."

I had announced an afternoon appointment for preaching in the same place, and thought from the size of the morning audience and the apparently good effect of the preaching upon them, that I would have a much larger congregation, and a better time at the second appointment. But to my surprise and mortification, I did not have more than twenty hearers, and when I cast about to know the cause, I learned that, according to custom, nearly the whole population of the neighborhood had by that hour of the day become too drunk to attend preaching. Such a variety of antics as they displayed beat anything I had ever witnessed. Next morning I found most of them sober and ready to work; and to show their appreciation of my ministerial services, they gave me a donation . . . of nearly one hundred dollars. . . .

I preached to a large assembly of miners one Sunday afternoon in the streets of Placerville, a flourishing mining city of six thousand inhabitants. In front of my goods-box pulpit stood a stagecoach, which was crowded to its utmost capacity with as many of my auditors as were fortunate enough to secure so good a seat.

I endeavored to show the multitude before me their unfitness for heaven in their unregenerated state, their utter want of sympathy with God or adaptation to the immunities of heaven. To illustrate the truth of my position I said: "If God should dispatch a rail-car train to the city of Placerville this afternoon to convey passengers direct to heaven, the conductor might whistle till the setting of the sun and not get one passenger. Heaven has no attractions for you. It is a place to which you don't want to go.

"Why, if the flaming steeds of Elijah's chariot of fire were hitched onto that stagecoach, and the driver cracked his whip for the heavenly country, every fellow in it would jump out"—and in a moment the coach was cleared; every man in it leaped for the street in an apparent fright from the apprehension that perhaps Elijah's horses might be hitched to the stage, and they taken off to glory, a place to which they did not wish to go.

Sabbath breaking and profane swearing are prominent in the catalogue of miners' offenses against the Lord. Sunday in the mines was remembered only as a day for trading, recreation, spreeing, business meetings and preparation for the business of the ensuing week. It was very common to see large cards hung up in boarding houses and business places, like this: "All bills paid up here on Sunday."

That was the day for miners to get their blacksmith work done, and lay in their supply of provisions for the week; the day for holding public meetings for the enactment of miners' laws or other municipal business; . . . and promiscuous masses of all sorts assembled at the hotels and drinking saloons to drink and spree without restraint. What was worse, the standard of moral law was thrown down and its authority denied. When we remember that a large majority of those men were educated in a Christian country, and that many had even been professors of religion, it is easy to see how quickly a Christian people will relapse into heathenism if deprived of the wholesome restraints and elevating influences of the Gospel. . . .

I went into the city of Sonora at nine o'clock one Saturday night, not knowing a man in the place; and finding the streets crowded with miners who had gathered in from all parts of the surrounding mountains, I felt a desire to . . . preach the Gospel to them. So I got a brother whom I chanced to meet to roll a goods-box into the street, nearly in front of a large crowded gambling house, and taking my stand, I threw out on the gentle zephyrs of that mild April night one of Zion's sweetest songs, which echoed among the hills and settled down on the astonished multitude like the charm of Orpheus.

My congregation packed the street from side to side. Good

order and profound attention prevailed while the truth, in the
most uncompromising terms, was being proclaimed. At the close
of the exercises many, strangers to me, who had heard me preach
in the streets of San Francisco, gave me a hearty greeting, among
them a notorious gambler who shook my hand and welcomed me
to the mountains.

I preached in Jamestown one night under similar circumstances. I got permission of a butcher to convert his meat block
into a pulpit; I tried to have the butcher himself converted, but
did not succeed in that. . . . Selecting the best point for a
crowd, I happened again to be in front of a large gambling house.
Some of the gamblers, thinking I was putting on too strong an
opposition line, took offense and tried to run me off the track.
They knew the character of the miners too well to attempt to
confront the preacher personally, so to try to scatter my audience,
they tied some tin pans to a dog's tail, and sent him off with a
clatter, they yelling after him.

Stopping short in the midst of my sermon, I said: "There they
go, poor fellows; they want to make their souls happy. Rather a
poor intellectual entertainment, tying tin pans to a dog's tail; but
I presume it's the best they can do, so we'll let them go and make
the most of it." By that time they were out of sight, out of hearing, and the attention of my audience stimulated and improved.
. . .

I think I never felt a greater thrill of pleasure in proclaiming a
free Gospel to the human varieties of California than I did one
Sunday morning a few years ago on Long Wharf in San Francisco. It happened that morning when the time came for my
wharf appointment that I was minus a text, but I met a brother
who said, "Good morning, Brother Taylor. What's the news this
morning?"

"Good news, my brother, good news! . . ."

Said I to myself, "I've got it." So on I went and took my stand
on the head of a whisky barrel in front of the worst rum hole in
the city; if there could be a worse one it was at the opposite
corner, just across the street. . . . I sung together a vast crowd

of such a variety of human kind as never was seen except in California. . . . When the songs ended, I said: "Good morning, gentlemen; I am glad to see you this bright Sabbath of the Lord. What's the news? Thank the Lord, I have good news for you this morning: 'Behold, I bring you good tidings of great joy, which shall be to all people.'"

I then addressed them as individual representatives of the different nations, thus: "My French brother, look here!" He looked with earnest eye and ear while I told him what Jesus had done for him and his people. "Brother Spaniard, I have tidings for you, señor," and told him the news, and requested him to tell his people. "My Hawaiian brother, don't you want to hear the news this morning? I have glad tidings of great joy for you, sir." I then told him the news. . . . "John Chinaman, you, John, there by that post, look here, my good fellow, I've got something to tell you," etc.

Thus I traveled, as it were, over all creation, calling by name all the different nations I could think of, recognizing their representatives before me, and I felt unspeakably happy in the fact that throughout creation's vast realm I could not find a rebel to whom I could not extend the hand of hearty Christian sympathy and say, I have good news to tell you, my brother, "glad tidings of great joy, which shall be to all people." . . .

Notwithstanding all past and present obstructions, the Church may command greater facilities for the conversion of the heathen in California than she can have in a foreign field. . . . With the proximity of California to the heathen millions of Asia, Japan, Oceanica, etc., and her constant intercommunication with them, I come to the deliberate conclusion that California is today, in the openings of Providence, the most important missionary field under the sun.

From *California Life Illustrated*, William Taylor (New York: Carlton and Porter, 1858).

XXXI

Friedrich Gerstäcker

While Protestantism was being given at least nominal recognition in California, Catholicism was entering a shocking state of degeneracy. The missions, as exemplified by San Francisco's Dolores, were a shambles, and the fine old buildings fast falling to ruins. Even the Indians who had remained in the sheltering shadows of the cloisters— sometimes out of loyalty, more often in sheer indolence—deserted to the lure of the gold mines. At Dolores a padre was still in residence, but after 1849 scarcely a handful of the faithful answered the call to morning mass or evening vespers.

Into the once prosperous community that had sprung up around the chapel moved derelict foreigners, ready to take shelter under any roof they could find in the Bay area. A section of the mission quarters was appropriated, without protest, as a public house, shabby, flea-ridden, and overpriced. Former craftsmen's shops were converted into saloons, gambling dens, and flophouses, and the new proprietors, eager for their share of the wealth that was flowing through San Francisco, added sacrilege to insult by turning Mission Dolores into a carnival. The saloon keepers banded together and instituted a lively program of horseracing, dances, wrestling matches, bear baits, bullfights, cockfights, though their real objective was to attract San Francisco gamblers to the bars, betting booths, and gaming tables.

Drawn by fliers advertising a spectacular bullfight, the German writer-vagabond Friedrich Gerstäcker (1816–1872) wandered out to the mission one Sunday in 1852 and in a single essay captured the real spirit of the place. After publishing a novel or two in Germany and a popular account of his wanderings over the Western Hemisphere, he was back in the United States with a commission from his government to prepare a manual or guide for prospective European emigrants to America. But, sidetracked by the gold rush, he had sailed off to the West Coast, and to the neglect of his commission was writing instead his *Scenes of Life in California*. The bullfight at Dolores was one of those scenes.

Gerstäcker considered the engagement a poor imitation of similar spectacles he had witnessed in Madrid and other Spanish cities. The arena, occupying the front of the mission grounds, was nothing but a great sand pit surrounded by a low, makeshift barricade, behind which natives and foreigners fought for standing room; the grandstand on one side was equally makeshift, though crowded with persons of quality or wealth; the first little brown bull brought into the ring was too frightened for combat; and the second, a huge, ferocious black beast, put the toreadors to flight, and in his first lunge crashed through the flimsy barricade, scattered the standees and took to the hills. Among the spectators, however, was the handsome, lithe, half-drunken Indian Valentin, who was equal to the occasion, dressed for it in the costume of a matador, and ready to give the assemblage its money's worth. Throwing away his bottle of brandy, he vaulted the barricade, leaped upon his horse, raced after the bull, and put on a show such as had never been witnessed in either Mexico City or Seville.

The Bull Fight at Mission Dolores

Valentin and his spirited horse, perceiving the bull a short distance before him, prepared himself for the chase that was to follow. Nose to the wind and neighing, there elapsed but a few seconds before the bull was overtaken; the horseman swung the lasso, whistling through the air, rapidly around his head two or three times. At the same moment, the horse, directed by the pressure of Valentin's leg, threw himself backward and opposed the whole of the weight of his body to the well-known pull of the captive. The bull finally made two bounds with greatest effort, for he felt the tightening of the terrible rawhide, but to break the hold that had caught him, the animal prisoner suddenly threw his head backward as if he wanted to snap his spine, then fell heavily to earth.

At this moment the other riders arrived and one of the Californians, seizing his lasso, was about to throw it over the horns of the animal so that, held from both sides, the bull could not attack anyone, but Valentin, heated by all the brandy that he had drunk and excited by the success of his chase, made a sign with his arms not to loosen the rope. Patting the neck of his panting and trembling horse, Valentin waited, a smile of triumph on his lips, for the first movement of his enemy, who was imprisoned but by no means subdued.

The bull, recovered from the dizziness that his fall had caused him, rose quickly and, seeing in his road this adversary bold enough to defy him, lowered his horns and plunged forward. This was the very thing that the Indian was expecting. Guiding the horse with his left hand, in which he held his mane, he galloped toward the side of the arena, keeping the lasso at full length and taking care not to be overtaken by the bull who followed him, growing more furious every instant.

Twice, seeing the uselessness of his efforts to overtake the horseman, the bull tried to turn aside, but always the lasso held him in his course, half forced, half voluntary. Each fruitless attempt of the animal served merely to increase his rage and to increase his ardor to pursue his tormentor, who continually escaped him.

It was thus that horse and rider, a truly fantastic pair, approached the arena under the eyes of the crowd of spectators, who were all shouting cries of admiration at the sight of the unbelievable daring of the Indian. The door of the ring had been opened wide by the Mexicans. From a distance Valentin already had made an excited sign that they leave the place free for him, and his fiery glance measured with a sort of anxiety the interior of the arena where he was taking his prisoner, now worked up to the last paroxysm of fury. The fence had been repaired and the place appeared satisfactory to the Indian.

Before entering the great door, behind which two men were standing ready to close it as soon as the bull would be inside, he stopped his horse short and waited with apparent tranquillity for his adversary, who came with horns lowered, and whose first bound could be but deadly. His horse, so gallant in the face of peril, was trembling; it tossed its beautiful head backward, but although without bridle, made not a single movement to avoid the danger that menaced it.

A frightened cry arose from almost every mouth when the bull appeared, his horns lowered, ready to sink them into the horse's flanks; but at that instant, guided by the hand of Valentin, the horse leaped into the arena and crossed it in a few bounds. The furious bull, closely pursuing, was about to horn the horse when, by an immense bound, the latter leaped the entrance barricade. We saw the long and supple figure of the Indian, who was holding himself by his knees to the saddle of his steed, fairly leap over the bull, who had been thrown several steps back when . . . his head had struck the beams and planks of the fence.

Then the Indian, leaping aside, shook the long black hair that was hanging in disorder over his face and we saw his eyes glitter with an expression of the savage joy that the pride of his triumph gave him. Valentin held in his right hand a little open knife, and in his left hand the lasso that he had cut; he presented both of them, laughing, to the spectators, who were not able to believe their eyes.

It would be useless to attempt to describe the cries of joy and admiration that resounded from the benches. It was with terror that they had seen what they took to be the end of the audacious Indian. That action, which in the mind of the public must have been his death stroke, was nothing but the legerdemain of the incomparable horseman. The applause did not cease.

On such occasions in California the audience does not content itself with clapping of the hands, but it gives to the performer who has successfully won the good graces of the public more substantial proofs of satisfaction. It is the custom in bull fights . . . to throw money to the toreadors. . . . Dollars, even ounces of gold, rain at times. . . . It was in this manner that the satisfaction of the public was made known to the Indian. The dollars came from all parts of the arena; some of them fell on the head of the bull, who, recovered from his heavy fall, was presenting anew his horned front to his victorious enemy.

"*Gracias, muchas gracias, caballeros,*" said the Indian, pleased when he saw the shower of gold. Recovering his hat, which at the moment of the leap of the horse had rolled on the ground, he began with the utmost coolness to gather the dollars, when the bull, full of wrath, recommenced the attack upon him.

"Look out! Look out! Valentin!" they cried to him from all sides; but the rash Indian deemed this scarcely worthy of his attention, and only turned his head from time to time to observe the movements of his aggressor. At the moment of attack he glided to one side like a snake, and must have already gathered not less than twenty dollars when the bull returned in a second fruitless attack.

The enthusiasm of the public grew increasingly at each of the movements of the Indian. More and more excited by his success and by the brandy, his eyes shone with an extraordinary brightness, and his whole person seemed to grow. The peril that all feared for him he had braved with a disdainful smile.

The bull himself seemed subdued before the tranquillity of the man. Convinced of his importance, he contented himself with plowing up the dirt with his horns and feet. "*Mira aqui, companero,*" the Indian said to him, laughing as he walked toward the beast, who was backing up for a greater plunge forward. "*Mira aqui,* do you see the beautiful dollars?" and taking them in his hat, he amused himself by counting them and throwing them in the sand before the nose of the furious bull.

"One, two, three, four—stop, *amigo;* come, do not be so lively or you will make me make a mistake—five, six, seven, eight—you see that I have generous sponsors—nine, ten, eleven, twelve, thirteen—oh, the devil!" and with that exclamation, which he made still laughing, Valentin was obliged to drop his hat, which the bull trampled under his feet, and to think of flight, for the sharp horns of the animal were menacing him closely.

Valentin, always rash, moved aside only enough to be out of

reach; then, recovering his hat, he resumed his occupation, while the bull ran bellowing around the arena.

He recommenced to count, throwing the dollars at the nose of the furious animal, one here, one there, making no attempt to avoid being horned other than by the light movements of his body, which gave the appearance of a dance. The enthusiasm of the audience was frantic; many and many a dollar rained into the arena. It was thus that our new toreador tired his enemy, and the monster allowed the feeble child of man to make sport of him with impunity. In the sand, the Indian, singing and dancing, counted his money. He shouted, he made the most unimaginable leaps which were interrupted every few seconds by an attack from the bull.

Meanwhile, the Mexican fighters, profoundly irritated and jealous of the triumphs of the redskin, remained mute witnesses. Suddenly one of them leaped into the arena and made a sign to the Indian to gather his silver and leave the place. The Mexican was going to renew the combat. His reception from the public was not very encouraging, for jeers and hisses greeted his entrance on the scene. Then the bull, seeing a new object against which to turn his fury, dropped his old enemy to precipitate himself upon the new arrival.

The latter, the most adroit of the hired fighters, waited tranquilly for the animal, and putting the point of his foot lightly on his head, he leaped nimbly over. This feat of daring gained some little sympathy from the unsettled crowd; the Mexicans, his countrymen, poured out their applause, which encouraged him to attempt something still more clever.

"Bueno, companero!" Valentin cried. However, he was not willing to allow the Mexican to take away the laurels of the day so easily. *"Bueno!* But that is just a joke, see!" And saying this, behold! Valentin faced the beast. As the bull lowered his head, Valentin, with one bound, put himself astride, face forward, and stayed there for not less than a minute, despite all the efforts of the furious animal to rid himself of his burden. This happened amidst the greatest applause.

At this sight the Mexican became pale with rage. "Is that all?"

he cried with a laugh full of spite, and when the bull, which did not deliver himself of his rider except when the latter voluntarily leaped down, rushed on him, the toreador tried to imitate the redskin in his feat. Anger, spite—have they deprived him of the coolness of which he had such great need in that struggle? In any case, he missed the leap; he made too great a one or fell too far behind, and the bull no sooner felt his enemy slip than he turned on the unfortunate toreador. Before the latter had time to recover himself, the bull took him on his horns and threw him high in the air, as he would have done to a little child.

"*Caremba!*" cried the Indian when he saw the animal, whose fury was increasing, take the body again on his horns, then trample it under his feet. "That is carrying the sport a little too far." And before any of the other combatants, who leaped the fence to the aid of their comrade, had been able to reach the bull, Valentin threw himself right between the two horns, exactly as if he were seeking death.

But the savage child of the mountains well knew what he was doing, and as a terrified cry from the spectators filled the air, he stood a few steps in front of the beast revealing in his right hand a short steel blade with which, at a single stroke, he cut the spinal marrow of the bull.

After that, in the middle of a thunder of applause, and under a rain of dollars, as you may well imagine, the Indian danced a fandango around the dead bodies of the man and animal.

From *Scenes of Life in California*, Friedrich Gerstäcker. Translated from the French by George Cosgrave (San Francisco: John Howell, 1942).

XXXII

James M. Hutchings

Although raucous little commercial centers and mining towns were mushrooming in California as if some devil-creator were pushing progress, vast mountain and desert tracts were still unexplored, still belonged to the Indians, and were tenanted solely by them. Magnificent Yosemite Valley was one of them. Long after its glory had been publicized, a few adventurers came forward to boast that they had been there first, but in the early 1850s Yosemite was unknown, unnamed.

Its real discovery was a by-product of the gold rush. The Indian inhabitants of the valley and tribes in the river basins west of the entrance heartily resented the encroachment of the white Argonauts, and demonstrated it in petty larceny and horse thieving among the settlements, in more serious marauding sorties and finally in a bold attack on a string of trading posts between the Fresno River and Mariposa Creek operated by an enterprising trader from San Francisco, James D. Savage. His stores were destroyed, clerks murdered, horses and cattle stolen.

In retaliation a company of volunteers was immediately formed either to wipe out the savages forever or herd them into a reservation which was hastily thrown up at Fresno by federal Indian commissioners. Under the banner of "Mariposa Battalion" the volunteers were ready to march early in the winter of 1850–51, with trader Savage, promoted to major, at their head. Their ultimate objective was the conquest of the Yosemite tribe that had been dieting too long on white men's horses; reputedly they lived in a mysterious valley deep in the Sierra, where they defended themselves by hurling rocks from towering cliffs upon any intruders.

En route to that valley the battalion surprised the villages of the minor Nootchu and Pohonochee tribes, rounded them up and sent them packing to what was little more than a concentration camp at Fresno. Then for weeks the Mariposa Battalion was stalled at a foothill encampment while repeated invitations were dispatched to the Yosemites to come out of the valley and surrender. The overtures were ignored until Savage issued a personal summons and ultimatum to old Chief Tenaya, whose name was already legend in California. To Savage's surprise he appeared in person the following day.

"My people do not want anything from the Great Father you tell me about," replied the chief to the major's offer of Uncle Sam's hospitality at Fresno. "The Great Spirit is our father, and he has always supplied us with all that we need. We do not want anything from white men. Our women are able to do our work. Go then; let us remain in the mountains where we were born, where the ashes of our fathers have been given to the winds. I have said enough!"

Under more forceful persuasion, Tenaya did finally agree to return and lead his tribesmen out. He was allowed to make the trip and shortly came back with assurances that his people would follow, but they failed to appear, and in exasperation Major Savage led his battalion into the valley, with Tenaya as guide. With the help of staff surgeon Dr. L. H. Bunnell, who accompanied the expedition, the story of the venture is told by James M. Hutchings (1820–1902) San Francisco journalist, founder of *Hutchings' California Magazine,* and later one of the first year-round residents and hotel proprietors of Yo Semitee—though the currently accepted spelling is substituted here for his.

The Discovery of Yosemite

The troops on the following morning made an early start with Major Savage in the advance, accompanied by Tenaya as guide. Deep snow, attended with the usual difficulties of making a trail through it, was soon encountered—and overcome by the rider in

Discovery of Yosemite

advance frequently falling out of line, and the next taking his place. By this old-fashioned method, a passably good horse trail was made over it, especially considering the rough and rocky country being traveled over.

About midway between camp and the valley, seventy-two of the Yosemites were met, forcing their way flounderingly through the snow, loaded down with children and wares, yet on their route to the place of general rendezvous. . . . This was at least partial proof that Tenaya was acting in good faith . . . but as his band was estimated to number over two hundred, the question very naturally arose, where were the remainder? . . . As Tenaya was a reluctant, if not an unwilling guide, one of his young braves was selected in his place and the old chief allowed to accompany his people to the camp.

After separating from the Indians, and before advancing many miles, the great valley opened before them like a sublime revelation. Dr. Bunnell, an eyewitness and participant in the honor, must be allowed to express his own sensations and to paint the graphic picture: "None but those who have visited this most wonderful valley can even imagine the feelings with which I looked upon the view that was there presented. The grandeur of the scene was but softened by the haze that hung over the valley—light as gossamer—and by the clouds which partially dimmed the higher cliffs and mountains.

"This obscurity of vision but increased the awe with which I beheld it, and as I looked a peculiarly exalted sensation seemed to fill my whole being, and I found my eyes in tears with emotion. To obtain a more distinct and *quiet* view, I had left the trail and my horse, and wallowed through the snow alone to a projecting granite rock. So interested was I in the scene before me that I did not observe that my comrades had all moved on, and that I would soon be left indeed alone.

"My situation attracted the attention of Major Savage, who was riding in the rear of the column. He hailed me from the trail below with, 'You had better wake up from that dream up there or you may lose your hair; I have no faith in Tenaya's statement that there are no Indians about here. We had better be moving; some of the murdering devils may be lurking along this trail to pick up stragglers.'

"I hurriedly joined the Major on the descent, and as other views presented themselves, I said with some enthusiasm: "If my hair is now required, I can depart in peace, for I have here seen the power and glory of a Supreme Being; the majesty of His handiwork is in that 'Testimony of the Rocks.' "

To the Mariposa Battalion, then, commanded by Major Savage is to be accorded the honor of first entering the Yosemite Valley, May 5 or 6th, 1851. It is true the writer has heard of various persons having visited it when prospecting for gold, as early as 1849, but no responsible data to establish the fact have yet come to his knowledge. . . . Their neglect to publish so marvelous a discovery to the world is presumable evidence of a lack of appreciation, or of an absorbed attention to other pursuits that utterly diverted it from this sublime theme. . . .

After the safe arrival of the command on the floor of the cliff-encompassed home of the "Grizzlies," as the Yosemites were invariably termed by the troops, it would seem that although supposed to be surrounded by hostile Indians, and that too in their much-vaunted stronghold, there evidently existed an utter absence of precaution, as of fear, inasmuch as all kinds of rollicking mirth and jollity held unchecked court in the lair of the enemy, and around a huge campfire on the very evening of their arrival. It was here, and under these circumstances, and on this occasion that the now famous valley received the musical name—Yosemite. . . .

In the early morning . . . when the order was given to fall in, every saddle was instantly occupied, and the advance commenced. . . . Smoke from a slumbering picket fire near El Capitan unmistakably revealed the presence of Indians, and that they knew of the advent of the whites, and were evidently watching their movements. The near vicinage of a large collection of Indian huts that had been but recently inhabited, and now gave evidence of hasty desertion, was proof positive that the game sought was near at hand. . . .

Far up the valley other manifest signs gave hopeful promise of nearness to the foe; but again delusive hope was to experience another dash of disappointment, as nothing but evidences in abundance of hasty departure were discoverable—except a very old woman . . . who when questioned of the whereabouts of her companions, curtly replied (in Indian), "You can hunt for them, if you want to see them!" Hunt they did for several days, but none was found, as the rocky talus over which the hostiles had made their escape left no tracks of their course.

On all hands and at every deserted camp were found large stores of Indian food, such as acorns, pine and chincapin nuts, grass seeds, wild oats scorched, dried caterpillars, roasted grasshoppers, sun-dried larvae and pupae of flies, obtained mostly from Mono Lake; homemade baskets of many sizes and patterns and for different uses; a few rabbit or squirrel-skin robes for bed coverings, obsidian (for arrow heads), pumice stone, salt, relics of clothing and trinkets, the picked bones of horses and mules, and other property stolen from the whites were found in liberal abundance—but not a single Indian was seen other than the old woman and the brave brought with them as guide.

Provisions becoming exhausted in the camp at Yosemite and the outlook for collecting the scattered Yosemites very discouraging without a prolonged search among the mountains around, after burning up the Indian food supplies, camp furniture and huts, as the only available means now at command for compelling a surrender, this unsuccessful campaign was closed by a return of the battalion to camp at the South Fork.

. . . Upon the arrival of the Yosemite expedition, it was determined to break up camp and convey such Indians as had been secured to the reservation on the Fresno. On their way thither the complement of the captives was increased about one hundred by the voluntary surrender of that number. . . . An appetizing march of several days brought the entire cavalcade to within a few miles of their intended destination. The general deportment of the Indians had been such as to successfully win the confidence of both officers and men, so that a strict guard over them was considered as altogether unnecessary.

Under these conditions, permission was asked for a large portion of the command to accompany Major Savage to the reservation [ahead of the slow-moving procession]. The Major finally assented to the proposition saying, "I do not suppose the Indians can be *driven* off, or be induced to leave, until they have had the feast I have promised; besides they will want to see some of the Commissioners' finery. I have been delighting their imaginations with descriptions of the presents in store for them."

Therefore Captain Boling with nine men as camp guard was the only force left. All apprehensions allayed, the kindly hearted Captain told his men to take their sleep and he would watch as he was not sleepy. "Toward morning I took another round," relates Captain Boling, "and finding the Indian camp wrapped in slumber, I concluded to take a little sleep myself until daylight. This now seems unaccountable to me, for I am extremely cautious in my habits. I confess myself guilty of neglect of duty; I should have taken nothing for granted. No one can imagine my surprise and mortification when I was told that the Indian camp was entirely deserted and that none were to be seen except the one asleep by our campfire."

Consternation was in every face, as not one of the three hundred and fifty captives, seen in such apparently peaceful slumber that night, was now left to explain the cause of their hasty departure. Effort in pursuit only disclosed their successful exodus and the utter hopelessness of one officer and nine men attempting to recapture them. No choice was left, therefore, other than for these to report themselves at headquarters and tell their own sad story.

The long-delayed arrival of the expected caravan at the reservation gave some cause for uneasiness there; but not one was prepared to realize the full force of such an appalling disclosure as that every one of the Indians, whom they had been months in collecting, were in a single night, and when within a few miles of the anticipated goal, all scattered abroad.

From *In the Heart of the Sierras*, J. M. Hutchings (Oakland: Pacific Press Publishing House, 1886).

XXXIII

J. D. Borthwick

Indians were no longer a problem for a booming valley crossroads rendezvous like Sacramento. Almost overnight the gold rush turned it into a city. Sutter's Fort and ranch had been a veritable haven for countless overlanders, a quiet rest stop where they could collect their wits after the Sierra crossing, before selecting their next destination. Now suddenly everything had changed. Three-quarters of all inland traffic to and from the mines converged there. Next to San Francisco it was the most important commercial center in California.

Besides saddle and vehicle traffic there was a steady flow of shipping from the Bay; even ships on the Atlantic side of the continent cleared ports directly for Sacramento. To the surprise of newcomers its waterfront had the appearance of a port, for wide levees had been thrown up on the river banks to keep rampaging winter floods out of the city, and these served also as wharves and supply depots where for half a mile were displayed sample wares and manufactures of a dozen countries.

Unlike most towns of the West, planning and design had gone into the construction of the city; it was rectangular—all streets running parallel to the river had been given numbers, the cross streets were given letters. J Street was the main street, laid out for a full mile, and several blocks of not unattractive brick buildings were already erected on it. They gave it the look of a midwest town, but the residential area was straight out of New England. The frame houses, gardens, and fences all had the Yankee accent of their builders.

The liveliest spot in Sacramento was the stagecoach depot on J Street, in front of the new three-story hotel. The glib London journalist and artist, J. D. Borthwick, paused there in 1852 to change coaches on his way to the mines. He was easily the most sophisticated and articulate globetrotter to appraise the early gold rush. His gibes were aimed in all directions, especially at the quaint emigrants with whom he hobnobbed. Nothing escaped his attention. He wrote waggishly of San Francisco and the mines, of Indians and Chinamen, of Western law and disorder, of grizzlies and the green world, of barrooms and bull-fights—and with particular relish of Sacramento and its stagecoach depot.

Tallyho for Hangtown

My stay in Sacramento on this occasion was limited to a few hours. I went to a large hotel, which was also the great staging house, and here I snoozed till about five o'clock, when, it being still quite dark, the whole house woke up into active life. About a hundred of us breakfasted by candlelight and, going out into the barroom while day was just dawning, we found turned out in front of the hotel about four-and-twenty four-horse coaches, all bound for different places in the mines. The street was completely blocked up with them, and crowds of men were taking their seats, while others were fortifying themselves for their journey at the bar.

The coaches were of various kinds. Some were light spring wagons—mere oblong boxes with four or five seats placed across them; others were of the same build but better finished and covered by an awning; and there were also numbers of regular American stagecoaches, huge high-hung things which carry nine inside upon three seats, the middle one of which is between the two doors.

The place which I had intended should be the scene of my first mining exploits was a village rejoicing in the suggestive appellation of Hangtown—designated, however, in official documents as Placerville. It received its name of Hangtown while yet in its infancy from the number of malefactors who had there expiated their crimes at the hands of Judge Lynch.

I soon found the stage for that place (it happened to be one of the oblong boxes) and, pitching in my roll of blankets, I took my seat and lighted my pipe that I might the more fully enjoy the scene around me. And a scene it was, such as few parts of the world can now show, and which would have gladdened the hearts of those who mourn over the degeneracy of the present age, and sigh for the good old days of stage-coaches.

Here, certainly, the genuine old mail coach, the guard with his tin horn, and the jolly old coachman with his red face, were not to be found; but the horses were as good as ever galloped with Her Majesty's mail. The teams were all headed the same way and, with their stages four or five abreast, occupied the whole of the wide street for a distance of sixty or seventy yards. The horses were restive and pawing and snorting and kicking; and passengers were trying to navigate to their proper stages through the labyrinth of wheels and horses, and frequently climbing over half a dozen wagons to shorten their journey.

Grooms were standing at the leaders' heads, trying to keep them quiet, and the drivers were sitting on their boxes, or seats rather, for they scorn a high seat, and were swearing at each other in a very shocking manner as wheels were locked and wagons were backed into the teams behind them, to the discomfiture of the passengers on the back seats, who found horses heads knocking the pipes out of their mouths.

In the intervals of their little private battles, the drivers were shouting to the crowds of passengers who loitered about the front of the hotel; for there as elsewhere people will wait till the last moment; and though it is more comfortable to sit than to stand, men like to enjoy their freedom as long as possible before resigning all control over their motions and charging with their precious persons a coach or a train on full cock and ready to go off and shoot them out upon some remote part of creation.

On each wagon was painted the name of the place to which it

ran; the drivers were also bellowing it out to the crowd, and even among such a confusion of coaches a man could have no difficulty in finding the one he wanted. One would have thought that the individual will and locomotive power of a man would have been sufficient to start him on his journey; but in this go-ahead country people who had to go were not allowed to remain inert till the spirit moved them to go; they had to be hurried up; and of the whole crowd of men who were standing about the hotel, or struggling through the maze of wagons, only one half were passengers; the rest were "runners" for the various stages, who were exhausting all their persuasive eloquence in entreating the passengers to take their seats and go.

They were all mixed up with the crowd, and each was exerting his lungs to the utmost. "Now then, gentlemen," shouts one of them, "all aboard for Nevada City. Who's agoin'? Only three seats left—the last chance today for Nevada City—take you there in five hours. Who's there for Nevada City?" Then catching sight of some man who betrays the very slightest appearance of helplessness, or of not knowing what he is about, he pounces upon him, saying, "Nevada City, sir?—this way—just in time," and seizing him by the arm, he drags him into the crowd of stages and almost has him bundled into that for Nevada City before the poor devil can make it understood that it is Coloma he wants to go to and not Nevada City.

His captor then calls out to some one of his brother runners who is collecting passengers for Coloma—"Oh Bill!—oh Bill!— where the devil are you?" "Hullo!" says Bill from the other end of the crowd. "Here's a man for Coloma!" shouts the other, still holding on to his prize in case he should escape before Bill comes up to take charge of him.

This sort of thing was going on all the time. It was very ridiculous. Apparently, if a hundred men wanted to go anywhere, it required a hundred more to despatch them. There was certainly no danger of anyone being left behind; on the contrary, the probability was that any weak-minded man who happened to be passing by would be shipped off to parts unknown before he could collect his ideas.

There were few opposition stages, excepting for Marysville and one or two of the larger places; they were all crammed full—and of what use these "runners" or "tooters" were to anybody was not very apparent, at least to the uninitiated. But they are a common institution with the Americans, who are not very likely to support such a corps of men if their services bring no return. In fact, it is merely part of the American system of advertising, and forcing the public to avail themselves of certain opportunities by repeatedly and pertinaciously representing to them that they have it in their power to do so.

In the States, to blow your own horn, and to make as much noise as possible with it, is the fundamental principle of all business. The most eminent lawyers and doctors advertise, and the names of the first merchants appear in the newspapers every day. A man's own personal exertions are not sufficient to keep the world aware of his existence, and without advertising he would be to all intents and purposes dead. Modest merit does not wait for its reward—it is rather too smart for that—it clamors for it, and consequently gets it all the sooner.

However, I was not thinking of this while sitting on the Hang-town stage. I had too much to look at, and some of my neighbors also took up my attention. I found seated around me a varied assortment of human nature. A New Yorker, a Yankee and an English Jack-tar were my immediate neighbors, and a general conversation helped to beguile the time till the "runners" had succeeded in placing a passenger upon every available spot of every wagon.

There was no trouble about luggage—that is an article not much known in California. Some stray individuals might have had a small carpet-bag—almost every man had his blankets—and the western men were further encumbered with their long rifles, the barrels poking into everybody's eyes, and the butts in the way of everybody's toes.

At last the solid mass of four-horse coaches began to dissolve. The drivers gathered up their reins and settled themselves down in their seats, cracked their whips and swore at their horses; the grooms cleared out the best way they could; the passengers shouted and hurrahed; the teams in front set off at a gallop; the rest followed them as soon as they got room to start, and chevied them up the street, all in a body, for about half a mile when, as soon as we got out of town, we spread out in all directions to every point of a semicircle, and in a few minutes I found myself one of a small isolated community, with which four splendid horses were galloping over the plains like mad.

No hedges, no ditches, no houses, no road, in fact. It was all a vast open plain as smooth as a calm ocean. We might have been steering by compass, and it was like going to sea, for we emerged from the city as from a landlocked harbor and followed our own course over the wide, wide world. The transition from the confinement of the city to the vastness of space was instantaneous; and our late neighbors, rapidly diminishing around us and getting hull down on the horizon, might have been bound for the uttermost parts of the earth for all we could see that was to stop them. . . .

The scene all around us was magnificent, and impressed one as much with his own insignificance as though he beheld the countries of the earth from the summit of a high mountain. Out of sight of land at sea one experiences a certain feeling of isolation: there is nothing to connect one's ideas with the habitable globe but the ship on which he stands, . . . but here we were upon an ocean of grass-covered earth dotted with trees and sparkling in the sunshine with the gorgeous hues of the dense patches of wild flowers, while far beyond the horizon of the plains there rose mountains beyond mountains. . . .

It was as if the circumference of the earth had been lifted up to the utmost range of vision and there melted into air. Such was the view ahead of us as we traveled toward the mines, where wavy outlines of mountains appeared one above the other, drawing together as they vanished, and at last indenting the sky with the snowy peaks of the Sierra Nevada.

From *Three Years in California or the Gold Hunters,* J. D. Borthwick (Edinburgh and London: W. Blackwood and Sons, 1857).

XXXIV

Harris Newmark

Compared to San Francisco and Sacramento, Los Angeles was still a lowly Mexican pueblo, existing largely on remnants of the impetus once given it by the mission friars. The gold rush was by-passing it. Not even a highway connected Los Angeles with the Bay area, on which it was dependent for almost everything except beef products; the only transportation of consequence between northern and southern California was an occasional schooner that dropped off freight and passengers at San Pedro. However, coaches plied regularly between that diminutive port and the pueblo, and travelers were few enough to assure fast, competitive service.

For the last leg of a journey more remarkable than J. D. Borthwick's, Harris Newmark (1834–1916), a German salesman of an odd commodity—bootblacking—boarded one of the Los Angeles coaches in the fall of 1853. He was a very humble figure, entertaining at the moment no higher ambition than to join his brother, who had preceded him to Los Angeles, as a dry goods clerk. However, Newmark soon acquired ambitions on a much larger scale. In the following years, as he watched the pueblo grow into a city, he predicted that Los Angeles would one day become "a world center, prominent in every field of endeavor." He played an important part in that development, became one of its leading merchants and its Pepys. But it was with something less than optimism that he rode the coach from San Pedro into Los Angeles in 1853 and surveyed the filthy, shabby, impoverished pueblo.

Pueblo of the Angels

Not a minute was lost between the arrival of passengers [at San Pedro] and the departure of coaches for Los Angeles in the early fifties. The competition developed a racing tendency that was the talk of the pueblo. The company that made the trip in the shortest time usually obtained, through lively betting, the best of advertising and the largest patronage, so that from the moment of leaving San Pedro until the final arrival in Los Angeles two and a half hours later, we tore along at breakneck speed. . . .

These roads never having been cared for, and still less inspected, were abominably bad, and I have often wondered that during such contests there were not more accidents. The stages were of the common Western variety, and four to six broncos were always a feature of the equipment. No particular attention had been given to the harness, and everything was more or less primitive. The stage was provided with four rows of seats, and each row as a rule was occupied by four passengers, the front row including the oft-bibulous driver; and the fare was five dollars.

Soon after leaving San Pedro we passed thousands of ground squirrels and, never having seen anything of the kind before, I took them for ordinary rats. This was not an attractive discovery, and when later we drove by a number of ranch houses and I saw beef cut into strings and hung up over fences to dry, it looked as though I had landed on another planet. I soon learned that dried beef or . . . *jerky* was an important article of food in Southern California. . . .

Having reached the Half-Way House, we changed horses; then we continued and approached Los Angeles by San Pedro Street, which was a narrow lane, possibly not more than ten feet wide, with growing vineyards bordered by willow trees on each side of the road. It was on a Sunday and in the midst of the grape season that I first beheld the City of the Angels; and to these facts in particular I owe another odd and unfavorable first impression of the neighborhood.

Much of the work connected with the grape industry was done by Indians and native Mexicans, or Californians, as they were called, and every Saturday evening they received their pay. During Saturday night and all day Sunday, they drank themselves into hilarity and intoxication, and this dissipation lasted until Sunday night. Then they slept off their sprees and were ready to work Monday morning.

During each period of excitement from one to three or four of these revelers were murdered. Never having seen Indians before, I supposed them to represent the citizenship of Los Angeles—an amusing error for which I might be pardoned when one reflects that nine out of forty-four of the founders of Los Angeles were Indians, and that . . . Los Angeles County in 1852 had about 3,700 domesticated Indians among a population of a little over 4,000 whites, and this mistake as to the typical burgher, together with my previous experiences, added to my amazement.

At last, with shouts and yells from the competing drivers, almost as deafening as the horn-blowing of a somewhat later date, and hailed apparently by every inhabitant and dog along the route, we arrived at the only real hotel in town, the Bella Union, where stages stopped and every city function took place. This hotel was a one-story adobe house . . . located on Main Street above Commercial. . . .

The charges for board at the Bella Union . . . were too heavy, so arrangements were made with a Frenchman named John La Rue, who had a restaurant on the east side of Los Angeles Street. . . . I paid him nine dollars a week for three more or less hearty meals a day, not including eggs—unless I provided them; in this case, he agreed to prepare them for me. . . . Nothing in Los Angeles, perhaps, has ever been cruder than this popular eating place. The room, which faced the street, had a mud floor and led to the kitchen through a narrow opening. Half a dozen cheap wooden tables, each provided with two chairs, stood against the walls. The tableclothes were generally dirty, and the knives and forks, as well as the furniture, were of the homeliest kind. The food made up in portions what it lacked in quality. . . .

What went most against the grain was the slovenliness of the proprietor himself. Flies were very thick . . . and one day I found a big fellow splurging in my bowl of soup. This did not, however, faze John La Rue. Seeing the struggling insect, he calmly dipped his coffee-colored fingers into the hot liquid and quite as serenely drew out the fly. . . .

In 1853 free-and-easy customs were in vogue in Los Angeles, permitting people in the ordinary affairs of life to do practically as they pleased. There were few if any restrictions. . . . As was the case in San Francisco, neither saloons nor gambling places were limited by law, and there were no regulations for their management. As many persons as could make a living in this manner kept such establishments. . . .

Through the most popular of these districts a newly found friend escorted me on the evening of my arrival in Los Angeles. The quarter was known by the euphonious title of Calle de los Negros—Nigger Alley. . . . Each side of the alley was occupied by saloons and gambling houses. Men and women alike were to be found there, and both sexes looked after the gaming tables, dealing monte and faro, and managing other contrivances that parted the good-natured and easy-going people from their money.

Those in charge of the banks were always provided with pistols, and were ready, if any emergency rose, to settle disputes on the spot; and only rarely did a case come up for adjustment before the properly constituted authorities. . . . Time was considered a very important element during the play, and sanguinary verdicts in financial disputes were generally rendered at once. Human life at this period was about the cheapest thing in Los Angeles, and killings were frequent.

Graded streets and sidewalks were unknown; hence, after heavy winter rains, mud was from six inches to two feet deep, while during the summer dust piled up to about the same extent. Few city ordinances were obeyed, for notwithstanding that a regulation of the City Council called on every citizen to sweep in front of his house to a certain point on Saturday evenings, not the slightest attention was paid to it.

Into the roadway was thrown all the rubbish. If a man bought a new suit of clothes, a pair of boots, a hat or a shirt, to replace a corresponding part of his apparel that had outlived its usefulness, he would think nothing, on attiring himself in the new purchase, of tossing the discarded article into the street, where it would remain until some passing Indian or other vagabond took possession of it. So wretched indeed were the conditions that I have seen dead animals left in the highway for days at a time, and can recall one instance of a horse dying on Alameda Street and lying there until a party of Indians cut up the carcass for food.

What made these street conditions more trying was the fact that on hot days roads and sidewalks were devoid of shade, except for that furnished by a few scattered trees or an occasional projecting veranda; while at night (if I except the illumination from the few lanterns suspended in front of barrooms and stores) thoroughfares were altogether unlighted. In those nights of dark streets and still darker tragedies, people rarely went out unless equipped with candle-burning lanterns. . . . Stores were lighted in the same manner.

At the time of my arrival, there was but one voting precinct and the polling place was located at the old municipal and county adobe. . . . Inside the room sat the election judges and clerks; outside a window stood the jam of voters. The window-sill . . . served as a table, upon it being placed a soap- or candle-box, into which a hole had been cut for the deposit of the votes.

There was no register, either great or small, and anyone could vote. . . . Aliens such as Mexicans, who had not even considered the question of taking out citizenship papers, were permitted to vote, while Indians and half-breeds, who were not eligible to citizenship at all, were irregularly given the franchise. The story is told of an election not far from Los Angeles at which a whole tribe of Indians voted; while on another occasion the names on a steamer's passenger list were utilized by persons who had already voted that very day once or twice! Cutting off the hair, shaving one's beard or mustache, reclothing or otherwise transforming the appearance of the voter—these were some of the tricks then practiced. . . .

Sonorans who had recently arrived from Mexico . . . were

easy subjects for the political manipulator. The various candidates, for example, would round up these prospective voters like so many cattle, confine them in corrals (usually in the neighborhood of Boyle Heights), keep them in a truly magnificent state of intoxication until the eventful morning, and then put them in stages hired . . . for the purpose; and from the time the temporary prisoners left the corral until their votes had been securely deposited, they were closely watched by guards. On reaching the voting place, the captives were unloaded from the stage like so much inanimate baggage, and turned over to the friends of the candidate to whom, so to speak, they belonged. One at a time these creatures were led to vote; and as each staggered to the ballot box, a ticket was held up and he was made to deposit it.

Once having served the purpose, he was turned loose and remained free until another election unless, as I have intimated, he and his fellows were again corralled and made to vote a second or even a third time the same day. . . .

At the time of my arrival, the Plaza, long the nucleus of the original settlement, was the center of life in the little community, and around it clustered the homes of many of those who were uppermost in the social scale. . . . The environment was not beautiful, a solitary pepper somewhat north of the Plaza being the only shade tree there; yet the general character of the homes was somewhat aristocratic. . . . There was no sign of a park: on the contrary, parts of the Plaza itself . . . were used as a dumping ground for refuse.

From time to time many church and other festivals were held at this square—a custom no doubt traceable to the Old World and to earlier centuries—but before any such affair could take place, requiring the erecting of booths and banks of vegetation in front of the neighboring houses, all rubbish had to be removed, even at the cost of several days' work. . . . The only church in Los Angeles at this time was that of *Nuestra* Señora la Reyna de los Angeles, known as Our Lady, the Queen of the Angels. . . . Not merely at the Plaza, but throughout Los Angeles, most of the houses were built of adobe, or mud mixed with straw. . . .

Zanja water was being used for irrigation when I arrived. A

system of seven or eight *zanjas,* or open ditches—originated, I
have no doubt, by the Catholic Fathers—was then in operation. . . . These small surface canals connected at the source
with the *zanja madre,* or mother ditch, on the north side of
town. . . . Water for domestic uses was an expensive luxury. Inhabitants living in the immediate neighborhood of *zanjas* or near
the river helped themselves, but their less fortunate brethren
were served by a carrier, who charged fifty cents a week for one
bucket a day, while he did not deliver at all on Sunday. . . .
This character was known as Bill the Waterman. . . . His somewhat rickety vehicle, drawn by two superannuated horses, slowly
conveyed the man and his barrel of about sixty gallons capacity
from house to house. . . .

Bill obtained his supply from the Los Angeles River, where at
best it was none too clean, in part owing to the frequent passage
of the river by man and beast. Animals of all kinds, including
cattle, horses, sheep, pigs, mules and donkeys, crossed and recrossed the stream continually, so that the mud was incessantly
stirred up, and the polluted product proved unpalatable. . . . To
make matters worse, the river and the *zanjas* were the favorite
bathing places, all the urchins of the hamlet disporting themselves there daily, while most of the adults frequently immersed
themselves. Both the yet unbridged stream and the *zanjas,* therefore, were repeatedly contaminated. . . .

People were not particular about keeping their places of business open all day. Proprietors would sometimes close their stores
and go out for an hour or two for their meals or to meet in a
friendly game of billiards. During the monotonous days when but
little business was being transacted, it was not uncommon for
merchants to visit back and forth and to spend hours at a time in
playing cards. . . .

Often have I seen the Mayor, therefore, long and lanky, seated
in my brother's store, tilted back in a chair against the wall or
merchandise, a cigar, which he never lighted, in his mouth, ex-
horting his hearers to be patriotic and to purchase city land at a
dollar an acre, thereby furnishing some of the taxes necessary to
lubricate the municipal machinery. Little did any of us realize as

we listened to this man, that in the course of another generation or so there would spring into life a prosperous metropolis whose very heart would be situated near where old Mayor Nichols was vainly endeavoring to dispose of thirty-five-acre bargains at thirty-five dollars each.

Condensed from *Sixty Years in Southern California, 1853–1913,* Harris Newmark (New York: Knickerbocker Press, 1916).

XXXV

Bret Harte

The drifters and dreamers who thronged into California's mountains in search of lucre during the 1850s were indeed richly endowed with an appetite for alcohol, a gift for gambling, the spirit of lawlessness, with greed, irreverence, and trigger-happiness, yet behind all this incivility there was always present—to those with the curiosity to look for it—a glow of human kindness. Bret Harte (1836–1902), who joined the westward procession in 1854, perhaps more than any other, gave a fair appraisal of the dual character of Sierra society. In every reprobate he usually managed to turn up some buried virtue, and he showed both sides of character in the yarns he spun. "I find men and women pretty much the same on Fifth Avenue as in Dutch Flat," he once declared.

Harte knew Fifth Avenue as intimately as he got to know Dutch Flat. He grew up in Albany and New York City, and did not reach California until he was eighteen. Besides prospecting with the toughest of the Argonauts in the West, he taught school, worked as a compositor in a printing shop, clerked in a drugstore and in the new United States Mint, spent all his spare time recording his impressions in experimental stories, and then helped to found and edit *Overland Magazine*, in which some of his finest writing was published. When he finally left San Francisco for the East in 1871, he was a literary celebrity.

That repute was gained in chronicling the life of gold towns like Poker Flat, Red Dog, Simpson's Bar, Calaveras, Angels Camp, Roaring

Camp, Chinese Camp. He found it unnecessary to invent completely original persons and places; those that existed were better than any that could be fabricated. He freely embroidered individual traits, juxtaposed facts, and recolored the particulars, but the germ for his stories came straight out of life.

"Tennessee's Partner" was such a story, originating from the exemplary friendship of two real, rough-hewn mining characters, Jason A. Chaffee and James B. Chamberlain. "Tennessee" of Sandy Bar was a hard-drinking gambler, absconder, crook, suspected thief, and finally a proven highway robber. Although his cabin companion and partner at the diggings—known to fellow miners only as "Tennessee's Partner" —deplored the deportment, nothing Tennessee could do ever shook his uncompromising loyalty. Even when Tennessee ran off with his companion's newly acquired bride—and quickly lost her—the Partner was the first to forgive him upon his return alone. But such affection for Tennessee was not shared by other residents of Sandy Bar, and after a bold, broad-daylight holdup, the culprit was pursued, soon captured, and brought back to the Bar for informal trial in the upper room of the stagecoach office.

Tennessee's Partner

It was a warm night. The cool breeze which usually sprang up with the going down of the sun behind the chaparral-crested mountain was that evening withheld from Sandy Bar. The little canyon was stifling with heated resinous odors, and the decaying driftwood on the Bar sent forth faint, sickening exhalations. The feverishness of the day and its fierce passions still filled the camp. Lights moved restlessly along the bank of the river, striking no answering reflection from its tawny current. Against the blackness of the pines the windows of the old loft above the express office stood our staringly bright; and through their curtainless panes the loungers below could see the forms of those who were even then deciding the fate of Tennessee. And above all this, etched on the dark firmament, rose the Sierra, remote and passionless, crowned with remoter passionless stars.

The trial of Tennessee was conducted as fairly as was consist-

ent with a judge and jury who felt themselves to some extent
obliged to justify, in their verdict, the previous irregularities of
arrest and indictment. The law of Sandy Bar was implacable, but
not vengeful. The excitement and personal feeling of the chase
was over; with Tennessee safe in their hands they were ready to
listen patiently to any defense, which they were already satisfied
was insufficient.

There being no doubt in their own minds, they were willing to
give the prisoner the benefit of any that might exist. Secure in the
hypothesis that he ought to be hanged on general principles, they
indulged him with more latitude of defense than his reckless
hardihood seemed to ask. The Judge seemed to be more anxious
than the prisoner, who, otherwise unconcerned, evidently took a
grim pleasure in the responsibility he had created.

"I don't take any hand in this yer game," had been his invari-
able, but good-natured reply to all questions. The Judge—who
was also his captor—for a moment vaguely regretted that he had
not shot him "on sight," that morning, but presently dismissed
this human weakness as unworthy of the judicial mind. Nevertheless, when there was a tap on the door, and·it was said that
Tennessee's Partner was there on behalf of the prisoner, he was
admitted at once without question. Perhaps the younger members
of the jury, to whom the proceedings were becoming irksomely
thoughtful, hailed him as a relief.

For he was not, certainly, an imposing figure. Short and stout,
with a square face, sunburned into a preternatural redness, clad
in a loose duck "jumper," and trousers streaked and splashed with
red soil, his aspect under any circumstances would have been
quaint, and was now even ridiculous. As he stooped to deposit at
his feet a heavy carpetbag he was carrying, it became obvious,
from partially developed legends and inscriptions, that the material with which his trousers had been patched had been originally intended for a less ambitious covering. Yet he advanced
with great gravity, and after having shaken the hand of each
person in the room with labored cordiality, he wiped his serious,
perplexed face on a red bandanna handkerchief, a shade lighter
than his complexion, laid his powerful hand upon the table to
steady himself, and thus addressed the Judge:

"I was passin' by," he began, by way of apology, "and I thought I'd just step in and see how things was gettin' on with Tennessee thar, my pardner. It's a hot night. I disremember any sich weather before on the Bar."

He paused a moment, but nobody volunteering any other meteorological recollection, he again had recourse to his pocket handkerchief, and for some moments mopped his face diligently.

"Have you anything to say in behalf of the prisoner?" said the Judge finally.

"Thet's it," said Tennessee's Partner in a tone of relief. "I come yar as Tennessee's pardner—knowing him nigh on four year, off and on, wet and dry, in luck and out o' luck. His ways ain't allers my ways, but thar ain't any p'ints in that young man, thar ain't any liveliness as he's been up to, as I don't know. And you sez to me, sez you—confidential-like, and between man to man—sez you, 'Do you know anything in his behalf?' and I sez to you, sez I—confidential-like, as between man and man—'What should a man know of his pardner?' "

"Is this all you have to say?" asked the Judge impatiently, feeling perhaps that a dangerous sympathy of humor was beginning to humanize the Court.

"Thet's so," continued Tennessee's Partner. "It ain't for me to say anything agin' him. And now, what's the case? Here's Tennessee wants money, wants it bad, and doesn't like to ask it of his old pardner. Well, what does Tennessee do? He lays for a stranger, and he fetches that stranger. And you lays for *him,* and you fetches *him;* and the honors is easy. And I put it to you, bein' a far-minded man, and to you, gentlemen, all, as far-minded men, ef this isn't so."

"Prisoner," said the Judge, interrupting, "have you any questions to ask this man?"

"No! no!" continued Tennessee's Partner, hastily. "I play this yer hand alone. To come down to the bedrock, it's just this: Tennessee, thar, has played it pretty rough and expensive-like on a stranger, and on this yer camp. And now, what's the fair thing? Some would say more; some would say less. Here's seventeen hundred dollars in coarse gold and a watch—it's about all my pile—and call it square!" And before a hand could be raised to prevent him, he had emptied the contents of the carpetbag upon the table.

For a moment his life was in jeopardy. One or two men sprang to their feet, several hands groped for hidden weapons, and a suggestion to "throw him from the window" was only overridden by a gesture from the Judge. Tennessee laughed. And apparently oblivious of the excitement, Tennessee's Partner improved the opportunity to mop his face again with his handkerchief.

When order was restored, and the man was made to understand, by the use of forcible figures and rhetoric, that Tennessee's offense could not be condoned by money, his face took a more serious and sanguinary hue, and those who were nearest to him noticed that his rough hand trembled slightly on the table. He hesitated a moment as he slowly returned the gold to the carpetbag, as if he had not yet entirely caught the elevated sense of justice which swayed the tribunal, and was perplexed with the belief that he had not offered enough.

Then he turned to the Judge, and saying, "This yer is a lone hand, played alone, and without any partner," he bowed to the jury and was about to withdraw when the Judge called him back. "If you have anything to say to Tennessee, you had better say it now." For the first time that evening the eyes of the prisoner and his strange advocate met. Tennessee smiled, showed his white teeth, and saying, "Euchred, old man!" held out his hand. Tennessee's Partner took it in his own, and saying, "I just dropped in as I was passin' to see how things was gettin' on," let the hand passively fall, and adding that "it was a warm night," again mopped his face with his handkerchief, and without another word withdrew.

The two men never again met each other alive. For the unparalleled insult of a bribe offered to Judge Lynch—who whether bigoted, weak or narrow, was at least incorruptible—firmly fixed in the mind of that mythical personage any wavering determination of Tennessee's fate; and at the break of day he was marched, closely guarded, to meet it at the top of Marley's Hill.

How he met it, how cool he was, how he refused to say anything, how perfect were the arrangements of the committee, were all duly reported, with the addition of a warning moral and example to all future evil-doers in the Red Dog *Clarion* by its editor, who was present, and to whose vigorous English I cheerfully refer the reader.

But the beauty of that midsummer morning, the blessed amity of earth and air and sky, the awakened life of the free woods and hills, the joyous renewal and promise of Nature, and above all, the infinite Serenity that thrilled through each, was not reported, as not being a part of the social lesson. And yet, when the weak and foolish deed was done, and a life, with its possibilities and responsibilities, had passed out of the misshapen thing that dangled between earth and sky, the birds sang, the flowers bloomed, the sun shone, as cheerily as before; and possibly the Red Dog *Clarion* was right.

Tennessee's Partner was not in the group that surrounded the ominous tree. But as they turned to disperse, attention was drawn to the singular appearance of a motionless donkey cart halted at the side of the road. As they approached, they at once recognized the venerable "Jenny" and the two-wheeled cart as the property of Tennessee's Partner—used by him in carrying dirt from his claim; and a few paces distant, the owner of the equipage himself, sitting under a buckeye tree wiping the perspiration from his glowing face.

In answer to an inquiry, he said he had come for the body of the "diseased," "if it was all the same to the committee." He didn't wish to "hurry anything"; he could "wait." He was not working that day; and when the gentlemen were done with the "diseased," he would take him. "Ef thar is any present," he added in his simple, serious way, "as would care to jine in the fun'l, they kin come." Perhaps it was from a sense of humor, which I have already intimated was a feature of Sandy Bar—perhaps it was from something even better than that; but two thirds of the loungers accepted the invitation at once.

It was noon when the body of Tennessee was delivered into the hands of his partner. As the cart drew up to the fatal tree, we noticed that it contained a rough, oblong box—apparently made from a section of sluicing—and half filled with bark and tassels of pine. The cart was further decorated with slips of willow, and made fragrant with buckeye blossoms.

When the body was deposited in the box, Tennessee's Partner drew over it a piece of tarred canvas, and gravely mounting the narrow seat in front, with his feet upon the shafts, urged the little donkey forward. The equipage moved slowly on, at that decorous pace which is habitual with "Jenny" even under less solemn circumstances. The men—half curiously, half jestingly, but all good-humoredly—strolled along beside the cart, some in advance, some a little in the rear of the homely catafalque. But, whether from the narrowing of the road or some present sense of decorum, as the cart passed on, the company fell to the rear in couples, keeping step, and otherwise assuming the external show of a formal procession. Jack Folinsbee, who had at the outset played a funeral march in dumb show upon an imaginary trombone, desisted, from a lack of sympathy and appreciation—not having, perhaps, your true humorist's capacity to be content with the enjoyment of his own fun.

The way led through Grizzly Cañon—by this time clothed in funereal drapery and shadows. The redwoods, burying their moccasined feet in the red soil, stood in Indian file along the track, trailing an uncouth benediction from their bending boughs upon the passing bier. A hare, surprised into helpless inactivity, sat upright and pulsating in the ferns by the roadside, as the cortege went by. Squirrels hastened to gain a secure outlook from higher boughs; and the bluejays, spreading their wings, fluttered before them like outriders, until the outskirts of Sandy Bar were reached, and the solitary cabin of Tennessee's Partner.

Viewed under more favorable circumstances, it would not have been a cheerful place. The unpicturesque site, the rude and unlovely outlines, the unsavory details, which distinguish the nest-building of the California miner, were all here, with the dreariness of decay superadded. A few paces from the cabin there was a rough enclosure, which, in the brief days of Tennessee's Partner's matrimonial felicity, had been used as a garden, but was now overgrown with fern. As we approached it, we were surprised to find that what had been taken for a recent attempt at cultivation was the broken soil about an open grave.

The cart was halted before the enclosure; and rejecting the offers of assistance with the same air of simple self-reliance he had displayed throughout, Tennessee's Partner lifted the rough coffin on his back, and deposited it, unaided, within the shallow grave. He then nailed down the board which served as a lid; and mounting the little mound of earth beside it, took off his hat, and slowly mopped his face with his handkerchief. This the crowd felt was a preliminary to speech; and they disposed themselves variously on stumps and boulders and sat expectant.

"When a man," began Tennessee's Partner slowly, "has been running free all day, what's the natural thing for him to do? Why, to come home. And if he ain't in a condition to go home, what can his best friend do? Why, bring him home! And here's Tennessee has been running free, and we brings him home from his wandering." He paused, and picked up a fragment of quartz, rubbed it thoughtfully on his sleeve, and went on: "It ain't the first time that I've packed him on my back, as you see'd me now. It ain't the first time that I brought him to this yer cabin when he couldn't help himself; it ain't the first time that I and 'Jinny' have waited for him on yon hill, and picked him up and so fetched him home, when he couldn't speak and didn't know me.

"And now that it's the last time, why—" he paused and rubbed the quartz gently on is sleeve—"you see it's sort of rough on his pardner. And now, gentlemen," he added abruptly, picking up his long-handled shovel, "the fun'l's over; and my thanks, and Tennessee's thanks, to you for your trouble."

Resisting any proffers of assistance, he began to fill in the grave, turning his back upon the crowd, that after a few moments' hesitation gradually withdrew. As they crossed the little ridge that hid Sandy Bar from view, some, looking back, thought they could see Tennessee's Partner, his work done, sitting upon the grave his shovel between his knees and his face buried in his red bandanna handkerchief. But it was argued by others that you couldn't tell his face from his handkerchief at that distance; and this point remained undecided.

In the reaction that followed the feverish excitement of that day, Tennessee's Partner was not forgotten. A secret investigation had cleared him of any complicity in Tennessee's guilt, and left only a suspicion of his general sanity. Sandy Bar made a point of calling on him, and proffering various uncouth, but well-meant kindnesses. But from that day his rude health and great strength seemed visibly to decline; and when the rainy season fairly set in, and the tiny grass blades were beginning to peep from the rocky mound above Tennessee's grave, he took to his bed.

One night when the pines beside the cabin were swaying in the storm, and trailing their slender fingers over the roof, and the roar and rush of the swollen river were heard below, Tennessee's Partner lifted his head from the pillow, saying, "It is time to go for Tennessee; I must put 'Jinny' in the cart"; and would have risen from his bed but for the restraint of his attendant.

Struggling, he still pursued his singular fancy: "There now, steady, 'Jinny'—steady, old girl. How dark it is! Look out for the ruts—and look out for him, too, old gal. Sometimes, you know, when he's blind drunk, he drops down right in the trail. Keep on straight up to the pine on the top of the hill. Thar—I told you so!—thar he is—coming this way, too—all by himself, sober, and his face a-shining. Tennessee! Pardner!"

And so they met.

From *The Luck of Roaring Camp and Other Sketches,* Bret Harte (Boston: Roberts Brothers, 1871).

XXXVI

Horace Greeley

"Go West, young man, go West," repeatedly exhorted the celebrated founder and editor of the New York *Tribune*, Horace Greeley (1811–1872), during the gold rush decade. Thousands upon thousands heeded his advice; anyone in need of an extra urge to hit the California trail harkened unto Horace Greeley. He alone was responsible for directing a migration of American youth westward.

Then in the summer of 1859 the editor, molder of national opinion, creator of statesmen, and himself a one-time candidate for the presidency of the United States, followed his own counsel and took to the road. He was no longer a young man, felt the bruises of the journey more sharply than his youthful precursors, and according to fellow travelers, evinced a certain nervousness on some of the more exciting stretches of the journey. But the coming of Horace Greeley was heralded as a major event in California, for he was regarded there as a foremost American.

He entered the state by way of Lake Tahoe and Echo Summit from Genoa, Nevada, late in July, was enormously impressed by the spectacular scenery and the Sierra highway that had been opened to traffic only three years before. He toured the mines and saw a few of the usual points of interest in northern California, but it was a hurried, almost cursory visit, punctuated with many speaking engagements.

Like every other journalist who made the trip, Greeley, of course, wrote a book about his experiences, and in it devoted a brief, constrained chapter to the stagecoach ride over the Sierra. The chapter was an unnecessary supplement, for long before the book came from the press the country knew more about that ride than Greeley. The original source of information was his coach driver, "Hank" Monk, a garrulous, rough-hewn, haughty madcap, a hound for self-aggrandizement, well aware of the fact that he was the most widely famed whipster on the Sierra run. Never before had he driven a more distinguished passenger, and he had no compunction about informing his following of how casually he could cope with celebrities.

"Just before I left Strawberry," Monk related in one of his least varnished accounts of the occasion, "Mr. Greeley called me to one side. 'Driver,' said he, 'can you get me to Placerville this evening by five o'clock, because the committee expect me, and I do not wish to disappoint them?'

" 'I'll get you there,' says I, and off we went. I drove to Dick's, eleven miles, in fifty-three minutes. . . . Just before I got to Dick's I looked into the coach and there was Greeley, his bare head bobbing, sometimes on the back and then on the front seat, sometimes in the coach and then out, then on the top and then on the bottom, holding on to whatever he could grab. Presently someone touched me on the back. 'Driver,' said a voice, 'I'm not particular for an hour or two!' 'Horace,' says I, 'keep your seat! I told you I would get you there by five o'clock, and by God I'll do it, if the axles hold!' And I did." As a reward for the punctuality, Monk claimed that Greeley bought him "the best suit of clothes he could find in Placerville."

Up and down his route Hank confided the yarn of how he had told off the great Greeley by commanding him to keep his seat, and it was so well received that he gradually elaborated upon the details, his speed, the precarious condition of the road, the terror of his passenger, and the bruises inflicted upon him. His auditors in turn hurried off to repeat the tale—adding further embellishments. Within weeks the entire nation was roaring with laughter at the expense of sedate Horace Greeley; the Sierra cliffs had gained considerable altitude; the editor had survived by the skin of his teeth; and his reward to Monk for saving him had become a very expensive gold watch.

Mark Twain later claimed that he heard the story with variations from "drivers, conductors, landlords, chance passengers, Chinamen and Indians" exactly 480 times while crossing the Sierra; he incorporated it in his lectures on California and for burlesque effect repeated it identically four times in one address. Artemus Ward expanded upon it, picturing Greeley bouncing "from one end of the coach to the other like a india-rubber ball," before his head burst through the roof. To Greeley's detriment, that version was published across the country, and even read before Congress in 1866, when a member of the House thought the editor needed to be put in his place. Joaquin Miller converted the story into a ballad, took the liberty of reversing the direction of the coach, tortured Horace unmercifully, and had him shouting to Hank that he didn't give a damn "whether I lecture in Nevada or not."

Greeley later asserted that "Hank" Monk, through repeating the anecdote, had done him "more injury than any other man in America." The incident, long since forgotten, ranked in the 1860s as one of the most famous rides in history, easily holding its own with the escapades of Paul Revere and Lady Godiva. But, alas, the popular renditions of the incident had little in common with the editor's own mild version.

One of the Finest Drives on Earth

We stopped but to dine in Genoa, then economized the residue of the daylight by pressing on fifteen miles to the point at which the California road enters the mountains by the side of the largest of the brooks which unite to form the Carson. Here we halted at a fair two-story house, the first one I had entered with the hope of resting in it since I left Salt Lake City. We had beds here—actual beds, and good ones—our first since Camp Floyd. Though our night was not a long one, for we were to start again at 4 A.M., I reckon good use was made of it by the four through passengers who had not lain down before since they left Shell Creek five days ago and nearly five hundred miles away. . . .

We were in motion again at the earliest dawn, for we had still about seventy-five miles of rugged mountain road to traverse before reaching this place [Placerville]. The Carson side of the road is not yet half made. . . . The expense of a good highway up the eastern slope of the Sierra must be a very heavy one. For that slope is here composed of granite—simple, naked rock—with scarcely a fraction of its surface thinly covered by soil.

Of course, no trees but evergreens can live—a very few small quaking asps in the bottoms of the ravines scarcely form an exception—while almost every rood is covered by giant, glorious pines. . . . In short, I never saw anything like so much nor so good timber in the course of any seventy-five miles' travel as I saw in crossing the Sierra Nevada. How greatly blessed California is in this abundance, I need not say.

The road over this pass—here claimed to be the lowest and most practicable of any over the Sierra Nevada—rises steadily for twelve or thirteen miles from our morning's starting point, then descends for two or three miles as abruptly to the valley of a brook which runs north into Lake Bigler, which in turn finds an outlet into Truckee River, whereby its waters are borne eastward into the desert and there dissipated. There is fine grass on Lake Bigler, and several hundred cows are kept there in summer, making butter for the California market. . . . Taking into account gold, timber and grass, the Sierra Nevada is probably the richest and most productive mountain chain on earth.

From the valley aforesaid, we rose again for two miles along a narrow road cut into the side of a mountain, with a precipitous declivity on the right. Then we began to descend once more beside a rivulet which leaped and laughed on its way to the Pacific. . . . But the road, even on this side, is for the most part eaten into the side of a steep mountain with a precipice of from five to fifteen hundred feet on one side and as steep an eminence on the other.

Yet along this mere shelf, with hardly a place to each mile where two meeting wagons can pass, the mail stage was driven at the rate of ten miles an hour (in one instance eleven), or just as fast as four wild California horses, whom two men could scarcely harness, could draw it. Our driver was, of course, skillful, but had he met a wagon suddenly on rounding one of the sharp points or projections we were constantly passing, a fearful crash was unavoidable.

Had his horses seen fit to run away (as they *did* run once, on the unhooking of a trace, but at a place where he had room to rein them out of the road on the upper side, and thus stop them),

I know that he could not have held them, and we might have been pitched headlong down a precipice of a thousand feet, where all the concern that could have been picked up afterward would not have been worth two bits per bushel. Yet at this breakneck rate we were driven for not less than four hours or forty miles, changing horses every ten or fifteen, and raising a cloud of dust through which it was difficult at times to see anything.

We crossed the south fork of the American River eighteen miles above this point, rising two or three miles immediately after to the summit of the ridge south, and thenceforward the road, nearly to this city, descends steadily a beautifully inclined ridge, and, but for the dust, would be one of the finest drives on earth. And right glad was I to find myself once more among friends, surrounded by the comforts of civilization, and with a prospect of occasional rest. I cannot conscientiously recommend the route I have traveled to summer tourists in quest of pleasure, but it is a balm for many bruises to know that I am at last in CALIFORNIA.

From *Overland Journey,* Horace Greeley (New York: C. M. Saxton, Baker and Co., 1860).

XXXVII

J. Ross Browne

A few months after Horace Greeley made his famous descent of the Sierra, journalist J. Ross Browne (1821–1875) took the same turnpike and was convinced that the great editor severely strained a metaphor in referring to it as "one of the finest drives on earth." It was April; the macadam of summertime had turned into a broad, knee-deep trough of mud and slush, and Browne minced no words in refuting Greeley's benediction.

The journalist's opinions had to be respected, too, for he had traveled much more widely than the editor, and was a reliable judge of roads. A son of Ireland, who migrated to Kentucky as a child, he had since slummed around much of the world, served for a time as short-hand reporter in the United States Senate, gone off on a whaling expedition, tried his hand at various other employments, and written about his experiences wittily. Later he was to receive an appointment as Minister to China, but in 1860 he had become disenchanted with his clerk's job in the San Francisco federal Treasury Department, and had elected to take a fling at mining.

The tide in California had turned: the same hordes that had swept west over the Sierra a decade earlier in search of gold were now moving east over the range to Washoe in search of silver. The territorial status of Nevada was then in the process of adjudication, and no two parties were in complete agreement on where they were going; some thought they were bound for the eastern outskirts of California,

others for the western outskirts of Utah. In any case, Placerville was
the take-off point, and on arriving there Browne concluded that the
town was distinctly Washoe-oriented.

"The streets were blocked up with crowds of adventurers all bound
for Washoe," he observed. "The gambling and drinking saloons were
crammed to suffocation with customers practising for Washoe. The
clothing stores were covered with placards offering to sell goods at
ruinous sacrifices to Washoe miners. The forwarding houses and
express offices were overflowing with goods and packages marked for
Washoe. The grocery stores were making up boxes, bags and bundles
of groceries for the Washoe trade. The stables were constantly starting
off passenger and pack trains for Washoe. . . . The newspapers were
full of Washoe. In short, there was nothing but Washoe to be seen,
heard or thought of. Every arrival from the mountains confirmed the
glad tidings that enormous quantities of silver were being discovered
daily in Washoe. Any man who wanted a fortune needed only to go
over there and pick it up."

Browne detailed every last particular and circumstance of his expedition, but he reserved his raciest prose to describe the advance up
the mountains and the night at Strawberry, a major stop on the trans-
Sierran journey, where the real character of the Washoe-minded crowd
was exposed.

The Inmates of Strawberry Flat

The road from Placerville to Strawberry Flat is for the most part
graded, and no doubt it is very good in the summer; but it would
be a violation of conscience to recommend it in the month of
April. The melting of the accumulated snow of the past winter
had practically washed it away, and what remained was deeply
furrowed by the innumerable streams that sought an outlet in the
ravines. In many places it seemed absolutely impracticable for
wheeled vehicles; but it is an article of faith with California
teamsters that wherever a horse can go a wagon can follow. There
were some exceptions to this rule, however, for the road was
literally lined with broken-down stages, wagons and carts, pre-

senting every variety of aspect from the general smash-up to the ordinary capsize.

Wheels had taken rectangular cuts to the bottom; broken tongues projected from the mud; loads of dry goods and whisky barrels lay wallowing in the general wreck of matter; stout beams cut from the roadside were scattered here and there, having served in vain efforts to extricate the wagons from the oozy mire. Occasionally these patches of bad road extended for miles, and here the scenes were stirring in the highest degree. Whole trains of pack mules struggled frantically to make the transit from one dry spot to another; "burros," heavily laden, were frequently buried up to the neck and had to be hauled out by main force.

Now and then an enterprising mule would emerge from the mud and, by attempting to keep the edge of the road, lose his foothold and go rolling to the bottom of the canyon, pack and all. Amidst the confusion worse confounded, the cries and maledictions of the vaqueros were perfectly overwhelming; but when the mules stuck fast in the mud and it became necessary to unpack them, then it was that the vaqueros shone out most luminously. They shouted, swore, beat the mules, kicked them, pulled them, pushed them, swore again; and when all these resources failed, tore their hair and resorted to prayer and meditation. . . . Should any future traveler be overcome by thirst and see a pair of ears growing out of the road, he will be safe in digging there, for underneath stands a mule, and on the back of that mule is a barrel of whisky.

The ascent of the mountains is gradual and continuous the entire distance to Strawberry. . . . In every gulch and ravine a tavern was in process of erection. Scarcely a foot of ground upon which man or beast could find a foothold was exempt from a claim. There were even bars with liquors offering a tempting place of refreshment to the weary traveler where no vestige of a house was yet perceptible. Board and lodging signs over tents not more than ten feet square were as common as blackberries in June; and on no part of the road was there the least chance of suffering from the want of whisky, dry goods or cigars.

An almost continuous string of Washoeites stretched "like a

great snake dragging its slow length along" as far as eye could reach. In the course of this day's tramp we passed parties of every description and color: Irishmen wheeling their blankets, provisions and mining implements on wheelbarrows; American, French and German foot passengers leading heavily laden horses or carrying their packs on their backs and their picks and shovels slung across their shoulders; Mexicans driving long trains of pack mules and swearing fearfully as usual to keep them in order; dapper-looking gentlemen, apparently from San Francisco, mounted on fancy horses; women in men's clothes mounted on mules or "burros"; Pike County specimens seated on piles of furniture and goods in great lumbering wagons; whisky peddlers with their bar fixtures and whisky on mule back, stopping now and then to quench the thirst of the toiling multitude; organ grinders carrying their organs; drovers riding, raving and tearing away frantically through the brush after droves of self-willed cattle designed for the shambles; in short, every imaginable class and every possible species of industry was represented in this moving pageant.

It was a striking and impressive spectacle to see, in full competition with youth and strength, the most pitiable specimens of age and decay—white-haired old men gasping for breath as they dragged their palsied limbs after them in the exciting race of avarice; cripples and hunchbacks; even sick men from their bed— all stark mad for silver. . . .

The day had opened fairly, but now there were indications of bad weather. It was quite dark when I reached a small shanty about four miles from Strawberry. Here I halted until my remaining comrade came up. The proprietor of the shanty was going into the tavern business and was engaged in building a large clapboard house. . . . I finally bribed him by means of a gold dollar to let us have a small piece of bread and a few swallows of tea. Thus refreshed, we resumed our journey.

Four miles more of slush and snow, up hill nearly all the way, across rickety bridges, over roaring cataracts, slippery rocks, stumps and brush, through acres of black oozy mire—and so dark a bat could scarcely recognize his own father. It was a walk to be remembered. . . . The rain poured down heavily, mingled with a cutting sleet; a doleful wind came moaning through the pines; our blankets were wet through and not a stitch upon our backs left dry; even my spare shirt was soaking the strength out of the plug of tobacco so carefully stowed away in its folds, and my paints were giving it what aid they could in the way of color.

Well, there is an end to all misery upon the earth, and so there was to this day's walk. A light at length glimmered through the pines, first faint and flickering, then a full blaze, then half a dozen brilliant lights, which proved to be campfires under the trees, and soon we stood in front of a large and substantial log house. This was the famous "Strawberry," known throughout the length and breadth of the land as the best stopping place on the route to Washoe, and the last station before crossing the summit of the Sierra Nevada.

The winter road for wheel vehicles here ended; and indeed it may be said to have ended some distance below, for the last twelve miles of the road seemed utterly impracticable for wagons. At least most of those I saw were fast in the mud and likely to remain there till the beginning of summer. Dark and rainy as it was, there were crowds scattered around the house, as if they had some secret and positive enjoyment in the contemplation of the weather.

Edging our way through, we found the barroom packed as closely as it could be without bursting out some of the walls; and of all the motley gangs that ever happened together within the space of twenty feet this certainly was the most extraordinary and the most motley. Dilapidated gentlemen with slouched hats and big boots, Jew peddlers dripping wet, red-shirted miners, teamsters, vaqueros, packers and traders swearing horribly at nothing; some drinking at the bar, some warming themselves before a tremendous log fire that sent up a reeking steam from the conglomerated mass of wet and muddy clothes—to say nothing of the boots and socks that lay simmering near the coals. . . . But chiefly remarkable in the crowd was the regiment of light infantry pressed in double file against the dining room door, awaiting the fourth or fifth charge at the table.

At the first tinkle of the bell, the door was burst open with a tremendous crash, and for a moment no battle scene in Waterloo, . . . no Crimean avalanche of troops dealing death and destruction around them, could have equaled the terrific onslaught of the gallant troops of Strawberry. The whole house actually tottered and trembled at the concussion, as if shaken by an earthquake. Long before the main body had assaulted the table, the din of arms was heard above the general uproar; the deafening clatter of plates, knives and forks, and the dreadful battle cry of "Waiter! Waiter! Pork and beans! Coffee, waiter! Beefsteak! Sausages! Potatoes! Ham and eggs—quick, waiter, for God's sake!"

It was a scene of destruction and carnage long to be remembered. I had never before witnessed a battle, but I now understood how men could become maddened by the smell of blood. When the table was vacated, it presented a shocking scene of desolation. Whole dishes were swept of their contents; coffee pots were discharged to their dregs; knives, forks, plates and spoons lay in a confused mass among the bones and mutilated remnants of the dead; chunks of bread and hot biscuit were scattered broadcast, and mince pies were gored into fragments; teacups and saucers were capsized; and the waiters, hot, red and steamy, were panting and swearing after their superhuman labors.

Half an hour more, and the battlefield was again cleared for action. This was the sixth assault committed during the evening; but it was none the less terrible on that account. Inspired by hunger, I joined the army of invaders this time, and by gigantic efforts of strength maintained an honorable position in the ranks. As the bell sounded—we broke! I fixed my eye on a chair, rushed through the struggling mass, threw out my hands frantically to seize it; but alas! it was already captured. A dark-visaged man who looked as if he carried concealed weapons on his person was seated in it, shouting hoarsely the battle cry of "Pork and beans! Waiter! Coffee, waiter!"

Up and down the table it was one gulping mass, jaws distended, arms stretched out, knives, forks and even the bare hands plunged into the enemy. Not a spot was vacant. I venture to assert that from the commencement of the assault till the capture and complete investment of the fortifications did not exceed five seconds. The storming of Malakoff and the fall of Sebastopol could no longer claim a place in history.

At length fortune favored the brave. I got a seat at the next onslaught and took ample satisfaction for the delay by devouring such a meal as none but a hardy Washoeite could be expected to digest. Pork and beans, cabbage, beefsteak, sausages, pies, tarts, coffee and tea, eggs, etc.—these were only a few of the luxuries furnished by the enterprising proprietor of the "Strawberry." May every blessing attend that great benefactor of mankind! . . . His house so far surpasses the Metropolitan or the St. Nicholas that there is no comparison in the relish with which the food is devoured.

In respect to sleeping accommodations there may be some difference in their favor. I was too late to secure a bed in the general bedroom upstairs, where two hundred and fifty tired wayfarers were already snoring in double-shotted bunks, 2×6; but the landlord was a man of inexhaustible resources. A private whisper in his ear made him a friend forever. He nodded sagaciously and led me into a small parlor, about 15×20, in which he gave my company of five what he called a "lay-out," that is to say, a lay-out on the floor with our own blankets for beds and covering. This was a special favor, and I would have cherished it in my memory for years, had not a suspicion been aroused in my mind before the lapse of half an hour that there were others in the confidence of mine host.

Scarcely had I entered upon the first nap when somebody undertook to walk upon me, commencing on my head and ending on the pit of my stomach. I grasped him firmly by the leg. He apologized at once in the most abject manner; and well for him that he did, for it is enough to incense any man to be suddenly roused up in that manner. The intruder, I discovered, was a Jew peddler. He offered me a cigar, which I smoked in token of amity; and in the meantime he turned in alongside and smoked another.

When daylight broke, I cast around to see what everybody was doing to create such a general commotion. I perceived that there were about forty sleepers all getting up. Boots, strongly scented with feet and stockings of every possible degree of odor, were lying loose in all directions; blankets, packs, old clothes and ragged shirts, and I don't know what all—a palpable violation of the landlord's implied compact. . . .

The Jew peddler had not undressed and, not to judge him harshly, I don't think he ever did undress. He was soon up, and left, as I suppose, while I was dressing. With him departed my stockings . . . valuable beyond gold and silver in this foot-weary land. I never saw them more. . . . I was delayed some hours in getting off, owing to the pressure of the forces at the breakfast table, but finally made a fair start for the summit.

From "A Peep at Washoe," J. Ross Browne, *Harper's New Monthly Magazine,* December 1860 and January 1861.

XXXVIII

Helen Hunt Jackson

All but ignored by the American emigrants, in their preoccupation with establishing themselves in the new state, were the old Spanish-Mexican families, who still regarded themselves as the rightful owners of California soil and were rapidly being dispossessed of it. To the real Californios the intruders seemed to come as conquerors, spoilers, imposters, and thieves, and the impression was further sustained by the arbitrary way in which official commissioners from Washington appropriated lands, discredited deeds, and summarily ousted tenants of long standing.

Hardly a voice was raised against these evictions until Helen Hunt Jackson (1830–1885), poet and essayist from Amherst, Massachusetts, moved West with her husband and witnessed the plight of the Mission Indians and their former landlords. So incensed was she by what she saw that she contrived to get a federal commission as special investigator of the situation. She turned in an exhaustive, shocking report, which was quickly shelved and forgotten. So she determined to make an appeal directly to the American public, as Harriet Beecher Stowe had done for the Southern slaves in *Uncle Tom's Cabin*.

The resulting novel, *Ramona*, proved almost as popular as *Uncle Tom*. Over the years it went into nearly 150 printings, and like Mrs. Stowe's novel, was converted into stage plays, pageants, eventually into three different moving picture versions, and commemorated in a perennially popular song. Behind young Ramona was romantic old

Señora Moreno, surviving mistress of the truncated Moreno Ranch, with its retinue of Mexican families and devoted Indian workhands. Here was symbolic fiction more eloquently disturbing than any factual document.

Señora Moreno

An exceedingly clever woman for her day and generation was Señora Gonzaga Moreno—as for that matter, exceedingly clever for any day and generation; but exceedingly clever for the day and generation to which she belonged. Her life, the mere surface of it, if it had been written, would have made a romance to grow hot and cold over: sixty years of the best of Old Spain, and the wildest of New Spain, Bay of Biscay, Gulf of Mexico, Pacific Ocean—the waves of them all had tossed destinies for the Señora. The Holy Catholic Church had had its arms round her from first to last; and that was what had brought her safely through, she would have said, if she had ever said anything about herself, which she never did—one of her many wisdoms.

So quiet, so reserved, so gentle an exterior never was known to veil such an imperious and passionate nature, brimful of storm, always passing through stress; never thwarted, except at peril of those who did it; adored and hated by turns, and each at the hottest. A tremendous force, wherever she appeared, was Señora Moreno; but no stranger would suspect it to see her gliding about in her scanty black gown, with her rosary hanging at her side, her soft dark eyes cast down, and an expression of mingled melancholy and devotion on her face. She looked simply like a sad, spiritual-minded old lady, amiable and indolent, like her race, but sweeter and more thoughtful than their wont. . . .

To the Señora it seemed as if there were no longer any people about the place. A beggarly handful, she would have said, hardly enough to do the work of the house, or of the estate, sadly as the latter had dwindled. In the General's day it had been a free-handed boast of his that never less than fifty persons, men, women and children, were fed within his gates each day; how many more, he did not care, nor know. But that time had indeed gone, gone forever. . . .

The Señora Moreno's house was one of the best specimens to be found in California of the representative house of the half barbaric, half elegant, wholly generous and freehanded life led there by Mexican men and women of degree in the early part of the century. . . . It was a picturesque life, with more of sentiment and gaiety in it, more also that was truly dramatic, more romance, than will ever be seen again on those sunny shores. The aroma of it all lingers there still; industries and inventions have not yet slain it; it will last out its century—in fact, it can never be quite lost, so long as there is left standing one such house as the Señora Moreno's.

When the house was built, General Moreno owned all the land within a radius of forty miles—forty miles westward, down the valley to the sea; forty miles eastward, into the San Fernando Mountains; and a good forty miles more or less along the coast. The boundaries were not very strictly defined; there was no occasion in those happy days to reckon land by inches.

It might be asked, perhaps, just how General Moreno owned all this land, and the question might not be easy to answer. It was not and could not be answered to the satisfaction of the United States Land Commission, which after the surrender of California undertook to sift and adjust Mexican land titles; and that was the way it had come about that the Señora Moreno now called herself a poor woman. Tract after tract, her lands had been taken away from her; it looked for a time as if nothing would be left. Every one of the claims based on deeds of gift from Governor Pio Pico, her husband's most intimate friend, was disallowed. They all went by the board in one batch, and took away from the Señora in a day the greater part of her best pasture lands.

They were lands which had belonged to the Bonaventura Mission, and lay along the coast at the mouth of the valley down which the little stream which ran past her house went to the sea; and it had been a great pride and delight to the Señora, when she was young, to ride that forty miles by her husband's side, all the way on their own lands, straight from their house to their own strip of shore. No wonder she believed the Americans thieves, and spoke of them always as hounds.

The people of the United States have never in the least realized that the taking possession of California was not only a conquering of Mexico, but a conquering of California as well; that the real bitterness of the surrender was not so much to the empire which gave up the country, as to the country itself which was given up. Provinces passed back and forth in that way, helpless in the hands of great powers, have all the ignominy and humiliation of defeat, with none of the dignities and compensations of the transaction.

Mexico saved much by her treaty, in spite of having to acknowledge herself beaten; but California lost all. Words cannot tell the sting of such a transfer. It is a marvel that a Mexican remained in the country; probably none did except those who were absolutely forced to it.

Luckily for the Señora Moreno, her title to the lands midway in the valley was better than those lying to the east and the west, which had once belonged to the missions of San Fernando and Bonaventura; and after all the claims, counterclaims, petitions, appeals and adjudications were ended, she still was left in undisputed possession of what would have been thought by any newcomer into the country to be a handsome estate, but which seemed to the despoiled and indignant Señora a pitiful fragment of one.

Moreover, she declared that she would never feel secure of a foot of even this. Any day, she said, the United States Government might send out a new Land Commission to examine the decrees of the first, and revoke such as they saw fit. Once a thief, always a thief. Nobody need feel himself safe under American rule. There was no knowing what might happen any day; and year by year the lines of sadness, resentment, anxiety and antagonism deepened on the Señora's fast aging face.

It gave her unspeakable satisfaction when the Commissioners, laying out a road down the valley, ran it at the back of her house instead of past the front. "It is well," she said. "Let their travel be where it belongs, behind our kitchens; and no one have sight of the front doors of our houses, except friends who have come to visit us." Her enjoyment of this never flagged. Whenever she saw, passing the place, wagons or carriages belonging to the hated Americans, it gave her a distinct thrill of pleasure to think that the house turned its back on them. She would like always to be able to do the same herself. . . .

The house was of adobe, low, with a wide veranda on the three sides of the inner court, and a still broader one across the entire front, which looked to the south. These verandas, especially those on the inner court, were supplementary rooms to the house. The greater part of the family life went on in them. Nobody stayed inside the walls except when it was necessary. All the kitchen work, except the actual cooking, was done here, in front of the kitchen doors and windows.

Babies slept, were washed, sat in the dirt, and played on the veranda. The women said their prayers, took their naps, and wove their lace there. Old Juanita shelled her beans there, and threw the pods down on the tile floor, till toward night they were sometimes piled up high around her, like corn husks at a husking. The herdsmen and shepherds smoked there, lounged there, trained their dogs there; there the young made love, and the old dozed. . . .

The arched veranda along the front was a delightsome place. It must have been eighty feet long at least. . . . Here the Señora kept her flowers, . . . fine geraniums, carnations, yellow-flowered musk . . . and many sorts of climbing vines. . . . Between the veranda and the river meadows, out on which it looked, all was garden, orange grove and almond orchard; the orange grove always green, never without snowy bloom or golden fruit; the garden never without flowers, summer or winter; and the almond orchard in early spring a fluttering canopy of pink and white petals, which, seen from the hills on the opposite side of the river, looked as if rosy sunrise clouds had fallen and become tangled in the treetops. On either hand stretched away other orchards— peach, apricot, pear, apple, pomegranate; and beyond these, vineyards. Nothing was to be seen but verdure or bloom or fruit at whatever time of year you sat on the Señora's south veranda. . . .

There stood on the veranda three carved oaken chairs and a carved bench, also of oak, which had been brought to the Señora for safe keeping by the faithful old sacristan of San Louis Rey at the time of the occupation of that Mission by the United States troops, soon after the conquest of California. Aghast at the sacrilegious acts of the soldiers, who were quartered in the very church itself and amused themselves by making targets of the eyes and noses of the saints' statues, the sacristan, stealthily, day by day and night after night, bore out of the church all that he dared to remove. . . . He carried them, a few at a time, concealed in the bottom of a cart under a load of hay or of brush to the house of the Señora. . . .

And so it came about that no bedroom in the Señora's house was without a picture or a statue of a saint or of a Madonna; and some had two; and in the little chapel in the garden the altar was surrounded by a really imposing row of holy and apostolic figures, which had looked down on the splendid ceremonies of the San Luis Rey Mission. . . . This chapel was dearer to the Señora than her house. . . .

Through wars, insurrections, revolutions, downfalls, Spanish, Mexican, civil, ecclesiastical, her standpoint, her poise, remained the same. She simply grew more and more proudly, passionately, a Spaniard and a Moreno; more and more stanchly and fiercely a Catholic and a lover of the Franciscans. . . .

As year by year she saw the ruin of the Missions steadily going on, their vast properties melting away like dew before the sun in the hands of dishonest administrators and politicians, the Church powerless to contend with the unprincipled greed in high places, her beloved Franciscan Fathers driven from the country or dying of starvation at their posts, she submitted herself to what, she was forced to admit, seemed to be the inscrutable will of God for the discipline and humiliation of the Church. . . .

Any race under the sun would have been to the Señora less hateful than the American. She had scorned them in her girlhood, when they came trading to post after post. She scorned them still. The idea of being forced to wage war with peddlers was to her too monstrous to be believed. In the outset she had no doubt that the Mexicans would win in the contest. "What!" she cried, "shall

we who won independence from Spain be beaten by these traders? That is impossible!" . . .

Out of such throes as these had been born the second nature
which made Señora Moreno the silent, reserved, stern, implacable
woman they knew, who knew her first when she was sixty. Of the
gay, tender, sentimental girl who danced and laughed with the
officers, and prayed and confessed with the Fathers forty years
before, there was small trace left now in the low-voiced, white-
haired, aged woman, silent, unsmiling, placid-faced.

Condensed from *Ramona*, Helen Hunt Jackson (Boston: Roberts Brothers,
1884).

XXXIX

Clarence King

In the 1860s, while redistribution and reassignment of old ranch and mission lands were still going on, serious efforts were also being made to reevaluate the natural resources of the state. In this the legislators took a prime interest; they wanted a thorough survey carried out to determine how much truth there was in tales of yet-undiscovered treasuries of gold and silver, gems, tin, sulphur, copper, and coal within their legislative jurisdiction.

To supervise the monumental project, and to accept the title of State Geologist, they brought in the Yale-trained geologist Josiah D. Whitney, who had completed similar surveys for other states and written the much-discussed book *The Metallic Wealth of the United States*. Sensibly he was also given full authority to assemble his own team of special assistants, and one of his early recruits was Clarence King (1842–1901), a foot-loose adventurer just out of Yale, who had headed for California, and happened to encounter a group of the survey party on the river steamer en route from Sacramento to San Francisco. He was hired on the spot, and proved to be a live wire of the team.

The geological survey made by Whitney and company over a period of a decade was never regarded in California as a complete success: they did not uncover any great new mineral wealth; they drafted important maps and reports, and set the stage for future, more comprehensive surveys, but lay critics got the impression that they were much more interested in climbing mountains and identifying new

landmarks with their names and names of their friends than with
practical prospecting. Indeed, to support that criticism, before the
geologists were through, a map of the High Sierra presented virtually a
muster of the survey members and their professional colleagues.

The state's highest elevation, Mount Whitney, memorialized the
director of the group, for example; Mount Conness commemorated the
Senator who had done the legislative groundwork for them; Mount
Hoffmann honored topographer Charles F. Hoffmann; Mount Brewer,
Professor William H. Brewer, Whitney's principal assistant; and
Mount King, the raw Yale recruit. The popular reluctance of Californians to shower with acclaim these well-paid scientists also stem-
med from the fact that they were prone to occasional error: Brewer
confused a generation of geography students by insisting that Mount
Shasta marked the highest point in the United States, and King
suffered the excruciating embarrassment of climbing and describing
what he supposed was Mount Whitney, only to be shown that he had
actually ascended Mount Langley.

But the courage and accomplishment of these mountaineer-geolo-
gists was not to be disparaged. They were the first scientists to penetrate the depths of the Sierra; out of their experience grew the whole
framework of the United States Geological Survey, with Clarence King
as its first director. In addition to remarkable physical vitality, King
also possessed broad intellect and genius as a colorful writer; nor did
he hesitate to stretch a point now and then to dramatize his ventures.
Mount Tyndall, named by King for the British physicist and Alpine
glacialist John Tyndall, was not an important Sierra peak, nor was it
later regarded as a difficult climb, but King, the first to conquer it with
mulepacker Richard Cotter in July 1864, drafted an account of the
ascent that read like an exciting expedition into the Himalaya.

Two Against Mount Tyndall

The Kings Canyon, which headed against our wall, seemed un-
traversable—no human being could climb along the divide; we
had then but one hope of reaching the peak [of Mount Tyndall],
and our greatest difficulty lay at the start. If we could climb down
to the Kern side of the divide and succeed in reaching the base of

the precipices which fell from our feet, it really looked as if we might travel without difficulty among the *roches moutonnées* to the other side of the Kern Valley, and make our attempt upon the southward flank of the great peak.

One look at the sublime white giant decided us. We looked down over the precipice, and at first could see no method of descent. . . . Cotter, with danger, edged his way along the wall to the east, and I to the west, to see if there might be some favorable point; but we both returned with the belief that the precipice in front of us was as passable as any of it. Down it we must.

After lying on our faces, looking over the brink ten or twenty minutes, I suggested that by lowering ourselves on the rope we might climb from crevice to crevice; but we saw no shelf large enough for ourselves and the knapsacks too. However, we were not going to give up without a trial; and I made the rope fast round my breast, and looping the noose over a firm point of rock, let myself slide gradually down to a notch forty feet below. There was only room beside me for Cotter, so I made him send down the knapsacks first. I then tied these together by the straps with my silk handkerchiefs and hung them off as far to the left as I could reach without losing my balance, looping the handkerchiefs over a point of rock. Cotter then slid down the rope, and with considerable difficulty, we whipped the noose off its resting place above, and cut off our connection with the upper world.

"We're in for it now, King," remarked my comrade, as he looked aloft, and then down; but our blood was up, and danger added only an exhilarating thrill to the nerves.

The shelf was hardly more than two feet wide, and the granite so smooth that we could find no place to fasten the lasso for the next descent; so I determined to try the climb with only as little aid as possible. Tying it round my breast again, I gave the other end into Cotter's hands, and he, bracing his back against the cliff, found for himself as firm a foothold as he could, and promised to give me all the help in his power. I made up my mind to bear no weight unless it was absolutely necessary; and for the first ten feet I found cracks and protuberances enough to support me, making every square inch of surface do friction duty, and hugging myself against the rocks as tightly as I could.

When within about eight feet of the next shelf, I twisted myself round upon the face, hanging by two rough blocks of protruding feldspar, and looked vainly for some further foothold; but the rock, beside being perfectly smooth, overhung slightly, and my legs dangled in the air. I saw that the next cleft was over three feet broad and I thought, possibly, I might, by a quick slide, reach it in safety without endangering Cotter. I shouted to him to be very careful and let go in case I fell, loosened my hold upon the rope and slid quickly down. My shoulder struck against the rock and threw me out of balance; for an instant I reeled over upon the verge, in danger of falling, but in the excitement, I thrust out my hand and seized a small alpine gooseberry bush, the first piece of vegetation we had seen. Its roots were so firmly fixed in the crevice that it held my weight and saved me.

I could no longer see Cotter, but I talked to him, and heard the two knapsacks come bumping along till they slid over the eaves above me and swung down to my station, when I seized the lasso's end and braced myself as well as possible, intending, if he slipped, to haul in slack and help him as best I might. As he came slowly down from crack to crack, I heard his hobnailed shoes grating on the granite; presently they appeared dangling from the eaves above my head. I had gathered in the rope until it was taut, and then hurriedly told him to drop. He hesitated a moment, and let go. Before he struck the rock I had him by the shoulder, and whirled him down upon his side, thus preventing his rolling overboard, which friendly action he took quite coolly.

The third descent was not a difficult one, nor the fourth; but when we had climbed down about two hundred and fifty feet, the rocks were so glacially polished and water-worn that it seemed impossible to get any farther. To our right was a crack penetrating the rock perhaps a foot deep, widening at the surface to three or four inches, which proved to be the only possible ladder. As the chances seemed to be rather desperate, we concluded to tie ourselves together, in order to share a common fate; and with a slack of thirty feet between us, and our knapsacks upon our backs, we climbed into the crevice, and began descending with our faces to the cliff.

This had to be done with unusual caution, for the foothold was about as good as none, and our fingers slipped annoyingly on the smooth stone; besides, the knapsacks and instruments kept a steady backward pull, tending to overbalance us. But we took pains to descend one at a time, and rest wherever the niches gave our feet a safe support. In this way we got down about eighty feet of smooth, nearly vertical wall, reaching the top of a rude granite stairway, which led to the snow; and here we sat down to rest, and found to our astonishment that we had been three hours from the summit.

After breathing a half-minute we continued down, jumping from rock to rock, and having by practice become very expert in balancing ourselves, sprang on, never resting long enough to lose the aplomb, and in this manner made a quick descent over rugged debris to the crest of the snow field, which for seven or eight hundred feet more swept down in a smooth, even slope of very high angle to the borders of the frozen lake.

Without untying the lasso which bound us together, we sprang upon the snow with a shout and glissaded down splendidly, turning now and then a somersault, and shooting out like cannon balls almost to the middle of the frozen lake. . . . The ice cracked in all directions. It was only a thin, transparent film, through which we could see deep into the lake. Untying ourselves, we hurried ashore in different directions, lest our combined weight should be too great a strain upon any point.

With curiosity and wonder we scanned every shelf and niche of the last descent. It seemed quite impossible we could have come down there, and now it actually was beyond human power to get back again. But what cared we? "Sufficient unto the day—" We were bound for that still distant, though gradually nearing, summit.

A very long, comparatively even snow slope, whose surface was pierced by many knobs and granite heads, giving it the aspect of an ice roofing fastened on with bolts of stone . . . stretched in far perspective to the summit. . . . Immense boulders were partly embedded in the ice just above us, whose constant melting left them trembling on the edge of a fall. It communicated no very pleasant sensation to see above you these immense missiles hanging by a mere band, and knowing that . . . you would be exposed to a constant cannonade. . . .

Melting began to liberate huge blocks, which thundered down past us, gathering and growing into small avalanches below. We did not dare climb one above another, according to our ordinary mode, but kept about an equal level, a hundred feet apart, lest, dislodging the blocks, one should hurl them down upon the other.

We climbed alternately up smooth faces of granite, clinging simply by the cracks and protruding crystals of feldspar, and then hewed steps up fearfully steep slopes of ice, zigzagging to the right and left to avoid the flying boulders. When midway up this slope we reached a place where the granite rose in perfectly smooth bluffs on either side of a gorge—a narrow cut or walled way leading up to the flat summit of the cliff. This we scaled by cutting ice steps, only to find ourselves fronted again by a still higher wall. Ice sloped from its front at too steep an angle for us to follow, but had melted in contact with it, leaving a space three feet wide between the ice and the rock. We entered this crevice and climbed along its bottom, with a wall of rock rising a hundred feet above us on one side and a thirty-foot face of ice on the other, through which light of an intense cobalt-blue penetrated.

Reaching the upper end, we had to cut our footsteps upon the ice again, and having braced our backs against the granite, climb up to the surface. We were now in a dangerous position: to fall into the crevice upon one side was to be wedged to death between rock and ice; to make a slip was to be shot down five hundred feet and then hurled over the brink of a precipice. In the friendly seat which this wedge gave me, I stopped . . . to enjoy the view.

The wall of our mountain sank abruptly to the left, opening for the first time an outlook to the eastward. Deep—it seemed almost vertically—beneath us we could see the blue water of Owens Lake, ten thousand feet down. The summit peaks to the north were piled in titanic confusion, their ridges overhanging the eastern slope with terrible abruptness. Clustered upon the shelves and plateaus below were several frozen lakes, and in all directions swept magnificent fields of snow.

The summit was now not over five hundred feet distant, and we started on again with the exhilarating hope of success. But if Nature had intended to secure the summit from all assailants, she could not have planned her defenses better; for the smooth granite wall which rose above the snow slope continued apparently quite round the peak, and we looked in great anxiety to see if there was not one place where it might be climbed. It was all blank except in one place; quite near us the snow bridged across the crevice and rose in a long point to the summit of the wall—a great icicle column frozen in a niche of the bluff—its base about ten feet wide, narrowing to two feet at the top.

We climbed to the base of this spire of ice, and with the utmost care began to cut our stairway. The material was an exceedingly compacted snow, passing into clear ice as it neared the rock. We climbed the first half of it with comparative ease; after that it was almost vertical, and so thin that we did not dare to cut the footsteps deep enough to make them absolutely safe. There was a constant dread lest our ladder should break off [it did, shortly after they had ascended it] and we be thrown either down the snow slope or into the bottom of the crevasse.

At last, in order to prevent myself from falling over backward, I was obliged to thrust my hand into the crack between the ice and the wall, and the spire became so narrow that I could do this on both sides; so that the climb was made as upon a tree, cutting mere toe holds and embracing the whole column of ice in my arms. At last I reached the top and with the greatest caution wormed my body over the brink, and rolling out upon the smooth surface of the granite, looked over and watched Cotter make his climb. He came steadily up, with no sense of nervousness, until he got to the narrow part of the ice, and here he stopped and looked up with a forlorn face to me; but as he climbed up over the edge the broad smile came back to his face and he asked me if it had occurred to me that we had by-and-by to go down again.

We had now an easy slope to the summit, and hurried up over rocks and ice, reaching the crest at exactly twelve o'clock. I rang my hammer upon the topmost rock; we grasped hands, and I reverently named the grand peak MOUNT TYNDALL.

From *Mountaineering in the Sierra Nevada*, Clarence King (Boston: James R. Osgood and Company, 1872).

XL

Artemus Ward

It was the quantitative transfusion of American citizenry from every existing state of the Union into the body politic of California that eased its transition from frontier dominion to full-blown statehood in less than a decade. Some of the other western wilderness regions took generations to attain an equivalent social and economic status, but gold and mass emigration accomplished it for California with immediacy. And the suddenly acquired adulthood of a state on the Pacific Coast challenged the whole nation to promote systems of communication and transportation that would help to incorporate it as an integral part of a united country.

Within a few months after the first overland stage reached California in 1857, a network of coaches was in operation; beginning in April 1860 a Pony Express rushed mail across the continent in days; and people had hardly become accustomed to the wonder of that speed when, in October 1861, a transcontinental telegraph line was completed; and that same year the Central Pacific Railroad Company of California was organized with the fantastic notion of bringing transcontinental passenger service at an early date.

But just as significant as these developments in communication and transportation was the constant flow of "culture" between East and West. San Franciscans already prided themselves in keeping *au courant* with fashions and affairs of Boston, New York, and Philadelphia; they subscribed to Eastern newspapers and magazines, were reading the latest books within a few months after publication; were applauding Broadway stars on tours to the Coast, prima donnas, noted recitalists, and lecturers only a season or two after they made headlines in the East. By the 1860s performing artists of all kinds were including San Francisco, the capital at Sacramento, and many of the gold towns in their itineraries.

For the sake of his own reputation, America's favorite humorist at midcentury, Artemus Ward (1845–1867), could not afford not to include California in his tours. His witticisms, first in the Cleveland *Plain Dealer* and New York's *Vanity Fair,* then on the lecture platform, had made him the rage of the country; Californians demanded his appearance.

Artemus, as everyone knew, was actually Charles Farrar Browne, a man from Maine who had capitalized on native Down East humor—understatement, overstatement, naive observations, tortured spellings, quaint dialect, twists of speech—and turned it into a fad. It was a brand new kind of Yankee humor which Browne and his copyist Mark Twain nationalized so effectively that it became a standard form of American wit, and later so commonplace that even the best of Artemus Ward on California of the 1860s appears a little trite and threadbare a century later.

Here to Amuse People

We reach San Francisco one Sunday afternoon. I am driven to the Occidental Hotel by a kind-hearted hackman who states that inasmuch as I have come out there to amuse people, he will only charge me five .dollars. I pay it in gold, of course, because greenbacks are not current on the Pacific Coast.

Many of the citizens of San Francisco remember the Sabbath day to keep it jolly; and the threatres, the circus, the minstrels and the music halls are all in full blast tonight. I "compromise" and go to the Chinese theatre, thinking perhaps there can be no great harm in listening to worldly sentiments when expressed in a language I don't understand.

The Chinaman at the door takes my ticket with the remark, "Ki hi-hi ki! Shoolah!" And I tell him that on the whole I think he is right.

The Chinese play is "continued," like a Ledger story, from night to night. It commences with the birth of the hero or heroine, which interesting event occurs publicly on the stage; and then follows him or her down to the grave, where it cheerfully ends.

Sometimes a Chinese play lasts six months. The play I am speaking of had been going on for about two months. The heroine had grown up into womanhood and was on the point, as I inferred, of being married to a young Chinaman in spangled pantaloons and a long black tail. The bride's father comes in with his arms full of tea chests and bestows them, with his blessing, upon the happy couple. As this play is to run four months longer, however, and as my time is limited, I go away at the close of the second act, while the orchestra is performing an overture on gongs and one-stringed fiddles.

The doorkeeper again says, "Ki hi-hi ki! Shoolah!" adding this time, however, "Chow-wow." I agree with him in regard to the *ki hi* and *hi ki*, but tell him I don't feel altogether certain about the *chow-wow*.

To Stockton from San Francisco.

Stockton is a beautiful town that has ceased to think of becoming a very large place and has quietly settled down into a state of supreme prosperity. I have my boots repaired here by an artist who informs me that he studied in the penitentiary; and I visit the lunatic asylum, where I encounter a vivacious maniac who invites me to ride in a chariot drawn by eight lions and a rhinoceros.

John Phoenix was once stationed at Stockton, and put his mother aboard the San Francisco boat one morning with the sparkling remark, "Dear mother, be virtuous and you will be happy."

Forward to Sacramento—which is the capital of the state and a very nice old town.

They had a flood here some years ago, during which several

blocks of buildings sailed out of town and have never been heard from since. A Chinaman concluded to leave in a washtub, and actually set sail in one of those fragile barks. A drowning man hailed him piteously, thus: "Throw me a rope, oh throw me a rope!" To which the Chinaman excitedly cried, "No have got— how can do?" and went on, on with the howling current. He was never seen more; but a few weeks after, his tail was found by some Sabbath-school children in the north part of the state.

I go to the mountain towns. The sensational mining days are over, but I find the people jolly and hospitable nevertheless. At Nevada I am called upon, shortly after my arrival, by an athletic, scarlet-faced man who politely says his name is Blaze. "I have a little bill against you, sir," he observes.

"A bill—what for?"

"For drinks."

"Drinks?"

"Yes, sir—at my bar. I keep the well-known and highly respected coffee house down street."

"But, my dear sir, there is a mistake—I never drank at your bar in my life."

"I know it, sir. That isn't the point. The point is this: I pay out money for good liquors, and it is people's own fault if they don't drink them. There are the liquors—do as you please about drinking them, *but you must pay for them!* Isn't that fair?"

His enormous body (which Puck wouldn't put a girdle round for forty dollars) shook gleefully while I read this eminently original bill.

Years ago Mr. Blaze was an agent of the California Stage Company. There was a formidable and well-organized opposition to the California Stage Company at the time, and Mr. Blaze rendered them such signal service in his capacity of agent that they were very sorry when he tendered his resignation.

"You are some sixteen hundred dollars behind in your accounts, Mr. Blaze," said the President, "but in view of your faithful and efficient services, we shall throw off eight hundred dollars of that amount."

Mr. Blaze seemed touched by this generosity. A tear stood in his eye and his bosom throbbed audibly.

"You *will* throw off eight hundred dollars—you *will?*" he at last cried, seizing the President's hand and pressing it passionately to his lips.

"I will," returned the President.

"Well, sir," said Mr. Blaze, "I'm a gentleman, *I am,* you bet! And I won't allow no stage company to surpass me in politeness. *I'll throw off the other eight hundred dollars, and we'll call it square!* No gratitude, sir—no thanks; it is my duty."

The distance from Sacramento to Atchison, Kansas, by the Overland stage route, is 2200 miles, but you can happily accomplish a part of the journey by railroad. The Pacific railroad is completed twelve miles to Folsom, leaving only 2188 miles to go by stage. This breaks the monotony; but as it is midwinter, and as there are well-substantiated reports of Overland passengers freezing to death, and of the Piute savages being in one of their sprightly moods when they scalp people, I do not—I may say that I do not leave the Capital of California in a lighthearted and joyous manner. But "leaves have their time to fall," and I have my time to leave, which is now.

We ride all day and all night, and ascend and descend some of the most frightful hills I ever saw. We make Johnson's Pass, which is 6752 feet high, about two o'clock in the morning, and go down the great Kingsbury grade with locked wheels. The driver, with whom I sit outside, informs me as we slowly roll down this fearful mountain road, which looks down on either side into an appalling ravine, that he has met accidents in his time and cost the California Stage Company a great deal of money—"because," he says, "juries is agin us on principle and every man who sues us is sure to recover. But it will never be so agin, not with *me,* you bet." . . .

It was frightfully dark. It was snowing withal, and notwithstanding the brakes were kept hard down, the coach slewed wildly, often fairly touching the brink of the black precipice.

"How is that?" I said.

"Why, you see," he replied, "that corpses never sue for damages, but maimed people do. And the next time I have an overturn I shall go round and keerfully examine the passengers. Them as is dead, I shall let alone; but them as is mutilated I shall finish with the king-bolt! Dead folks don't sue. They ain't up to it."

Thus with anecdote did this driver cheer me up.

From *Artemus Ward: His Travels* (New York: Carleton, 1865).

XLI

Mark Twain

Artemus Ward traveled under a handicap on his Western tour: he had such a tight lecture schedule that there was little time for sight-seeing or collecting stories from the natives. From San Francisco he raced on to engagements at Stockton, Sacramento, and Nevada City, then east to Salt Lake City. But he did pause long enough en route for a chat with another budding humorist named Samuel Clemens (1835–1910), then working for the Virginia City *Enterprise* in Nevada. The meeting was providential, for it was the encouragement given on that occasion by the popular lecturer that helped propel a virtually unknown Samuel Clemens into a renowned Mark Twain. Thereafter the Virginia City reporter seemed to pattern his life after Artemus Ward's and he soon eclipsed him at his own game.

Clemens was almost thirty at the time, but no one as yet took him very seriously as a literary figure; he was better known as a Mississippi pilot, printer, gold prospector, and dabbler in Nevada silver mine stocks, or as an irresponsible, roving small town paragrapher. "The Celebrated Jumping Frog of Calaveras County" had not yet catapulted him to glory; he had not been to the Sandwich Islands to gather material for the lectures that were to popularize him as a superb entertainer; he had not produced a book, nor a story that could command more than regional interest.

In the spring of 1864 he moved down from the mountain country to San Francisco to take a cub reporting job on the *Morning Call*. "It was

fearful drudgery—" he wrote, "soulless drudgery—and almost destitute of interest. It was an awful slavery for a lazy man." He was
frustrated, dejected, bored; and to add to his misery, the silver mines
in which he had speculated failed disastrously, leaving him almost
penniless.

Eight years later—after the Calaveras frog had hopped into the
national limelight, after his tours to the Sandwich Islands and the Holy
Land, after he had settled down in the East—he recalled with a
degree of stoicism the unpleasant reportorial experience in San Francisco, freely embroidered the truth of his economic plight as well as his
"butterfly idleness," and incorporated the episode in *Roughing It*.
During those months on his beat for the *Morning Call* he covered
everything from police courts to opera, which seldom inspired jocular-
ity. The one event that produced his most amusing yarn was a civic
tragedy—the "great earthquake" of October 1864.

No Better Place to Die Than This

It was just after noon on a bright October day. I was coming
down Third Street [in San Francisco]. The only objects in motion
anywhere in sight in that thickly built and populous quarter were
a man in a buggy behind me and a street car wending slowly up
the cross street. Otherwise, all was solitude and a Sabbath
stillness.

As I turned the corner around a frame house, there was a great
rattle and jar, and it occurred to me that here was an item!—no
doubt a fight in that house. Before I could turn and seek the door,
there came a really terrific shock; the ground seemed to roll under
me in waves, interrupted by a violent joggling up and down, and
there was a heavy grinding noise as of brick houses rubbing
together.

I fell up against the frame house and hurt my elbow. I knew
what it was now, and from mere reportorial instinct, nothing else,
took out my watch and noted the time of day. At that moment a
third and still severer shock came, and as I reeled about on the
pavement trying to keep my footing, I saw a sight! The entire

front of a tall four-story brick building in Third Street sprung
outward like a door and fell sprawling across the street, raising a
dust like a great volume of smoke! And here came the buggy—
overboard went the man, and in less time than I can tell it the
vehicle was distributed in small fragments along three hundred
yards of street. One could have fancied that somebody had fired a
charge of chair rounds and rags down the thoroughfare.

The street car had stopped, the horses were rearing and plunging, the passengers were pouring out at both ends, and one fat
man had crashed half way through a glass window on one side of
the car, got wedged fast and was squirming and screaming like an
impaled madman. Every door of every house as far as the eye
could reach was vomiting a stream of human beings; and almost
before one could execute a wink and begin another, there was a
massed multitude of people stretching in endless procession down
every street my position commanded. Never was solemn solitude
turned into teeming life quicker.

Of the wonders wrought by "the great earthquake" these were
all that came under my eye; but the tricks it did elsewhere, and
far and wide over the town, made toothsome gossip for nine days.
The destruction of property was trifling—the injury to it was
widespread and somewhat serious.

The "curiosities" of the earthquake were simply endless. Gentlemen and ladies who were sick, or were taking a siesta, or had
dissipated till a late hour and were making up lost sleep, thronged
into the public streets in all sorts of queer apparel, and some
without any at all. One woman who had been washing a naked
child ran down the street holding it by the ankles as if it were a
dressed turkey. Prominent citizens who were supposed to keep
the Sabbath strictly rushed out of saloons in their shirt sleeves,
with billiard cues in their hands. Dozens of men, with necks
swathed in napkins, rushed from barber shops, lathered to the
eyes or with one cheek clean shaved and the other still bearing a
hairy stubble.

Horses broke from stables, and a frightened dog rushed up a
short attic ladder and out onto a roof, and when his scare was
over had not the nerve to go down again the same way he had

gone up. A prominent editor flew down stairs in the principal hotel with nothing on but one brief undergarment—met a chambermaid and exclaimed: "Oh, what *shall* I do! Where shall I go!"

She responded with naive serenity: "If you have no choice, you might try a clothing store!"

A certain foreign consul's lady was the acknowledged leader of fashion, and every time she appeared in anything new or extraordinary the ladies in the vicinity made a raid on their husbands' purses and arrayed themselves similarly. One man who had suffered considerably and growled accordingly was standing at the window when the shocks came, and the next instant the consul's wife, just out of the bath, fled by with no other apology for clothing than—a bath towel! The sufferer rose superior to the terrors of the earthquake and said to his wife: "Now *that* is something *like!* Get out your towel, my dear!"

The plastering that fell from ceilings in San Francisco that day would have covered several acres of ground. For some days afterward groups were eying, and pointing men stood about many a building, looking at long zig-zag cracks that extended from the eaves to the ground. Four feet of the tops of three chimneys on one house were broken square off and turned around in such a way as to completely stop the draft.

A crack a hundred feet long gaped open six inches wide in the middle of one street and then shut together again with such force as to ridge up the meeting earth like a slender grave. A lady sitting in her rocking and quaking parlor saw the wall part at the ceiling, open and shut twice like a mouth, and then—drop the end of a brick on the floor like a tooth. She was a woman easily disgusted with foolishness, and she arose and went out of there.

One lady who was coming down stairs was astonished to see a bronze Hercules lean forward on its pedestal as if to strike her with its club. They both reached the bottom of the flight at the same time—the woman insensible from the fright. Her child, born some little time afterward, was club-footed. However—on second thought—if the reader sees any coincidence in this, he must do it at his own risk.

The first shock brought down two or three huge organ pipes in one of the churches. The minister, with uplifted hands, was just closing the services. He glanced up, hesitated, and said: "However, we will omit the benediction!"—and the next instant there was a vacancy in the atmosphere where he had stood.

After the first shock an Oakland minister said: "Keep your seats! There is no better place to die than this"—And added after the third: "But outside is good enough!" He then skipped out the back door.

Such another destruction of mantel ornaments and toilet bottles as the earthquake created, San Francisco never saw before. There was hardly a girl or a matron in the city but suffered losses of this kind. Suspended pictures were thrown down, but oftener still, by a curious freak of the earthquake's humor, they were whirled completely around with their faces to the wall!

There was a great difference of opinion, at first, as to the course or direction the earthquake traveled, but water that splashed out of various tanks and buckets settled that. Thousands of people were made so seasick by the rolling and pitching of floors and streets that they were weak and bedridden for hours, and some for even days afterward. Hardly an individual escaped nausea entirely. The queer earthquake—episodes that formed the staple of San Francisco gossip for the next week would fill a much larger book than this.

From *Roughing It*, Mark Twain (Hartford: American Publishing Company, 1872).

XLII

Alta California

It is sorely regrettable that humorists like J. Ross Browne, Artemus Ward, and Mark Twain could not have been prevailed upon to linger in California, for here was a climate made to order for the quipster, the natural home of the practical joke and the philosophy of the absurd; nothing was too sacred to be spared the barbs of the jester—righteousness, motherhood, patriotism, disaster, even the Civil War that was then wracking the rest of the nation. In California any funnyman could flourish, but the real professionals preferred to take a look, gather up their notes, and then hurry off to give California the laugh on the other side of the continent, leaving the home field to the amateurs.

A typical lugubrious subject perennially accorded the light touch was the state's proneness to highway robbery. Actually holdups were not much more common in California than in enlightened Eastern states, in Great Britain, Italy, Greece, or Mongolia, but the open spaces and secluded canyons of the West offered a more colorful setting for these improprieties, and therefore made a more memorable story. So highway robbery went down in folklore as a peculiarly Western institution—seasoned almost always with a bit of drollery, regardless of the bloodshed or magnitude of the take. It was a joke on someone.

Normally the bloodshed, the amount confiscated, and the horrendous character of the robbers increased proportionately with each telling, whether oral or printed. Rarely was there a dispassionate, objective witness to present the unadulterated facts. But in 1864, for a robbery that incorporated all of the ordinary elements, San Francisco's major newspaper, *Alta California,* did obtain a fairly collected, chatty, first-person account. The hoax in this case purportedly was at the expense of the Confederate Army. However, "Captain Ingraham," chief of the brigands, was shortly rounded up, brought to justice, and identified as none other than an ex-sheriff of Monterey County. That display of short arms in the Sierra foothills was about as close as California ever came to shooting participation in the Civil War then gripping North and South.

Stand and Deliver!

In all your roamings by land and sea, were you ever robbed or have you ever enjoyed the sensation of meeting with a knight of the road, and heard his "Stand and deliver"? Judging from my brief experience in such a situation, not met with in the Campana of Italy, the Abrazzi or Pyrenees, but here in California on the Western slope, the sensation is not the most pleasant or desirable. . . . I was one of the company of fourteen who left Carson, Nevada Territory, on Friday morning last, bound for San Francisco. Another stagecoach accompanied us, and we were about twenty-eight travelers in all.

We were bound over the Placerville route, and nothing occurred beyond the usual incidents of travel until we reached a point about fourteen miles from Placerville, California—that is, about one and a quarter miles east of the "Thirteen Mile House." The driver of the first stage was Blair. Our vehicle which was No. 2, was driven by Charley Watson. About 10 P.M., just as we turned the bend of the road, we found that Blair's stage was standing in our front, and someone called out, "Hold on," or he would fire. Thinking that some accident had occurred to the forward coach, Watson reined up.

As the stage stopped, I, being an inside passenger, looked out at the window and heard someone say, "We won't detain you but a moment; all we want is Wells, Fargo and Co.'s treasure," at the same time assuring the passengers that no harm was intended them if they would remain quiet. Here was a dramatic situation—robbers in our front and for all we knew on all our surroundings. Prudence dictated silence—and I can assure you that it was with some difficulty that prudence prevailed.

The robbers took possession of the treasure in the forward boot, three sacks of bullion in all, and then ordered the driver to proceed. The gang surrounding the stage were seven in number, armed with revolvers, I think two pistols each, and I assure you pistols never before appeared so formidable to me as well as to others, for in the dark the bores seemed at least as large as six-pounders. One of the crowd had a rifle or gun.

While this was going on, the gang ordered the forward stage to proceed, and on its start a shot was fired, which created considerable excitement among them. They came up to our stage, some of them remarking that they ought to shoot us all, but our driver coolly remarked that no shot had been fired from his stage and consequently no harm ought to reach his passengers. Watson, the driver, on hearing the shot, requested the passengers not to fire, as we were on the grade, and as the shot had already startled the leaders, a second might send them over, and we would all be dashed to pieces.

The gang surrounded us, presenting their weapons, and I noticed that one man had a tin cup and bowie knife slung to him in addition to a revolver in each hand, leveled at the driver.

At this time one of the robbers advanced, claiming to be the Captain, who informed us as follows: "Gentlemen, I will tell you who we are. We are not robbers, but a company of Confederate soldiers. Don't act foolish. We don't want anything of the passengers. All we want is Wells, Fargo and Co.'s treasure to assist us to recruit for the Confederate Army." The spokesman was a tall, raw-boned and slim man, who spoke with confidence, as if he understood the business he was engaged in.

In response to the demand, Watson threw out two sacks, but on some of the gang's intimating that it was not all, one of them got up on the boot and produced another sack of bullion and the wooden box containing the Genoa express, way bills, etc. He also found a small box of express freight, which he judged from its weight was valuable, and it was consequently confiscated.

. . . We had four ladies with us, and of course they were alarmed. One of them, however, exhibited grit of the right kidney. She was a young lady of between sixteen and seventeen, and exhibited considerable cuteness, as well as bravery. With woman's tact and curiosity, she immediately commenced a conversation with the so-styled captain of the band. . . . As they leveled their weapons on us and stated that they were Confederate soldiers, she asked if they had a flag. The reply was *yes.* She said she would like to see it. They answered that it was not convenient to show it, as they were busy now.

She then led them into a regular talk, asking them divers questions, among which, if they would take all the bullion, how they could carry it off; what they were going to do with it, etc. To all of which, replies were given. During the talk the robber's pistol would approach the lady's face, on which she requested him to lower it, as it might go off accidentally. The robber, *à la Fra Diablo,* acquiesced, stating that they were all Southern gentlemen and preferred to protect rather than injure ladies.

After the robbers had secured the treasure, they asked the passengers if they would not contribute a few dollars to assist the cause of the Confederacy. The lady then asked one of them if they would take greenbacks, at the same time remarking that she had a five-cent postal currency in her pocket, but would not give it up without a fight—plucky that! That gentlemanly robber replied that he wanted no greenbacks, as they had no need of that class of currency.

The robbers then informed us that we were at liberty to depart, but gave us warning that if a shot was fired, they would immediately return it. They ordered the driver to go ahead, and as we did, the gang lowered their weapons and we had a fair sight of the muzzles. The relief was great . . . as all the arms the passengers had were one revolver and a couple of derringers. (Mem. —Don't travel Eastward without a full armament.)

On our departure, one of the passengers asked our Joan d'Arc why she asked the robbers so many questions, when she ingenuously replied that she desired to obtain a hearing of the natural voices of the robbers, as well as a sight of their faces (they were masked) as some of the passengers might, if they did not recognize them, at least identify them in the future. She was smarter than we men were at any rate—and I might add, considerably more self-possessed.

. . . The [Captain] gave a receipt to Watson, the purport of which was as follows—"June-1864-. This is to certify that I have received of Wells Fargo and Co. the sum of——dollars, said account to be used in securing enlistments in this State for the Confederate service.

Henry M. Ingraham
Captain in Command C.S.A."

From "The Late Highway Robbery on the Placerville Route," *Alta California,* July 3, 1864.

XLIII

Oscar Lewis

In 1853—more than three years before the first wagon road over the Sierra was opened, four years before the first overland stage reached San Diego, and seven years before a Pony Express introduced eight-day mail service between Missouri and California—Congress voiced its interest in a transcontinental railroad by ordering that a route be surveyed at once. Politics and North-South animosity delayed effective action for years: geography, climate, and the engineers dictated that the rails be strung across the South, and Northerners, who would be supplying most of the capital for construction of the road, were loath to grant such a boon to slave states. The outbreak of the Civil War confirmed the need for at least a military railway linking the Atlantic and Pacific and decreed that it would have to be in the North in defiance of intemperate climate, rugged terrain, and the opinion of engineers.

The major obstacle for the northern route was the Sierra Nevada Range. Surveyors found a feasible grade across the Rockies, but scaling the one hundred and thirty miles of precipitous heights in the Sierra presented the most formidable problem ever faced by road builders anywhere.

The resolution of that challenge became one of the most exciting dramas in the annals of engineering. It was told again and again by participants in the struggle, by lay spectators and tramp tourists, by annalists who later patched together assorted accounts, but never

any better than it was related by California historian Oscar Lewis
(1893–   ) in *The Big Four,* a worthy companion volume for some
twenty other books written by him on the West.

The quartet who masterminded the rail construction over the mountains were a wholesale grocer, Leland Stanford; a dry goods merchant,
Charles Crocker; and two partner-proprietors of a hardware store,
Mark Hopkins and Collin P. Huntington. All were unknowns outside
their limited business and political circles before they became rail
entrepreneurs, and all four became wheeler-dealers of wealth as a
result of their efforts. High in the cast, too, were Theodore Judah, who
was largely responsible for mapping the line over the Sierra; J. H.
Strobridge, construction superintendent under Charles Crocker; and
Crocker's older brother, "E. B.," head of the Central Pacific's legal
department. And in the background of the drama was a host of indispensables, the thousands of coolies—"Crocker's pets"—recruited in
China as the principal labor force, and an army of diehards, detractors,
and carpers in San Francisco and elsewhere, who insisted that no train
could ever mount the Sierra or who were dead set against giving it a
try, because a rail line would be detrimental to their private interests.

Congress then added a major element of suspense by parceling out
the construction of the transcontinental route to two companies: the
Union Pacific working from the eastern terminus and the Central
Pacific working from Sacramento. It was made a great game, with one
company playing for high stakes against the other, since both were
granted an initial subsidy of $16,000 per mile over level terrain,
$48,000 in the mountains, and a land grant of 12,800 acres to go with
every mile of road completed, with the option, of course, of operating
and exploiting their respective sections of the line.

The crucial three years for the Central Pacific came between mid-
1865 and mid-1868, when its competitor was adding as much as a mile
a day in the flat country to the east and "Crocker's pets" were advancing over the Sierra by inches. All this was prelude to the final joining of
the two lines at Promontory, Utah, on May 10, 1869.

Over the Hump

By midsummer of 1865 trains were running, three a day each
way, to Illinoistown (soon renamed Colfax in honor of a visit

from Grant's Vice-President), while men and equipment were concentrated on the line ahead. The job was entering its difficult phase. In April 2,000 men and 300 wagons and carts had constituted Crocker's force. Six months later it had been increased to 6,000 men, mostly Chinese, and 600 teams. With plenty of money to spend and plenty of men, rapid headway was being made at last. That summer the Sacramento *Union* reviewed the road's activities and pronounced it "the largest construction enterprise in the world, not excepting the Suez Canal." Crocker, more confident than ever that he had been cut out for a leader, announced to the world: "The work goes bravely on."

There were many who wondered that so large a man could be so tireless. In later years dozens retained the memory of his large figure slouched on the back of a steaming horse, weaving continuously back and forth over the line, roaring orders, finding fault; in his own words, "stopping along wherever there was anything going amiss and raising old nick with the boys." . . . "Everyone was afraid of me," he recalled with pride. "I was just looking for someone to find fault with all the time." . . .

Only once a month was his appearance among the construction crews greeted with pleasure. His big sorrel mare then labored under an additional burden, two leather saddle-bags, bulging with coins. The big boss—"Cholly Clocker" to the Orientals—rode into the midst of a group, produced a paper and called off the names of the men. As each stepped forward he dipped into the saddle-bags—gold on one side, silver on the other—and dropped the coins into the lifted palm. It was a chore he insisted on doing himself. Riding up the noisy canyon with a hundred and fifty pounds of gold and silver in his saddle-bags appealed to his sense of the dramatic, and its distribution periodically confirmed a pleasant sense of power. Later he was to remark in sincere admiration: "My faculty of leadership developed more and more as I grew older."

But fifty miles of line had yet to be built before the summit was reached, and some of the problems were hardly suspected. Beyond Secrettown the climb to the snow-covered crest began in earnest; the grade stakes veered upward along the slanting side of the American River canyon, and the stream dropped far below. Meantime, surveying parties ran scores of experimental lines ahead, and here and there made minor changes in Judah's survey, avoiding occasional deep fills, substituting a wooden trestle for a cut through granite, trying—without success—to effect changes in the route that would materially lessen construction costs or reduce grades and curvature.

Throughout the summer of 1866, "Crocker's pets," six thousand strong, swarmed over the upper canyon, pecking methodically at the broken rock of the cuts, trooping in long lines beneath their basket hats to pour wheelbarrow loads of debris down the canyonside, threading precarious paths with seventy-pound kegs of black powder suspended from both ends of bamboo poles, refreshing themselves at intervals with sips of tea kept near at hand in whisky kegs emptied and abandoned by their white confreres. The Chinese were presently found to be adept at the back-breaking work of drilling and placing blasts, by then a major part of the work, for the upper ridges were scraped clear of soil by the winter deposits of ice. The reverberations of the heavy blasts echoed at decreasing intervals through the canyons, and the consumption of black powder rose to five hundred kegs a day.

Track-layers followed close behind the graders, and locomotives pushed strings of flatcars loaded with construction iron, lumber, explosives, food, drink and more men to the railhead. Cape Horn, a sheer granite buttress, proved the most formidable obstacle of the year; its lower sides dropped away in a thousand-foot vertical cliff that offered no vestige of a foothold. The indomitable Chinese were lowered from above on ropes, and there, suspended between sky and earth, chipped away with hammer and chisel to form the first precarious ledge, which was then laboriously deepened to a shelf wide enough to permit the passage of the cars. Three years later when overland trains crept cautiously along this ledge, passengers gazed straight down from their windows into thin air.

Cape Horn was successfully passed in May 1866. Dutch Flat . . . was reached in July. Later that summer Crocker, Stanford and Hopkins, hoping to convince still-skeptical Coast financiers that they were building no mere feeder for their trans-Sierran wagon road, celebrated the opening of the track to Alta. Ten carloads of citizens from Sacramento and the bay arrived over the rails, gathered about tables set in the open air, and with appetites sharpened by the altitude ate a luncheon "worthy of Delmonico's" and made their choice of three beverages: lemonade for the ladies, ice water for the hypothetical teetotalers, and a concoction named Pacific Railroad punch for all the rest. Thus fortified, the visitors listened to nine speeches. . . .

The progress continued. In November the company's time-tables in California newspapers were again revised, as Cisco, ninety-four miles from Scramento and nearly six thousand feet high, became the new terminus. Two trains were operated each way; the running time was five and a half hours, an average of about sixteen miles an hour, and the passenger fare was $9.40. Twenty-eight miles of track were built during 1866, at a cost of slightly less than eight million dollars.

Cisco was fourteen miles from the summit and eleven hundred feet below. To build this section . . . the company engineers had to overcome difficulties new to railroad builders anywhere. One problem was the extreme hardness of the granite of the upper ridges, through which the road must pass in almost con-tinuous tunnels and deep cuts. Here heavy blasts spurted back through the drill holes, leaving rock undamaged. The points of picks and chisels flattened against its flinty surface. Their usual equipment useless, the engineers adopted a late scientific dis-covery. Presently a Swedish chemist, one Swansen, was installed to manufacture on the spot a temperamental new substance called nitroglycerin. Its characteristics were imperfectly known and accidents were frequent; moreover, the cause of premature blasts could only be guessed at, for the explosions usually obliter-ated both evidence and witnesses. . . .

Summit Tunnel, a quarter-mile bore through the granite back-bone of the mountain, emphasized the inadequacy of the rock-drilling equipment then in use. Begun in midsummer of 1866 and pushed with all possible speed, it was a solid year in the building. Not only was the work tackled from both ends, but a shaft was chipped out from above so that work could proceed outward from the middle. Thus on four fronts Chinese crowded shoulder to shoulder and, working in twelve-hour shifts, chipped and hacked at the steel-like rock faces—and advanced at an average rate of eight inches a day.

At San Francisco, Stanford and Hopkins and E. B. Crocker received reports of this snail-like progress and compared them with news of the Union Pacific, then just hitting its stride in the easy advance across the prairies of eastern Nebraska. They foresaw their rival making good its boast to build to the California state line, leaving the Western company only the costly and unproductive road across the mountains. . . .

When the first locomotive nosed its way through the east portal of the summit bore, signalizing the conquest of the Sierra's crest, it marked the end of the first phase of construction. Nearly five years had passed since the wet afternoon at Sacramento when ground was broken, and the line was still where its enemies had predicted it would end—"lost in the clouds of the Sierra." Another full year, 1867, was to pass before the tracks would reach the state line and flatten out on the floor of the Nevada plateau.

The prospect of building in the desert heat could hardly have been distasteful to Crocker and his thousands of workmen, for they had already had far more than their share of sub-zero weather. The winter of 1864-5 had been abnormally mild. . . . The next winter was a different story. Construction work by then was mostly above the six-thousand-foot mark—and the winter was as severe as any on record. Snow fell in quantity as early as October, and the next five months saw an almost continuous succession of storms.

As ground froze and the tracks and construction line were blanketed under an icy mass fifteen feet thick, the work slowed down to a walk. Crocker, wrapped in furs like an Eskimo, patrolled the line continually; the work must go bravely on. It went on, even though nearly half his force of nine thousand were needed to keep the line clear of snow. . . . The mileage race with the Union Pacific was on in earnest and the Western forces could not afford to slow down. The snow-bound thousands continued

Railroad over the Sierra

the struggle straight through from November to May. Chinese in day and night shifts shoveled continuously to help keep the completed line open, but drifts formed faster than they and the steam plows could remove them. In the end the section above Cisco had to be abandoned.

Before winter was half over, work in the open had become impossible and thousands of half-frozen Chinese were shipped back to Sacramento or over the summit to the lower levels of the eastern slope. Only in the tunnels and deep cuts could construction go on, and even there the difficulties mounted. Food, powder, fuel and all construction materials were laboriously packed in from Cisco. By January the task of keeping paths open between camps and the line was abandoned. Tunnels were dug beneath forty-foot drifts, and for months three thousand workmen lived curious mole-like lives, passing from work to living quarters in dim passages far beneath the snow's surface.

This eerie existence was complicated by constant danger, for as snows accumulated on the upper ridges, avalanches grew frequent, their approach heralded only by a brief thunderous roar. A second later a work crew, a bunkhouse, sometimes an entire camp, would go hurtling at a dizzy speed down miles of frozen canyons. Not until months later were the bodies recovered; sometimes groups were found with shovels or picks still clutched in their frozen hands.

Those sent ahead to clear the roadway down the east slope found conditions not much easier. In the heavily wooded Truckee River canyon, clearing the frozen ground for the graders proved a huge task. Sugar pines eight feet and more in diameter were felled, their trunks cut in sections and rolled out of the way, while heavy blasts were planted beneath their stumps, which were blown skyward in abrupt fountains of flying wood, frozen earth and pungent black smoke.

To supply this outpost army, thousands of tons of equipment, material and provisions had to be hauled on sleds from Cisco over the summit to Donner Lake. Three locomotives, iron for forty miles of road, and forty cars were among the items freighted on sleds over the ridge, then loaded on wagons at Donner Lake and drawn down rutted, muddy roads to Truckee. The distance from Cisco to Truckee was only twenty-eight miles, but the expenditure in effort and dollars was enormous.

Months later, as spring thaws began to reduce the mountains of snow, Crocker and Strobridge moved their crews back to the summit and began chipping down through solid ice to the abandoned cuts and fills. The upper few miles of completed line on the west slope were presently cleared and Cisco again became a way station. The assault was resumed and intensified. Throughout 1867 twelve thousand workmen crowded along the forty-mile front from the summit to the eastern base of the mountains, hacking at the cuts and tunnels above Donner Lake, grading the roadbed down the steep slopes of Truckee Canyon. Tunnel No. 9 at Donner Lake and the adjacent deep cuts through solid granite proved tediously slow. Before that seven-mile gap could be closed and a connection made with the tracks ahead, winter again closed in and the experiences of a year before were repeated.

The construction record for 1867—a scant forty miles, twenty-five of which were still unconnected with the main line—was not encouraging to the four partners, who were casting growingly anxious eyes at the Union Pacific. That year the rival road built six times as many miles as the Central; its officials planned to reach Ogden, five hundred miles beyond its railhead, by the end of 1868. Faced by the loss of hundreds of miles of easy construction across Nevada and Utah—where the government subsidy was easily twice the cost of building—the partners nonetheless could do little to remedy the situation. . . . Cisco once more became the terminus, and the slow process of sledding over the summit had to be resumed. . . .

Because no other means of keeping the tracks open could be devised, construction of a long series of snowsheds was begun. During the next two years a dozen sawmills and two hundred carpenters were continuously busy putting up the heavily timbered galleries that eventually covered thirty-seven of the upper forty miles of the road. A year or two later, when tourists began passing over the line, it was these sheds and not the vastly more difficult cuts and tunnels that aroused their admiration.

During the winter of 1867–8 work was pushed on the unclosed gap above Donner Lake, while rails were laid down the eastern slope and graders pushed into the sage-covered desert beyond. But until the gap could be closed all hope of successfully competing for mileage with the Union Pacific was futile. . . . At the first hint of warmer weather, thousands of coolies were moved back to the summit to reopen the line above Cisco and to clear the ground for the uncompleted section. The bosses, from Crocker down, drove them unmercifully, but removing the thick crust of ice proved a colossal task. It engaged the picks and wheelbarrows of six thousand Chinese for weeks before the frozen roadbed was exposed and track-laying could begin.

June of 1868 was well advanced before the rails joined and the tracks at last were made continuous from Sacramento to the state line. Immediately freight trains packed with supplies and materials started rolling down the eastern mountainside and out upon the Nevada desert.

From *The Big Four,* Oscar Lewis (New York: Alfred A. Knopf, 1959).

XLIV

Samuel Bowles

Just as the Central Pacific construction was reaching the Sierra foothills in 1865, two conspicuous standard bearers of the nation's Republican Party, the Honorable Schuyler Colfax, Speaker of the House of Representatives, and Samuel Bowles (1826–1878), editor of one of the country's most influential newspapers, the Springfield, Massachusetts, *Republican,* teamed up to cross the continent, "simply to see the country, to study its resources, to learn its people and wants"—Colfax in the interests of government, Bowles in the interests of newspaper journalism.

They were among the first tourists to make the trip without ulterior motives, and everywhere had a difficult time persuading people they met that they were not performing "some secret governmental service; to see how they should be taxed; to relocate the Pacific Railroad; to make a bargain with the Mormons; to regulate the distant states—at least to speculate in mines and buy corner lots."

Once they convinced their public that they were merely on a junket, the response was warm and enthusiastic. The Congressman made countless speeches, had towns and streets named for him, and did so well for himself politically that he was soon to be elected Vice President of the United States. Bowles wrote the diary of the trip for his newspaper—fluently, vividly, rhetorically, often appearing to have borrowed some of his companion's eloquence.

Golden Pathway to the Golden Gate

Across the Continent! The Great Ride is finished. Fifteen hundred miles of railroad, two thousand of staging, again sixty miles of railway, and then one hundred and fifty miles by steamboat down the Sacramento River, and the goal is reached, the Continent is spanned. Seven weeks of steady journeying, within hail of a single parallel line from east to west, and still the Republic! Still the old flag . . . still the same Fourth of July—better than all, still the same people, with hearts aglow with the same loyalty and pride in the American Union, and the same purpose and the same faith for its future.

Greater the wonder grows at the extent of the Republic; but larger still our wonder at the mysterious but unmistakable homogeneity of its people. San Francisco, looking westward to the Orient for greatness, cooling its summer heats with Pacific breezes, thinks the same thoughts, breathes the same patriotism, burns with the same desires that inspire New York and Boston, whose outlook is eastward, and which seem to borrow their civilization with their commerce from Europe.

Sacramento talks as you do in Springfield; Nevada, over the mountains, almost out of the world, anticipates New England in her judgments, and makes up her verdict, while those close to the "Hub of the Universe" are looking over the testimony.

It is this that is the greatest thing about our country; that makes it the wonder of nations, the marvel of history—the unity of its people in ideas and purpose; their quick assimilation of all emigration—come it so far or so various; their simultaneous and similar currents of thought, their spontaneous, concurrent formation and utterance of a united Public Opinion. This is more than extent of territory, more than wealth of resource, more than beauty of landscape, more than variety of climate and productions, more than marvelous material development, more than cosmopolitan population, because it exists in spite of them, and conquers them all by its subtle electricity.

It is very interesting, indeed, to stand amid this civilization of half a generation; to see towns that were not in 1850, now wearing an old and almost decaying air; to walk up and down the close-built streets of this metropolis, and doubt whether they look most like Paris or New York, Brussels or Turin; to count the ocean steamers in the bay, or passing out through the narrow crack in the coast hills beautifully called the Golden Gate, and wonder as you finish your fingers where they all came from and are going to; to find an agriculture richer and more various than that of Illinois; to feast the senses on a horticulture that marries the temperate and torrid zones, and makes of every yard and garden and orchard one immense eastern greenhouse; to observe a commerce and an industry that supply every comfort, minister to every taste and fill the shops with every article of convenience and luxury that New York or Paris can boast of, and at prices as cheap as those of the former city today; to find homes more luxurious than are often seen in the eastern States, and to be challenged unsuccessfully to name the city whose ladies dress more magnificently than those of San Francisco.

None of this surprises me. I had large ideas of the Pacific Coast and its development; and I long ago gave up being surprised at any victories of the American mind and hand over raw American matter. Still, Nevada and California, with towns and cities of two to fifteen years' growth, yet today all full-armed in the elements of civilization, wanton with the luxuries of the senses, rich in the social amenities, supplied with churches and schools and libraries, even affecting high art, are wonderful illustrations of the rapidity and ease with which our people organize society and State, and surround themselves with all the comforts and luxuries of metropolitan life. The history of the world elsewhere offers no parallel to these. . . .

A railroad track . . . is now laid about forty miles from Sacramento, or nearly to Placerville. . . . The track is fast ascending the Sierras on its progress eastward. . . . To feel the importance of the Pacific Railroad, to measure the urgency of its early completion, to become impatient with government and contractor at every delay in the work, you must come across the Plains and the mountains to the Pacific Coast. Then you will see half a Continent waiting for its vivifying influences.

You will witness a boundless agriculture, fickle and hesitating for lack of the regular markets this would give. You will find mineral wealth immeasurable, locked up, wastefully worked or gambled away, until this shall open to it abundant labor, cheap capital, wood, water, science, ready oversight, steadiness of production—everything that will make mining a certainty and not a chance.

You will find the world's commerce with India and China eagerly awaiting its opportunities. You will see an illimitable field for manufactures unimproved for want of its stimulus and its advantages. You will feel hearts breaking, see morals struggling slowly upward against odds, know that religion languishes; feel, see and know that all the sweetest and finest influences and elements of society and Christian civilization hunger and suffer for the lack of this quick contact with the Parent and Fountain of all our national life.

It is touching to remember that between Plains and Pacific . . . through all our long journey, the first question asked of us by every man and woman we have met, whether rich or poor, high or humble, has been, "When do you think the Pacific Railroad will be done?" or, "Why don't or won't the government, now the war is over, put the soldiers to building this road?"—and their parting appeal and injunction as well, "Do build this Pacific Road for us as soon as possible." We wait, everything waits for that. . . . It is the hunger, the prayer, the hope of all these people. . . .

Men of the East! Men of Washington! You have given the toil and even the blood of a million of your brothers and fellows for four years, and spent three thousand million dollars to rescue one section of the Republic from barbarism and from anarchy; and your triumph makes the cost cheap. Lend now a few thousand of men and a hundred millions of money to create a new Republic, to marry to the Nation of the Atlantic an equal if not greater Nation of the Pacific.

Anticipate a new sectionalism, a new strife, by a triumph of the arts of Peace that shall be even prouder and more reaching than the victories of your Arms. Here is payment of your great debt; here is wealth unbounded; here the commerce of the world; here the completion of a Republic that is continental; but you must come and take them with the Locomotive!

From *Across the Continent,* Samuel Bowles (Springfield: Bowles and Company, 1865).

XLV

Ambrose Bierce

The post-Civil War generation in the East could boast of an impressive list of journalistic arbiters of the stature of Samuel Bowles; the West had one, Ambrose Bierce (1842–1913?), and he hailed from Ohio. After the War he chose San Francisco as his rostrum, and except for a few years in London and Washington, remained there for the rest of his life, raging against everything that came within his vision—a bitter satirist, brutal nihilist, morbid cynic.

His shafts were directed at all civilized humanity. Nothing cheered him. He jeered, insulted, and ridiculed the Bay City, yet he was lionized in return and regarded as a sort of West Coast Samuel Johnson. Nor was his influence limited to California. Before he had spoken American literature had been predominantly cheerful and optimistic. Bierce broke with tradition. He was the forerunner of "the angry men" in American letters.

He conducted newspaper columns, edited journals, and contributed to San Francisco periodicals and to popular Eastern magazines. His bitterness poured out in articles, editorials, short stories, news stories, translations, critiques, fables, and assorted collections of all these. Then in 1913 his career suddenly and mysteriously terminated: he went to Mexico and vanished without a trace from the society he had so long excoriated.

For years San Franciscans were subjected almost daily to the gibes in his newspaper columns. Examples of his wit were then gathered up, edited, disguised, augmented, and published in little volumes like *Cobwebs from an Empty Skull* and *Nuggets and Dust Panned Out in California,* under the pseudonym Dod Grile. Speaking for himself in all likelihood, the "editor" of the latter commented in an introduction: "Doubtless a riper experience would have taught him to somewhat repress the tendency to sneer at what others are accustomed to regard with veneration." But actually his newspaper commentaries, so frequently evidencing his obsession with the macabre, were the gentlest of his gibes.

Satirist at Large

The annual wrangle about the celebration of Fourth of July was terminated by the appointment of a President of the Day, a Grand Marshal, and other officers. One thing seems to have been neglected, namely the selection of a competent person to superintend the fireworks—a Pyrotechnician Extraordinary, as it were. We trust we shall not be accused of nepotism if we nominate Mr. Satan to that important office. He is in every way qualified, is a permanent resident of the city, has had some experience in fireworks, and is a most enthusiastic patriot. Besides, he is a gentleman of engaging manners and urbane disposition, a popular politician and owns property here. As to his honesty, it is above the average.

Our virtuous press professes grief at the discovery of another gigantic fraud upon the public treasury. We know better. A fraud is a thing your journalist dotes upon. He makes merry with it as a pig tosses a wisp of straw, and dallies with it as an elephant wraps his lithe trunk lovingly about the loins of a sleek puppy. To breathe an atmosphere of gigantic fraud is an editor's heaven on earth. It affords him an opportunity to display his loftiest public virtues, to get rid of the withering sarcasm that is spoiling in stock, to speak of the "influence of the press," to platitudinize, to make a donkey of himself, and provoke a sublime indifference in the object of his attacks. It is very jolly to be an editor under such creditable circumstances, and see men go on year after year robbing the public treasury under the very nose of a united and influential press.

Mrs. Harrow, the wife of a Methodist minister was lassoed by a party of native Californians, and dragged about until her life is despaired of. This is a direct result of the abolition of bull fights; the native Californian mind demands some relaxation from the cares and anxieties of a highway robbery, and the Irish have used up all the available Chinese.

A popular method of practical joking consists of going out with empty pockets on a dark night and getting knocked on the head and "robbed" by some needy garroter. The discomfiture of the operator is a thing to be enjoyed, but it is neither courteous nor equitable to play pranks upon those whose necessities compel them to rob, while our own only constrain us to cheat. There is such a thing as etiquette, even between the rival branches of the same profession.

California has not only the finest climate in the world, sir, and the biggest trees above ground, but she boasts the most elastic babies in creation. One of these compressible innocents fell off a balcony twenty-five feet in height yesterday, and, striking on a stone sidewalk, was caught on the second bound by a gentleman passing that way. Upon receiving her darling, the mother anxiously remarked that she feared the careless thing would get hurt some day at that business. We trust not.

An Indian was killed the other day on the San José railroad by the cowcatcher of the engine tearing the top of his head off. A savage of our acquaintance hearing of the accident remarked: "Ugh! Paleface git evum on Injun. Steam scalp-'em knife, ugh!"— and the dusky representative of a perishing race shaded his eyes with his hand, and looked across the western wave at the setting sun with an expression of sentimental acquiescence, acquired by long practice in allegorical engravings.

We like the Indians they raise in Fresno County. They are of a sanguinary yet discriminating turn of mind. None of your howling, tearing and wantonly blood-letting savages, but cool, temperate, judicial-minded aborigines, aiming to do even-handed justice by fitting each crime with a punishment nicely adjusted to the magnitude of the offense. To illustrate:

Mr. Dougherty, having reason to suspect that one of them might advantageously be dispensed with, walked up to him and discharged a pistol into his belly. The stricken aborigine clinched with his assailant, wrested the weapon from his clinging fingers, and with it pounded him upon the pate until the warlike Dougherty lay limp and peaceful along the mead, no longer zealous in his own Indian policy. Now the Red Man began to be sensible of a hurt, and suspended further punishment to await the result of his injuries. Seating himself alongside the passive Caucasian, he made a careful and critical examination of his own wound by pushing his finger into the hole. He was constrained to admit that it was mortal. Then rose that Indian with the look of one who has a high and holy duty to perform, and very little time to perform it in. He repossessed his hand of the discarded firearm, and wrought upon Mr. Dougherty a full, final and perfect retribution. This savage then died; and in death his features wore a peaceful smile, as of one who has discharged both barrels of his duty, and been killed by the recoil.

A roll containing one thousand dollars in gold coin has been paid over the counter of Wells, Fargo and Company's Express Office, in mistake for a forty-dollar roll of silver. This raises a curious question of law: if the man to whom it was paid shall break his neck hastening to the office to have the mistake rectified, can the careless clerk be adjudged guilty of manslaughter?

From *Nuggets and Dust Panned Out in California by Dod Grile*. Collected and loosely arranged by J. Milton Sloluck (London: Chatto and Windus [c. 1872]).

XLVI

Charles Nordhoff

The physical expansion of San Francisco and other coastal or inland cities would have been slowed to a crawl if it had not been for the abundance of building material with which California was blessed. Mexicans, of course, would have made do with adobe, and the necessary mud and straw was available almost anywhere, but men of Anglo-Saxon heritage were not at home until they could live and carry on their business behind more substantial walls of brick or boards. Brickyards—only a little better ordered than the untidy backyard native facilities for producing adobe—sprang up around all the larger towns. But the most popular material for quick California construction was wood—redwood.

The lumbermen who supplied that finished redwood were a distinct class of immigrant who entered the state so unobtrusively that they were never even recognized as immigrants. They came all the way from the state of Maine, and some of them took so long in crossing the continent that the journey occupied two generations. They migrated the slow, hard way, through the woods of the northern tier of states, chopping their way, and leaving behind them new fields where forests had been. After cleaning out the tallest of the Maine pine, they moved west to the upper reaches of the Connecticut River valleys, on to the Appalachians of New York and Pennsylvania, to the big timber of the Great Lakes, Michigan, Wisconsin, and Minnesota, and then to the Northwest and California.

For more than three thousand miles they carried with them their Maine ways and lingo, Maine tools, appetites, and lumbering technique—peaveys, broad axes, oxsleds, salt pork, beans, flapjacks, red flannels, mackinaws, muzzle-loaders, deacon seats, and profanity. Not until they reached California did they alter their lumbering methods appreciably, and then only because the climate, the size of the trees, and the Chinese who joined them decreed it.

Charles Nordhoff (1830–1901) was the first Eastener to describe the real drama of the California big-tree lumbering operations. Born in Germany, brought up in Ohio, he surrendered to the lure of the sea, as did his more famous grandson Charles, co-creator of the *Bounty* trilogy. Nordhoff joined the United States Navy at the age of fourteen and furthered his nautical indoctrination with sea wanderings as a whaler, and as crewman on fishing smacks. *Nine Years a Sailor* and *Stories of the Island World* were products of those youthful years afloat.

Then he made an abrupt switch to newspaper journalism, specializing in political reporting, and it was in 1872 and 1873, between jobs with the New York *Evening Post* and the New York *Herald* that he took time off for another voyage to the Pacific, including the customary triangle—San Francisco, Honolulu, and the Columbia River. Much of his itinerary he had covered before, but the survey of the redwood lumbering country was something new in his experience. He noted that the choppers from Maine and China were very wasteful, but the coast forests were then so extensive that their eventual destruction never so much as occurred to him.

Big Trees of the Big River Country

Some years ago, before there was a wagon road between Cloverdale and Mendocino City, or Big River, as it is more commonly called up here on the northern coast, the mail was carried on horse—or more usually on muleback; and the mail rider was caught on one stormy and dark night upon the road and found himself unable to go farther. In this dilemma he took refuge, with his mule and the United States mails, in a hollow redwood, and man and mule lay down comfortably within its shelter. They had room to spare indeed, as I saw when the stage driver pointed out the tree to me and kindly stopped until I examined it.

At a road-side inn I found that they roofed over a hollow stump, and used it as a capacious storeroom.

All these were large trees, of course; but there is no reason to believe that they were the biggest of their kind; and when you have traveled for two or three days through the redwood forests of the northern coast of California you will scarcely be surprised at any story of big trees.

The redwood seems to be found only near the coast of California; it needs the damp air which comes from the sea and which blows against the mountain slopes, which the tree loves. The coast, from fifty miles north of San Francisco to the northern border of Humboldt County, is a dense redwood forest; it is a mountainous and broken country, and the mountains are cut at frequent intervals by streams, some but a few miles in length, others penetrating into the interior by narrow cañons forty or fifty miles, and dividing in their upper waters into several branches.

The man who wondered at the wisdom of Providence in causing great rivers to flow past large cities would be struck with admiration at the convenient outflow of these streams; for upon them depends the accessibility of the redwood forests to the loggers and sawmill men who are busily turning these forests into lumber. At the mouth of every stream is placed a sawmill; and up these little rivers . . . loggers are busy chopping down huge trees, sawing them into lengths and floating them down to the mills. . . . The sawmills are mostly on so large a scale that about every one grows up a village or town, which usually contains several saloons or grogshops, one or two billiard rooms, a rude tavern or two, a doctor or two, several stores, and in some cases a church. . . .

Where the little sawmill rivers enter the sea, there is usually a sort of roadstead—a curve of the shore, not enough to make a harbor, but sufficient to give anchorage and a lee from the prevailing northwest wind, which makes it possible, by different devices, to load vessels. . . . The expedients for loading are often novel and ingenious. For instance, at Mendocino the lumber is loaded on cars at the mill and drawn by steam up a sharp incline, and by horses off to a point which shelters and affords anchorage for schooners. This point is perhaps one hundred feet above the water line, and long wire-rope stages are projected from the top and suspended by heavy derricks. The car runs to the edge of the cliff; the schooner anchors under the shipping stage one hundred feet below, and the lumber is slid down to her, a man standing at the lower end to check its too rapid descent with a kind of brake.

When a larger vessel is to be loaded, they slide the lumber into a lighter, and the ship is loaded from her. The redwood is shipped not only to California ports, but also to China and South America. . . . Vessels are frequently lost in spite of all precautions; for when the wind changes to southwest, the whole Pacific Ocean rolls into these roadsteads; and when a gale is seen approaching, the crews anchor their ships as securely as they can and then go ashore. It has happened in Mendocino harbor that a schooner has been capsized at her anchorage by a monstrous sea; and Captain Lansing told me that in the last twenty years he had seen over a hundred persons drowned in that port alone.

The waves have cut up the coast in the most fantastic manner . . . and there are caves innumerable, some with extensive ramifications. I was shown one such cave at Mendocino City into which a schooner, drifting from her anchor, was sucked during a heavy sea. As she broke from her anchors, the men hoisted sail, and the vessel was borne into the cave with all sail set. Her masts were snapped off like pipestems, and the hull was jammed into the great hole in the rock, where it began to thump with the swell so vehemently that two of the frightened crew were at once crushed on the deck by the overhanging ceiling of the cave. Five others climbed out hurriedly over the stern, and there hung on until ropes were lowered to them by men on the cliff above, who drew them up safely. . . . The next morning the vessel was so completely broken to pieces that not a piece the size of a man's arm was ever found of her hull. . . .

The real curiosity of this region is a logging camp, . . . an assemblage of rude redwood shanties, gathered about one larger shanty, which is the cookhouse and dining hall, and where usually two or three Chinamen are at work over the stove, and setting table. The loggers live well; they have excellent bread, meat, beans, butter, dried apples, cakes, pies and pickles; in short, I have dined at worse places.

A camp is divided into "crews"; a crew is composed of from twenty to twenty-six men, who keep one team of eight or ten oxen busy hauling the logs to water. A "crew" consists of teamsters, choppers, chain tenders, jack-screw men (for these logs are too heavy to be moved without such machinery), swampers, who build the roads over which the logs are hauled, sawyers, and barkers. A teamster, I was told, received seventy dollars per month, a chopper fifty dollars, chain tenders and jack-screw men the same, swampers forty-five dollars, sawyers forty dollars and barkers, who are usually Indians, one dollar a day, and board besides, for all. The pay is not bad, and as the chances to spend money in a logging camp are not good, many of the men lay up money and by and by go to farming or go home. They work twelve hours a day.

A man in Humboldt County got out of one redwood tree lumber enough to make a house and barn, and to fence in two acres of ground. A schooner was filled with shingles made from a single tree. One tree in Mendocino, whose remains were shown to me, made a mile of railroad ties. Trees fourteen feet in diameter have been frequently found and cut down. . . . A tree four feet in diameter is called undersized in these woods; and so skillful are the woodchoppers that they can make the largest giant of the forest fall just where they want it, or as they say, they "drive a stake with the tree."

To chop down a redwood tree, the chopper does not stand on the ground, but upon a stage sometimes twelve feet above the ground. Like the sequoia, the redwood has a great bulk near the ground, but contracts somewhat a few feet above. The chopper wants only the fair round of the tree, and his stage is composed of two stout staves, shod with a point at one end, which is driven into the tree. The outer ends are securely supported; and on these staves he lays two narrow, tough boards, on which he stands, and

Redwood lumbermen

which spring at every blow of his axe. It will give you an idea of the bulk of these trees when I tell you that in chopping down the larger ones two men stand on the stage and chop simultaneously at the same cut, facing each other.

They first cut off the bark, which is from four to ten, and often fifteen inches thick. This done, they begin what is called the "undercut"—the cut on that side toward which the tree is meant to fall; and when they have made a little progress, they, by an ingenious and simple contrivance, fix upon the proper direction of the cut, so as to make the tree fall accurately where they want it. This is necessary on account of the great length and weight of the trees and the roughness of the ground, by reason of which a tree carelessly felled may in its fall break and split to pieces, so as to make it entirely worthless. This happens not infrequently, in spite of every care. . . .

The "undercut" goes in about two-thirds the diameter. When it is finished, the stage is shifted to the opposite side, and then it is a remarkable sight to see the tall, straight mass begin to tremble as the axe goes in. It usually gives a heavy crack about fifteen minutes before it means to fall. The chopper thereupon gives a warning shout, so that all may stand clear—not of the tree, for he knows very well where that will go, and in a cleared space men will stand within ten feet of where the top of the tree is to strike, and watch its fall; his warning is against the branches of other trees which are sometimes torn off and flung to a distance by the falling giant, and which occasionally dash out men's brains.

At last the tree visibly totters, and slowly goes over; and as it goes, the chopper gets off his stage and runs a few feet to one side. Then you hear and see one of the grandest and most majestic incidents of forest life. There is a sharp crack, a crash, and then a prolonged thunderous crash, which, when you hear it from a little distance, is startlingly like an actual and severe thunder peal. To see a tree six feet in diameter, and one hundred and seventy-five feet high, thus go down, is a very great sight, not soon forgotten. . . .

In one logging camp I visited, there remained a stump fourteen feet high. At this height the tree was fourteen feet in diameter, perfectly round and sound, and it had been sawn into seventeen logs, each twelve feet long. The upper length was six feet in diameter. Probably the tree was three hundred feet long, for the top for a long distance is wasted.

So many of the trees and so many parts of trees are splintered or broken in the fall that the master of a logging camp told me he thought they wasted at least as much as they saved: and as the mills also waste a good deal, it is probable that for every foot of this lumber that goes to market, two feet are lost. A five-foot tree occupies a chopper from two and a half to three and a half hours, and to cut down a tree eight feet in diameter is counted a day's work for a man.

When the tree is down, the sawyers come. Each has a long saw; he removes the bark at each cut with an axe, and then saws the tree into lengths. It is odd enough to go past a tree and see a saw moving back and forward across its diameter without seeing the man who moves it, for the tree hides him completely from you, if you are on the side opposite him. Then come the barkers with long iron bars to rip off the thick bark; then the jack-screw men, three or four of whom move a log about easily and rapidly, which a hundred men could hardly budge. They head it in the proper direction for the teamsters and chain men, and these then drag it down to the water over roads which are watered to make the logs slide easily; and then, either at high tide or during the winter freshets, the logs are run down to the mill.

The Maine men make the best woodchoppers, but the logging camp is a favorite place also for sailors; and I was told that Germans are liked as workmen about timber. . . .

At present prices it pays to haul logs in the redwood country only about half a mile to water; all trees more distant than this from a river are not cut; but the rivers are in many places near each other, and the belt of timber left standing, though considerable, is not so great as one would think. . . .

Accidents are frequent in a logging camp, and good surgeons are in demand in all the sawmill ports, for there is much more occasion for surgery than for physic. Men are cut with axes, jammed by logs, and otherwise hurt, one of the most serious dangers arising from the fall of limbs torn from standing trees by a falling one. Often such a limb lodges or sticks in the high top of a tree until the wind blows it down, or the concussion of the woodcutters axe, cutting down the tree, loosens it. Falling from such a height as two hundred or two hundred and fifty feet, even a light branch is dangerous. . . .

When you leave the coast for the interior, you ride through mile after mile of redwood forest. Unlike the firs of Oregon and Puget Sound, this tree does not occupy the whole land. It rears its head from a jungle of . . . other trees; and I doubt if as many as fifty large redwoods stand upon a single acre. I was told that an average tree would turn out about fifteen thousand feet of lumber, and thus even thirty such trees to the acre would yield nearly half a million feet.

From *Northern California, Oregon and the Sandwich Islands,* Charles Nordhoff (New York: Harper and Brothers, 1874).

XLVII

Walt Whitman

The thunder of the falling Mendocino redwoods was heard on the opposite side of the continent by Walt Whitman (1819–1892), the Brooklyn newspaper editor and poet who was raising a nationwide literary storm over the merits of his "free verse," with its long psalmodic lines and daring subject matter, which he published in repeated and ever-expanding editions of a volume entitled *Leaves of Grass*.

Whitman would hardly qualify as a California poet, for he never penetrated the West farther than Colorado, but he was better informed on what was taking place on the Pacific shores than many a long-time resident. He was the all-American songster, soon to be recognized as that, and acclaimed, too, for the incalculable influence he exerted on younger generations of poets. In his Eastern perspective, the felling of the redwoods symbolized merely a step in the preparation of "standing-ground" for a burgeoning race—a making of clearings for future agriculture and industry, not unlike what had already taken place in Massachusetts, Maine, or Michigan. Here was evolving a first fulfillment in "the promise of thousands of years."

Song of the Redwood Tree

1.

A California song,
A prophecy and indirection, a thought impalpable to breathe as
       air,
A chorus of dryads, fading, departing, or hamadryads departing,
A murmuring, fateful, giant voice, out of the earth and sky,
Voice of a mighty dying tree in the redwood forest dense.

Farewell my brethren,
Farewell O earth and sky, farewell you neighboring waters,
My time is ended, my term has come.

Along the northern coast,
Just back from the rock-bound shore and the caves,
In the saline air from the sea in the Mendocino country,
With the surge for base and accompaniment low and hoarse,
With crackling blows of axes sounding musically driven by strong
       arms,
Riven deep by the sharp tongues of the axes, there in the redwood
       forest dense,
I heard the mighty tree its death-chant chanting;
The choppers heard not, the camp shanties echoed not,
The quick-ear'd teamsters and chain and jack-screw men heard
       not,
As the wood-spirits came from their haunts of a thousand years to
       join the refrain,
But in my soul I plainly heard.

Murmuring out of its myriad leaves,
Down from its lofty top rising two hundred feet high,
Out of its stalwart trunk and limbs, out of its foot-thick bark,
That chant of the seasons and time, chant not of the past only but
       the future.

You untold life of me,
And all you venerable and innocent joys,
Perennial hardy life of me with joys 'mid rain and many a summer
        sun,
And the white snows and night and the wild winds;
O the great patient rugged joys, my soul's strong joys unreck'd by
        man,
(For know I bear the soul befitting me, I too have consciousness,
        identity,
And all the rocks and mountains have, and all the earth),
Joys of the life befitting me and brothers mine,
Our time, our term has come.

Nor yield we mournfully majestic brothers,
We who have grandly fill'd our time;
With Nature's calm content, with tacit huge delight,
We welcome what we wrought for through the past,
And leave the field for them.

For them predicted long,
For a superber race, they too to grandly fill their time,
For them we abdicate, in them ourselves ye forest kings!
In them these skies and airs, these mountain peaks, Shasta,
        Nevadas,
These huge precipitous cliffs, this amplitude, these valleys, far
        Yosemite,
To be in them absorb'd, assimilated.

Then to a loftier strain,
Still prouder, more ecstatic rose the chant,
As if the heirs, deities of the West,
Joining with master-tongue bore part.

Not wan from Asia's fetiches,
Nor red from Europe's old dynastic slaughter-house,
(Area of murder-plots of thrones,
        with scent left yet of wars and scaffolds everywhere,)

But come from Nature's long and harmless throes, peacefully
   builded thence,
These virgin lands, lands of the Western shore,
To the new culminating man, to you, the empire new,
You promis'd long, we pledge, we dedicate.

You occult deep volitions,
You average spiritual manhood, purpose of all, pois'd on yourself,
   giving not taking law,
You womanhood divine, mistress and source of all, whence life
   and love and aught that comes from life and love,
You unseen moral essence of all the vast materials of America,
   (age upon age working in death the same as life,)
You that, sometimes known, oftener unknown, really shape and
   mould the New World, adjusting it to Time and Space,
You hidden national will lying in your abysms, conceal'd but ever
   alert,
You past and present purposes tenaciously pursued,
   may-be unconscious of yourselves,
Unswerv'd by all the passing errors, perturbations of the surface;
You vital, universal, deathless germs, beneath all creeds, arts,
   statutes, literature,
Here build your homes for good, establish here, these areas en-
   tire, lands of the Western shore,
We pledge, we dedicate to you.

For man of you, your characteristic race,
Here may be hardy, sweet, gigantic grow, here tower proportion-
   ate to Nature,
Here climb the vast pure spaces unconfined, uncheck'd by wall or
   roof,
Here laugh with storm or sun, here joy, here patiently inure,
Here heed himself, unfold himself, (not others' formulas heed,)
   here fill his time,
To duly fall, to aid, unreck'd at last,
To disappear, to serve.

Thus on the northern coast,
In the echo of teamsters' calls and the clinking chains,
        and the music of choppers' axes,
The falling trunk and limbs, the crash, the muffled shriek, the
        groan,
Such words combined from the redwood-tree, as of voices ec-
        static, ancient and rustling,
The century-lasting, unseen dryads, singing, withdrawing,
All their recesses of forests and mountains leaving,
From the Cascade range to the Wahsatch, or Idaho far, or Utah,
To the deities of the modern henceforth yielding,
The chorus and indications, the vistas of coming humanity,
        the settlements, features all,
In the Mendocino woods I caught.

2.

The flashing and golden pageant of California,
The sudden and gorgeous drama, the sunny and ample lands,
The long and varied stretch from Puget Sound to Colorado south,
Lands bathed in sweeter, rarer, healthier air, valleys and moun-
        tain cliffs,
The fields of Nature long prepared and fallow, the silent, cyclic
        chemistry,
The slow and steady ages plodding, the unoccupied surface
        ripening, the rich ores forming beneath;
At last the New arriving, assuming, taking possession,
A swarming and busy race settling and organizing everywhere,
Ships coming in from the whole round world,
        and going out to the whole world,
To India and China and Australia and the thousand island para-
        dises of the Pacific,
Populous cities, the latest inventions, the steamers on the rivers,
        the railroads, with many a thrifty farm, with machinery,
And wool and wheat and the grape, and diggings of yellow gold.

3.

But more in you than these, lands of the Western shore,
(These but the means, the implements, the standing-ground,)
I see in you, certain to come, the promise of thousands of years,
        till now deferr'd,
Promis'd to be fulfill'd, our common kind, the race.

The new society at last, proportionate to Nature,
In man of you, more than your mountain peaks or stalwart trees
        imperial,
In woman more, far more, than all your gold or vines, or even
        vital air.

Fresh come, to the new world indeed, yet long prepared,
I see the genius of the modern, child of the real and ideal,
Clearing the ground for broad humanity, the true America,
        heir of the past so grand,
To build a grander future.

From *Leaves of Grass,* Walt Whitman (Camden, N.J.: Author's Edition, 1876).

XLVIII

Isabella Lucy Bird

While the Central Pacific was under construction, Truckee, on the eastern slope of the Sierra, had developed into a lusty lumbering center more important than any camp in the Mendocino country, and after supplying millions of board feet for the snowsheds and trestles on the rail line, it kept thriving. Truckee was distinctly a man's town; it was no place for a lady who valued her reputation. But peripatetic Isabella Lucy Bird (1831–1904), the emancipated British globetrotter, horsewoman, and correspondent, was not one to be bothered by California's social conventions. To her San Francisco was a "weariness" and a "clang"; Sacramento "very repulsive." So she headed straight for Truckee.

Miss Bird did not come to California to visit, sightsee, or size up the place; she was merely passing through en route to the Rockies, New York, and England after a cruise to Australia and the Sandwich Islands. On this trip, late in the summer of 1873, she planned to do most of her American touring in the Colorado mountains and had little time to waste on California; Truckee would be her only stop of consequence.

Under any ordinary standards of travel Miss Bird would have been totally disqualified from either invading or evaluating such a masculine realm: she was an invalid, inflicted with an incurable spinal disorder, and she was the daughter of a conservative clergyman. But despite these handicaps, she set out to see the world on adventure

[329]

after adventure, traveling at a pace that would have outdistanced a Phineas Fogg. Ill health was never permitted to interfere with her journeys, many of which were in the interest of good works—establishment of hospitals in remote countries, aiding underprivileged humanity in a big way, organizing mass emigration movements. India, Tibet, Kashmir, Canada, Persia, New Zealand, Palestine, Japan, China, and Korea were all included in her itineraries. So remarkable was her career that she was elected a Fellow of the Royal Geographical Society —the first woman so honored. Accordingly, there was nothing extraordinary about the brief appearance of this lone woman in the male-oriented backwoods of California—and as was her habit, no sooner had she arrived at a spot that she wanted to explore than she was astride a horse cantering off by herself.

The Trail to Tahoe

The cars drew up in a street [at Truckee]—if street that could be called which was only a wide, cleared space intersected by rails, with here and there a stump, and great piles of sawn logs bulking big in the moonlight, and a number of irregular clapboard, steep-roofed houses, many of them with open fronts, glaring with light and crowded with men. We had pulled up at the door of a rough Western hotel with a partially open front, being a barroom crowded with men drinking and smoking, and the space between it and the cars was a moving mass of loafers and passengers.

On the tracks, engines tolling heavy bells were mightily moving, the glare from their cyclopean eyes dulling the light of a forest which was burning fitfully on a mountain side; and on open spaces great fires of pine logs were burning cheerily with groups of men around them. A band was playing noisily, and the unholy sound of tom-toms was not far off. Mountains—the Sierras of many a fireside dream—seemed to wall in the town, and great pines stood out sharp and clear against a sky in which a moon and stars were shining frostily.

It was a sharp frost at that great height, and when an "irrepressible nigger," who seemed to represent the hotel establishment, deposited me and my carpetbag in a room which answered for "the parlor," I was glad to find some remains of pine knots still alight in the stove. A man came in and said that when the cars were gone he would try to get me a room, but they were so full that it would be a very poor one. The crowd was solely masculine. It was then 11:30 P.M., and I had not had a meal since 6 A.M., but when I asked hopefully for a hot supper with tea, I was told that no supper could be got at that hour; but in half an hour the same man returned with a small cup of cold weak tea and a small slice of bread, which looked as if it had been much handled.

I asked the Negro factotum about the hire of horses and presently a man came in from the bar who, he said, could supply my needs. This man, the very type of a Western pioneer, bowed, threw himself into a rocking chair, drew up a spittoon beside him, cut a fresh quid of tobacco, began to chew energetically, and put his feet, cased in miry high boots, into which his trousers were tucked, on the top of the stove. He said he had horses which would both "lope" and trot, that some ladies preferred the Mexican saddle, that I could ride alone in perfect safety; and after a route had been devised, I hired a horse for two days. This man wore a pioneer's badge as one of the earliest settlers in California, but he had moved on as one place after another had become too civilized for him. "But nothing," he added, "was likely to change much in Truckee."

I was afterward told that the usual regular hours of sleep are not observed there. The accommodation is too limited for the population of 2,000, which is masculine mainly, and is liable to frequent temporary additions, and beds are occupied continuously, though by different occupants, throughout the greater part of the twenty-four hours. Consequently I found the bed and room allotted to me quite tumbled looking. Men's coats and sticks were hanging up, miry boots were littered about, and a rifle was in one corner. There was no window to the outer air, but I slept soundly, being only once awoke by an increase of the same din in which I had fallen asleep, varied by three pistol shots fired in rapid succession.

This morning Truckee wore a totally different aspect. The

crowds of the night before had disappeared. There were heaps of
ashes where the fires had been. A sleepy German waiter seemed
the only person about the premises; the open drinking saloons
were nearly empty; and only a few sleepy-looking loafers hung
about in what is called the street. It might have been Sunday, but
they say that it brings a great accession of throng and jollity.
Public worship has died out at present; work is discontinued on
Sunday, but the day is given up to pleasure.

Putting a minimum of indispensables into a bag and slipping on
my Hawaiian riding dress [a loose-fitting jacket, ankle-length skirt
and full Turkish trousers gathered into frills over riding boots],
over a silk skirt and a dust cloak over all, I stealthily crossed the
plaza to the livery stable, the largest building in Truckee, where
twelve fine horses were stabled in stalls on each side of a broad
drive. My friend of the evening before showed me his "rig," three
velvet-covered side saddles almost without horns.

Some ladies, he said, used the horn of the Mexican saddle, but
none "in the part" rode cavalier fashion. I felt abashed. I could
not ride any distance in the conventional mode and was just going
to give up this splendid "ravage" when the man said, "Ride your
own fashion; here at Truckee, if anywhere in the world, people
can do as they like." Blissful Truckee! In no time a large gray
horse was "rigged out" in a handsome silver-bossed Mexican
saddle with ornamental leather tassels hanging from the stirrup
guards and the housing of black bear's skin.

I strapped my silk skirt on the saddle, deposited my cloak in
the cornbin and was safely on the horse's back before his owner
had time to devise any way of mounting me. Neither he nor any
of the loafers who had assembled showed the slightest sign of
astonishment, but all were as respectful as possible.

Once on horseback my embarrassment disappeared and I rode
through Truckee, whose irregular, steep-roofed houses and shanties, set down in a clearing and surrounded closely by mountain
and forest, looked like a temporary encampment; passed under
the Pacific Railroad; and then for twelve miles followed the
windings of the Truckee River, a clear, rushing mountain stream,
in which immense pine logs had gone aground, not to be floated

off till the next freshet. . . . All was bright with that brilliancy of sky and atmosphere, that blaze of sunshine and universal glitter which I never saw until I came to California, combined with an elasticity in the air which removes all lassitude and gives one spirit enough for anything. On either side of the Truckee great sierras rose like walls, castellated, embattled, rifted, skirted and crowned with pines of enormous size, the walls now and then breaking apart to show some snow-slashed peak rising into a heaven of intense, unclouded, sunny blue. . . .

At this altitude of 6,000 feet . . . I feasted my eyes on pines which . . . are really gigantic, attaining a height of 250 feet. . . . Pines cleft the sky; they were massed wherever level ground occurred; they stood over the Truckee at right angles, or lay across it in prostrate grandeur. Their stumps and carcasses were everywhere; and smooth "shoots" on the sierras marked where they were shot down as "felled timber," to be floated off by the river. To them this wild region owes its scattered population, and the sharp ring of the lumberer's axe mingles with the cries of wild beasts and the roar of mountain torrents.

. . . I met nobody and passed nothing on the road but a freight wagon drawn by twenty-two oxen, guided by three fine-looking men, who had some difficulty in making room for me to pass their awkward convoy. After I had ridden about ten miles the road went up a steep hill in the forest, turned abruptly, and through the blue gloom of the great pines which rose from the ravine in which the river was then hid, came glimpses of two mountains, about 11,000 feet in height, whose bald gray summits were crowned with pure snow. It was one of those glorious surprises in scenery which make one feel as if one must bow down and worship.

The forest was thick and had an undergrowth of dwarf spruce and brambles, but as the horse had become fidgety and scary on the track, I turned off in the idea of taking a short cut, and was sitting carelessly shortening my stirrup when a great, dark, hairy beast rose, crashing and snorting, out of the tangle just in front of me. I had only a glimpse of him and thought my imagination had magnified a wild boar, but it was a bear.

The horse snorted and plunged violently as if he would go down to the river, and then turned, still plunging, up a steep bank, when, finding that I must come off, I threw myself off on the right side, where the ground rose considerably, so that I had not far to fall. I got up covered with dust, but neither shaken nor bruised. It was truly grotesque and humiliating.

The bear ran in one direction and the horse in another. I hurried after the latter, and twice he stopped till I was close to him, then turned round and cantered away. After walking about a mile in deep dust, I picked up first the saddle blanket and next my bag, and soon came upon the horse, standing facing me and shaking all over. I thought I should catch him then, but when I went up to him he turned round, threw up his heels several times, rushed off the track, galloped in circles, bucking, kicking and plunging for some time, and then throwing up his heels as an act of final defiance, went off at full speed in the direction of Truckee . . . while I trudged ignominiously along in the dust, laboriously carrying the bag and saddle blanket.

I walked for nearly an hour, heated and hungry, when to my joy I saw the ox-team halted across the top of the gorge and one of the teamsters leading the horse toward me. The young man said that, seeing the horse coming, they had drawn the team across the road to stop him . . . and had just saddled one of their own horses to go in search of me. He brought me some water to wash the dust from my face and resaddled the horse, but the animal snorted and plunged for some time before he would let me mount, and then sidled along in such a nervous and scared way that the teamster walked for some distance by me to see that I was "all right." He said that the woods in the neighborhood of Tahoe had been full of brown and grizzly bears for some days, but that no one was in danger from them. I took a long gallop beyond the scene of my tumble to quiet the horse, who was most restless and troublesome.

Then the scenery became truly magnificent and bright with life. . . . The gorge opened, and this mountain-girdled lake lay before me, with its margin broken up into bays and promontories, most picturesquely clothed by huge sugar pines. It lay dimpling and scintillating beneath the noonday sun, as entirely unspoilt as fifteen years ago when its pure loveliness was known only to trappers and Indians. . . . On its margin I found an irregular wooden inn, with a lumber wagon at the door, on which was the carcass of a large grizzly bear, shot behind the house this morning. . . . Bewitched by the beauty and serenity of Tahoe, I have remained here sketching, reveling in the view from the veranda and strolling in the forest. . . . The beauty is entrancing. . . .

As night came on, the cold intensified, and the stove in the parlor attracted everyone. A San Francisco lady, much "got up" in paint, emerald green velvet, Brussels lace and diamonds, rattled continuously for the amusement of the company, giving descriptions of persons and scenes in a racy Western twang without the slightest scruple as to what she said. In a few years Tahoe will be inundated in summer with similar vulgarity. . . .

I dreamt of bears so vividly that I woke with a furry death hug at my throat, but feeling quite refreshed. When I mounted my horse after breakfast the sun was high and the air so keen and intoxicating that, giving the animal his head, I galloped up and down hill feeling completely tireless. Truly that air is the elixir of life. I had a glorious ride back to Truckee. . . . My horse was so excitable that I avoided the center of Truckee and skulked through a collection of Chinamen's shanties to the stable. . . . Truckee was at the height of its evening revelries—fires blazing out of doors, barrooms and saloons crammed, lights glaring, gaming tables thronged, fiddle and banjo in frightful discord, and the air ringing with ribaldry and profanity.

Precisely at 11 P.M. the huge Pacific train, with its heavy bell tolling, thundered up to the door of the Truckee House, and on presenting my ticket at the double door of a "Silver Palace" car, the slippered steward, whispering low, conducted me to my berth—a luxurious bed three and a half feet wide, with a hair mattress on springs, fine linen sheets and costly California blankets. The twenty-four inmates of the car were all invisible, asleep behind rich curtains. . . . Four silver lamps, hanging from the roof and burning low, gave a dreamy light. On each side of the center passage rich rep curtains, green and crimson, striped with gold, hung from silver bars running near the roof, and trailed on the soft Axminster carpet. The temperature was carefully kept at 70°. It was 29° outside. Silence and freedom from jolting were secured by double doors and windows, costly and ingenious arrangements of springs and cushions, and a speed limited to eighteen miles an hour.

As I lay down, the gallop under the dark pines, the frosty moon, the forest fires, the flaring lights and roaring din of Truckee faded as dreams fade.

From *A Lady's Life in the Rocky Mountains*, Isabella L. Bird (New York: G. P. Putnam's Sons, 1881).

XLIX

Kate Douglas Wiggin

Almost simultaneous to Miss Bird's trip across the state came another vivacious equestrienne, Kate Douglas Wiggin (1859–1923), distinguished educator, writer, actress, musician, lecturer, traveler, and associate of the great literati of her day. But Kate's career was then all ahead of her; she was in her early teens and in no hurry to explore any country except the surroundings of Santa Barbara, her "Paradise on earth."

She came from the land of the lumbermen—from Bar Mills, Maine, where her stepfather was a highly respected and prosperous, but indisposed, country doctor. In medical circles, California was just beginning to be recognized as an ideal asylum for valetudinarians who could afford the transcontinental train fare, and when the doctor finally diagnosed his ailment as "a little weakness of the lungs," he prescribed Santa Barbara as the future home for himself and family.

Young Kate immediately fell in love with the old mission town, and if her stepfather's prescription had effected the cure he hoped for, she would undoubtedly have been victimized by its spell, would have continued to enjoy a life of ease, married a respectable rancher or local businessman and lived in happy freedom from renown. But after investing all the family fortune in Santa Barbara real estate, the doctor suddenly died, the bottom dropped out of the land boom, and a wife and three children were left penniless.

Kate immediately found it necessary to assume responsibility for the financial welfare of the family. She took on a job as church organist, not daring to admit that she had never before touched the keys of an organ; she started writing children's stories for St. Nicholas Magazine, never before having written anything longer than a letter; then, as a complete amateur in the field of education, she turned to teaching, and organized the first free kindergarten on the Pacific Coast.

In rapid succession after that came international fame in other fields and as author of Rebecca of Sunny Brook Farm and creator of Mother Carey, Penelope, Patsy, Timothy, and a long cast of characters beloved by generations of children around the world. But through all her remarkable career she always remembered the years in Santa Barbara before the death of her stepfather as "the most irresponsible, delightful, entirely healthful and enchanting" part of her life.

Paradise on Earth

No words can describe the loveliness of Santa Barbara with its semi-tropical atmosphere, its luxuriance of foliage and flowers, its lovely semicircle of mountains, its blue, blue sea!

I had been used to the deep snows and late reluctant springs of Maine. In California, when the rains had ceased, April was a revelation of beauty hitherto unimagined. We had a pleasant house, although there were no positively unpleasant ones to be found, for where fuchsias and geraniums climb up and hang over the fences, and rosebushes, staggering under the wealth of bloom, hide all defects of architecture or lack of paint, the enchanted eye refuses to find a flaw.

On and near the foothills and in the canyons the wild hyacinths were out, lupins and poppies, too, and acres upon acres of baby blue eyes in damp hollows and shady places. There was a breath of sweetness from budding fruit trees, fragrance of orange blossoms, and every poor man's garden was the equal of a millionaire's conservatory.

The sun was never shy, surly, indifferent or capricious; he seemed to have an adequate idea of his duty in the world. So also had the myriads of stars (there seemed to be thousands more than in New England); and as for the moon—that orb is responsible for enough mischief in temperate climes, but the Southern California moon is in a class by itself. This assertion may not be entirely scientific, but its admirers, or those who have been affected by its rays, will swear that the moon is far brighter, bigger, yellower, and more dangerous, than elsewhere, and that it is suspended in its clear blue canopy of sky in a way unlike other moons in other skies.

There was good society in Santa Barbara, both for young and old. There were few dances save those under the famous grapevine in the Montecito Valley, because there was so much bathing and horseback riding, so many picnics in the Cathedral Oaks and along the many trails through the canyons, so many suppers on the beach—in short, such a habit of living out of doors morning, noon and evening, that there was little time for indoor gaieties.

Our attending squires were charming companions, mostly Eastern college men of good family, sometimes looking (not too energetically) for bargains in fruit farms and sheep ranches; now and then needing a soft climate for some slight throat trouble; oftentimes merely resting a season after stupendous intellectual labors at Harvard or Yale.

How stimulating were our horseback rides on the beach at low tide; our country gallops along trails leading through towering groves of wild yellow mustard to some hospitable ranch for luncheon, our return winding up in a hilarious attempt to "lope" twelve abreast down Santa Barbara's main street, a dangerous and reckless experiment that never ended in, though it often appeared to presage, a universal slaughter of the inhabitants.

My little white bronco, Blanquita, was saddled and tied to the horse block every morning, and I frequently rode in the afternoon a *palomino* horse from the livery stable, hard of mouth and heavy of foot, but strong and handsome.

That we never had any accidents worth mentioning shows our horsemanship, for almost all broncos "buck" when so disposed, and to keep one's seat while they are clambering up some slippery mountain trail with loose sand and rolling pebbles underfoot means something in the way of pluck and ability. It was a free, eager, venturesome joyous life altogether, and if I had a dozen daughters I should like those born in the East to have a breath of the West, while I would send California girls to the East for a year or two.

From *My Garden of Memory: An Autobiography*, Kate Douglas Wiggin (Boston and New York: Houghton Mifflin Company, 1923).

L

John Muir

Ever since the expulsion of the scholarly Spanish mission padres, California had been bereft of its full quota of intellectual nourishment. Men of learning and culture were so vastly outnumbered by ragtag throngs whose consummate interest was in gold, gambling, and a good time that savants were commonly regarded as mavericks. Outside a few places like Santa Barbara and San Francisco, Californians were not very hospitable to collegians, philosophers, and prophets.

Naturalist John Muir (1838–1914) was not the first to discover this. He reached California in 1868 at the age of thirty, much more interested in the scenery of the West than its society. To convivial Californians he was all too obviously a loner and a sophist, and his rich Scotch brogue, which student years at the University of Wisconsin had failed to erode, helped to set him apart. In order to get into the back country, he took a job as sheepherder, only to learn that he hated sheep with a passion, for they were devouring the very greenery he had come to worship. That same enmity soon extended to all other agents that were disfiguring the landscape—especially mankind.

Muir became a recluse among a predominantly gregarious people; a campaigner for the unpopular cause of conservation; a lone voice decrying the destroyers of natural beauty in an era when everyone else was devoting his energies to slashing forests, clearing meadows, and disrupting watersheds in the interests of mining, agriculture, and industry. Eventually Muir retreated to Yosemite Valley for long periods where he would not have to observe the ravages of his fellow beings.

For a long generation Muir was the state's most outspoken conservationist, the crusader for national parks and reservations, the author of half a dozen classics on the California wilds, a man whom future generations of Americans would revere because he, almost single-handed, had made possible a publicly owned Yosemite, a relatively unscathed Lake Tahoe, and preserves of a few clumps of Big Trees.

To most of his contemporaries, however, John Muir was a queer, crazy fanatic. While sane folks of the high mountains were cozying up to their stoves during a blizzard, likely as not he was out wading in the drifts, reveling in the wonderland of snow; while normal outdoorsmen were stalking game with a gun, he was playing St. Francis, chattering with a squirrel, tossing grain to the birds, tempting an unfriendly grizzly to come a friendly foot closer to him; while citizens of Sacramento were hysterically fighting the great floods of 1874–75, he was wandering upstream in the rain, soaked to the skin, ecstatically enjoying the thrash of windswept trees, the drama and excitement of the storm, the rush of the very waters that were inundating California's capital city.

Storms Are Fine Speakers

Strange to say, the greatest floods [of the Sierra] occur in winter, when one would suppose all the wild waters would be muffled and chained in frost and snow. The same long, all-day storms of the so-called Rainy Season in California that give rain to the lowlands, give dry frosty snow to the mountains. But at rare intervals warm rains and warm winds invade the mountains and push back the snow line from 2000 feet to 8000, or even higher, and then come the big floods.

I was usually driven down out of the High Sierra about the end of November, but the winter of 1874 and 1875 was so warm and calm that I was tempted to seek general views of the geology and topography of the basin of Feather River in January. And I had just completed a hasty survey of the region and made my way

down to winter quarters when one of the grandest flood-storms
that I ever saw broke on the mountains.

I was then in the edge of the main forest belt at a small foothill
town called Knoxville, on the divide between the waters of the
Feather and Yuba rivers. The cause of this notable flood was
simply a sudden and copious fall of warm wind and rain on the
basins of these rivers at a time when they contained a considerable quantity of snow. The rain was so heavy and long-sustained
that it was of itself sufficient to make a good wild flood, while the
snow which the warm wind and rain melted on the upper and
middle regions of the basins was sufficient to make another flood
equal to that of the rain. Now these two distinct harvests of flood
waters were gathered simultaneously and poured out on the plain
in one magnificent avalanche. . . .

It is a pity that but few people meet and enjoy storms so noble
as this in their homes in the mountains, for, spending themselves
in the open levels of the plains, they are likely to be remembered
more by the bridges and houses they carry away than by the
beauty or the thousand blessings they bring to the fields and
gardens of Nature.

On the morning of the flood, January 19th, all the Feather and
Yuba landscapes were covered with running water, muddy torrents filled every gulch and ravine, and the sky was thick with
rain. The pines had long been sleeping in sunshine; they were
now awake, roaring and waving with the beating storm, and the
winds sweeping along the curves of hill and dale, streaming
through the woods, surging and gurgling on the tops of rocky
ridges, made the wildest of wild storm melody.

It was easy to see that only a small part of the rain reached the
ground in the form of drops. Most of it was thrashed into dusty
spray like that into which small waterfalls are divided when they
dash on shelving rocks. Never have I seen water coming from the
sky in denser or more passionate streams. The wind chased the
spray forward in choking drifts, and compelled me again and
again to seek shelter in the dell copses and back of large trees to
rest and catch my breath.

Wherever I went, on ridges or in hollows, enthusiastic water still flashed and gurgled about my ankles, recalling a wild winter flood in Yosemite when a hundred waterfalls came booming and chanting together and filled the grand valley with a sealike roar.

After drifting an hour or two in the lower woods, I set out for the summit of a hill 900 feet high, with a view to getting as near the heart of the storm as possible. In order to reach it I had to cross Dry Creek, a tributary of the Yuba that goes crawling along the base of the hill on the northwest. It was now a booming river as large as the Tuolumne at ordinary stages, its current brown with mining mud washed down from many a "claim," and mottled with sluice-boxes, fence rails and logs that had long lain above its reach.

A slim foot-bridge stretched across it, now scarcely above the swollen current. Here I was glad to linger, gazing and listening, while the storm was in its richest mood—the gray rain-flood above, the brown river-flood beneath. The language of the river was scarcely less enchanting than that of the wind and rain; the sublime overboom of the main bouncing, exultant current, the swash and gurgle of the eddies, the keen dash and clash of heavy waves breaking against rocks, and the smooth, downy hush of shallow currents feeling their way through the willow thickets of the margin. And amid all this varied throng of sounds I heard the smothered bumping and rumbling of boulders on the bottom as they were shoving and rolling forward against one another in a wild rush, after having lain still for probably a hundred years or more.

The glad creek rose high above its banks and wandered from its channel out over many a briery sandflat and meadow. Alders and willows waist-deep were bearing up against the current with nervous trembling gestures, as if afraid of being carried away, while supple branches, bending confidingly, dipped lightly and rose again, as if stroking the wild waters in play. . . .

Nor was the flood confined to the ground. Every tree had a water system of its own, spreading far and wide like miniature Amazons and Mississippis.

Toward midday, cloud, wind and rain reached their highest development. The storm was in full bloom, and formed, from my commanding outlook on the hilltop, one of the most glorious views I ever beheld. As far as the eye could reach, above, beneath and around, wind-driven rain filled the air like a vast waterfall. Detached clouds swept imposingly up the valley, as if they were endowed with independent motion and had special work to do in replenishing the mountain wells, now rising above the pine tops, now descending into their midst, fondling their arrowy spires and soothing every branch and leaf with gentleness in the midst of all the savage sound and motion. . . .

I watched the gestures of the pines while the storm was at its height, and it was easy to see that they were not distressed. Several large Sugar Pines stood near the thicket in which I was sheltered, bowing solemnly and tossing their long arms as if interpreting the very words of the storm while accepting its wildest onsets with passionate exhilaration. The lions were feeding. . . .

Calms like sleep come upon landscapes just as they do on people and trees, and storms awaken them in the same way. In the dry midsummer of the lower portion of the range the withered hills and valleys seem to lie as empty and expressionless as dead shells on a shore. Even the highest mountains may be found occasionally dull and uncommunicative as if in some way they had lost countenance and shrunk to less than half their real stature. But when the lightnings crash and echo in the canyons, and the clouds come down wreathing and crowning their bald snowy heads, every feature beams with expression and they rise again in all their imposing majesty.

Storms are fine speakers, and tell all they know, but their voices of lightning, torrent and rushing wind are much less numerous than the nameless still, small voices too low for human ears; and because we are poor listeners we fail to catch much that is fairly within reach. Our best rains are heard mostly on roofs and winds in chimneys; and when by choice or compulsion we are pushed into the heart of a storm, the confusion made by cumbersome equipments and nervous haste and mean fear prevent our hearing any other than the loudest expressions. . . .

Toward the middle of the afternoon the main flood cloud lifted along its western border, revealing a beautiful section of the Sacramento Valley some twenty or thirty miles away, brilliantly sun-lighted and glistening with rain sheets as if paved with silver. Soon afterward a jagged blufflike cloud with a sheer face appeared over the valley of the Yuba, dark-colored and roughened with numerous furrows like some huge lava table. The blue Coast Range was seen stretching along the sky like a beveled wall, and the sombre, craggy Marysville Buttes rose impressively out of the flooded plain like islands out of the sea.

Then the rain began to abate and I sauntered down through the dripping bushes revelling in the universal vigor and freshness that inspired all the life about me. How clean and unworn and immortal the woods seemed to be!—the lofty cedars in full bloom laden with golden pollen and their washed plumes shining; the pines rocking gently and settling back into rest, and the evening sunbeams spangling on the broad leaves of the madroños. . . . Every moss that had ever lived seemed to be coming crowding back from the dead to clothe each trunk and stone in living green. The steaming ground seemed fairly to throb and tingle with life . . . and innumerable green and yellow buds were peeping and smiling everywhere.

As for the birds and squirrels, not a wing or tail of them was to be seen while the storm was blowing. Squirrels dislike wet weather more than cats do; therefore they were at home rocking in their dry nests. The birds were hiding in the dells out of the wind, some of the strongest of them pecking at acorns and manzanita berries, but most were perched on low twigs, their breast feathers puffed out and keeping one another company through the hard time as best they could.

When I arrived at the village about sundown, the good people bestirred themselves, pitying my bedraggled condition as if I were some benumbed castaway snatched from the sea, while I in turn, warm with excitement and reeking like the ground, pitied them for being dry and defrauded of all the glory that Nature had spread round about them that day.

From *The Mountains of California,* John Muir (New York: Century Company, 1903).

LI

Robert Louis Stevenson

Less than thirty years after the start of the gold rush, upland California was littered with the ruins of an abandoned civilization, frowzy, dilapidated, debris-strewn ghost towns left to the mercy of the elements and the marauding of time, wild life, and human prowlers. There were more deserted towns than in any other region of the modern world. Silverado, on the slope of Mount Saint Helena in the Coast Range, was a fair example. It had once been a prosperous, riproaring mining village; in 1880 it was totally derelict. But in the summer of that year, life and a kind of immortality were restored to Silverado through the person of one of the century's foremost English writers, Robert Louis Stevenson (1850–1894).

The principal distinction Stevenson had earned at the time was through his vagabond books—the recounting of a canoe trip through Belgium and France in *An Inland Voyage*, and *Travels with a Donkey in the Cévennes*. *Treasure Island*, *Kidnapped*, *Dr. Jekyll and Mr. Hyde*, *The Master of Ballantrae* were all far in the offing. Complications of circumstance brought him to California. Three years earlier, in the sleepy little art colony of Grez, France, he had met the rather charming, vivacious wife of a California prospector and political ne'er-do-well of the West, Mrs. Samuel C. (Fanny) Osbourne. The amorous intrigue that followed was interrupted by Fanny's decision in 1878 to return to California, either to patch things up with the husband, who had virtually deserted her, or to seek a divorce.

Within a few months after her arrival in California, Stevenson received a persuasive plea to join her. Almost immediately he took
passage for New York, and there boarded the slow transcontinental
train for San Francisco. The voyage across the Atlantic was later
chronicled in *The Amateur Emigrant* and the dreary rail trip in *Across
the Plains.* He found Fanny at Monterey, where he took time out from
a cautious courtship to write his essay, "The Old Pacific Capital"; then
followed her to Oakland, where she was finally divorced from Osbourne. The persistent suitor and Fanny were married on May 19,
1880.

Before leaving England, Stevenson had confided to a friend: "I
want—a holiday; I want to be happy; I want the moon or the sun or
something. I want the object of my affections badly anyway; and a big
forest; and fine breathing, sweating, sunny walks; and the trees all
crying aloud in a summer wind, and a camp under the stars."

He found just what he was looking for at Silverado, where the two
spent their honeymoon as squatters in a ghost town. It was the kind of
eerie but enchanting hideaway that suited Stevenson's nature to perfection. "One feels more Stevenson in the air at Silverado," commented
biographer J. C. Furnas, "than anywhere else except in Edinburgh and
environs."

The Silence of Silverado

We followed a good road along the hillside through the forest,
until suddenly that road widened out and came abruptly to an
end. A canyon, woody below, red, rocky and naked overhead, was
here walled across by a dump of rolling stones, dangerously steep,
and from twenty to thirty feet in height. A rusty iron chute on
wooden legs came flying, like a monstrous gargoyle, across the
parapet. It was down this that they poured the precious ore; and
below here the carts stood to wait their lading, and carry it mill-
ward down the mountain.

The whole canyon was so entirely blocked . . . that we could
only mount by lengths of wooden ladder fixed in the hillside.
These led us round the farther corner of the dump; and when
they were at an end, we still persevered over loose rubble and

wading deep in poison oak, till we struck a triangular platform
filling up the whole glen, and shut in on either hand by bold
projections of the mountain. Only in front the place was open like
the proscenium of a theatre, and we looked forth into a great
realm of air, and down upon treetops and hilltops, and far and
near on wild and varied country.

The place still stood as on the day it was deserted: a line of iron
rails with a bifurcation; a truck in working order; a world of
lumber, old wood, old iron; a blacksmith's forge on one side, half
buried in the leaves of dwarf madronas; and on the other, an old
brown wooden house.

Fanny and I dashed for the house. It consisted of three rooms,
and was so plastered against the hill that one room was right
atop of another, that the upper floor was more than twice as large
as the lower, and that all three apartments must be entered from
a different side and level. Not a window sash remained. The door
of the lower room was smashed, and one panel hung in splinters.
We entered that and found a fair amount of rubbish: sand and
gravel that had been sifted in there by the mountain winds;
straw, sticks and stones, a table, a barrel; a plate rack on the wall;
two home-made bootjacks, signs of miners and their boots. . . .

The room immediately above could only be entered by a plank
propped against the threshold, along which the intruder must
foot it gingerly, clutching for support to sprays of poison oak, the
proper product of the country. Herein was on either hand a triple
tier of beds where miners had once lain; and the other gable was
pierced by a sashless window and a doorless doorway opening on
the air of heaven, five feet above the ground. As for the third
room, which entered squarely from the ground level, but higher
up the hill and further up the canyon, it contained only rubbish
and the uprights for another triple tier of beds.

The whole building was overhung by a bold, lionlike red rock.
Poison oak, sweet bay trees, calycanthus, brush and chaparral
grew freely but sparsely all about it. In front, in the strong sunshine, the platform lay overstrewn with busy litter as though the
labors of the mine might begin tomorrow in the morning.

Following back into the canyon among the mass of rotting

plant and through the flowering bushes, we came to a great crazy staging with a wry windlass on the top; and clambering up, we could look into an open shaft, leading edgeways down into the bowels of the mountain, trickling with water and lit by some stray sun gleams. . . . But in the tunnel a cold, wet draught tempestuously blew. Nor have I ever known that place otherwise than cold and windy.

Such was our first prospect of Juan Silverado. I own I had looked for something different: a clique of neighborly houses on a village green, we shall say, all empty to be sure, but swept and varnished; a trout stream brawling by; great elms or chestnuts humming with bees and nested in by song birds; and the mountains standing round about as at Jerusalem. Here mountain and house and the old tools of industry were all alike rust and downfalling. The hill was here wedged up, and there poured forth its bowels in a spout of broken mineral; man with his picks and powder, and nature with her own great blasting tools of sun and rain, laboring together at the ruin of that proud mountain.

The view up the canyon was a glimpse of devastation; dry red minerals sliding together, here and there a crag, here and there dwarf thicket clinging in the general glissade, and over all a broken outline trenching on the blue of heaven. Downward indeed, from our rock eyrie we beheld the greener side of nature; and the bearing of the pines and the sweet smell of bays and nutmegs commended themselves to our senses. . . .

The lower room had been the assayer's office. The floor was thick with debris—part human from the former occupants; part natural, sifted in by mountain winds. In a sea of red dust there swam or floated sticks, boards, hay, straw, stones and paper; ancient newspapers above all . . . and bills of the Silverado boarding house, some dated Silverado, some Calistoga Mine. . . . We scraped some of the rougher dirt off the floor and left it. That was our sitting room and kitchen, though there was nothing to sit upon but the table, and no provision for a fire except a hole in the roof of the room above, which had once contained the chimney of a stove.

To the upper room we now proceeded. There were the

eighteen bunks in a double tier, nine on either hand, where from eighteen to thirty-six miners had once snored together all night long. . . . There was the roof, with a hole in it through which the sun now shot an arrow. There was the floor, in much the same state as the one below, though, perhaps there was more hay, and certainly there was the added ingredient of broken glass, the man who stole the window frames having apparently made a miscarriage with this one. . . . The one bright arrow of day in that gaunt and shattered barrack made the rest look dirtier and darker, and the sight drove us at last into the open. . . .

I set to work with pick and shovel, and deepened the pool behind the shaft, till we were sure of sufficient water for the morning; and by the time I had finished, the sun had begun to go down behind the mountain shoulder, the platform was plunged in quiet shadow and a chill descended from the sky. Night began early in our cleft. . . . There was no stove, of course, and no hearth in our lodging, so we betook ourselves to the blacksmith's forge across the platform. . . . For a while it was even pleasant in the forge, with a blaze in the midst and a look over our shoulders on the woods and mountains where the day was dying like a dolphin. . . .

We turned, with our last spark of courage, to the bedroom. We had improved the entrance, but it was still a kind of rope walking; and it would have been droll to see us mounting, one after another, by candlelight, under the open stars. . . . Two lowest bunks . . . we roughly filled with hay for that night's use . . . and when we were once in bed, we lay, awaiting sleep, in a haunted, incomplete obscurity. At first the silence of the night was utter. Then a high wind began in the distance among the tree-tops, and for hours continued to grow higher; . . . yet here in our open chamber we were fanned only by gentle and refreshing draughts, so deep was the canyon, so close our house was planted under the overhanging rock. . . .

I must try to convey some notion of our life, of how the days passed and what pleasure we took in them, of what there was to do and how we set about doing it in our mountain hermitage. The

house, after we had repaired the worst of the damages, and filled
in some of the doors and windows with white cotton cloth, became a healthy and pleasant dwelling place, always airy and dry,
and haunted by the outdoor perfumes of the glen.

Within, it had the look of habitation, the human look . . .
with the beds made, the plates on the rack, the pail of bright
water behind the door . . . and perhaps the table roughly laid
against a meal—a man's order, the little clean spots that he
creates to dwell in, were at once contrasted with the rich passiv-
ity of nature. And yet our house was everywhere so wrecked and
shattered, the air came and went so freely, the sun found so many
portholes, the golden outdoor glow shone in so many open chinks,
that we enjoyed at the same time some of the comforts of a roof
and much of the gaiety and brightness of al fresco life. A single
shower of rain, to be sure, and we should have been drowned out
like mice. But ours was a California summer, and an earthquake
was a far likelier accident than a shower of rain.

Trustful of this fine weather, we kept the house for kitchen and
bedroom, and used the platform as our summer parlor. The sense
of privacy . . . was complete. We could look over the dump on
miles of forest and rough hilltop; our eyes commanded some of
Napa Valley, where the train ran, and the little country town-
ships sat so close together along the line of the rail. But there was
no man to intrude. . . .

So our days, as they were never interrupted, drew out to the
greater length; hour melted insensibly into hour; the household
duties, though they were many, and some of them laborious,
dwindled into mere islets of business in a sea of sunny daytime;
and it appears to me, looking back, as though the far greater part
of our life at Silverado had been passed propped upon an elbow
or seated on a plank, listening to the silence that there is among
the hills. . . .

To walk at all was a laborious business; the foot sank and slid,
the boots were cut to pieces, among sharp, uneven, rolling stones.
. . . If water were to be drawn, the water carrier left the house
along some tilting planks that we had laid down, and not laid
down very well. These carried him to that great highroad, the

railway; and the railway served him as far as the head of the shaft. But from thence to the spring and back again he made the best of his unaided way, staggering among the stones and wading in low growth of the calycanthus, where the rattlesnakes lay hissing at his passage. Yet I liked to draw water. It was pleasant to dip the gray metal pail into the clean, colorless, cool water; pleasant to carry it back with the water lipping at the edge, and a broken sunbeam quivering in the midst. . . .

It was only with the return of night that any change would fall on our surroundings. . . . Indeed, it would be hard to exaggerate the pleasure that we took in the approach of evening. . . . I would be fevered and weary of the staring sun; and just then he would begin courteously to withdraw his countenance, the shadows lengthened, the aromatic airs awoke, and an indescribable but happy change announced the coming of the night.

The hours of evening, when we were once curtained in the friendly dark, sped lightly. Even as with the crickets, night brought to us a certain spirit of rejoicing. It was good to taste the air; good to mark the dawning of the stars, as they increased their glittering company; good, too, to gather stones and send them crashing down the chute, a wave of light. It seemed, in some way, the reward and the fulfillment of the day. . . .

Many a night I have strolled about the platform, taking a bath of darkness before I slept. . . . [Inside] a single candle in the neck of a pint bottle was the only illumination; and yet the old cracked house seemed literally bursting with the light. It shone keen as a knife through all the vertical chinks; it struck upward through the broken shingles; and through the eastern door and window; it fell in a great splash upon the thicket and the overhanging rock. You would have said a conflagration, or at least a roaring forge; and behold, it was but a candle.

Or perhaps it was yet more strange to see the procession moving bedward round the corner of the house, and up the plank that brought us to the bedroom door; under the immense spread of the starry heavens, down in a crevice of the giant mountain, these few human shapes, with their unshielded taper, made so disproportionate a figure in the eye and mind.

But the more he is alone with nature, the greater man and his doings bulk in the consideration of his fellowmen. Miles and miles away upon the opposite hilltops, if there were any hunter belated or any traveler who had lost his way, he must have stood and watched and wondered from the time the candle issued from the door of the assayer's office till it mounted the plank and disappeared again into the miner's dormitory.

From *The Silverado Squatters*, Robert Louis Stevenson (Boston: Roberts Brothers, 1884).

LII

Mary Austin

California seemed to be crowded with destroyers intent on defacing the land: unsuccessful speculators who abandoned settlements like Silverado and let nature do what it could to curtain the ruins; miners who invariably left chaos and upheaval behind them; lumbermen who were stripping the mountainsides, inviting catastrophic fires and floods; railroaders who were blasting unsightly cuts and rockslides along the green slopes; men of commerce who were turning graceful shorelines into ugly slum-backed waterfronts; sheepmen who were encouraging their flocks to grub pleasant pastures into desert wastes. All these were unpopular with nature lovers and utopians who took the long-range view of California, but none suffered quite the scathing diatribes that were directed at the sheepmen.

Sheep raising was one of California's oldest vocations. The little flocks originally driven from Mexico by the padres proliferated until well over a million sheep were being tended by Indian shepherds on the mission ranges in 1825. But the sheep were ill-bred, shaggy, wild, bony creatures that threatened to become almost extinct after the missions were desegregated.

Twenty years later, however, three hundred hybrids arrived from New England, driven on the hoof three thousand miles across the continent, and these were soon augmented by other fine flocks imported by ship. They thrived from the start, and for the next half century sheep raising was the most profitable agricultural pursuit in the state. Hundreds of Basques, Frenchmen, and Portuguese were brought in as herdsmen to assist the Indians and Mexicans. By the 1870s California was supporting a six-million-dollar woolen industry.

But the sheep were scavengers and, to anyone except the sheepmen, a scourge. Millions of them grazed the valleys clean in winter, and then were driven into the Sierra to do the same in the mountain meadows. To John Muir, who put in a season as a herder and hated every hour of it, they were "hoofed locusts," "poor, helpless, misbegotten, semi-manufactured creatures born out of time and place, made less by God than man." "Incredible numbers are driven into the mountain pastures every summer," he stormed, "and in order to make easy paths and to improve the pastures, running fires are set everywhere to burn off the old logs and underbrush. . . . The fires of sheepmen probably form more than 90 per cent of all destructive fires that sweep the woods."

However, the sheep and the shepherds found a less prejudiced ally in Mary Austin (1868–1934), a liberally educated poet, essayist, critic, and amateur anthropologist from Illinois, who had accompanied her husband West and discovered in New Mexico and California wonderful Indian and Spanish cultures in need of a champion. She became that champion. From her pen poured volume after sympathetic volume—all so well received back East that many a critic regarded hers as "the only literary voice in California worth listening to."

Often the voice had a sentimental catch in it, but it enunciated the romance, the tragedy, the excitement of every phase of the old way of life in California. And, probably to the discomfort of John Muir, she extracted stirring yarns for her books even from the sheepherders.

They Steered a Course by the Stars

You should have seen Don José Jesús letting his cigarette die out between his fingers as he told the story of his Long Drive, young vigor and the high, clean color of romance lightening the becoming portliness of middle years. Even then you would miss something in not being able to pronounce his name with its proper soft elisions and insistent rhythm, José Jesús Lopez.

Señor Lopez began to be major-domo of the sheep at Tejon in

'74, shaped to his work by much experience in the Southwest. In
'79, that year of doubtful issues, he left La Liebre on the desert
side to drive ten thousand sheep to Cheyenne. He had with him
twelve men, none too well seasoned to the work, and a son of the
only Henry Ward Beecher for his bookkeeper. . . . Beecher left
him before accomplishing the adventure . . . but there is no
doubt Don José Jesús proved himself the better man.

They went out, I say, by La Liebre, northward across the Antelope Valley when the *chili-cojote* was in bloom and began to
traverse the Mojave Desert. Well I know that country! A huge
fawn-colored hollow, drawn on its borders into puckery hills,
guttered where they run together by fierce, infrequent rains;
mountains rear on its horizons out of tremulous deeps of air, with
mile-long beds of lava simulating cloud shadows on their streaked
sides.

Don Jesús went with his sheep in parted bands, like Jacob
taking out his flocks from Padanaram, dry camp upon dry camp,
one day like to every other. If they saw any human traces on that
journey, it might have been the Owens Valley stage whirling on
the thin, hard road, or the twenty-mule ore wagons creaking in
from the plain of Salt Wells, stretching far and flat.

All trails through that country run together in the gorge of
Little Lake, untwining on their separate errands as they open out
toward Coso. Don José kept on northward until he had brought
the ten thousand to pasture in the river bottom below Lone Pine,
where the scar of the earthquake drop was still red and raw.
Enough Spanish Californians had been drawn into that country
by Cerro Gordo and neighboring mines to make entertainment for
so personable a young man as Don José Jesús, dancing in the
patios at moonrise with the señoritas and drinking their own
vintages with courteous dons.

The flock rested hereabout some weeks and passed up the east
side of the valley loiteringly, finally crossing through the White
Mountains to Deep Springs Valley, thus far with no ill fortune.
That was more than could be laid to most adventurers into that
region. A little before that time John Barker had foraged as far
north with twenty-two thousand sheep, retiring disgustedly with

nine thousand. Said he, "Where we camped we left the ground kicking with dying sheep."

This was the time of the great drouth, when season after season the rains delayed, flinging themselves at last in wasteful fury on a baked, impervious soil. Rack-boned cattle died in the trails with their heads toward the place of springs, and thousands of flocks rotted in the dry ravines. Lopez took his sheep by the old Emigrant Trail, southward of the peak I watch daily, lifted clear white and shining above the summer haze, and came into the end of Deep Springs.

The feed in that country is bunch grass with stubby shrubs, shoulder high to the sheep. The ten thousand passed here and reached Piper's in good condition, having drunk last in Owens Valley. Piper was a notable cattleman of those parts, annexing as much range as could be grazed over from the oasis where his ranch house stood, and looked with the born distrust of the cowman on the sheepherder. Notwithstanding, the manners of Don José won him permission to keep the sheep along the stream side until they should have their fill of water. But sheep are fastidious drinkers, and the water of Piper's Creek was not to their liking.

Now observe, the flock had come over a mountain range and across a considerable stretch of sandy and alkali-impregnated soil since last watering, but they would not drink. Lopez hoped for a living stream at Pigeon Springs, but here the drouth had fevered all the land and left a caked and drying hole. Now they pushed the fagged and footsore sheep toward Lida Valley, where there was a reservoir dammed up for a mine, for there is gold in that country and silver ore, very precious; but an imp of contrarity had been before them, and though the sheep were pushed into it and swam about in the pool sullenly, they would not drink.

All that country was strange to Don José Jesús, bewildering whitey-brown flanks of hill and involved high mesas faced by dull blue mountain ridges exactly like all other dull blue ridges. A prospector, drifted in from the outlying camps, reported abundance of feed and water at a place called Stonewall. Lopez sent men forward with picks and shovels to make a drinking place while he came on slowly with the flock, but after two days he met his men returning. No water, said they, but a slow dribble from the cracks of seepage in the stone wall.

Now they turned the flock aside toward Stone Cabin, footsore, with heaving flanks and shrunken bellies. At home they might feed a winter long on the rain-bedewed tall pastures without drink, but here in the desert where the heat and dryness crumple men like grass in a furnace, the sheep, though traveling by night, suffered incredibly. All through the dark they steered a course by the stars that swung so low and white in the desert air; morning and evening they fed as they might on the dry sapless shrubs, and at noon milled together in the sand. Each seeking protection for its head under the body of another, they piled hot and close and perished upon their feet. Made senseless by heat and thirst, they strayed from the trail-weary herders.

Lopez, following such a band of estrays into the fawn and amethyst distances, at the end of two days had lost all his water and, persisting to the end of the third day, began to fail. His men, not finding him where he had appointed a meeting, returned to his point of starting and took up the clue of his tracks; following until they saw him through a field glass, at last, going forward dizzily in the bluish light of dawn. They had no more than come up with him, when at the relieving touch of water in his parched throat, he fell away into a deep swoon of exhaustion.

For three hours his spirit ebbed and tugged in the spent body while the men sheltered him in their own shadows from the sun and waited, as they of the desert know how to wait its processes and occasions. At last, having eaten and drunk again, he was able to make the remaining thirty miles to camp and bring in his sheep to Stone Cabin, where there was a well of fresh, sweet drink. They had come a hundred and thirty miles with the flock all waterless; and Don José Jesús laughed when he told it. He had companioned with thirst; failure had stalked him in the bitter dust; he had seen death camping on his trail; and after six and twenty years he laughed, a little as a woman laughs for remembered love. By which I take it, he is a man to whom the taste of work is good.

The flock drifted northward across Nevada until they came to where sixty feet of Snake River roared in the way. Indian agents, it seems, exist merely to fill agencies. At any rate, the one in charge of the Bannock Reservation would mediate neither for Señor Lopez nor the Indians. "Anyway you fix it, if you get into trouble," said the agent, "don't look to me."

Lopez set a guard about his horses and his camp, sought for El Capitan and dealt with him as man to man. Twenty-four hours to go through on his feet with his sheep, his wagon and his men; ten Indians to be paid in silver to aid at the river ford: that was the bargain he made with the chief of the Bannocks. Judge then his consternation as he came to the river border in the morning with the last of his bands to find three hundred braves in possession of the camp. They ate everything in sight with the greatest cheerfulness. But El Capitan reassured him, "You pay only for ten."

When there was plainly no more to be eaten, the chief laid the hollow of his hand to his mouth and lifted a long cry like a wolf's howl. Instantly three hundred braves had stripped and plunged into the icy swell of the ford. The chuckle of their laughter was louder than the rush of its waters. Shouting, they drew into two lines, beating the water with their hands.

When the herders brought up the sheep, one and another of them was plunged into the living chute. As they struck the water they were shot forward by long arms; the shoulder of one sheep crowded the rump of another. *Spat! Spat!* went the vigorous, brown arms. The swish of the river, cloven by the stream of sheep, was like the rip of water in closed sluices. The wall of shining bodies swayed with the current and withstood it. "As I live and breathe," says Don José Jesús, "ten thousand sheep went over in half an hour."

The herders, swimming over, formed the dripping flocks into bands and pushed them forward, for the point where the play of savages turns to plundering is easily passed. Lopez called up El Capitan, and the chief called up the ten. Two dollars and a half of silver money went to the chief, and one dollar and a half to each of his men. The rest of the two hundred and ninety naked Bannocks, having swum the wagons over, played on unconcernedly as boys in the freezing river. Within less than their allotted twenty-four hours, López was clear of the reservation. Some stragglers still stuck to his trail, bent on thieving, and one, professing himself son of the chief, rode after them threateningly, demanding a toll, but was appeased with two dollars in silver, and the flock turned eastward across the tablelands.

All this Iliad of adventure leads merely to the transfer of the flock by sale at Cheyenne—squalid and inadequate conclusion! No, but these are the processes by which the green bough of the man-strain renews itself in the suffocating growth of trade. Not that you should have mutton, but that nature should have men. It was so she put the stamp of efficiency on Señor Lopez, who is now at Tejon as major-domo of the cattle.

From *The Flock*, Mary Austin (Boston and New York: Houghton, Mifflin and Company, 1906).

LIII

Joaquin Miller

Few of the contributors to nineteenth-century California literature *belonged* to the West; they were transients, visitors, short-term residents, loath to cast their lot completely with this frontier society. Joaquin Miller (1841–1913) belonged—despite protracted periods of self-imposed exile. He was an authentic member of the horde of Westward-Ho emigrants that moved to the coast to stay, and was actually born in a covered wagon on his way West, though it was not until 1852 that his family completed the trek across the continent, to settle in Willamette Valley, Oregon.

Joaquin had been christened "Cincinnatus"; Mexican traveling companions on his early Western adventures gave him the pseudonym, allegedly borrowing it from the famed bandit, Joaquin Murietta, who ever after was one of Miller's heroes. Those independent adventures began at the age of fourteen when he slipped away from his parents in Willamette Valley and headed south for California; for the rest of his life there were few periods when he was not engaged in some equally rash pursuit.

He prospected for gold, fought in the Indian wars—*with* the Indians as well as against them; went on long trading expeditions with Mexican friends to Arizona and Mexico; helped establish a short-lived "Indian republic" for oppressed redmen on Mount Shasta; was in turn a renegade and a patriot, a stagecoach rider and newspaper editor, a miner's attorney and a frontier judge, writer of harassing letters to assorted editors, author of farfetched autobiographical sketches, of prose fiction, essays, plays, quantities of verse, and a few fine poems.

Not until 1871 was he accepted as a gifted poet, and then it was in England rather than in the United States. For years he had pretentiously aspired to be known as "the American Byron," but neither Easterners nor Westerners were ready to accord him any such honor. England welcomed, cheered, and feted him as the frontier philosopher, "the poet of the Sierras," the long-haired, top-booted lyricist of the West, and some of the glow from this British acclaim inevitably followed him back to Boston, New York, and then San Francisco.

Eventually he established himself on a sprawling hilltop estate, called "The Hights," overlooking Oakland and San Francisco Bay, where he fancied himself the leader of a native poetical movement, a seer, prophet, "the Moses of the Golden Gate," and where he wrote copiously—too copiously—with inadequate premeditation, inadequate editing, with careless rhyme, measure, and choice of word. He turned out superb lines, but was prone to bury them in otherwise trite utterance.

He and "The Hights" became favored tourist attractions of the Bay area, but people sought him out more as a "character" than a great poet. During his heyday Californians as a people were inclined toward temerity, impetuosity, and slipshod artistry. Miller let that spirit work its way into the structure of his poetry. Particularly in his California verse, he fell far short of becoming "the American Byron."

In San Francisco

Lo! here sit we mid the sun-down seas
    And the white sierras. The swift, sweet breeze
Is about us here; and the sky so fair
    Is bending above in its azaline hue,
    That you gaze and you gaze in delight, and you
See God and the portals of heaven there.

Yea, here sit we where the white ships ride
    In the morn, made glad and forgetful of night,
The white and the brown men side by side

In search of the truth, and betrothed to the right;
For these are the idols, and only these,
Of men that abide by the sun-down seas.

The brown brave hand of the harvester,
    The delicate hand of the prince untried,
The rough hard hand of the carpenter,
    They are all upheld with an equal pride;
And the prize it is his to be crown'd of blest,
Prince or peon,who bears him best.

Yea, here sit we by the golden gate,
    Not demanding much, but inviting you all,
Not publishing loud, but daring to wait,
    And great in much that the days deem small;
And the gate it is God's, to Cathay, Japan,—
And who shall shut it in the face of man?

Shadows of Shasta

In the place where the grizzly reposes,
    Under peaks where a right is a wrong,
I have memories richer than roses,
    Sweet echoes more sweet than a song;

Sounds sweet as the voice of a singer
    Made sacred with sorrows unsaid,
And a love that implores me to linger
    For the love of dead days and their dead.

But I turn, throwing kisses, returning
    To strife and to turbulent men,
As to learn to be wise, as unlearning
    All things that were manliest then.

Yosemite

Sound! sound! sound!
O colossal walls and crown'd
In one eternal thunder!
Sound! sound! sound!
O ye oceans overhead,
While we walk, subdued in wonder,
In the ferns and grasses, under
And beside the swift Merced!

Fret! fret! fret!
Streaming, sounding banners, set
On the giant granite castles
In the clouds and in the snow!
But the foe he comes not yet,—
We are loyal, valiant vassals,
And we touch the trailing tassels
Of the banners far below.

Surge! surge! surge!
From the white Sierra's verge,
To the very valley blossom.
Surge! surge! surge!
Yet the song-bird builds a home,
And the mossy branches cross them,
And the tasselled tree-tops toss them
In the clouds of falling foam.

Sweep! sweep! sweep!
O ye heaven-born and deep,
In one dread, unbroken chorus!
We may wonder or may weep,—
We may wait on God before us;
We may shout or lift a hand,—
We may bow down and deplore us,
But may never understand.

Beat! beat! beat!
We advance, but would retreat
From this restless, broken breast
Of the earth in a convulsion.
We would rest, but dare not rest,
For the angel of expulsion
From this Paradise below
Waves us onward and . . . we go.

The Men of Forty-nine

Those brave old bricks of forty-nine!
What lives they lived! what deaths they died!
A thousand cañons, darkling wide
Below Sierra's slopes of pine
Receive them now. And they who died
Along the far, dim, desert route—
Their ghosts are many. Let them keep
Their vast possessions. The Piute,
The tawny warrior, will dispute
No boundary with these. And I
Who saw them live, who felt them die,
Say, let their unplow'd ashes sleep,
Untouch'd by man, on plain or steep.

. . .

They sought, yea, they did find their rest.
Along that long and lonesome way,
These brave men buffet'd the West
With lifted faces. Full were they
Of great endeavor. Brave and true
As stern Crusader clad in steel,
They died afield as it was fit.
Made strong with hope, they dared to do
Achievement that a host today
Would stagger at, stand back and reel,
Defeated at the thought of it.

What brave endeavor to endure!
What patient hope, when hope was past!
What still surrender at the last,
A thousand leagues from hope! how pure
They lived, how proud they died!
How generous with life! The wide
And gloried age of chivalry
Hath not one page like this to me.

. . .

Yea, I remember! The still tears
That o'er uncoffin'd faces fell!
The final, silent, sad farewell!
God! these are with me all the years!
They shall be with me ever. I
Shall not forget. I hold a trust.
They are part of my existence. When
Swift down the shining iron track
You sweep, and fields of corn flash back,
And herds of lowing steers move by,
And men laugh loud, in mute distrust,
I turn to other days, to men
Who made a pathway with their dust.

From *Poems of Joaquin Miller* (Boston: Roberts Brothers, 1889), and *Complete Poetical Works of Joaquin Miller* (San Francisco: Whitaker and Ray Company, 1904).

LIV

Robert Frost

By birth Robert Frost (1874–1963) belonged to the West. He was born in San Francisco, son of a Yankee schoolteacher, and had he remained there he might well have become a far more celebrated poet of the Pacific Coast than Joaquin Miller, rather than laureate of New England. But immediately after his father's death in 1885, the family returned to the East—a few weeks after Robert's eleventh birthday.

In adult years Frost made many journeys back to his native state, though he never seemed to regard these as sentimental pilgrimages to his boyhood home. California, nevertheless, left its impression on him, and forty years after the first departure from San Francisco he included in his volume *West-running Brook* two graphic reminiscences of his youth: "Once by the Pacific" and "A Peck of Gold." To both were affixed the half-facetious annotation, "As of about 1880."

Once by the Pacific

The shattered water made a misty din.
Great waves looked over others coming in,
And thought of doing something to the shore
That water never did to land before.

The clouds were low and hairy in the skies,
Like locks blown forward in the gleam of eyes.
You could not tell, and yet it looked as if
The shore were lucky in being backed by cliff,
The cliff in being backed by continent;
It looked as if a night of dark intent
Was coming, and not only a night, an age.
Someone had better be prepared for rage.
There would be more than ocean-water broken
Before God's last *Put out the Light* was spoken.

As of about 1880.

A Peck of Gold

Dust always blowing about the town,
Except when sea-fog laid it down,
And I was one of the children told
Some of the blowing dust was gold.

All the dust the wind blew high
Appeared like gold in the sunset sky,
But I was one of the children told
Some of the dust was really gold.

Such was life in the Golden Gate:
Gold dusted all we drank and ate,
And I was one of the children told,
"We all must eat our peck of gold."

As of about 1880.

From *West-running Brook,* Robert Frost (New York: Henry Holt and Company, 1928).

LV

Lincoln Steffens

The democratic spirit of the West was making room even for a cult of intellectuals and creative artists by the 1870s and 1880s. But these cultists, as was their custom anywhere else, clung together and tended to gravitate toward San Francisco, where they could comfort one another, quarrel, lock horns, self-admire, and criticize each other's ideas in their own little Bohemia. The reverberations they produced were noisy and out of all proportion to their actual numbers, but with convictions as varied as those of free-swinging Ambrose Bierce, Joaquin Miller, and John Muir, there was bound to be a racket.

Many of these Golden Gate Bohemians—young men with fresh insight, poetasters and bibliophiles, artists, classicists, and literati—sought refuge in San Francisco because they were at loggerheads with their families and communities in some other part of the world, and were sure that they could find there a freer freedom of expression. In their new-found haunts they formed tight fraternal groups devoted to the arts and creativity, lionized visiting liberal spirits from the other side of the continent, served as a claque for performing artists on tour, and inaugurated local journals like *Golden Era, The Californian,* and *Overland Monthly.*

Occasionally they drew into their circles allies from across the Bay in Berkeley, where the College of California, founded in 1860, had been elevated to a state university. But the two did not yet have much in common. Berkeley could hardly be regarded as a fount of original thinking; it was a small, undistinguished institution, slow to gather academic momentum, and hampered by its own unsophisticated students, who had an unfortunate inclination to bring to the campus all the rough-and-tumble deportment of their hometowns. Nevertheless, the University and San Francisco's Bohemia together were contributing to California's maturity and were exerting refreshing influences.

Lincoln Steffens (1866–1936) was exposed to both influences and could speak for both. Born in San Francisco, brought up in Sacramento, graduated from a good military academy, and backed by a family of highly creditable social standing, all his early indoctrination had been slanted to prepare him for entrance to the University in 1884. And despite that preparation and backing, he was turned down—a rejection that spoke well, perhaps, for the admission standards that the institution was attempting to maintain, considering that the candidate in his adulthood was to become author of half a dozen outstanding volumes exposing municipal and political corruption, a sensational muckraker, and editor successively of *McClure's, The American,* and *Everybody's* magazines. "I failed Greek, Latin, and enough other subjects to put me off for a year," Steffens confided.

He spent that year of grace among the arty set of San Francisco, being tutored formally by a spirited San Francisco classicist, Evelyn Nixon, and informally by Nixon's Bohemian friends, "a maddening lot of cultivated, conflicting minds, . . . four to ten of them, all Englishmen, all Oxford and Cambridge men, all exiles, and all interested in any and all subjects, which they discussed with knowledge, with the precise information of scholarship, and with no common opinions on anything." They represented the offbeat intellects that had gathered around the Golden Gate, and Steffens found them so stimulating that the college education which followed was a complete letdown by comparison.

The Privileged Vices of Berkeley

The University of California was a young, comparatively small institution when I was entered there in 1885 as a freshman. Berkeley, the beautiful, was not the developed villa community it is now; I used to shoot quail in the brush under the oaks along the edges of the college grounds. The quail and the brush are gone now, but the oaks are there and the same prospect down the hill over San Francisco Bay out through the Golden Gate between the low hills of the city and the high hills of Marin County.

My class numbered about one hundred boys and girls, mostly boys, who came from all parts of the State and represented all sorts of people and occupations. There was, however, a significant uniformity of opinion and spirit among us, as there was, and still is, in other, older colleges. The American is molded to type early. And so are our college ways. We found already formed at Berkeley the typical undergraduate customs, rights and privileged vices which we had to respect ourselves and defend against the faculty, regents, and the State government.

One evening, before I had matriculated, I was taken out by some upper classmen to teach the president a lesson. He had been the head of a private preparatory school and was trying to govern the private lives and the public morals of university "men" as he had those of his schoolboys. Fetching a long ladder, the upper classmen thrust it through a front window of Prexy's house and, to the chant of obscene songs, swung it back and forth, up and down, round and round, till everything breakable within sounded broken and the drunken indignation outside was satisfied or tired.

This turned out to be one of the last battles in the war for liberty against that president. He was allowed to resign soon thereafter and I noticed that not only the students but many of the faculty and regents rejoiced in his downfall and turned with us to face and fight the new president when, after a lot of politics, he was appointed and presented. We learned somehow a good deal about the considerations that governed our college government. They were not only academic. The government of a university was—like the State government and horse-racing and so many other things—not what I had been led to expect. And a college education wasn't either, nor the student mind. . . .

My expectations of college life were raised too high by Nixon's Saturday nights. I thought, and he assumed, that at Berkeley I would be breathing in the atmosphere of thought, discussion and some scholarship; working, reading, and studying for the answers to questions which would be threshed out in debate and conversation. There was nothing of the sort. . . .

There were no moot questions in Berkeley. There was work to do, knowledge and training to get, but not to answer questions. I found myself engaged, as my classmates were, in choosing courses. The choice was limited and, within the limits, had to be determined by the degree we were candidates for. My questions were philosophical, but I could not take philosophy, which fascinated me, till I had gone through a lot of higher mathematics, which did not interest me at all.

If I had been allowed to take philosophy, and so discovered the need and the relation of mathematics, I would have got the philosophy and I might have got the mathematics, which I miss now more than I do the Hegelian metaphysics taught at Berkeley. . . . No one ever developed for me the relation of any of my required subjects to those that attracted me; no one brought out for me the relation of anything I was studying to anything else, except, of course, to that wretched degree. Knowledge was absolute, not relative, and it was stored in compartments, categorical and independent. The relation of knowledge to life, even to student life, was ignored, and as for questions, the professors asked them, not the students; and the students, not the teachers, answered them—in examinations. . . .

Students selected subjects or teachers for a balance of easy and hard, to fit into their time and yet "get through." I was the only rebel of my kind, I think. . . . What I wanted to know was buried deep under all this "college stuff" which was called "shop." It had nothing to do with what really interested us in common. Having chosen our work and begun to do it as a duty, we turned to the socially important question: which fraternity to join.

The upper classmen tried to force our answers. They laid aside their superiority to "rush" those of us whose antecedents were known and creditable. It was all snobbish, secret, and exclusive. I joined a fraternity out of curiosity: What were the secrets and mystic rites? I went blindfold through the silly initiation to find

that there were no secrets and no mysteries, only pretensions and
bunk, which so disgusted me that I would not live at the clubhouse, preferring for a year the open doors of a boarding house.

The next great university question was as to athletics. . . . I
went with the other freshmen to the campus to be tried out for
football, baseball, running, jumping, etc. Caught by the college
and class spirit, I hoped to give promise of some excellence. Baseball was impossible for me; I had been riding horses when the
other boys were preparing for college on the diamond. I had
learned to run at the military academy and in the first freshman
tests I did one hundred yards enough under eleven seconds to be
turned over to an athletic upper classman for instruction. Pointing up to Grizzly Peak, a high hill back of the college, he said:
"All you need is wind and muscle. Climb that mountain every day
for a year; then come back and we'll see."

I did not climb Grizzly Peak every day, but I went up so often
that I was soon able to run up and back without a halt. At the end
of the year I ran around the cinder track so long that my student
instructor wearied of watching me, but, of course, I could not
do a hundred yards much under twelve seconds. Muscle and
wind I had, but all my physical reactions were so slow that I was
of no social use in college athletics. . . .

I shone only in the military department. The commandant, a
U.S. Army officer, seeing that I had previous training, told me off
to drill the awkward squad of my class, and when I had made of
them the best-drilled company in college, he gave me the next
freshman class to drill. In the following years I was always drill-
master of the freshmen and finally commanded the whole cadet
corps. Thus I led my class in the most unpopular and meaningless
of undergraduate activities. I despised it myself, prizing it only
for the chances it gave me to swank and, once a week, to lord it
over my fellow students, who nicknamed me the "D.S."—damn
stinker. . . .

All other student enthusiasms, athletics, class and college politics, fashions, and traditions I laughed at and damped. I was a
spoilsport. I was mean, as a horse is mean, because I was un-
happy myself. I could be enthusiastic in a conversation about

something we were learning, if it wasn't too cut and dried; we
had such talks now and then at the clubhouse in my later years.
But generally speaking we were discussing the news or some
prank of our own.

One night, for example, we sallied forth to steal some chickens
from Dr. Bonte, the popular treasurer of the university. I crawled
into the coop and selected the chickens, wrung their necks, and
passed them out with comments to the other fellows who held the
bag. "Here," I said, "is the rooster, Dr. Bonte himself; he's tough,
but good enough for the freshmen. Next is a nice fat hen, old Mrs.
Bonte. This one's a pullet, Miss Bonte," and so on, naming each of
the Bonte girls, till we were interrupted.

There was a sound from the house, the lights flashed in the
windows, and—someone was coming. The other fellows ran, and
I—when I tore myself out—I ran too. Which was all right
enough. But when I caught up with the other thieves, I learned
that they had left the sack of chickens behind!

Our Sunday dinner was spoiled, we thought, but no: the next
day the whole fraternity was invited to dinner at Dr. Bonte's on
Sunday. We accepted with some suspicion, we went in some embarrassment, but we were well received and soon put at our ease
by Dr. Bonte, who explained that some thieves had been frightened while robbing his roost. "They were not students, I take it,"
he said. "Students are not so easily frightened; they might have
run away, but students would have taken the bag of chickens
with them. I think they were niggers or Chinamen."

So seated hospitably at table we watched with deep interest
the great platter of roasted chickens borne in and set down before
Dr. Bonte, who rose, whetted his carving-knife, and turning first
to me said: "Well, Steffens, what will you have, a piece of this old
cock, Dr. Bonte? Or is he too tough for any but the freshmen?
Perhaps you would prefer the old hen, Mrs. Bonte, or, say, one of
the Bonte girls."

I couldn't speak. No one could; and no one laughed, least of all
Dr. Bonte, who stood there, his knife and fork in the air, looking
at me, at the others, and back at me. He wanted an answer; I
must make my choice, but I saw a gleam of malicious humor in

his eye; so I recovered and I chose the prettiest of the girls, pointing to the tenderest of the pullets. Dr. Bonte laughed, gave me my choice, and we had a jolly, ample dinner.

We talked about that, we and the students generally, and the faculty—we discussed that incident long enough and hard enough to have solved it, if it had been a metaphysical problem. We might have threshed out the psychology of thieves, or gamblers, but no. We liked to steal, but we didn't care to think about it, not as stealing.

And some of us gambled. We had to get money for theaters, operas, and other expenses in the city. I had only my board, lodging, and clothes paid for by my father, and others had not even that. We played cards, therefore, among ourselves, poker and whist, so that a lucky few got each month about all the money all the other hard-ups had, and so had all the fun. We played long, late, and hard, and for money, not sport. The strain was too great.

One night my roommate, sunk low in his chair, felt a light kick on one of his extended legs; a second later there were two kicks against his other leg. Keeping still and watching the hands shown down, he soon had the signal system of two men playing partners, the better hand staying in the game. We said nothing but, watching, saw that others cheated, too.

We knew well an old professional gambler from the mining camps who was then in San Francisco. We told him all about it. "Sure," he said, "cheating will sneak into any game that's played long enough. That's why you boys oughtn't to gamble. But if you do, play the game that's played. Cards is like horse racing. I never bet a cent except I know, and know how, the game is crooked."

Having advised against it, he took us around to the gambling houses and the race course and showed us many of the tricks of his trade, how to spot and profit by them—if we must play. "Now you won't need never to be suckers," he said. "And ye needn't be crooks either," he added after a pause.

But we had it in for our opponents. We learned several ways to cheat; we practiced them till we were cool and sure. After that our "luck" was phenomenal. We had money, more than we needed. In my last two years at the university I had a salary as military instructor at a preparatory school in the town, and my roommate, the adopted son of a rich gold miner, had a generous allowance. But we went on playing and cheating at cards for the excitement of it, we said, but really it was for the money.

And afterward, when I was a student in Germany, I played on, fair, but hard—and for money I did not need, till one night at the Café Bauer in Berlin, sitting in a poker game that had been running all night, an American who had long been playing in hard luck, lost a large amount, of which I carried away more than my share. The next day we read in the papers that when he got home he had shot himself. I have never gambled since—at cards.

It is possible to get an education at a university. It has been done; not often, but the fact that a proportion, however small, of college students do get a start in interested, methodical study, proves my thesis.

From *The Autobiography of Lincoln Steffens* (New York: Harcourt, Brace and Company, 1931).

LVI

John R. Spears

Intellectualism was not yet superseding California industry. Gold mining had seen its best days, but all manner of productive enterprises were taking its place: woolen mills, tanneries, shipbuilding, refineries for raw Hawaiian sugar, flour mills, fruit canneries, iron foundries, meat-packing plants, wineries, even experimental electric power plants and oil refineries. But the most unexpected and colorful industry of all sprang up in that contemptible desert wilderness known as Death Valley, in 1882. That was the year crazy prospectors began hauling immense loads of a snowy-white substance out of the depths of the hated valley.

The glistening cargo was known to the chemists as $Na_2B_4O_7 \cdot 10H_2O$, to mineralogists as tincal, to industry as sodium tetraborate, and to desert dealers as "cottonball crude"; to housewives it was soon to be known as borax. Until the ponderous wagons started moving it out of Death Valley it had been expensive stuff, costing as much as twenty-five cents an ounce at the drugstore. Borate of soda had been sparingly used since ancient times by glassmakers, metal craftsmen, and dyers; it was far too rare and costly to be used in ordinary kitchens.

For a hundred years the principal supply had come from Tibet, packed over the Himalaya passes on the backs of sheep; then it had been discovered nearer civilization in the swamps of Tuscany, and more recently in places like Turkey, Chile, and Argentina. But in Death Valley there was enough to corner the world market. Within a few months borax was to be displayed on the grocer's shelves rather than the druggist's.

John R. Spears (1850–1936), a feature writer for the New York *Sun*, accustomed to traveling anywhere from Greenland to Central America on special assignments, first became acquainted with the household variety of borax while shopping in a grocery store. His eye was caught by a fascinating white box picturing "a half-mile string of desert mules" hauling a gigantic van. It reminded him that a fellow reporter had suggested to him more than a year before that the place to go for a really exciting story was "the borax deserts of the Pacific Coast." The illustration on the white box convinced him. He set out without delay, and never had occasion to complain that the borax packers were over-advertising their product.

Twenty-mule-team Traffic

The largest, most capacious and most economical wagons ever built were manufactured in the Mojave Desert, for use in Death Valley. . . . There is probably nothing like desert transportation in all the world. I got my first glimpse of it at the Nevada Salt and Borax Company's works at Rhodes' Marsh. . . . The works for producing borax from the crude material found in the marsh there used nut pine as fuel, and the wood was cut on a mountain top twelve miles away, piled up on a bench at the head of a canyon and drawn thence in wagons to the works.

One of those wagons was standing empty in a wood yard when I visited the marsh and, although not the largest in use, it was a sight to make an Eastern teamster gasp. The tops of the wheels came just level with the eyes of a tall man. . . .

The woodsman of the East counts his load great when he has piled two cords on the easy-running bobsleds in winter time, but here the wood hauler piles from five to six cords on each wagon, couples two of them together, and draws the train down the rocky defiles and winding canyons of the mountainside and across the sandy plains, where the wheels of an ordinary Eastern farm wagon, with its load, would cut in six inches deep.

Of course, no one pair of horses, nor any combination of horses known to Eastern teamsters, could move, let alone haul such a load. The swell young gentlemen who handle the ribbons over two pairs of horses in front of a Newport coach, and the dignified driver guiding four pairs of heavy grays before a New York City safe truck, think themselves drivers of rare skill, and so they are. But the fuel driver of the desert commonly drives twelve horses with the aid of a single rope, in place of reins, and never has less than ten before him. And yet he is but "a raw-hide" driver when compared with those who had charge of the Death Valley borax teams.

When, in 1883, the manufacture of borax was . . . undertaken at the marsh in Death Valley, . . . J. S. W. Perry . . . who had before that been employed in Mojave in the borax business, was put at work organizing a system of transportation over the desert, which should be adequate for the safe handling of all the product of the Death Valley region.

Some of the difficulties in the way of carrying out the company's plans may be mentioned, but scarce described so as to be fully comprehended by one who has not seen the desert to be crossed. Between Mojave and the valley proper there were but three springs of water. The road from the railway station led away over the sandy plain, in an easterly direction, toward a peak locally known as Granite Mountain [or Pilot Butte]. . . . It was just fifty and one-half miles across this desert—a desert where the sand-laden wind forever blows and the sun pours down with intolerable fierceness in summer—to the first spring, which was called Black Water.

Beyond Black Water, six and one-half miles away, was Granite Spring at the foot of Pilot Butte; and the next spring was Lone Willow, twenty-six miles away, at the foot of one of the peaks of the Panamint Range. These last two spaces between springs were comparatively short distances, but the next dry space was worst of all, for it was fifty-three miles to Mesquite Well near the lower end of Death Valley.

And yet experience had demonstrated that a loaded team could travel only from fifteen to seventeen miles in a day. There was, of course, but one way in which those fifty-mile stretches could be crossed, and that was by hauling water for men and animals for the three days required in the passage between springs. Nor was that all. The desert does not produce a mouthful of food of any kind. Grain and hay had to be hauled as well as water.

There were other obstacles along the trail. It is a mountainous country. The road leaves Death Valley by what is known as Windy Gap. This gap is really what is known in that country as a wash. It is the bed of torrents that come pouring down after a cloud-burst on the mountain top. Volumes of water, in foaming waves twenty feet high, are said to be common enough, and others much higher are told about by the white Arabs.

When a wave has passed, boulders are found scattered in all directions, gullies are cut out, and at the best only a bed of yielding sand is found for the wheels to roll over. Worse yet, this bed of sand rises on an average grade of one hundred feet to the mile for forty miles, while the grade for short distances is four times as much.

The entire length of this desert road between Death Valley and Mojave is 164½ miles. There was, of course, in all that distance no sign of human habitation. In case of sickness, accident or disaster, either to themselves or the teams, the men could not hope for help until some other team came along over the trail.

The first thing done by Mr. Perry was to obtain, by inspection or correspondence, the dimensions of all varieties of great wagons used by Pacific coast freighters. With these and the load carried by each wagon spread out before him, he proceeded to design the wagons.

The task he had set for himself was the building of ten wagons so large that any of them would carry at least ten tons. The reader who is familiar with railroads . . . must have seen these legends painted on the sides of freight cars: "Capacity 28,000 lbs.," "Capacity 40,000 lbs.," (rarely) "Capacity 50,000 lbs." With this in mind, consider that these wagons for hauling borax out of Death Valley were to haul ten tons, or half a car load each—that a train of two wagons was to carry a load, not for one of the old-style, but for one of the modern, well-built freight cars, and carry the load, too, not over a smooth iron tramway, but up and down the rocky defiles and canyons of one of the most precipitous mountain ranges in the world, the Panamint.

Because these were probably the largest wagons ever used and because they were and still are completely successful, [I give] their dimensions in detail. . . . The hind wheel was seven feet in diameter, and its tire was eight inches wide and an inch thick. The forward wheel was five feet in diameter, with a tire like that on the rear wheel. The hubs were eighteen inches in diameter, by twenty-two inches long. The spokes were made of split oak, five and one half inches at the butt. . . . The forward axle-trees were made of solid steel bars, three and a quarter inches square in cross section, while the rear axles were three and a half inches square.

The wagon beds were sixteen feet long, four feet wide and six feet deep. The tread of the wagon—the width across the wheels —was six feet. Each wagon weighed 7,800 pounds, and the cost of the lot was about $9,000, or $900 each. . . .

While the wagons were building, the road had to be divided up into what might be called days' journeys. . . . Ten stations were established at intervals along the whole route, where the teams could stop for the night when coming in loaded to Mojave, while certain other stations were established for resting places on the way out of Death Valley, these last being located with a view of making a team travel further when light than when loaded.

So far as possible these stations were established at the few springs found along the route. Elsewhere dry camps had to be made. Here the natural lack of water was overcome by a system of wheeled water tanks, very much like the tanks of street sprinklers. These were made to hold 500 gallons each, and were towed by the teams from the springs to the dry camps and from the dry camps back to the springs to be filled again when empty. They were necessarily made of iron because a wooden tank would dry out and fall to pieces when partly empty. . . .

At all the stations from two to four feed boxes were built of lumber, each large enough to hold four bales of hay and six bags of barley. . . . The teams bound out to the valley filled the feed boxes, and then emptied them coming in. The greatest distance made by a team in cool winter weather, on a down-grade with no load, was twenty-two miles. The shortest run for hot weather was about fourteen miles.

But it should be said here that for the three months in the heat of the summer, from the middle of June until the middle of September, no teaming could be done at all. It was not possible for either man or beast to stand the terrific heat of even the Mojave Desert, not to mention Death Valley.

The teams consisted of eighteen mules and two horses. . . . The horses and mules are harnessed up in pairs. The horses are attached to the wagon at the tongue, and a great, handsome 2,800-pound team it is—gentle, obedient and strong as a locomotive. Ahead of them stretch the mules, their double trees geared to a chain that leads from the forward axle. The most civilized pair are placed in the lead and the next in intelligence just ahead of the tongue, while the sinful and fun-loving and the raw-hides fill in between.

The nigh leader has a bridle with the strap from the left jaw shorter than the other, and from this bridle runs a braided cotton rope a half an inch in diameter, through fair-leaders on each mule to the hand of the driver, who sits on a perch on the front end of the wagon box just eight feet above the ground. That rope is known as the jerk-line and its length is not far from 120 feet. The team that draws the desert freight train stretches out for more than a hundred feet in front of the wagon. . . .

To see a Death Valley teamster soar up over the front wheel to his perch, tilt his hat back on a rear corner of his head, gather in the slack of the jerk-line, loosen the ponderous brake, and awaken the dormant energies of the team with "Git up,—— —— you; git up," is the experience of a tourist's lifetime. And when at the end of a journey the teamster pulls up beside the dump with the mules in a line so straight that a stretched string would touch the ear of every mule on either side of the chain, as has often been done, one wants to be introduced and shake hands, as with "one whom lesser minds make boast of having seen."

And when one sees the mules settle forward in their collars, feeling gently of their load until at last the chain stretches as firm as an iron bar, and with one accord start the train of well-nigh 60,000 pounds weight almost as though it was naught, he wants to be introduced and shake hands with the mules too. . . . Their intelligence is such that he would be proud of a speaking acquaintance with them, but if he knew the mules, he would be a little shy about getting within hand-shaking range.

It is wonderfully interesting, too, to watch the mules as they turn a sharp corner in a canyon, or on a trail where it rounds a sharp turn on the mountain side. Span after span, near the end of the tongue, often without a word from the driver, will jump over the long chain and pull away on a tangent that the heavy load may be dragged around. Even then the novice wonders how they succeed, for some of the curves are so sharp that the leaders pull in one direction while the wagons are traveling very nearly in an opposite one.

. . . In freighting over the desert with a twenty-animal team every driver has an assistant called a swamper. The swamper's duties are multifarious. On a down-grade he climbs to a perch on the rear wagon and puts on the brake; on the up-grade he reasons with and throws rocks at the indolent and obstreperous mules. As mealtime approaches he kicks dead branches from the grease bush along the route and pulls up sagebrush roots for fuel. When the outfit stops, he cooks the food while the driver feeds the animals, and when the meal is over, washes the dishes, which, with the food, are carried in a convenient box in the wagon.

. . . The bill of fare served at a desert freight camp includes bacon, bread and beans for a foundation, with every variety of canned goods known to the grocery trade for the upper strata. They carry Dutch ovens for their baking, pans for frying and tin kettles for stewing. On the whole, however, they do not eat much fancy canned stuff, and a cobbler made of canned peaches serves for both pie and cake.

They rarely carry liquor for use on the road. I observed that empty bottles on some of the desert trails were as thick as good resolutions on the road to Sheol, but the teamster did not empty or leave them there. They had served to cheer the road for gentle-

Twenty-mule-team transportation

men en route to inspect Breyfogle, Gunsight lead and Peg-Leg mines. . . . This is not to say, however, that the teamster is a disciple of Neal Dow or the Woman's Christian Temperance Union.

While the five trains were running regularly between Death Valley and Mojave, the chief care of Superintendent Perry was to keep them moving regularly. He had the road so divided that the teams went out to the valley, got loaded, and returned to Mojave on the twentieth day at 3 o'clock with a precision that was remarkable. At Mojave the teamster was allowed to have the rest of the day and night to himself, and it usually happened that when the hour of starting came next day, he rolled in instead of soared to his perch, and then, as he blinked his eyes and pawed the jerk-line said: "Git hep-th-th-th-th yougithop."

It is a matter of record that the mules understood him, nevertheless—that, in fact, these long-eared, brush-tailed tugs of the desert never did but once fail to understand the driver, no matter what his condition. On that occasion the driver, instead of getting drunk, had gone to hear an evangelist preach and had been converted. Next morning, it is said, when he mounted the wagon and invited the team to go on, the mules, with one accord, turned their heads over their shoulders, cocked forward their ears and stared at him. He had omitted the customary *emphasis* from his command. . . .

The life of a teamster on the desert is not only one of hardship, it is in places extremely dangerous. . . . There are grades down the mountains like the one, for instance, on the road from Granite Spring toward Mojave, where the plunge is not only steep, but the road bed is as hard as a turnpike. The load must go down, and so when the brink is reached, the driver throws his weight on the brake of the front wagon, the swamper handles the brake on the rear one, and away they go, creaking and groaning and sliding till the bottom is reached.

If the brake holds, all is well, but now and then a brake block gives way and such a race with death as then begins cannot be seen elsewhere. With yells and curses, the long team is started in a gallop, an effort is made to swing them around up the mountainside, a curve is reached, an animal falls, or a wheel strikes a rock or a rut and, with thunderous crash over go the great wagons, and the teamster who has stuck to his post goes with them. There are many graves on the desert of men who died with their boots on, but some of them hold men who were killed while striving to guide a runaway freight team in a wild dash down the side of a desert mountain.

From *Illustrated Sketches of Death Valley,* John R. Spears (Chicago and New York: Rand, McNally and Company, 1892).

LVII

Rudyard Kipling

In one way or another the lion's share of the state's industrial profits flowed into gay, garish, heterogeneous San Francisco, a city that was spilling out over its sand dunes faster than census takers could tally the population and count the habitations. Planted firmly on the upper edge of the business district, as if to check progress of occidental industry in that direction, stood Chinatown, already virtually a city within a city; it overran Dupont and Sacramento streets, Grant Avenue and Stockton, and was rapidly outclassing other quarters of the metropolis in glamor and exotic fascination. Chinatown was one section of San Francisco that no visitor ever missed.

It immediately caught the imagination of twenty-four-year-old Rudyard Kipling (1865–1936), who paused at the Golden Gate for a few weeks on his way home from India to England by way of the United States in 1889. He could not forget that Englishmen had once held a stake in northern California, and at first he was shocked by what the Americans were doing to New Albion. To the reserved, cultivated Britisher, San Francisco seemed to be inhabited by barbarians—boorish, vulgar, extravagantly uncouth.

He checked in at the Palace Hotel, that "seven-storied warren of humanity with a thousand rooms in it," tenanted by men in frock coats and top hats—"but they all spat. They spat on principle. The spittoons were on the staircases, in each bedroom . . . but they blossomed in chiefest splendor round the Bar, and they were all used, every reeking

[388]

one of 'em"; he explored the waterfront and the harbor yachting center, was belatedly admitted as guest at the Bohemian Club and to some of the more palatial homes, where he confessed that he fell in love "with about eight American maidens—all perfectly delightful till the next one comes into the room"; he rode the cable cars, poked into public bars and gambling houses, and finally decided that he was very fond of San Francisco and San Franciscans, despite their shortcomings.

"San Francisco has only one drawback," he concluded. " 'Tis hard to leave. When . . . I 'cut that city by the sea' it was with regrets for the pleasant places left behind, for the men who were so clever, and the women who were so witty, for the 'dives,' the beer halls, the bucket shops, and the poker halls where humanity was going to the Devil with shouting and laughter and song and the rattle of dice boxes." But Kipling's most memorable and exciting San Francisco venture was in Chinatown.

Three Stories Underground

A man took me round the Chinese quarter of San Francisco, which is a ward of the city of Canton set down in the most eligible business quarter of the place. The Chinaman with his usual skill has possessed himself of good brick fire-proof buildings and, following instinct, has packed each tenement with hundreds of souls, all living in filth and squalor. . . . That cursory investigation ought to have sufficed; but I wanted to know how deep in the earth the Pigtail had taken root. Therefore I explore the Chinese quarter a second time and alone, which was foolishness.

No one in the filthy streets (but for the blessed sea breezes San Francisco would enjoy cholera every season) interfered with my movements, though they asked for *cumshaw*. I struck a house about four stories high full of celestial abominations, and began to burrow down, having heard that these tenements were constructed on the lines of icebergs—two-thirds below sight level.

Downstairs I crawled past Chinamen in bunks, opium smokers, brothels and gambling dens, till I reached the second cellar—was, in fact, in the labyrinths of a warren. Great is the wisdom of the

Chinaman. In time of trouble that house could be razed to the ground by the mob, and yet hide all its inhabitants in brick-walled and wooden-beamed subterranean galleries, strengthened with iron-framed doors and gates.

On the second underground floor a man asked for *cumshaw* and took me downstairs to yet another cellar, where the air was as thick as butter, and the lamps burned little holes in it not more than an inch square. In this place a poker club had assembled and was in full swing. The Chinaman loves "pokel," and plays it with great skill, swearing like a cat when he loses. Most of the men round the table were in semi-European dress, their pigtails curled up under billy-cock hats. One of the company looked like a Eurasian, whence I argued that he was a Mexican—a supposition that later inquiries confirmed.

They were a picturesque set of fiends and polite, being too absorbed in their game to look at the stranger. We were all deep down under the earth, and save for the rustle of a blue gown sleeve and the ghostly whisper of the cards as they were shuffled and played, there was no sound. The heat was almost unendurable. There was some dispute between the Mexican and the man on his left. The latter shifted his place to put the table between himself and his opponent, and stretched a lean yellow hand toward the Mexican's winnings.

Mark how purely man is a creature of instinct. Rarely introduced to the pistol, I saw the Mexican half rise in his chair and at the same instant found myself full length on the floor. None had told me that this was the best attitude when bullets are abroad. I was there prone before I had time to think—dropping as the room was filled with an intolerable clamor like the discharge of a cannon.

In those close quarters the pistol report had no room to spread any more than the smoke—then acrid in my nostrils. There was no second shot, but a great silence in which I rose slowly to my knees. The Chinaman was gripping the table with both hands and staring in front of him at an empty chair. The Mexican had gone, and a little whirl of smoke was floating near the roof.

Still gripping the table, the Chinaman said, "Ah!" in the tone that a man would use when, looking up from his work suddenly, he sees a well-known friend in the doorway. Then he coughed and fell over to his own right, and I saw that he had been shot in the stomach.

I became aware that, save for two men leaning over the stricken one, the room was empty; and all the tides of intense fear, hitherto held back by intenser curiosity, swept over my soul. I ardently desired the outside air. It was possible that the Chinamen would mistake me for the Mexican—everything horrible seemed possible just then—and it was more than possible that the stairways would be closed while they were hunting for the murderer.

The man on the floor coughed a sickening cough. I heard it as I fled, and one of his companions turned out the lamp. Those stairs seemed interminable, and to add to my dismay there was no sound of commotion in the house. No one hindered, no one even looked at me. There was no trace of the Mexican. I found the doorway and, my legs trembling under me, reached the protection of the clear cool night, the fog and the rain.

I dared not run, and for the life of me I could not walk. I must have effected a compromise, for I remember the light of a street lamp showed the shadow of one half skipping—caracoling along the pavements in what seemed to be an ecstasy of suppressed happiness. But it was fear—deadly fear. Fear compounded of past knowledge of the Oriental—only other white man—available witness—three stories underground—and the cough of the Chinaman now some forty feet under my clattering boot heels.

It was good to see the shop fronts and electric lights again. Not for anything would I have informed the police, because I firmly believed that the Mexican had been dealt with somewhere down there on the third floor long ere I had reached the air. . . . My ill-considered flight brought me out somewhere a mile distant from the hotel; and the clank of the lift that bore me to a bed six stories above ground was music to my ears. Wherefore I would impress it upon you who follow after, do not knock about the Chinese quarters at night and alone. You may stumble across a picturesque piece of human nature that will unsteady your nerves for half a day.

From *American Notes*, Rudyard Kipling (New York: Manhattan Press, c.1892).

LVIII

Hildegarde Hawthorne

Compared to San Francisco, the growth of Los Angeles came by halting fits and starts. During the rancho period virtually all of southern California was under the feudal sway of a handful of Mexican cattle barons, and they did nothing to elevate the ugly pueblo. After the American takeover, Los Angeles developed into the most lawless, rip-roaring frontier village of the West, commonly maligned as "Los Diablos." For a period in the 1850s it chalked up the record average of a murder per day, and no one appeared to be unduly concerned.

Two decades later it was beginning to be a little more civilized—until an aroused white mob attacked its Chinatown and slaughtered nineteen Chinese in one sally. The event made headlines across the country— the first national recognition Los Angeles had ever received; in fact, it created such a shock wave that the reverberations shook Angelenos into a state of temporary sobriety. But it was the coming of the railroad that marked the first emergence of the pueblo into a modern city.

That emergence was summarized by Hildegarde Hawthorne (d. 1952), poet, essayist and biographer of Emerson, Longfellow, Oliver Wendell Holmes, as well as of her famed New England grandfather Nathaniel Hawthorne. Born in New York and a resident of the East for most of her life, she did not travel West to stay until she reached her mature years. She was quickly recognized as one of California's leading commentators and social historians.

Hoop-la for L.A.

In 1876, when the railways finally reached Los Angeles, it was a dusty, unpaved town, with wooden sidewalks where there were any. In the winter rains it was a sea of mud. Small horse-drawn streetcars, oxcarts, covered wagons and one- or two-horse surreys and phaetons took care of the traffic, where the saddle was not preferred.

Outside town limits the orange groves spread haphazardly, the vineyards vying with them. Here and there in the American section fussy wooden buildings, surrounded by lawns decorated with iron fountains and dogs or deer, housed proud owners. In the Plaza, surrounded by its rows of clipped Monterey cypresses, huddled the idlers of the Mexican part of town, Sonora Town as they called it then, to distinguish it from the ever-extending American section.

The Mexicans were still far the more numerous, but the Americans were richer and they were the ruling class. Along the river, houses were scattered on both banks, and in the center of town there were several three-story business blocks. At night street lamps, each fed from its own small gas tank, made illumination.

Minor financial panics held the city back for a while after the longed-for advent of the railway; droughts did deadly work; smallpox took its toll. But gradually things brightened; out in the broad valleys the farmers were producing increasing crops on the fertile land; irrigation projects increased. By 1882 oranges, lemons, peaches, olives, plums and almonds were bringing in splendid returns. There were apples, plums, pears, figs and walnuts, great orchards of them.

Wheat, corn and hay to feed both the people and the domestic stock, grazing as it did over the grass and wild-oat pastures of the hills before the sun burned them dry, flourished. Six wineries were turning the grapes into wine, one of them the largest in the world. Milk, butter, eggs, honey—a list to make any country jealous. Desert stretches lay between the productive areas. But the promise was great. . . .

With 1883 the Southern Pacific's advertisements of the home advantages of that part of California began to take effect. In that year five thousand new settlers came into the region, Los Angeles benefiting in trade and wealth. In 1885 the Santa Fe Railway came into the city and immediately set out to bring the Southern Pacific to heel in the matter of rates for passengers and freight.

The first rush, the gold rush, had drawn men to San Francisco. The second rush, the land rush, brought families to Los Angeles. The war of the railroad rates went on until you could get to Los Angeles from the Mississippi River for fifteen, for five dollars. The hordes poured in, real-estate values leaped; the boom was on. This became vast by 1884.

Hoop-la!

Before the end of 1887 the population had risen from 1,200 to 100,000. Subdivisions sprang up while you turned your back and people crowded into them, paying incredible prices for lots. Landowners were chased by eager purchasers; lots changed hands even in the now returned churches. Orange and other fruit groves and orchards were ruthlessly cut down, and on the bare ground shanties gave evidence of the new crop of houses about to sprout.

Towns, so-called, were laid out in every direction—later to become that extended and scattered Los Angeles. . . . The newspapers laid the groundwork for later Hollywood advertising in their impassioned phrases. Excursions, with lunch and ice water thrown in, were offered free, even a band included. Prices rose with the yells, and the Los Angeles throats were sounding brass.

Suddenly in 1888 the boom went bang. Within a month or two the fools who had been on the way in were on the way out. The climate took a hand, turning vicious in several ways at once, and a couple of earthquakes shook already shaken nerves. Three thousand persons a month were fleeing Los Angeles. The owners of untold acres of land listed for taxes in the papers could not be found, were for that matter unknown. Rank weeds covered agricultural land; the trees planted on it died for lack of water; the houses crumbled. The real-business men and honest bankers of the city were on the edge of despair. Woe, woe, woe!

It was then that the Santa Fe Railway for one, and Harrison Grey Otis for the other, took hold in earnest to create a real population, real homes, real farms and to bring in a sane population. In the late fall of 1888, Otis formed the Chamber of Commerce of Los Angeles. . . .

A couple of years later the famous "Permanent Exhibit" of Southern California produce was set up in Chicago. It was a whiz and met with instantaneous success. The Santa Fe did its bit by carrying all the stuff free in a baggage car attached to its best train. The Chamber did the selecting and packing, and Los Angeles engaged herself to pay ten thousand dollars for a continuous display during the first year. Orators stood beside fruit and vegetables talking, handing out literature, generally making whoopee. Pamphlets were spread over the entire country.

By 1900 Los Angeles was back in the hundred-thousand-population class again, none of them fly-by-nights, most of them good solid Middle Westerners. Not an exposition in any city but carried a grand splurge from Los Angeles, with every sort of delicious fruit and giant vegetable, and the climate was praised as far as high heaven.

The Middle Westerner especially was fascinated, he who had endured the blizzards of winter, the deluges of spring, the burning summers of his own whatever state. If he had money and youth, he came to buy and to grow. If he had money and was old, he came to rest and go right on living. If he were an invalid, he came to be cured—and usually was. He brought his wife and family along if he had them. Often, too, he or she brought some queer religious leaning along, or a whole sect came in a lump.

They began coming in 1890; they have been coming ever since. But the Middle West itself does not care for Los Angeles, calls it names, tries to call its bluff and to nail its lies, for the city of the Angeles does not always keep itself pure of sin in these directions. No matter. The farmers and little shop keepers, the businessmen who have given up business, the delicate who dread another frozen winter, continue to build bungalows or statelier mansions according to circumstances . . . to the foothills and the sea, there to abide until death does them part.

A very large percentage among these people know only two places, the one they came from, and Los Angeles. Like all converts they have a fanatic devotion to their new love. From their throats flow unending songs of praise, and if you do not agree with them that Los Angeles is the greatest, wisest and most beautiful of cities, their rage can become quite noticeable.

From *Romantic Cities of California,* Hildegarde Hawthorne (New York: D. Appleton-Century, 1939).

miner in Los Angeles to another. No one has ever been able to tell how the information got out, but when the news that the brand-new Wedge Mine had got for one week's product of ore some $18,000, the miners all over southern California were wild at once. . . . Before the middle of October there were more than 1,200 men on the scene. When November came, the number had grown to 2,500.

The heat in the region was severe in September and October, and on many days the temperature rose to 110° in the shade, and sometimes 118°. The only food obtainable was canned meats, vegetables, stale breadstuffs and pork and beans. No climate or disagreeable facts about life and diet ever deterred a gold miner. The hot, alkali, sandy waste for miles was traversed over by ardent, restless prospectors. Lawyers, ranchmen, orchardists, merchants, boys from college, teachers, Mexicans, Yankees and people of all nationalities, except Chinese and Indians, joined in twos or threes or alone in the feverish search for outcroppings of rock wherein to locate a gold mine.

Every canyon within a hundred miles of the Rand ledges was searched through and through; every protruding rock and every hummock of rotten granite was blasted or dug open in the eager search for veins of gold quartz. A few men died of hunger and privation on the desert. Before November some 800 mining claims were posted in the Randsburg district. Up to date 4,300 claims have been made in . . . an area of some fifteen square miles. . . .

In three months Randsburg changed from a desert waste to as lively a mining town as there is in the world. It has grown faster than even Tombstone in 1879, or the Comstock in 1869. . . . "This is the richest gold camp *on top* I ever knew," said Colonel George Ellison, who is in Randsburg, fresh from South Africa, and was formerly of the Treadwell Mine in Alaska. . . . "If the ledges now being developed extend a thousand or more feet in the ground, this will be the greatest mining town the world has ever seen—notwithstanding the fierce summer heat. I've seen this week chunks from four mines here that have assayed at the rate of $3,800 a ton."

The artist who visits Randsburg will find an abundance of vivid local color. The town has four rough wooden buildings called hotels. At each of them there is a call every night for accommodations by over a hundred men, while but fifty men may have the privilege of paying one dollar each for sleeping in bunks arranged in tiers of four, one above the other, and looking at will through the cracks between the boards upon the moonlight scene across the barren stretch of sands. There are five restaurants—all built in the last thirty days—where meals are served at long counters of planed redwood lumber as high as one's chin.

Hundreds of men have paid fifty cents a night for the use of blankets out on the hillsides these cool winter weeks. In and about the town are some seven hundred tents, for, on the desert, camping is more agreeable than living in any house. The dance halls and saloons that follow closely in the wake of every rush to a new mining camp are numerous. The most stately building is the dance hall. It is recruited from San Francisco and Los Angeles, and the proprietors do a land-office business seven nights a week. Saloons are built in short rows here and there about the town on the desert. The saloons number twenty-four, and the scarcity of all lumber for knocking together some sort of a structure is the only reason there are no more of them.

Three years ago F. M. Mooers, formerly a newspaper man in Brooklyn, went out from Los Angeles to get information about placer mines at Goler for a series of newspaper articles. He became interested in the life of a mining camp and abandoning reportorial work, went to work with a pick and shovel for the Goler Company. On days when there was no work, he and a friend, C. A. Burcham, found pleasure in studying the volcanic formation of the rocks and hills about them. They conceived the idea that the golden flakes that they washed from the Goler gravel must originally have come from the ledge of gold-bearing ore in that region.

The old miners laughed, and said that practical mining had long ago exploded such a theory. Nevertheless, Mooers and Burcham became the more convinced that there were ledges of gold-bearing ore in that region, covered by sand and sun-baked soil, and they continued their search. For months in 1895 they traveled about in a lumber wagon drawn by mules across the desert and among the mountains and along the foothills. Every day they prospected from dawn until dark.

Many times they were about to give up their search because of their suffering for lack of food and water. One night in October of 1895 Mooers and Burcham slept in a desolate dry canyon. The next morning while they were foraging for grease-roots with which to cook their breakfast, Burcham came across a bit of protruding rock. He went back to the wagon, got his hammer, as he had done thousands of times before, and knocked off a chunk of the rock.

He and Mooers looked it over. The gold was sticking out in pin-head particles. Both men could hardly believe their eyes. Another chunk was knocked from the butte. Mooers and Burcham sat down and looked it over with their pocket magnifying glass. "Burch, we've struck it!" cried Mooers. "There's no need to look further. All we've got to do is to shovel the whole mountain into a stamp mill and barrel up our gold."

There was no further thought of breakfast in camp that day. An assayer in Los Angeles subsequently found that the first chunk of rock taken out was worth in gold $9.50. It was the size of a large cabbage. For weeks Mooers and Burcham kept their find a secret. They went over and over the mountain until they believed they knew all the best ledges in it. These ledges are known as the Rand Mines. They called in an experienced quartz miner, John Singleton, and with him located some eight mines there. Then, when they had made good titles to their finds, they called in capital, and they have since been developing their group of mines. Several times they have had offers of hundreds of thousands of dollars for a half-interest in the property. The first week in February they shipped to the San Francisco smelters $58,000 worth of ore.

There are other men who have gone to Randsburg poor, and whose lucky strokes of the hammer on ledges have made them rich. There's Dan Kelsey who was a teamster on a wagon that used to haul borax from Death Valley to Mojave. He hauled lumber to the Rand Mine last July, before the richness of the rocks there was known by more than a hundred persons. He was used to the drought of the blistering desert, and dared much where other men would be timid.

He spent two weeks following "float" from a ledge up Yucca Canyon. He hammered and pecked his way for six miles, and one Sunday he chipped off a piece of quartz that made his eyes swim at the sight of the golden flecks. That piece of rock is now exhibited in a bank in Los Angeles, and it led to Dan's getting a partner to invest $20,000 for a half-interest. With this capital two tunnels have been blasted into the ledge for 145 feet, and every pound of the rock has sold at good prices. The mine, known as the Blue Daisy, was sold early in December for $170,000, with which Daniel Kelsey and family have now gone on a tour of Europe.

Last spring Cyrus Drouillard was eking out a bare existence as a country constable in Kern County. He went over to what is now Randsburg one day last June to serve some legal papers. He saw what the Rand Mine was doing and lost no time in going out to prospect in that region. He spent several weeks in prowling about the foothills searching for signs of mineral wealth. He risked thirst and hunger, and slept where night overtook him, only to follow up a lead at daybreak.

One evening as he was munching on his lonely supper of dried corned meat and crackers, he saw a mass of "live" rock at his elbow that looked more promising than any he had seen in several days. It was too dark to do much investigating that night, so he simply drilled a hole a few inches deep that evening, and the next morning put in a small dynamite candle. When the charge had been exploded, he ran back to see what his blast had revealed. His trained eyes told him he had at last made his stroke of fortune.

Where that charge of dynamite blew out a projecting rock, out on the yellow blistering sands of the Mojave Desert, six miles east of Randsburg, Cy Drouillard located the St. Elmo Mine. He has had several offers of $300,000 for the property, but he declines to listen to any offers, and says it is worth millions to him. That may seem strange to the average reader when the information is added that the shaft into St. Elmo Mine is down but about 180 feet, and the only works about it are a common windlass, a length of wire cable and a few ore buckets.

From "Randsburg, A Desert Mining Town," Henry G. Tinsley. *Harper's Weekly,* March 6, 1897.

LX

Edwin Markham

Inconsistent as it appeared—against the tendency of Californians to consider the best Indians dead Indians, the best Chinese those that were holed up in their ghettos, the best Mexicans those who were content to serve as laborers or vaqueros—the state was developing a social consciousness. Voices were raised occasionally in favor of applying the much-talked-about American democratic principles to the downtrodden races in their midst.

The most eloquent voice was that of Edwin Markham (1852–1940) and the brunt of his message was contained in six lines of a single poem, "The Man with the Hoe":

> Bowed by the weight of centuries he leans
> Upon his hoe and gazes on the ground,
> The emptiness of ages in his face,
> And on his back the burden of the world.
>
> . . .
>
> O masters, lords and rulers in all lands,
> Is this the handiwork you give to God?

Few poems in American literature ever created quite the commotion that was stirred by "the hoe-poem," as it was called at the time. First published in the San Francisco *Examiner* in 1899, it was reprinted in newspapers and magazines across the country, hailed as "the battle cry for the next thousand years"; it generated so much praise and reproach that daily for six months the *Examiner* ran a full page of letters, parodies, approbation, and denunciation; it was shortly translated into a score of languages and circulated in as many countries. The poem brought Markham instant renown.

Until the date of its publication, its author had lived in obscurity in California, as a sheepherder, vaquero, blacksmith, field hand, farmer, occasional versifier, and, after belated attendance at San Jose State Normal School, as teacher and principal in Oakland. Fairly overwhelmed with homage, the principal soon resigned, moved to New York and lived there the rest of his life.

"The Man with the Hoe," of course, was composed as an impassioned commentary on Millet's popular painting of the same subject, a rebuke to mankind for placing the burden of labor upon the backs of the "plundered peasant." It was addressed to the world—not particularly to Californians—as was his other poetry. In fact, Markham as a poet did not concern himself conspicuously with questions of morality. Most of his verse about the West dealt with nostalgic recollections and pleasant images of his youthful years as sheepherder, cowboy, and amateur naturalist.

A Mendocino Memory

Once in my lonely, eager youth I rode,
With jingling spur, into the clouds' abode—
Rode northward lightly as the high crane goes—
Rode into the hills in the month of the frail wild rose,
To find the soft-eyed heifers in the herds,
Strayed north along the trail of nesting birds,
Following the slow march of the springing grass,
From range to range, from pass to flowering pass.

. . .

I climbed the canyon to a river-head,
And looking backward saw a splendor spread,
Miles beyond miles, of every kingly hue
And trembling tint the looms of Arras knew—

A flowery pomp as of the dying day,
A splendor where a god might take his way.

And farther on the wide plains under me,
I watched the light-foot winds of morning go,
Soft shading over wheat-fields far and free,
To keep their old appointment with the sea.
And farther yet, dim in the distant glow,
Hung on the east a line of ghostly snow.

After the many miles an open space
Walled by the tules of a perished lake;
And there I stretched out, bending the green brake,
And felt it cool against my heated face.
My horse went cropping by a sunny crag,
In wild oats taller than the antlered stag
That makes his pasture there. In gorge below
Blind waters pounded boulders, blow on blow—
Waters that gather, scatter and amass
Down the long canyons where the grizzlies pass,
Slouching through manzanita thickets old,
Strewing the small red apples on the ground,
Tearing the wild grape from its tree-top hold,
And wafting odors keen through all the hills around.

. . .

The Rock-Breaker

Pausing he leans upon his sledge, and looks—
    A labor-blasted toiler;
So have I seen, on Shasta's top, a pine
    Stand silent on a cliff,
Stript of its glory of green leaves and boughs,
    Its great trunk split by fire,

Its gray bark blackened by the thunder-smoke,
   Its life a sacrifice
To some blind purpose of the destinies.

On the Suisun Hills

Long, long ago I was a shepherd boy,
My young heart touched with wonder and wild joy.
Once in my happy country far away,
One dear December day,
On green Sierran hills at fall of sun,
We shepherds came with singing, every one
Bearing a fragrant pack
Of manzanita boughs upon the back.
And soon the watch-fires kindled on the height
Were darting scarlet prongs against the night;
While all the huddled sheep
Were lying still, save one belated ewe
Bringing her lost lamb in with loud ado.
And by the crackling boughs our dogs asleep
Were startling with short barks
Or pricking pointed ears in little harks,
Chasing a dream-coyote down the steep.

. . .

Joy of the Hills

I ride on the mountain tops, I ride;
I have found my life and am satisfied.
Onward I ride in the blowing oats,
Checking the field-lark's rippling notes—
   Lightly I sweep
   From steep to steep:

Over my head through the branches high
Come glimpses of a rushing sky;
The tall oats brush my horse's flanks;
Wild poppies crowd on the sunny banks;
A bee booms out of the scented grass;
A jay laughs with me as I pass.

I ride on the hills, I forgive, I forget
    Life's hoard of regret—
    All the terror and pain
    Of the chafing chain.
    Grind on, O cities, grind:
    I leave you a blur behind.
I am lifted elate—the skies expand:
Here the world's heaped gold is a pile of sand.

Let them weary and work in their narrow walls:
I ride with the voices of waterfalls!

I swing on as one in a dream—I swing
Down the airy hollows, I shout, I sing!
The world is gone like an empty word:
My body's a bough in the wind, my heart a bird!

In Poppy Fields

Here the poppy hosts assemble:
How they startle, how they tremble!
All their royal hoods unpinned
Blow out lightly in the wind.
Here is gold to labor for;
Here is pillage worth a war.

Men that in the cities grind,
Come! before the heart is blind.

In Death Valley

There came gray stretches of volcanic plains,
Bare, lone and treeless, then a bleak lone hill,
Like to the dolorous hill that Dobell saw.
Around were heaps of ruins piled between
The Burn o' Sorrow and the Water o' Care;
And from the stillness of the down-crushed walls
One pillar rose up dark against the moon.
There was a nameless Presence everywhere;
In the gray soil there was a purple stain,
And the gray reticent rocks were dyed with blood—
Blood of a vast unknown Calamity.
It was the mark of some ancestral grief—
Grief that began before the ancient Flood.

In High Sierras

There at a certain hour of the deep night,
A gray cliff with a demon face comes up,
Wrinkled and old, behind the peaks, and with
An anxious look peers at the Zodiac.

"A Mendocino Memory" from *Lincoln and Other Poems* by Edwin Markham (New York: McClure, Phillips and Company, 1901); "Joy of the Hills," "The Rock-Breaker," "In Poppy Fields," "In Death Valley," and "In High Sierras" from *The Man with the Hoe and Other Poems* by Edwin Markham (New York: Doubleday and McClure Company, 1899).

LXI

Frank Norris

Everywhere in California incredible change was taking place—everywhere, it seemed, except in Death Valley, and even there a seldom frequented cart path snaked from the borax works down part of its length. But that path meant scarcely more than would a scratch on the face of the moon; Death Valley had been altered little since the day Lewis Manly led his straggling group of overlanders out of it. It was the ultimate in places of escape, for pursuers would avoid it like the plague.

It was just the setting Frank Norris (1870–1902) needed for the final chapters of his novel *McTeague*. A man of the world, born in Chicago, educated in Paris, at Harvard and Berkeley, he took up residence in San Francisco after completing his formal education, and began experimenting there with the kind of blunt realism he found in the contemporary French writer and social reformer Emile Zola. *McTeague* was the first product of that experiment and it shocked the country when it was first published in 1899. Here were aspects of paradisiacal California—from sordid slums to burning desert—that had never before been revealed.

Dr. McTeague had been a respected San Francisco dentist before he was exposed as a quack, before he ran off with the fiancée of his best friend and confidant Marcus Schouler, married, degraded, and finally murdered her. A posse of sheriffs and deputies had tracked the doctor across the breadth of California, but when he sought refuge in Death

Valley, they declined to follow. Only Marcus, propelled by a passion
for revenge, would risk that. Into the depths of Death Valley he cautiously followed the brute McTeague, who to the last incongruously
carried with him one symbol of his former sensitivity—a caged canary.

To the Bitter End

Far behind [McTeague], the Panamint hills were already but
blue hummocks on the horizon. Before him and upon either side,
to the north and to the east and to the south, stretched primordial
desolation. League upon league the infinite reaches of dazzling
white alkali laid themselves out like an immeasurable scroll un-
rolled from horizon to horizon; not a bush, not a twig relieved
that horrible monotony.

Even the sand of the desert would have been a welcome sight;
a single clump of sagebrush would have fascinated the eye; but
this was worse than the desert. It was abominable, this hideous
sink of alkali, this bed of some primeval lake lying so far below
the level of the ocean. The great mountains of Placer County had
been merely indifferent to man; but this awful sink of alkali was
openly and unreservedly iniquitous and malignant.

McTeague had told himself that the heat upon the lower slopes
of the Panamint had been dreadful; here in Death Valley it
became a thing of terror. There was no longer any shadow but his
own. He was scorched and parched from head to heel. It seemed
to him that the smart of his tortured body could not have been
keener if he had been flayed.

"If it gets much hotter——" he muttered, wringing the sweat
from his thick fell of hair and mustache, "if it gets much hotter, I
don' know what I'll do." He was thirsty, and drank a little from
his canteen. "I ain't got any too much water," he murmured,
shaking the canteen. "I got to get out of this place in a hurry,
sure."

By eleven o'clock the heat had increased to such an extent that
McTeague could feel the burning of the ground come prickling

and stinging through the soles of his boots. Every step he took
threw up clouds of impalpable alkali dust, salty and choking, so
that he strangled and coughed and sneezed with it. "*Lord!* what a
country!" exclaimed the dentist.

An hour later the mule stopped and lay down, his jaws wide
open, his ears dangling. McTeague washed his mouth with a
handful of water and for a second time since sunrise wetted the
flour sacks about the bird cage. The air was quivering and
palpitating like that in the stokehold of a steamship. The sun,
small and contracted, swam molten overhead. "I can't stand it,"
said McTeague at length. "I'll have to stop and make some kinda
shade."

The mule was crouched upon the ground, panting rapidly, with
half-closed eyes. The dentist removed the saddle and unrolling
his blanket, propped it up as best he could between him and the
sun. As he stooped down to crawl beneath it, his palm touched
the ground. He snatched it away with a cry of pain. The surface
alkali was oven-hot; he was obliged to scoop out a trench in it
before he dared to lie down.

By degrees the dentist began to doze. He had had little or no
sleep the night before, and the hurry of his flight under the
blazing sun had exhausted him. But his rest was broken; between
waking and sleeping, all manner of troublous images galloped
through his brain. He thought he was back in the Panamint hills
again. . . . Something was following him . . . something dark
crawling upon the ground, an indistinct gray figure, man or brute,
he did not know. Then he saw another and another; then another.
A score of black, crawling objects were following him, crawling
from bush to bush, converging upon him. "*They*" were after him,
were closing in upon him, were within touch of his hand, were at
his feet—*were at his throat.*

McTeague jumped up with a shout, oversetting the blanket.
There was nothing in sight. For miles around the alkali was
empty, solitary, quivering and shimmering under the pelting fire
of the afternoon's sun. But once more the spur bit into his body,
goading him on. There was to be no rest, no going back, no pause,
no stop. Hurry, hurry, hurry on. . . . "I *can't* go on," groaned

McTeague, his eyes sweeping the horizon behind him. "I'm beat out. I'm dog tired. I ain't slept any for two nights." But for all that he roused himself again, saddled the mule, scarcely less exhausted than himself, and pushed on once more over the scorching alkali and under the blazing sun.

From that time on, the fear never left him, the spur never ceased to bite, the instinct that goaded him to flight never was dumb; hurry or halt, it was all the same. On he went, straight on, chasing the receding horizon, flagellated with heat, tortured with thirst, crouching over, looking furtively behind, and at times reaching his hand forward, the fingers prehensile, grasping as it were toward the horizon that always fled before him.

The sun set upon the third day of McTeague's flight; night came on; the stars burned slowly into the cool dark purple of the sky. The gigantic sink of white alkali glowed like snow. McTeague, now far into the desert, held steadily on, swinging forward with great strides. His enormous strength held him doggedly to his work. Sullenly, with his huge jaws gripping stolidly together, he pushed on. At midnight he stopped. "Now," he growled with a certain desperate defiance, as though he expected to be heard, "now, I'm going to lay up and get some sleep. You can come or not."

He cleared away the hot surface alkali, spread out his blanket, and slept until the next day's heat aroused him. His water was so low that he dared not make coffee now, and so he breakfasted without it. Until ten o'clock he tramped forward, then camped again in the shade of one of the rare rock ledges, and "lay up" during the heat of the day. By five o'clock he was once more on the march.

He traveled on for the greater part of that night, stopping only once toward three in the morning to water the mule from the canteen. Again the red-hot day burned up over the horizon. Even at six o'clock it was hot. "It's going to be worse than ever today," he groaned. "I wish I could find another rock to camp by. Ain't I ever going to get out of this place?"

There was no change in the character of the desert. Always the same measureless leagues of white-hot alkali stretched away toward the horizon on every hand. Here and there the flat, dazzling surface of the desert broke and raised into long low mounds, from the summit of which McTeague could look for miles and miles over its horrible desolation. No shade was in sight. Not a rock, not a stone broke the monotony of the ground. Again and again he ascended the low unevenness, looking and searching for a camping place, shading his eyes from the glitter of sand and sky.

He tramped forward a little farther, then paused at length in a hollow between two breaks, resolving to make camp there.

Suddenly there was a shout. "Hands up. By damn, I got the drop on you!"

McTeague looked up. It was Marcus.

"Hands up!" shouted Marcus a second time. "I'll give you three to do it in. One, two——"

Instinctively McTeague put his hands above his head.

Marcus rose and came toward him over the break. "Keep 'em up," he cried. "If you move 'em once I'll kill you, sure." He came up to McTeague and searched him, going through his pockets; but McTeague had no revolver, not even a hunting knife. "What did you do with that money, with that five thousand dollars?"

"It's on the mule," answered McTeague sullenly.

Marcus grunted and cast a glance at the mule, who was standing some distance away, snorting nervously and from time to time flattening his long ears. . . . "Got any water?" he demanded.

"There's a canteen of water on the mule."

Marcus moved toward the mule and made as if to reach the bridle rein. The mule squealed, threw up his head and galloped to a little distance, rolling his eyes and flattening his ears. Marcus swore wrathfully.

"He acted that way once before," explained McTeague, his hands still in the air. "He ate some locoweed back in the hills before I started."

For a moment Marcus hesitated. While he was catching the mule McTeague might get away. But where to, in heaven's name? A rat could not hide on the surface of that glistening alkali, and besides, all McTeague's store of provisions and his priceless supply of water were on the mule. Marcus ran after the mule, revolver in hand, shouting and cursing. But the mule could not be caught. He acted as if possessed, squealing, lashing out and galloping in wide circles, his head high in the air. . . . McTeague came up. "He's eatun some locoweed," he repeated. "He went kinda crazy once before."

"If he should take it into his head to bolt and keep on running——" Marcus did not finish. A sudden great fear seemed to widen around and enclose the two men. Once their water was gone, the end would not be long.

Already the sense of enmity between the two had weakened in the face of a common peril. Marcus let down the hammer of his revolver and slid it back into the holster. The mule was trotting ahead, snorting and throwing up great clouds of alkali dust. . . . "He's clean crazy," fumed Marcus, panting and swearing. . . .

Then began an interminable pursuit. Mile after mile under the terrible heat of the desert sun the two men followed the mule, racked with a thirst that grew fiercer every hour. A dozen times they could almost touch the canteen of water, and as often the distraught animal shied away and fled before them. At length Marcus cried: "It's no use; we can't catch him, and we're killing ourselves with thirst. We've got to take our chances." He drew his revolver from his holster, cocked it and crept forward.

"Steady, now," said McTeague; "it won't do to shoot through the canteen."

Within twenty yards Marcus paused, made a rest of his forearm and fired. "You've *got* him," cried McTeague. "No, he's up again. Shoot him again. He's going to bolt."

Marcus ran on, firing as he ran. The mule, one foreleg trailing, scrambled along, squealing and snorting. Marcus fired his last shot. The mule pitched forward upon his head, then rolling sideways, fell upon the canteen, bursting it open and spilling its entire contents into the sand. Marcus and McTeague ran up. . . . There was no water left. . . . "We're dead men," said Marcus.

McTeague looked from him out over the desert. Chaotic desolation stretched from them on either hand, flaming and glaring with the afternoon heat. There was the brazen sky and the

leagues upon leagues of alkali, leper white. There was nothing
more. They were in the heart of Death Valley. "Not a drop of
water," muttered McTeague, "not a drop." . . .

Marcus ground his teeth. "Done for," he muttered; "done for.
. . . Well, we can't stop here; we got to go somewhere. . . .
Anything we want to take along with us from the mule? We
can——"

Suddenly he paused. In an instant the eyes of the two doomed
men had met as the same thought simultaneously rose in their
minds. The canvas sack with its five thousand dollars was still
tied to the horn of the saddle. Marcus had emptied his revolver at
the mule, and though he still wore his cartridge belt, he was for
the moment as unarmed as McTeague. "I guess," began Mc-
Teague, coming forward a step, "I guess, even if we are done for,
I'll take—some of my truck along."

"Hold on," exclaimed Marcus with rising aggressiveness. "Let's
talk about that. . . . You're my prisoner, do you understand?
You'll do as I say." Marcus had drawn the handcuffs from his
pocket and stood ready with his revolver held as a club. ". . .
Don't you lay your finger on that sack."

Marcus barred McTeague's way, white with passion. Mc-
Teague did not answer. His eyes drew to two fine, twinkling
points, and his enormous hands knotted themselves into fists, hard
as wooden mallets. He moved a step nearer to Marcus, then another. Suddenly the men grappled and in another instant were
rolling and struggling upon the hot white ground. McTeague
thrust Marcus backward until he tripped and fell over the body
of the dead mule. The little bird cage broke from the saddle with
the violence of their fall and rolled upon the ground, the flour
bags slipping from it. McTeague tore the revolver from Marcus's
grip and struck out with it blindly. Clouds of alkali dust, fine and
pungent, enveloped the two fighting men, all but strangling them.

McTeague did not know how he killed his enemy, but all at
once Marcus grew still beneath his blows. Then there was a
sudden last return of energy. McTeague's right wrist was caught;
something clicked upon it; then the struggling body fell limp and
motionless with a long breath.

As McTeague rose to his feet, he felt a pull at his right wrist; something held it fast. Looking down, he saw that Marcus in that last struggle had found strength to handcuff their wrists together. Marcus was dead now; McTeague was locked to the body. All about him, vast, interminable, stretched the measureless leagues of Death Valley.

McTeague remained stupidly looking around him, now at the distant horizon, now at the ground, now at the half-dead canary chittering feebly in its little gilt prison.

From *McTeague*, Frank Norris (New York: Boni and Liveright, 1899).

LXII

Jack London

For more than three quarters of a century, before bridges spanned San Francisco Bay and the Golden Gate, one of the boasted attractions of the Bay region was the system of ferries that carried commuters, shoppers, and visitors between the major cities hugging the shores. The crossing provided a relaxing half hour for scanning the newspapers, for a few hands at the card tables, exchanges of local gossip, a sandwich and cup of coffee, or idle survey of the coastline from the upper deck.

Few vicissitudes of tide or weather were permitted to alter schedules. Departure and arrival times were immutable; ferries ran on time in foul weather and fair, over placid waters or against rip currents, through high winds and pea soup fog. The fogs that billowed in unheralded through the Golden Gate were perhaps the worst hazard with which the ferry skippers had to contend, particularly when the Bay was congested with traffic.

The collision of a ferry and commercial vessel in one of these blinding fogs is the plot propellant for *The Sea Wolf* by Jack London (1876–1916). Essays and poems by the score were written about San Francisco Bay fogs in all their moods, and as rehearsals of the tragedies they produced, but no one ever pictured the atmosphere more vividly than London in the opening chapter of his novel—fog as seen and felt by ferry passengers in the throes of disaster near the turn of the century. The cold, wet, gray fogs seemed to hold a very personal

[418]

significance to London, for he was exposed to them during all his early life.

Over a period of scarcely more than a decade and a half, Jack London wrote a phenomenal fifty books, most of which in some way were autobiographical. He could draw from a wealth of first-hand experience. Born in the slums of San Francisco and brought up in Oakland, he knew the Bay area intimately, as he later knew intimately such disparate regions as the Klondike, Japan, the South Seas, and Mexico. At seventeen he shipped out as an able seaman to Japan and the Bering Sea. In turn he was an oyster pirate, an early gold digger in the Klondike rush, a correspondent in the Russo-Japanese War and in the 1914 Mexican War. His personal adventures were both romantic and realistic. He incorporated those qualities into fiction peopled with characters he had known, spiced with incidents the like of which he had witnessed, and set in backgrounds where he had lived.

In *The Sea Wolf* London unmistakably identified himself with the victim of the San Francisco Bay collision, who is picked up by the schooner *Ghost* and impressed as a crewman under the brutal command of Captain Wolf Larsen for a seal-hunting expedition to the North Pacific.

From Out of the Fog

I sometimes facetiously place the cause of it all to Charley Furuseth's credit. He kept a summer cottage in Mill Valley, under the shadow of Mount Tamalpias, and never occupied it except when he loafed through the winter months and read Nietzsche and Schopenhauer to rest his brain. When summer came on, he elected to sweat out a hot and dusty existence in the city and to toil incessantly. Had it not been my custom to run up to see him every Saturday afternoon and to stop over till Monday morning, this particular January Monday morning would not have found me afloat on San Francisco Bay.

Not but that I was afloat in a safe craft, for the *Martinez* was a new ferry-steamer, making her fourth or fifth trip on the run between Sausalito and San Francisco. The danger lay in the heavy fog which blanketed the bay, and of which, as a landsman,

I had little apprehension. In fact, I remember the placid exalta-
tion with which I took up my position on the forward upper deck,
directly beneath the pilot-house, and allowed the mystery of the
fog to lay hold of my imagination. A fresh breeze was blowing,
and for a time I was alone in the moist obscurity—yet not alone,
for I was dimly conscious of the presence of the pilot, and of what
I took to be the captain, in the glass house above my head.

I remember thinking how comfortable it was, this division of
labor which made it unnecessary for me to study fogs, winds,
tides and navigation, in order to visit my friend who lived across
an arm of the sea. It was good that men should be specialists, I
mused. The peculiar knowledge of the pilot and captain sufficed
for many thousands of people who knew no more of the sea and
navigation than I knew.

On the other hand, instead of having to devote my energy to
the learning of a multitude of things, I concentrated it upon a few
particular things, such as, for instance, the analysis of Poe's place
in American literature—an essay of mine, by the way, in the
current *Atlantic*. Coming aboard, as I passed through the cabin, I
had noticed with greedy eyes a stout gentleman reading the *Atlantic*, which was open at my very essay. And there it was again,
the division of labor, the special knowledge of the pilot and
captain which permitted the stout gentleman to read my special
knowledge on Poe while they carried him safely from Sausalito to
San Francisco.

A red-faced man, slamming the cabin door behind him and
stumping out on the deck, interrupted my reflections, though I
made a mental note of the topic for use in a projected essay which
I had thought of calling "The Necessity for Freedom: A Plea for
the Artist." The red-faced man shot a glance up at the pilot-
house, gazed around at the fog, stumped across the deck and back
(he evidently had artificial legs), and stood still by my side, legs
wide apart, and with an expression of keen enjoyment on his face.
I was not wrong when I decided that his days had been spent on
the sea.

"It's nasty weather like this here that turns heads gray before
their time," he said, with a nod toward the pilot-house.

"I had not thought there was any particular strain," I answered. "It seems as simple as A, B, C. They know the direction by compass, the distance and the speed. I should not call it anything more than mathematical certainty."

"Strain!" he snorted. "Simple as A, B, C! Mathematical certainty!"

He seemed to brace himself up and lean backward against the air as he stared at me. "How about this here tide that's rushin' out through the Golden Gate?" he demanded, or bellowed, rather. "How fast is she ebbin'? What's the drift, eh? Listen to that, will you? A bell-buoy, and we're a-top of it! See 'em alterin' the course!"

From out of the fog came the mournful tolling of a bell, and I could see the pilot turning the wheel with great rapidity. The bell, which had seemed straight ahead, was now sounding from the side. Our own whistle was blowing hoarsely, and from time to time the sound of other whistles came to us from out of the fog.

"That's a ferry-boat of some sort," the newcomer said, indicating a whistle off to the right. "And there! D'ye hear that? Blown by mouth. Some scow schooner, most likely. Better watch out, Mr. Schooner-man. Ah, I thought so. Now hell's a-poppin' for somebody!"

The unseen ferry-boat was blowing blast after blast, and the mouth-blown horn was tooting in terror-stricken fashion.

"And now they're payin' their respects to each other and tryin' to get clear," the red-faced man went on, as the hurried whistling ceased.

His face was shining, his eyes flashing with excitement, as he translated into articulate language the speech of the horns and sirens. "That's a steam siren a-goin' it over there to the left. And you hear that fellow with a frog in his throat—a steam schooner as near as I can judge, crawlin' in from the Heads against the tide."

A shrill little whistle, piping as if gone mad, came from directly ahead and from very near at hand. Gongs sounded on the *Martinez*. Our paddle-wheels stopped, their pulsing beat died away, and then they started again. The shrill little whistle, like the chirping of a cricket amid the cries of great beasts, shot through the fog from more to the side and swiftly grew faint and fainter. I looked to my companion for enlightenment.

"One of them dare-devil launches," he said. "I almost wish we'd sunk him, the little rip! They're the cause of more trouble. And what good are they? Any jackass gets aboard one and runs it from hell to breakfast, blowin' his whistle to beat the band and tellin' the rest of the world to look out for him, because he's comin' and can't look out for himself! Because he's comin'! And you've got to look out, too! Right of way! Common decency! They don't know the meanin' of it!"

I felt quite amused at his unwarranted choler, and while he stumped indignantly up and down I fell to dwelling upon the romance of the fog. And romantic it certainly was—the fog, like the gray shadow of infinite mystery, brooding over the whirling speck of earth; and men, mere motes of light and sparkle, cursed with an insane relish for work, riding their steeds of wood and steel through the heart of the mystery, groping their way blindly through the Unseen, and clamoring and clanging in confident speech the while their hearts are heavy with incertitude and fear.

The voice of my companion brought me back to myself with a laugh. I too had been groping and floundering, the while I thought I rode clear-eyed through the mystery.

"Hello; somebody comin' our way," he was saying. "And d'ye hear that? He's comin' fast. Walking right along. Guess he don't hear us yet. Wind's in wrong direction."

The fresh breeze was blowing right down upon us, and I could hear the whistle plainly, off to one side and a little ahead.

"Ferry-boat?" I asked.

He nodded, then added, "Or he wouldn't be keepin' up such a clip." He gave a short chuckle. "They're gettin' anxious up there."

I glanced up. The captain had thrust his head and shoulders out of the pilot-house, and was staring intently into the fog as though by sheer force of will he could penetrate it. His face was anxious, as was the face of my companion, who had stumped over to the rail and was gazing with a like intenseness in the direction of the invisible danger.

Then everything happened, and with inconceivable rapidity. The fog seemed to break away as though split by a wedge, and the bow of a steamboat emerged, trailing fog-wreaths on either side like seaweed on the snout of Leviathan. I could see the pilot-house and a white-bearded man leaning partly out of it, on his elbows. He was clad in a blue uniform, and I remember noting how trim and quiet he was. His quietness, under the circumstances, was terrible. He accepted Destiny, marched hand in hand with it, and coolly measured the stroke. As he leaned there, he ran a calm and speculative eye over us, as though to determine the precise point of the collision, and took no notice whatever when our pilot, white with rage, shouted, "Now you've done it."

On looking back, I realize that the remark was too obvious to make rejoinder necessary.

"Grab hold of something and hang on," the red-faced man said to me. All his bluster had gone, and he seemed to have caught the contagion of preternatural calm. "And listen to the women scream," he said grimly—almost bitterly, I thought, as though he had been through the experience before.

The vessels came together before I could follow his advice. We must have been struck squarely amidships, for I saw nothing, the strange steamboat having passed beyond my line of vision. The *Martinez* heeled over, sharply, and there was a crashing and rending of timber. I was thrown flat on the wet deck, and before I could scramble to my feet I heard the scream of the women. This it was, I am certain—the most indescribable of blood-curdling sounds—that threw me into a panic.

I remembered the life-preservers stored in the cabin, but was met at the door and swept backward by a wild rush of men and women.

What happened in the next few minutes I do not recollect, though I have a clear remembrance of pulling down life-preservers from the overhead racks, while the red-faced man fastened them about the bodies of an hysterical group of women. This memory is as distinct and sharp as that of any picture I have seen. It is a picture, and I can see it now—the jagged edges of the hole in the side of the cabin, through which the gray fog swirled and eddied; the empty upholstered seats, littered with all the evidences of sudden flight, such as packages, hand satchels, umbrellas, and wraps; the stout gentleman who had been reading my essay, encased in cork and canvas, the magazine still in his hand, and asking me with monotonous insistence if I thought there was any danger; the red-faced man, stumping gallantly around on his artificial legs and buckling life-preservers on all comers; and finally, the screaming bedlam of women.

This it was, the screaming of the women, that most tried my nerves. It must have tried, too, the nerves of the red-faced man, for I have another picture which will never fade from my mind. The stout gentleman is stuffing the magazine into his overcoat pocket and looking on curiously. A tangled mass of women, with drawn, white faces and open mouths, is shrieking like a chorus of lost souls; and the red-faced man, his face now purplish with wrath, and his arms extended overhead as in the act of hurling thunderbolts, is shouting, "Shut up! Oh, shut up!"

I remember the scene impelled me to sudden laughter, and in the next instant I realized I was becoming hysterical myself; for these were women of my own kind, like my mother and sisters, with the fear of death upon them and unwilling to die. And I remember that the sounds they made reminded me of the squealing of pigs under the knife of the butcher, and I was struck with horror at the vividness of the analogy. These women, capable of the most sublime emotions, of the tenderest sympathies, were open-mouthed and screaming. They wanted to live, they were helpless, like rats in a trap, and they screamed.

The horror of it drove me out on deck. I was feeling sick and squeamish, and sat down on a bench. In a hazy way I saw and heard men rushing and shouting as they strove to lower the boats. It was just as I had read descriptions of such scenes in books. The tackles jammed. Nothing worked. One boat lowered away with the plugs out, filled with women and children and then with water, and capsized. Another boat had been lowered by one end, and still hung in the tackle by the other end, where it had been abandoned. Nothing was to be seen of the strange steamboat which had caused the disaster, though I heard men saying that she would undoubtedly send boats to our assistance.

I descended to the lower deck. The *Martinez* was sinking fast, for the water was very near. Numbers of the passengers were leaping overboard. Others, in the water, were clamoring to be taken aboard again. No one heeded them. A cry arose that we were sinking. I was seized by the consequent panic, and went over the side in a surge of bodies. How I went over I do not know, though I did know, and instantly, why those in the water were so desirous of getting back on the steamer. The water was cold—so cold that it was painful. The pang, as I plunged into it, was as quick and sharp as that of fire. It bit to the marrow. It was like the grip of death. I gasped with the anguish and shock of it, filling my lungs before the life-preserver popped me to the surface. The taste of the salt was strong in my mouth, and I was strangling with the acrid stuff in my throat and lungs.

But it was the cold that was most distressing. I felt that I could survive but a few minutes. People were struggling and floundering in the water about me. I could hear them crying out to one another. And I heard, also, the sound of oars. Evidently the strange steamboat had lowered its boats. As the time went by I marvelled that I was still alive. I had no sensation whatever in my lower limbs, while a chilling numbness was wrapping about my heart and creeping into it. Small waves, with spiteful foaming crests, continually broke over me and into my mouth, sending me off into more strangling paroxysms.

The noises grew indistinct, though I heard a final and despairing chorus of screams in the distance and knew that the *Martinez* had gone down. Later—how much later I have no knowledge—I came to myself with a start of fear. I was alone. I could hear no calls or cries—only the sound of the waves, made weirdly hollow and reverberant by the fog. A panic in the crowd, which partakes of a sort of community of interest, is not so terrible as a panic when one is by oneself; and such a panic I now suffered.

Whither was I drifting? The red-faced man had said that the tide was ebbing through the Golden Gate. Was I, then, being carried out to sea? And the life-preserver in which I floated? Was it not liable to go to pieces at any moment? I had heard of such things being made of paper and hollow rushes which quickly became saturated and lost all buoyancy. And I could not swim a stroke. And I was alone, floating, apparently, in the midst of a gray primordial vastness. I confess that a madness seized me, that I shrieked aloud as the women had shrieked, and beat the water with my numb hands.

How long this lasted I have no conception, for a blankness intervened, of which I remember no more than one remembers of troubled and painful sleep. When I aroused, it was as after centuries of time; and I saw, almost above me and emerging from the fog, the bow of a vessel, and three triangular sails, each shrewdly lapping the other and filled with wind. Where the bow cut the water there was a great foaming and gurgling, and I seemed directly in its path.

I tried to cry out, but was too exhausted. The bow plunged down, just missing me and sending a swash of water clear over my head. Then the long, black side of a vessel began slipping past, so near that I could have touched it with my hands. I tried to reach it, in a mad resolve to claw into the wood with my nails, but my arms were heavy and lifeless. Again I strove to call out, but made no sound.

The stern of the vessel shot by, dropping, as it did so, into a hollow between the waves; and I caught a glimpse of a man standing at the wheel, and of another man who seemed to be doing little else than smoke a cigar. I saw the smoke issuing from his lips as he slowly turned his head and glanced out over the water in my direction. It was a careless, unpremeditated glance, one of those haphazard things men do when they have no immediate call to do anything in particular, but act because they are alive and must do something.

But life and death were in that glance. I could see the vessel being swallowed up in the fog; I saw the back of the man at the wheel, and the head of the other man turning, slowly turning, as his gaze struck the water and casually lifted along it toward me. His face wore an absent expression, as of deep thought, and I became afraid that if his eyes did light upon me he would nevertheless not see me. But his eyes did light upon me, and looked squarely into mine; and he did see me, for he sprang to the wheel, thrusting the other man aside, and whirled it round and round, hand over hand, at the same time shouting orders of some sort. The vessel seemed to go off at a tangent to its former course and leapt almost instantly from view into the fog.

I felt myself slipping into unconsciousness, and tried with all the power of my will to fight off the suffocating blankness and darkness that was rising around me. A little later I heard the stroke of oars, growing nearer and nearer, and the calls of a man. When he was very near I heard him crying, in vexed fashion, "Why in hell don't you sing out?" This meant me, I thought, and then the blankness and darkness rose over me.

From *The Sea Wolf,* Jack London (New York: Macmillan Co., 1904).

LXIII

Gelett Burgess

As might be expected, informal versifiers of California were unfailingly partial to acclamation of their own geographic attractions, home traditions, and local lore: gold, Indians, stagecoach holdups, yellow poppies, redwoods, Pacific tides, Chinamen, missions, mountains. But the most familiar lines ever penned in the West—more widely known even than "the hoe-poem"—concerned none of these. They were written in 1895 about a nonindigenous purple cow:

> I never saw a purple cow—
> I never hope to see one;
> But I can tell you anyhow,
> I'd rather see than be one.

In fact, "The Purple Cow" was quoted so widely and so frequently that its author, Gelett Burgess (1866–1951), felt obliged two years later to compose a sequel:

> Ah, yes, I wrote "The Purple Cow"—
> I'm sorry now I wrote it;
> But I can tell you anyhow
> I'll kill you if you quote it.

Burgess hailed from Boston, where he earned, from the Massachusetts Institute of Technology, a scientific degree that was never to prove very useful to his line of creativity. His start in publishing came as an illustrator, not as author. After winning a reputation as a clever draftsman, he began dashing off entertaining paragraphs—and a great deal of nonsense—to accompany his drawings.

In San Francisco soon after his graduation from M.I.T. in 1887, he wrote a whimsical column for the *Examiner* and in 1895 took on the editorship of a short-lived little magazine called the *Lark*. "The Purple Cow," which appeared in the first issue, brought the editor embarrassment, as well as fame; he wanted to be remembered for something a little more distinguished than that four-line jingle. The ambition was at least partially attained with publication of books such as *The Gage of Youth, Goops and How to Be Them, Are You a Bromide?, The Maxims of Methuselah,* and *Why Men Hate Women.*

Next to "The Purple Cow," Californians remember him most for his "Hyde Street Grip," about the cable cars of San Francisco, where "grip" once referred both to the tramway itself and to the device by which the car was attached to the endless cable that drew it, and where the conductor (who earned 22¢ an hour in the early 1900s) was known as the gripman. To riders of the "grip" that poem still conveys an essence of the life and spirit of San Francisco at the turn of the century.

Hyde Street Grip

Oh, the rain is slanting sharply, and the Norther's blowing cold;
When the cable strands are loosened, she is nasty hard to hold;
There's little time for sitting down and little time for gab,
For the bumper guards the crossing, and you'd best be keeping
      tab!
Two-and-twenty "let-go's" every double trip—
It takes a bit of doing, on the Hyde Street Grip!

Throw her off at Powell Street, let her go at Post,
Watch her well at Geary and at Sutter, when you coast,
Easy at the Power House, have a care at Clay,
Sacramento, Washington, Jackson, all the way!
Drop the rope at Union, never make a slip—
The lever keeps you busy, on the Hyde Street Grip!

Foot-brake, wheel-brake, slot-brake and gong,
You've got to keep 'em working, or you'll soon be going wrong!
Rush her on the crossing, catch her on the rise,
Easy round the corners, when the dust is in your eyes!
And the bell will always stop you, if you hit her up a clip—
You are apt to earn your wages, on the Hyde Street Grip!

North Beach to Tenderloin, over Russian Hill,
The grades are something giddy, and the curves are fit to kill!
All the way to Market Street, climbing up the slope,
Down upon the other side, hanging to the rope;
But the sight of San Francisco, as you take the lurching dip!
There is plenty of excitement, on the Hyde Street Grip!

Oh, the lights are in the Mission, and the ships are in the Bay;
And Tamalpais is looming from the Gate, across the way;
The Presidio trees are waving, and the hills are growing brown,
And the driving fog is harried from the Ocean to the town!
How the pulleys slap and rattle! How the cables hum and whip!
Oh, they sing a gallant chorus, on the Hyde Street Grip!

When the Orpheum is closing, and the crowd is on the way,
The conductor's punch is ringing, and the dummy's light and
        gray;
But the wait upon the table by the Beach is dark and still—
Just the swashing of the surges on the shore below the mill;
And the flash of Angel Island breaks across the channel rip,
As the hush of midnight falls upon the Hyde Street Grip.

From *A Gage of Youth,* Gelett Burgess (Boston: Small, Maynard and Company, 1901).

LXIV

Charles Caldwell Dobie

In a brief fifty years San Francisco had spread out over the sand hills south of the Golden Gate to become one of the great cities of the world, the pride of the West, and the finest port metropolis on the Pacific shores of the Americas. It was hardly an idyllic city—it had grown too fast to be that. The uninitiated could get lost in its maze of streets and alleys, and a great many of those thoroughfares bisected quarters that were anything but beautiful, orderly, or sanitary. But those very deficiencies somehow added to the charm of the place, and the magnificent natural setting compensated for occasional ugliness. The city was bursting with enterprise; it had spirit, character, even a touch of nobility. San Franciscans had reason to be proud of their city—on April 17, 1906.

Three days later it was a smoking ruin. Earthquake and the Great Fire had very nearly leveled it.

Everyone who lived through that catastrophe was ever after possessed by a hankering to tell his personal tale of survival. There were as many stories as there were people, all more or less true, all different, yet all one. Thousands of them got into print, some narrated in a spirit of braggadocio, some with more appropriate humility or resignation; others calculated to stir compassion, to appall, to build up an ego and a hero.

No one told his experiences with more objectivity, calmness and restraint than Charles Caldwell Dobie (1881–1943), San Francisco

native and resident, for many years one of the city's top-ranking novel-
ists, playwrights, and literary observers, who as a boy peddled that old
periodical of the West, *The Argonaut,* through San Francisco streets,
and rose to be one of its leading contributors and its editor.

Forty-eight Hours of Red Terror

Premonitions of disaster seemed singularly lacking in San Francisco on the evening of April 17, 1906. Spring was in the full flush
of its enchantment and the only audible rumblings came from
nothing more portentous than carriage wheels bumping over the
cobbled streets toward the Grand Opera House. San Francisco
was in a gala mood, as she always was when keyed to the excitement of an opera season. This year Caruso was the star . . .
billed to sing Don José to Olive Fremstad's Carmen. This . . .
was not on my list. So I retired early, setting my alarm clock with
the prudence of a man young enough to sleep past the hour of
rising. This proved to be an unnecessary precaution. Something
much more effective than an alarm clock was scheduled to
awaken me.

I came out of a thick slumber with the confused notion that I
was on a bucking horse. The plunging continued, followed by a
deafening roar. I jumped out of bed to run down the hall to my
mother's room. But the swaying of the house flung me from one
wall to the other, very much as a passenger aboard an ocean liner
would be flung by a heavy sea. Then quite suddenly the vibra-
tions ceased.

Fortunately it was daylight—in the neighborhood of five
o'clock. The family ran to the front windows and looked out. A
fine dust from crumbling chimneys filled the air. But the frame
houses of the quarter in which we lived were standing valiantly.
We had all felt earthquakes before, and ordinarily after the shock
was over we were disposed to joke about it. But this time we
knew we had passed through an earthquake that was no joking
matter. Although even at this point we did not realize just how
serious matters were. Particularly, as an inspection of our apart-

ment disclosed no damage beyond cracked plaster and one shattered vase.

We were not a family disposed to alarm after danger had passed, and so we dressed, lit a fire in the kitchen stove, and sat down to a cup of coffee. It never occurred to us that the chimney might be cracked and that we could set fire to the house in consequence. We noticed that the water trickled out of the faucet very slowly, but we were not disposed to be captious about a reluctant water spout on such a morning. By this time it was six o'clock. My brother and I discussed the matter of going down to our respective offices. We were not due to work until nine. We decided to take a turn about town in the meantime.

The streets were filled with excited people making ominous predictions. But we declined to share their pessimism. We felt that the worst was over, although disturbing plumes of black smoke began to appear upon the horizon. But what was a fire or two? San Francisco had one of the most efficient fire departments in the country. The fires would be under control in a half-hour. At this point neither one of us remembered the trickle of water that had so slowly filled the coffee pot a half-hour before.

By this time we had reached the top of Nob Hill. It was here that we received our first shock. A few years before, a huge dome had been tacked on to the City Hall to provide the faithful with jobs. This dome stood up in the morning sunlight divested of every brick that had covered its steel nakedness. More than that, the black plumes of smoke were increasing. At a dozen different points they were smudging the sky line. A man said: "The water supply has been cut off!" Another told us that Chief Sullivan of the Fire Department had been killed.

Catton, Bell and Company, the firm I worked for, had offices in the Merchants Exchange Building on California Street at the foot of Nob Hill. Thither we went, somewhat sobered by the news that had come to our ears. The streets were littered with bricks from falling chimneys, fragments of shattered cornices, with here and there the front wall of a cheaply constructed building piled up on the sidewalk. But, on the whole, the city was still standing gallantly.

The earthquake had thrown the entire elevator system of the Merchants Exchange out of commission. I started to climb the stairs. Another sharp earthquake shock routed my intentions. Like most fools I wanted to be out on the street when the earth trembled, when, as a matter of fact, the interior of a steel-frame building was perhaps the safest place a man could find on such an occasion.

My brother was employed by the Mutual Savings Bank on Market Street. We decided to move in that direction. Our way led us through the shopping district. Here we found every plate-glass front completely shattered. But it was not until we reached Union Square that we began to get a sense of portentous disaster. The square was swarming with refugees from the "South of Market" districts. This was the cheap, poor quarter of the town and many of the wretches who had fled from the flames looked as if they had not faced the morning sunlight for years. They were like rats startled out of their holes, this beer-sodden, frowsy crew of dreadful men and still more dreadful women. A breed that has passed out of American life completely—red-faced, bloated, blowsy.

It was eight o'clock when we reached the Mutual Bank. This building was on the north side of Market Street. Opposite, an inferno was raging. The cheap lodging houses of Third Street were shooting up flames, walls were crumbling, explosions were throwing debris into the air. On the corner of Third and Market Streets stood the Call Building. It was one of San Francisco's first skyscrapers—a "fireproof" building. We watched the intense heat smash window after window. In the wake of each shattered pane would follow a burst of flame, a cloud of smoke. In ten minutes the building was doomed. Now, for the first time, we began to be truly apprehensive. If stone and steel and concrete could burn like a cigar box, what hope was left? More than this, we knew by this time that the pessimists were right: there was no water. The earthquake had dislocated and smashed the main pipeline.

We walked a block to the Palace Hotel. Here everything was calm to the point of absurdity. In the lobby the Chinese servants in their immaculate white duck uniforms were dusting off the furniture. Most of the tourists had undoubtedly turned over and gone to sleep again, secure in conviction that the cosmic prank of the morning was a weekly occurrence. Only the native San Franciscans and the great Enrico Caruso were unduly alarmed. And even then it was only Mr. Caruso who was in tears. He swore on that fateful morning that wild horses would never drag him back to San Francisco. And they never did. Apparently he preferred the volcanic earthquakes of his native Italy to the fault-line earthquakes of California. . . .

Most people, even those whose roofs the fire had not yet burned away, slept out of doors that night. But not our family. My mother's sense of personal privacy made her willing to chance the hazard of four walls. What followed had all the elements of delirium. We dozed, fully clothed, to a solemn undercurrent of marching feet. The fire had reached Chinatown and our house was on Jackson Street, in the path of the steady stream of Orientals fleeing to points of safety. At dawn the exodus was at its height. They came, silently, with the fatalistic calm of the Far East—dragging trunks, chests, go-carts, baby buggies, wicker baskets, piled high with household goods. The woman who lodged beneath us was from the South. That morning I met her peering out at the disheveled stream. "It's like Sherman's March through Georgia!" she said, and her lips quivered with the memory of that horror.

We made a fire in the garden. We had learned the hazard of cracked chimneys. . . . After breakfast we decided to seek out a vantage point where we could watch the progress of the flames. From indications, the fire was creeping toward us from every side but the west. My mother insisted on going with us. She had bought, only a few days before, a street gown in the latest mode. It had sleeves, elbow length, and a pair of long black kid gloves added to its distinction. When she came downstairs to join us she was flaunting this new costume. She even had a veil drawn tightly across her face. Her cheeks were smudged and unwashed, her hair a bit snarled. But otherwise her toilette was irreproachable. In spite of the desperate situation, the three of us laughed, and, thus refreshed, we went forth to learn the worst.

The worst was very bad indeed. The fire was creeping up the

slopes of Nob Hill within a dozen blocks of our home. We sat in
the shadow of the bonanza missions of the incredible seventies
and watched the blue-black menace snake up the heights. The
lawns, the sidewalks, the roadways, were crowded with as silent a
throng, I think, as I shall ever witness.

The entire downtown section, built of stone, brick and concrete, had been devoured as completely as if some insatiable
monster had crept over it. It was a frame city that was being
attacked now. One hope for the doomed city was the usual brisk
afternoon wind to spring up from the west. A scant hour of April
rain would have beaten out the flames. Even a thick blanket of
fog might have smothered them. But the sky smiled down in blue,
sardonic calm, as if to pay us back for every idle protest that we
had ever lodged against wind and weather. . . .

We arrived at our house to find a soldier ringing at our door to
warn us out of the district. Martial law had been proclaimed by
the mayor and the military was in command, closing up saloons,
shooting down looters, clearing threatened quarters of their inhabitants. On every side our neighbors were making ready to flee.
Many of them were at that moment digging holes in their back
yards in which they were burying their silver and treasure.

We tied all our clothes and bedding into bundles with rope
filched from a clothes line. These we slung over our shoulders. A
huge basket my brother and I carried between us—piled with
personal effects. My brother commented many times upon the
heaviness of the basket. He did not know until we had reached
our destination that I had hidden a collection of rare German
beer mugs that had been my boyish delight between the layers of
blankets. Nor did he suspect the volume on "Italian Gardens" by
Edith Wharton and illustrated by Maxfield Parrish, which I had
tucked under my arm. It had been given me the week before and
I was loath to leave the history of so much loveliness behind.

My mother went on ahead, in her smart gown with the long
black gloves, carrying the family canary and a large cream-col-
ored pitcher made by Wedgwood that my grandmother had
brought across the Isthmus of Panama in the fifties. For some
reason we were not unduly cast down. At least we had the cour-

age, the hope, the absurdity, if you will, to save some of the unessentials. And I have always treasured the picture of my mother on that fateful morning in her new dress, with a dotted veil drawn tautly across her shapely nose, carrying a canary and a Wedgwood pitcher to safety. The dauntlessness of San Francisco shone through the unconscious gallantry of her gesture. . . .

We set up a camp in the de Bretteville garden and hung the canary in a rosebush. As we entered the gate we met Madame Emma Eames and a trio of other opera stars leaving. A continuous stream of people looking for an oasis in a desert of flames came and went all afternoon. It was as if our friends were holding a reception. That evening we dined off cold canned spaghetti washed down with hot coffee which we shared with other refugees who had crept into the inclosure. In the matter of serving coffee, my beer mugs, even at this early hour, justified themselves.

All night the writhing flames danced their dance of destruction. The boom of dynamite began to shake the earth, now. It was rumored that the navy was blowing up blocks at a time so as to leave nothing in the path of the red monster. Our shelter stood upon sloping ground and we could see the bay alive with glittering ferry boats carrying thousands away from the doomed city. The docks through some miracle had been spared and this made flight an easy matter.

About three o'clock in the morning the block containing our home burned up. The suspense was over—for us at least. We threw ourselves down upon our blankets and fell into fitful slumber, while all about us sparks and embers rained in a continuous downpour. We woke to stifling heat. A pall of smoke obscured the sun. The fire was moving relentlessly toward our safety zone. But all this did not prevent our silly canary from singing out his pleasure at this new home in the rosebush.

We held a family council. The decision was that I should take my mother over on the Tiburon ferry to Belvedere where my brother maintained a houseboat. My brother was to stay behind to help our friends save their home. Sparks and falling embers were the chief dangers, and vigilance might bring victory. We stored our belongings in the basement and walked along sizzling pavements to the Ferry Building. My mother still wore her long black gloves, but her fingers were poking through them and her dotted veil had a rent in it. She carried her irrepressible canary in one hand and her Wedgwood pitcher in the other.

It was now Friday. The earthquake had occurred on Wednesday morning, but forty-eight hours of red terror had almost wiped out the memory of that cosmic insolence. . . .

That night was the most horrid of all, in spite of the fact that my mother and I were far removed from the flames. The city glowed in the distance like an angry dragon belching out fire and brimstone. And the heavy thunders from the relentless war upon conflagration, which the navy was waging with guncotton, kept up until dawn. At noon the next day my brother showed up. The de Bretteville house had been saved and with it our bedding and the book on "Italian Gardens." The fire had been halted at Van Ness Avenue, which filled my mother with such elation that she trudged straightway to the village store in Tiburon and bought the last dozen clothespins remaining in stock, to the great envy and amazement of our refugee neighbors who began at once to quarrel over who should be the first to borrow them—showing what a relative thing wealth is.

If you are a lover of statistics you will find a rich yield of interesting figures in the story of the San Francisco earthquake and fire. You will learn among other things that the "shake" lasted one minute and five seconds and that it was caused by a subterranean landslide or slip of faulty ground along 400 miles of coast line. You will likewise discover that the flames destroyed over 2,500 acres of improvements or about 500 city blocks. The value of property destroyed is confusing and the estimates run all the way from its assessed value of some $50,000,000 to a more generous estimate which reached ten times that amount. But one set of figures is incontrovertible—the amount of insurance paid out, $163,713,330, to be exact.

Perhaps the most interesting of all is the degree of heat thrown off by the flames which made so vast and altogether satisfactory a bonfire possible. This has been fixed at 2,700 degrees Fahrenheit, and explains why bulwarks of stone and steel crumbled like dust before its blast. However open to controversy any other of San Francisco's claims to superiority are, there is no doubt about her preëminence in the matter of fires. With six previous disasters by flames to her credit, she finally put on a show that crowded out the heroic attempts of Mrs. O'Leary's cow to give Chicago first place in conflagration finals.

It would be unfair not to mention the generosity which San Francisco met at the hands of the world. Within twenty-four hours after word went out that San Francisco was burning, relief trains by the hundreds were started on their way with food supplies. Not a soul went hungry, even for a day. More than this, the Red Cross received nearly $10,000,000 for San Francisco relief. It was a heartening testimonial to the place which San Francisco held in the affections of all who knew its own generous impulses.

This start toward rehabilitation did much to put spirit into the people. Before the ashes had cooled, they were rolling up their sleeves for the greatest feat of the city's career—or the career of any city in the world's history.

From *San Francisco: A Pageant*, Charles Caldwell Dobie (New York: Appleton-Century, 1939).

LXV

Will Irwin

Within hours San Francisco had become a place haunted with terror, a Sodom and Gomorrah. Few sober-minded citizens in the days immediately following the Great Fire cared to predict unequivocally that the city would ever be rebuilt on its former scale. Who would be so foolhardy as to advocate restoring a city that might at any hour again be shaken to the ground and consumed in another inferno?

The nation and the world wept at the passing of San Francisco. Will Irwin (1873–1948) drafted its obituary. He possessed the right sense of drama and the right historical perspective. Though he was with the New York *Sun* on the other side of the continent, he knew San Francisco intimately from his years as an undergraduate at Stanford, and he loved it. In 1906 he was recognized principally as a circumspect reporter and foreign correspondent. His stirring exhortations on the state of world society, his biographies and drama collaborations were still to come, but he was widely respected and trusted; when Will Irwin expressed pessimism about the future of San Francisco, his readers were likely to appropriate his doubt as theirs.

The City That Was

The old San Francisco is dead.

The gayest, lightest hearted, most pleasure-loving city of the western continent, and in many ways the most interesting and romantic, is a horde of refugees living among ruins. It may be rebuilt; it probably will; but those who have known that peculiar city by the Golden Gate, have caught its flavor of the Arabian Nights, feel that it can never be the same.

It is as though a pretty, frivolous woman had passed through a great tragedy. She survives, but she is sobered and different. If it rises out of the ashes, it must be a modern city, much like other cities and without its old atmosphere. . . .

One usually entered San Francisco by way of the Bay. Across its yellow flood, covered with the fleets from the strange seas of the Pacific, San Francisco presented itself in the hill panorama. Probably no other city in the world, excepting perhaps Naples, could be so viewed at first sight. It rose above the passenger, as he reached dockage, in a succession of hill terraces.

At one side was Telegraph Hill, the end of the peninsula, a height so abrupt that it had a one-hundred-and-fifty-foot sheer cliff on its seaward frontage. Further along lay Nob Hill, crowned with the Mark Hopkins mansion, which had the effect of a citadel, and in later years by the great white Fairmount. Further along was Russian Hill, the highest point. Below was the business district, whose low site caused all the trouble.

Except for the modern buildings, the fruit of the last ten years, the town presented at first sight a disreputable appearance. Most of the buildings were low and of wood. In the middle period of the '70's, when a great part of San Francisco was building, the newly rich perpetrated some atrocious architecture. In that time, too, everyone put bow windows on his house to catch all of the morning sunlight that was coming through the fog; and those little houses, with bow windows and fancy work all down their fronts, were characteristic of the middle-class residence districts.

Then the Italians, who tumbled over Telegraph Hill, had built as they listed and with little regard for streets, and their houses hung crazily on a side hill which was little less than a precipice. The Chinese, although they occupied an abandoned business district, had remade their dwellings Chinese fashion, and the Mexicans and Spaniards had added to their houses those little balconies without which life is not life to a Spaniard.

Yet the most characteristic thing after all was the coloring. The sea fog had a trick of painting every exposed object a sea gray, which had a tinge of dull green in it. This, under the leaden sky of a San Francisco morning, had a depressing effect on first sight and afterward became a delight to the eye. For the color was soft, gentle and infinitely attractive in mass. . . .

With the hills, with the strangeness of the architecture and with the green-gray tinge over everything, the city fell always into vistas and pictures, a setting for the romance which hung over everything, which has always hung over life in San Francisco since the padres came and gathered the Indians about Mission Dolores.

And it was a city of romance and a gateway to adventure. It opened out on the mysterious Pacific, the untamed ocean; and through the Golden Gate entered China, Japan, the South Sea Islands, Lower California, the West Coast of Central America, Australia. There was a sprinkling, too, of Alaska and Siberia. From the windows on Russian Hill one saw always something strange and suggestive creeping through the mists of the bay.

It would be a South Sea Island brig, bringing in copra, to take out cottons and idols; a Chinese junk after sharks' livers; an old whaler, which seemed to drip oil, home from a year of cruising in the Arctic. Even the tramp windjammers were deep-chested craft, capable of rounding the Horn or of circumnavigating the globe; and they came in streaked and picturesque from their long voyaging.

In the orange-colored dawn which always comes through the mists of that bay, the fishing fleet would crawl in under triangular lateen sails; for the fishermen of San Francisco Bay are all Neopolitans who have brought their customs and sail with lateen rigs stained an orange brown and shaped, when the wind fills them, like the ear of a horse.

Along the waterfront the people of these craft met. "The smelting pot of the races," Stevenson called it; and this was always the city of his soul. There were black Gilbert Islanders, almost indistinguishable from Negroes; lighter Kanakas from Hawaii or Samoa; Lascars in turbans; thickset Russian sailors; wild Chinese with unbraided hair; Italian fishermen in tam o' shanters, loud shirts and blue sashes; Greeks; Alaska Indians; little Bay Spanish-Americans; together with men of all the European races.

These came in and out from among the queer craft, to lose themselves in the disreputable, tumbledown, but always mysterious shanties and small saloons. In the back rooms of these saloons South Sea Island traders and captains, fresh from the lands of romance, whaling masters, people who were trying to get up treasure expeditions, filibusters, Alaskan miners, used to meet and trade adventures.

There was another element, less picturesque and equally characteristic, along the waterfront. San Francisco was the back eddy of European civilization—one end of the world. The drifters came there and stopped, lingered a while to live by their wits in a country where living after a fashion has always been marvelously cheap. These people haunted the waterfront and the Barbary Coast by night, and lay by day on the grass in Portsmouth Square. . . .

The Barbary Coast was a loud bit of hell. No one knows who coined the name. The place was simply three blocks of solid dance halls, there for the delight of the sailors of the world. On a fine busy night every door blared loud dance music from orchestras, steam pianos and gramophones, and the cumulative effect of the sound which reached the street was chaos and pandemonium. . . .

Until the last decade almost anything except the commonplace and the expected might happen to a man on the waterfront. The cheerful industry of shanghaiing was reduced to a science. A citizen taking a drink in one of the saloons which hung out over the water might be dropped through the floor into a boat, or he might drink with a stranger and wake in the forecastle of a whaler bound for the Arctic. . . . This life of the floating population lay apart from the regular life of the city, which was distinctive in itself. . . .

The greatest beauty show on the continent was the Saturday afternoon matinee parade in San Francisco. . . . From two o'clock to half-past five, a solid procession of Dianas, Hebes and

Junos passed and repassed along the five blocks between Market and Powell and Sutter and Kearney—the "line" of San Francisco slang. Along the open-front cigar stores, characteristic of the town, gilded youth of the cocktail route gathered in knots to watch them. There was something Latin in the spirit of this ceremony—it resembled church parades in Buenos Ayres. . . . One caught the type and longed sometimes for the sight of a more ethereal beauty—for the suggestion of soul which belongs to a New England woman on whom a hard soil has bestowed a grudged beauty—for the mobility, the fire, which belongs to the Frenchwoman. . . . It was the beauty of Greece.

With such a people life was always gay. If the fairly Parisian gaiety did not display itself on the streets, except in the matinee parade, it was because the winds made open-air cafes disagreeable at all seasons of the year. The life careless went on indoors or in the hundreds of pretty estates—"ranches," the Californians called them—which fringe the city.

San Francisco was famous for its restaurants and cafes. Probably they were lacking at the top; probably the very best, for people who do not care how they spend their money, was not to be had. But they gave the best fare on earth, for the price, at a dollar, seventy-five cents, a half a dollar, or even fifteen cents. . . . The eating was usually better than the surroundings. Meals that were marvels were served in tumbledown little hotels. . . .

The city never went to bed. There was no closing law, so that the saloons kept open nights and Sundays at their own sweet will. Most of the cafes elected to remain open until two o'clock in the morning at least. . . .

Hospitality was nearly a vice. As in the early mining days, if they liked the stranger, the people took him in. At the first meeting the San Francisco man had him put up at the club; at the second, he invited him home to dinner. As long as the stranger stayed, he was being invited to week-end parties at ranches, to little dinners at this or that restaurant and to the houses of his new acquaintances, until his engagements grew beyond hope of fulfillment. Perhaps there was rather too much of this kind of thing.

At the end of a fortnight a visitor with a pleasant smile and a good story left the place a wreck. This tendency ran through all grades of society—except, perhaps, the sporting people who kept the tracks and the fighting game alive. These also met the stranger—and also took him in. . . .

Over by the ocean and surrounded by cemeteries in which there are no more burials, there is an eminence which is topped by two peaks and which the Spanish of the early days named after the breasts of a woman. The unpoetic Americans had renamed it Twin Peaks. At its foot was Mission Dolores, the last mission planted by the Spanish padres in their march up the coast, and from these hills the Spanish looked for the first time upon the golden bay.

Many years ago someone set up at the summit of this peak a sixty-foot cross of timber. Once a high wind blew it down, and the women of the Fair family then had it restored so firmly that it would resist anything. It has risen for fifty years above the gay, careless, luxuriant and lovable city, in full view from every eminence and from every valley. It stands tonight above the desolation of ruins.

The bonny, merry city—the good, gray city—O that one who has mingled the wine of her bounding life with the wine of his youth should live to write the obituary of Old San Francisco!

Condensed from *The New York Sun*, April 21, 1906, reprinted in booklet form under the title *The City That Was, A Requiem of Old San Francisco* (New York: B. W. Huebsch, 1906).

LXVI

Sinclair Lewis

San Francisco was rebuilt rather than restored—and rebuilt with more foresight and finesse than went into the original. When the city again began to take shape, the shacks were gone, as were much of the Victorian gingerbread, the ostentatious palaces, and a great many of the dives, dens, and back alleys. The new metropolis looked into the future; there was an air of stability, permanence, and conservatism in the business blocks, the hotels, public buildings, and big private residences. It was a sobered city. Nevertheless, the builders made sure that it was not too sober; they insisted conscientiously that it also stand as a pleasure city.

In 1910, a full decade before he published *Main Street*, the sensationally popular satire on small-town life of the Middle West, Sinclair Lewis (1885–1951) paid his respects to the rejuvenated city and appraised the success of the reconstruction. Casting himself as one of the local master builders, exhausted from his efforts and in need of a holiday, he toured San Francisco and its environs, on foot, by buggy, by the new horseless carriage, in search of re-creative facilities, and flippantly recited their virtues, as though he were a paid agent of the Chamber of Commerce. Lewis demonstrated incidentally the racy irreverence that later made *Babbitt, Arrowsmith, Elmer Gantry*, and *Dodsworth* famous, and their author the most discussed novelist in the United States and the first American recipient of the Nobel Prize in literature.

[446]

New Fountain of Youth

The Master Builder had wielded men, while the men wielded steel and cement, for the four years "since." Then the doctor had his say: "My dear man, you've been working too hard and you're going to pot unless you get your nerves tuned up. Try Tahiti."

"I will not," answered the Master Builder. "I won't leave my brand-new six-foot bathtub for all your surfboards. If I must be a child again, I'll stay right here in San Francisco and see if they've made any new playthings since the fire. I've been too busy to brush the brick dust off my jacket and look for the rebuilt theatres, almost. But The Wife, she knows!"

He told The Wife, and ended gloomily, "Now lead us to the rejuvenating merriment."

"Very well. I've been wondering how long it would be before you'd stop being a crab—walking backward through life. We'll start with the theatres."

As they were whirled to their show in a taxicab, the Master Builder exclaimed, still resentful, "Now here you are, in spite of all the doctor-men say about working too hard. Where'd you play-folks be if we hadn't been building—building theatres and garages and taxicab companies. Doesn't look much like fire and disaster, does it, to ride in one of these rigamajigs? . . . Why, there's so many taxicabs and private cars in town, a dealer was telling me that the chauffeurs have an association with about five hundred members. Oh, we've been building in lots of things besides stone."

"Yes, in cafes, and Spanish dancers, for instance. We'll see La Castillaña tonight after the show."

They did. They wandered along the New White Way, from the Portolá to Techau Tavern—Tait's—the Bismarck—the Odeon—the St. Francis—the Palace—peeping in at each, till The Wife reported that careful investigation indicated that another claret lemonade would cause a Central American revolution in the stomatic regions.

As they rode home, at an unheavenly hour, the Master Builder spoke something after this wise, or unwise: "By Jove! They talk about their blooming old lights of Lunnon Town. Lights of Market Street for me! Good, eh? And later we'll see some of the little French and Italian places. Distinctly San Franciscan. From the architecture of a ravioli at Coppa's to the architecture of the Laurel Court at the Fairmont, there's nothing like San Francisco for laughter, edible and bottled and painted up *onto* walls! And the people don't sit around stiffly, startled into a feeling of vague guilt by the phenomenon of having a good time."

The Goodman halted, realizing that his adoption of pleasure for hobby was rather recent.

With a feeling of infinite luxury, he slept late next day, Sunday, and they did not start on what The Wife called "Laughter Lesson II" till afternoon, when they went autoing to the beach. From the terrace of the New Cliff House they watched the absurdly grave and bearded sea lions waltz through ethereally blue waves. They looked up the training quarters of a world-famed pugilist, and dropped in at the mild little roadhouses along the perfect boulevard, where their auto wheels whirred silkenly, and wandered up into the gardens of Sutro Heights, whose highest rampart overlooked the enormous yellow crescent of hard beach, edged with sunny foam and scattered with colorful picnicking parties—overlooked the vast sweep of sea—from Golden Gate to Far Cathay!

"Great Saints!" cried the Master Builder. "*Is* it good to be out of office? *Is* this a pleasure city? Look at those people down there in the Seeing San Francisco car. Even such untrained aliens are handed one of the cheerfulest pleasures—sightseeing. We must have some of that, eh? Takes a native not to know his own city."

"Yes. We must. How long is it since you've looked at the Mission Dolores and imagined the padres were there again? I thought so. Likewise imagine soldiers at Fort Winfield Scott as in the old days. And watch the bathers at Brighton Beach."

"But now let's go down and picnic on the beach among the pro-le-tar-i-at!" suggested the Master Builder.

They purchased a lunch-in-er-paper and trotted gaily down to the peopled sands. The air was sweet and the small girls, paddling gingerly, were funny and frolicsome. Their lunch was flavored with the Salt of Life as well as the salt of the sea.

"Lord but the people here do enjoy themselves," the Builder said as they rode home through Golden Gate Park. "Track meet at the Stadium, eh? Lemme tell you, Lady, Old Greece lives again when you have a temple—free, public—to graceful, strong young manhood like that."

"And you, revered sir," smiled The Wife, "had better get your 'strong young manhood' back again. You may just dismiss the chauffeur and take me for a row on Stow Lake."

With sunset among the pines on Strawberry Hill, they slid softly among the lily pads, like the swans about them. They had tea afterward in the Japanese Garden—tea reminiscent of fairy fields of Nippon served in a little shrine of the God Oolong, set among dwarf bridges and stone idols.

As they strolled down the great avenue toward the park entrance, slow shadows of dusk drifted across meadow vistas. The crowd which had been hearing the Sunday afternoon band concert was still filing happily homeward. The Master Builder hummed "La Paloma" cheerfully and insisted on stopping to feed the lazy bears, in which feeding he was aided and abetted by, Item: one clean small boy; Item: one dirty small boy, and Item: one Englishman of title, traveling incognito. The Builder was very content.

Long months, now, he had been accustomed to go down to the office on Sunday "just to run through a few letters"—which running was a Marathon for length. It was good to be free, even to be lugged off to vespers by The Wife. Nevertheless, on Monday morning he was restless and wanted to sneak off for a bit of the just-running-through. . . . "I don't want to get too much of a good thing," complained the prisoner. "I'll get bored to death if I overwork this fool pleasure stunt."

"Now you see here. You won't get bored. I could find an entirely different game for you every day for three months in this town. Today we'll jaunt to the suburbs—go down to San Mateo and see the polo at El Palomar Field. You used to be a horseman, dear," she added wistfully. "We used to have some rather nice rides together. There's a wonderful game today, a team of English army officers versus the crack 'Blingum' players. Then tomorrow we'll go a-fishing, either out at Ocean Beach—casting through the surf—or over at Sausalito."

The Master Builder admitted Her Honor's wisdom when he had fished and watched the polo and tramped with her for a couple of miles, from San Mateo, up El Camino Real, the highway where rode splendid dons and exquisite ladies in the days before the gringoes came. Consequently, it was easy for The Wife to lead him out for a whole-day excursion across the bay. They wandered among the Mill Valley villas, perched like playhouses on slopes above the redwoods, and then went jogging up Mount Tamalpais on the little railway, which wound like a politician.

From the summit there was a view which made the Builder whoop. Far out, beyond a four-master heading for the Golden Gate, beyond the Farallone Islands, the gaze swept over the magnificent seascape. San Francisco was out-rolled in another direction; and purple, proud Mount Diablo brooded over the historic Carquinez Straits and watched the silver course of the Sacramento River. "Yes," remarked the Builder, "and likewise there are the Suisun Flats to be considered, which doth remind me that I was ass enough not to go duck hunting in the land of the tules last spring. Canvasbacks! Yum!"

They dined at the tavern atop the mountain and took the last train down. On the deck of the ferry boat they watched San Francisco, set on its Roman hills, grow large as they approached, and its regal guard of lights flash into more brilliant battalions. Angel Island and Alcatraz were spots of dusky mystery; and the breeze had the mystery of the health of out-of-doors.

The Wife announced that they would vary the sport by another glimpse of the night side of town; and they "did" Fillmore Street, the avenue of lights and Mardi Gras gaiety, of derelict Mexican restaurants and—nickelodeons! It seemed improper not to have confetti flying here under the quadruple arches of lights.

The towers and the scenic railroad's runway at "The Chutes" glowed before them. "Come on!" the Builder cried. "I want to get joggled on the Human Roulette Wheel, and look upon the Small Brothers in the Hotel de Monk."

The Wife explained to him with care that it was not at all decent for a man of his dignity to be seen flying down the Chutes and coasting the Devil's Slide, and gaping at open-air acrobats, but the Master Builder was obdurate. When they left "The Chutes," he was even seized by a notion that it was his duty to attend either an all-night masquerade at the Auditorium or go roller skating; and she had to wile him home.

Trusting him out alone, she sent him next night to an exhibition contest between two of the greatest billiard players in the world. Once seated in the big, beautiful room, he heard at his elbow, "Well, well! Haven't seen you at any sports for quite sometime." The voice belonged to an acquaintance of his more leisurely days before the fire.

"No, I've been pretty busy building. The only sport I've looked at the last year has been a ball game at Recreation Park, and the horse races at Emeryville. Great races. Got Jaurez beat a mile. Oh, say—you ought to know—where are the gymnasiums now? I'm on a sort of vacation—"

The acquaintance named a dozen. "This is getting to be about the best-equipped town in the country for sports," he added. "And the sport comes here. Prize fights, of course. All there are. And take Marathon races, for instance. Taking a kind of layoff, are you? Well, don't forget the college sports—and St. Mary's and Santa Clara, as well as the U.C. and Stanford, or the soccer football league. Well, here come the champs."

At breakfast next morning the Master Builder announced himself a confirmed sporting person now.

"Yes," said The Wife. "But I won't let you become that only. Be a gent, with emphasis on the waistcoat, indeed! Bein' as it's rainy, today you're to do the opposite sort of pleasures with me. See the bookstores and the rest."

The Master Builder was astonished to find just how much the shops of luxuries had been rebuilt. A picture store with an Italian courtyard, smacking of dreamy Verona, a half-dozen bookstores, a music shop where they listened to a piano-player concert—with heads turned lest highbrow acquaintances should spy them— these were their rainy-day diversions.

"Now," said the Builder, as they sat at hot chocolate in a delightfully rococo little shop—an echo of Paris, "let's go to one of those continuous-moving-picture-and-vaudeville palaces on Market Street."

"Aren't you *ashamed* of yourself."

"Nope. And if it weren't growing late, I'd want to emulate the tourists and spend an hour down at the State Board of Trade's exhibits at the Ferry Building—see the mining display and the stereopticon views of orange trees. But here's the sunshine again. Cummon!"

As they roamed up Grant Avenue among the smart shops, he glanced up the hill to the glittering pagodas of Chinatown and remarked, "There's something we've been neglecting. Let's go see if Chinkville has become the real thing again."

A jade and teak-wood salon was discovered for their dinner, with a joss house across the street from the balcony where they ate. "B'lieve this *is* better than it was before the fire," mused the Builder, as they left the Chinese theatre. "Cleaner. Glad those old shacks are gone. These buildings give 'em more chance to tog out in purple and gold. Look at that little Chinese girl. Wish I could wear lavender silk trousers embroidered in silver!"

"You want to notice some of the lower tones, too, you gaudy male. See how quaint this alley is, with overhanging balconies and a Chinawoman furtively slipping through it. Well, put quotation marks on that if you want to. But see this Jap art store. Aren't those the most exquisite grays and browns in those prints? Come away! You have the symptoms of the spending mania in that left eye. Or—we won't have a cent left for Italian town tomorrow. And you know we want to dine at the Fior d'Italia on pastes and spaghetti and see where the literati—and the near-literati—do congregate at Sanguenetti's."

The Master Builder was so frisky a Builder by now that The Wife began taking him on long tramps, after having tested him by the ascent of Telegraph Hill, above Italian town and above studio land—a real Quartier Latin. From Buena Vista heights they saw the new city before them, with scarcely a trace of the fire. They climbed the Twin Peaks, and wandered through Richmond, and along the Pacific Heights with its castle homes. Then he was, at last, graduated into the tennis-playing class. In the Golden Gate Park courts and the grounds of the Alta Plaza, from whose pleateau they could see Lone Mountain with its great, mysterious cross standing solitary, they played and loafed and played, till the Master Builder was not missing *every* serve.

He took to swimming too, and splashed in the salt-water tanks of the Sutro Baths, and the new Lurline, built in Roman-wise. He had already been renewing habit in his two clubs, and was looking forward to the Bohemian Club jinks, that pageant in an outdoor cathedral whose pillars were redwoods. Now he edged his way into one of the four golf clubs and trotted through long afternoons over the Presidio links in the great Government reservation. Old friendships with army people were renewed there; and he was even seen at post tiffin and the Presidio shops.

"Why, you'll be teaching your teacher," The Wife laughed, as they cantered through the park together. "You're getting almost too athletic and social for me."

"Well, let's have a quiet day tomorrow then. I say, do you remember what we used to do in courtin' days, before there were motor cars? Go buggy riding! We'll just do that tomorrow."

Through the Oakland and Berkeley streets of leisurely homes, past the University campus and the dignity of the Greek Theatre they went a-buggy riding, a long, lazy, dreamy ride, with the sun bright on the leaves of the eucalyptus and soft in the pepper-tree foliage. Finally they drove to the golden hills beyond and stood at gaze looking over to the peaks of the dimly seen High Sierras, while the Master Builder said: "Guess I'm ready for a diploma in the course in getting young now. Weren't the Spaniards chumps to think the Fountain of Youth was in the tropics! For it's by the Golden Gate, and we've found it, eh?"

From "A San Francisco Pleasure Cure," Sinclair Lewis. *Sunset Magazine,* April 1910.

LXVII

E. Roscoe Shrader

During the years that San Francisco was recovering from its holocaust, Los Angeles was having its troubles too. With a population rapidly approaching that of the northern city, it was suffering from severe growing pains, violent labor revolts, land booms and recessions, arguments over harbor location, disfiguration from the scattering of some 1400 oil derricks about the city, water shortages, and drought. Among all the problems, the water shortage was the most serious. Los Angeles was in danger of being parched off the map.

The water predicament was not remedied until Owens Valley, almost 250 miles from the city, was appropriated, and a monumental system of dams, concrete ditches, steel conduits, mountain tunnels, siphons, and power stations was constructed to bring Sierra water to the kitchen taps, bathrooms, and lawns of Los Angeles—on November 5, 1913.

To residents of Owens Valley, who had also coveted that water for local irrigation, the confiscation of their rivers was the most ignominious act of land piracy in California history; to Angelenos it was an act of courage, and the construction of the aqueduct "the most titanic struggle ever undertaken by any municipality." Even outsiders compared it to the better publicized ditch then being dug across the Isthmus of Panama.

What made the California enterprise so impressive was not the mere length of the ditch, but the terrain in which it was constructed. The water had to be carried along steep mountain sides broken every few miles by gulches and river beds, down which thundered seasonal freshets that could demolish any ordinary work of man; it had to cross barren, waterless, roadless sections of the Mojave Desert for scores of miles; it had to be conveyed over mountain ranges and under mountain ranges; and, worst of all, it had to be piped up and down almost perpendicular slopes of canyons too wide to be bridged. Moreover, much of the terrain was all but inaccessible. Mule trails, railroads, telephone and power lines, and water systems to supply the builders, all had to be constructed before the ditch digging could start. It was an epoch-making operation, too, because it utilized some of the first big power machinery, like caterpillar tractors and steam shovels—then conspicuously awkward and outsized—ever employed on remote excavation work.

The region was so isolated that the nearest settlement to be found for a base of operations was the little wind-swept watering stop of Mojave, at that time a town of not more than a dozen permanent structures. Into Mojave the artist-journalist E. Roscoe Shrader, free lance for *Scribner's Magazine,* wandered in 1911, when the work was at its height. This was the town where the major problems were being tackled: problems of engineering, problems of logistics, problems of transportation, labor problems. From Mojave he toured the "stakes," the line of the aqueduct, and vividly recorded both in words and in sketches high points of the "Titanic struggle."

A Ditch in the Desert

"It's always blowin' in Moharvey," I was informed by a leather-brown citizen of that desert metropolis. Personal experience confirmed him entirely. There is nothing to stop it, for Mojave squats low and alone in a vast plain of sand, which rears only a useless growth of greasewood, cactus and sage. It boasts a couple of "cement block" buildings, but for the most part frame structure and tents anchored to stout poles line its streets. A scarce half-dozen in number, these, after the short space of a couple of blocks, discouraged-like, blur themselves in the scorched surrounding barrier of nothingness. The municipal board of Mojave needs to go to no expense for street sweepers, for the ever-present wind keeps its thoroughfares clear and clean to the hard-baked surface. . . .

Mojave for nearly a half century has been an important port of the great American Desert. It has outfitted numberless Jasons who have fared forth from its shelter to search for golden treasure. It has received the wagon trains of ore rumbling down from mines in the barren northern mountains.

Some five years ago prospectors of a new order came to Mojave. From the rapidly growing community [of Los Angeles] across the Coast Range to the southward, they came in search of water, much more precious to that community than silver or gold. . . . So the prospecting engineers made their way across the desert, past Death Valley, the lowest point in the United States, and up among the noble Sierra Nevadas to the base of Mount Whitney, our highest land. On the sides of this great watershed lie perpetual snows, which constantly feed the valleys below with an abundance of pure water . . . but to place this water in Los Angeles was plainly a daring, tremendous task. . . . The real tussle of the job was to bring the ditch through the Mojave. . . .

Thus it was that the dusty little town in the midst of the desert awoke one day to find itself important. It was as if an army of conquest had made it its headquarters. Tons of freight and machinery were deposited at its dingy station. Each day's trains brought detachments of men, engineers in khaki and corduroy and high boots; laborers, if they had the fare. If no fare was possessed, whole squads hoofed it in along the railroad. Out over the old stage road went straining ten-mule teams, and along the line of stakes straggling through the desert reaches arose the first camps of construction, the shining white of their canvas making a new note of color in the pervading grayness. . . .

Each division over the course of the aqueduct now has its camp capital, from which post the division engineer controls the activities of its several subsidiary construction camps. The system of the project making every bunkhouse, messhall or corrugated iron warehouse alike, does not keep each camp from investing itself with an individuality of its own. Among these, Cinco in the "Jaw-bone" lies panting on the lifting slope of the valley, exposed to the full strength of the sun; Boulder, camped high, overlooks the plain, its structures dwarfed among great monumental rocks which give Boulder Mountain its name; lovely Grapevine, amid a scrap of verdure in the great cup of a canyon, one of the precious water holes, shelters its lucky inhabitants in envied desert lux-uriance.

What is it that brings this young engineer chap out here in these lone places? . . . He represents a new impulse in the world. It is not that of a soldier, nor that of the discoverer, and yet it may be a touch of both. It is with the discoverer's instinct that he finds his course, and the general's planning that he breaks through opposing barriers. But above these . . . is the impulse to make useful useless places, to loose the powers lying long latent in our great natural resources. . . .

He has a complex army of men under his control. Clerks and draughtsmen, mechanics and miners, and the rank and file, the hobos. "Stakers," as these well-known gentlemen are termed on the ditch, make up the general mass of laborers. They come in from somewhere and work a while at a camp. Then, leaving with their roll of blankets and a bottle of water, foot it to the camp below, there to repeat the performance, and so on out to the comforts of civilization. It is said the aqueduct is being built by hobo labor. . . .

High on the mountain side you see an even scratch of familiar gray—the ditch. Zigzagging to and from it are the smaller scratches of workmen's trails. . . . Where all these marks come together is—camp. . . . The camp is strongly built for one whose existence will no doubt terminate with the completion of the aqueduct. The office building, with its quarters for the engineer and assistants, and its comfortable, shielding porches, stands under a huge cottonwood tree beside the creek. The camp store, of mongrel architecture, half canvas, half wood, is just across the stream. All the necessaries of desert life are there, from clothing to tobacco. In a row stand the bunkhouses, rough, strong, but comfortable, a room for each two men. Built to protect the men from an unmerciful summer sun, they are prepared to withstand, paradoxical though it may appear, the desert's winter cold. In that season the mercury drops at times to within ten degrees of zero.

The system of the camp is complete to its hospital. . . . A surgeon is in charge, with a hospital steward for assistant. He is ready, as the engineer, to travel at a call to any of his division camps. . . . Warehouses and machine shops—the hospitals for the mechanical beasts of the aqueduct—the steam shovel, the caterpillar traction engine, and the drill—are of corrugated iron. Stout barns and corrals are constructed for the livestock.

Breaking a way for the circling streak of conduit above the camp is one of the big shovels. In use throughout the work, these are driven both by steam and electricity. A steam shovel is no uncommon sight today, but the effect produced by one of the big mechanical monsters, high-perched against the glare of the desert's dead mountain side, comes differently. It seems almost as though you had been transported to some ancient period, and that black thing up there, with hoarse snorts and dipping, swaying beak, was one of the prehistoric animals making a gritty meal.

The steel-tusked shovel leans into the ditch, and with a few stertorous puffs from the engine, noses about for a mouthful. Into the rock it plunges, with rattle of chains and the screeching grit of steel on rock. A rapid series of puffs, and it rears swiftly into the air, dust clouds streaming in its wake. Swaying out over the rim of the ditch, with a grin of its gaping jaws, it drops the load. A few stones, finding no lodgement on the side, go on down to the valley in great skips and bounds, but before their clatter has ceased the shovel is again in the ditch.

This time it rises with a huge rock in its clutches, and swings over to a bunch of attendants on the bank, who jump forward with crowbars and perform a monstrous dental operation. The rock it is bringing up from the ditch is placed on the outer side, thus strengthening that side, and laying the foundation for a road for patrol when the work is completed.

Perched out on the great beam at his levers and "trip rope," like an East Indian mahout astride the neck of his elephant, sits the

Los Angeles Aqueduct

master of the metal brute. At will he can make it dig or lift, push, pull or bump.

"How on earth did you ever get it up there?" I asked.

To get one of those shovels over here when we first started work *was* somewhat of a trick," replied my friend. "Then we had to take it apart at the railroad, get the sections over by mule team and assemble them again on the mountain. Now, since we've got the "caterpillars," we can hitch two or three of 'em onto a shovel and snake it up to the base, where there is an easy slope. Then we get it up to the ditch on its own steam. Simple enough, you see." . . .

Ahead of the shovel is a gang of drillers using "hand steel." These men prepare for blasts, by which the surface is shot just enough to break the rock and to ease the progress of the shovel. Following in its wake come men who complete by hand the shaping of the ditch. Then a force of carpenters build the moulds, and the reenforcing steel is placed. The concrete pourers follow, carrying the liquid stone from mixer to moulds, and beyond them the finished conduit appears gray-white, with curious rib-fashioned cover. In a long swinging curve it follows a recession in the mountain side, to appear boldly against the distance on the adjacent promontory. Lost from sight and again to be seen in ever diminishing proportions, it makes its tortuous way until it reaches the gulf of a great desert canyon.

Here is a place where the engineer sat himself down and with knitted brows turned his imagination loose. To span the gap would require an enormous structure five hundred feet high, a mile or more wide. Multiplied by the numerous times this condition confronts him would mean the aqueduct's cost sailing into the impossible. To carry the aqueduct to the head of the canyon and back again down the other side was for the same reason not to be considered. There was nothing to do but to go straight over the side to the canyon's bottom and climb again "to grade" on the opposing wall—so he traced on his plans a letter V and throughout the aqueduct's course these gigantic initials are being set up.

A number are built of steel to withstand the terrible force of water falling from great heights, and are called in technical terms "inverted syphons." Some of them will approach two miles in length, and about fifteen miles in all of this novel construction will be required. This makes up a little load of steel of over eighteen thousand tons to be carried across the desert.

Transportation by mule team, shortly after the work began, was seen to be expensive and ineffectual . . . so the "caterpillar" traction engine was pressed into the service of the ditch to navigate the sea of sage and sand. . . . Perched in the rear, up under a flapping canvas canopy, sits the helmsman of this new "ship of the desert." . . . A "caterpillar" slowly topping a rolling wave of the desert floor, with broad-tired freighters grinding heavily in tow, joins itself in your mind to all traditional forms of desert travel. But when you see its burden, equal to that of a dozen caravans . . . and when the horrible racket of its muffled motor beats in your ears, you finally confess: "This belongs to today. It is different. It is new." . . .

None the less spectacular and daring are the methods adopted to get men and material to the different points inaccessible by road or trail. There are thrills to be had from the dipping over a declivity on a little car tethered to a strand of cable, at the mercy of an engineer, hand on lever, beside his "drum" at the top; and the sensations of aerial travel in an enlarged package carrier strung across the gap of a canyon. . . . Securely anchored in a huge mass of rock on the canyon side is a series of big bolts and steel cables. These, by gigantic knots and bolted clamps, hold a single cable, a mere spider's thread between the mighty walls, swinging upward five hundred feet to the other side. . . .

The cable begins to sing, and along its length a speck is seen swinging downward. Descending, enlarging, it soon scrapes on the platform—the car of the system. This is a stout wooden affair, with two sides about a foot high. The ends are open. . . . "Come on, let's go up," invites the host. . . . The signal to hoist is given, and the car swings out over the canyon. The camp buildings below take on the proportions of chicken coops. . . . The car keeps rising; the camp below is but a toy. . . . Why is it that those wretched chaps standing calmly by have to discuss a runaway load of machinery which smashed to flinders at the bottom the week before; or the ways and means of saving oneself if the traction cable should break? . . .

At last, after a terrible moment of giddy swinging beside the upper landing, [the passengers] climb out on a terrace cut in the mountain's side. Here are supported the machine shops, power installations and housing for the mules attendant on a tunnel opening into the canyon wall.

Doubly isolated in the heart of the mountain, a good dozen city squares distant, is a little knot of human energy slowly fretting its way with vibrating steel through the flinty core. The tunnel needs no timbering. It is piercing some of the hardest rock known. At the portal nothing can be heard of the activity at the "breast." The way is rough, over a narrow-gauge track and lengths of snaky air tubes. The tunnel's air is cooler and begins to take on a clinging dampness.

A faint burr falls on the ear from the blackness ahead. It rises louder, a clatter, a racket, and then, as the obscurity resolves itself into mysterious moving forms, becomes a dreadful din, the clamor of a whole battery of Gatlings in swift discharge. This is the drill shift. Two machines are raised on a platform, attacking the upper part of the rock, a man, grime-streaked, at each. Braced mute against the vibrating drills, their eyes strain forward as though they can see the mysterious line which the transit men have pointed for them through the mountain. They work amid the eternal furor of battle. Nothing can be heard until the drills are changed. All orders must be given by signs. . . .

There is unity in this effort against the rock which shows well-developed team work among the men. Like football players, they press forward together against the opposition. The work has, in truth, been made a great game for the men by the aqueduct builders. The excavation, whether tunnel or conduit, in rock or clay, is classified, and a ten-day average progress set for each. A gang, when it exceeds the average, receives a bonus. The men in rock, where five feet gained to a shift is reckoned an honorable accomplishment, strain as hard for the extra inch as the sprinter who endeavors to clip a fraction of a second from his record. . . .

The drillers, through with their attack on the rock, charged the holes with powder and "shot." . . . After having examined everything about the "breast" to see that nothing was left to prevent a successful "shot," all the workers, with the exception of two, started back through the tunnel. At a word from the foreman, they began "spitting" the coiling lengths of fuse, which marked in crude geometrical design, the work of the drillers. We tarried an instant, just long enough to see this "Christmas tree" sputtering away in the face of the rock. "I guess you won't care to stay for the rest of the celebration," my friend said. "But you don't need to hurry, for we've got five minutes to get out of range."

Well down the tunnel and safe around a curve, we presently heard the muffled "bump-bump-bump" of the distant exploding charges. Careful count was kept of the shots to see that none had missed. The "Christmas tree" had, with the force of giants, obeyed the will of its masters. Amidst the gray boiling clouds of smoke and gases we found the rock well broken up and thrown out in a well-ordered mass. . . .

The members of the "mucking gang," tin lunch buckets in hand, are waiting at the platform to "go on" when the car . . . returns from its perilous soaring. A big, cool, gray shadow comes creeping over the canyon from the western wall, and begins to climb the other side, absorbing as it goes that rim of flaming cadmium. Up the street arises the clamor of a massive triangle, beaten by a signficant individual in bare brown arms and an apron sometime white. . . . The throng at the door . . . disappears within the savory-odored mess hall.

In the reviving coolness of evening the office porch becomes the club room, the social parlor of the camp. Groups at one end, with guitar or mandolin, are doing "close harmony" with old college songs. Down the porch rail is a border of broad, tan-shirted backs and grimy mountain boots twined about the braces. On the steps sit dusky figures, elbows across knees or sprawling back. . . . Over all is drawn a broad band of star-dotted sky between canyon walls, hushed and looming. The talk going round cannot wander far from the ditch . . . or what they'll all do when the "durned old thing is finished." . . . Gradually the groups break up, the porch becomes deserted and all is quiet in the desert night.

Down in the camp's draughting rooms are maps and blueprints, covered with curves and angles and figures. Up in the mountains and across the mesas the great bore is repeating them in proportions unerring and heroic. Section is joining section, tunnel is meeting tunnel; here a siphon links together the opposing arteries, and there a great reservoir stands ready with open gates.

Soon a great day will come for the city, a day when the "staker" will swing his blankets to back and fill the water bottle for the last time; when miners and engineers will lay aside their tools and troop back to civilization. The turbines of the huge powerhouses will begin to turn, and a flood from the far Sierras will pour forth to quench the thirst of the Southland.

From "A Ditch in the Desert," E. Roscoe Shrader, *Scribner's Magazine,* May 1912.

LXVIII

George Sterling

Eight years after the Great Fire of San Francisco, scarcely a trace of the destruction was visible. A new city stood in place of the old. According to California custom, such an achievement had to be publicized. The world should be shown how the men of the West reacted to an urgent challenge. And since no better way of advertising great civic accomplishments had then been devised, San Francisco had to stage a monumental fair or exposition; like nothing else, a formal exposition would focus the attention of the world on the resurrected city. Then the idea was expanded to incorporate the celebration of another notable event of the Western Hemisphere: a world's fair would be timed to coincide with the opening of the Panama Canal.

Along the waterfront adjacent to the old Presidio rose a complex of eleven magnificent palaces, all harmoniously related, with low Byzantine domes, red tile roofs, portals, columns, and walls in muted colors—though somewhat dominated by an architectural wedding cake, the Tower of Jewels, shimmering with glass gems, and the majestic Palace of Fine Arts. It was a show worthy of San Francisco.

The Panama Canal was opened to traffic on August 15, 1914; the Panama-Pacific International Exposition opened six months later, on February 20, 1915. On hand for the grand occasion was the Carmel poet, George Sterling (1869–1926), California's laureate of the period, to intone a dedicatory ode.

Exposition Ode

*(On the opening of the Panama-Pacific International
Exposition, San Francisco, February 1915)*

Be ye lift up, O gates of sea and land,
          Before the host that comes,
Not, as of old, with roar of hurrying drums,
And blaze of steel, and voice of war's command!
Legions of peace are at thy borders now,
O California, and ranks whose eyes
Behold the deathless star upon thy brow
          And know it leads to love.
Wherefore, give thou thy banners to the skies,
And let the clarions of thy conquest sound!
          For thine is holy ground,
          And from thy heavens above
Falls tenderly a rain of life, not death.
          Thy sons have found
Again the rivers of that Paradise
And valleys where the fig and olive grow,
          Wherefrom, one saith,
Man journeyed forth in tears, and long ago.

Be ye lift up, O gates of many halls,
          That house, sublime,
The trophies and the nobler spoils of Time!
From where the Orient in friendship calls
          Across her ocean-roads—
          From Africa's abodes—
From seas whose purple bore the keels of Tyre—
          From islands west and north—
From lands that see the white Andean walls—
From those frontiers of thunder and of fire
That compass Europe now, hath man sent forth

The fruitage of his labor and his art.
Behold the greatness of his mind and heart
    Who so can strive
    And, though the earthquake rive,
And War, with mailed hands at the race's throat,
Confirm the terrors that the prophets wrote
And all the stars have seen since Christ was born,
Can so bear witness to the soul within!
Yea! from Earth's mire of ignorance and sin
    He marches with the morn,
And lays a new commandment on the sea,
Bidding it set the continents apart,
And of the trackless heavens is he free.
Yet those are but the lesser of his dreams,
When the white vision of the Future gleams,
    And Music in his heart
Makes for a while the seraph he shall be;
For he would sway the sun's effulgent beams,
Vassal to that diviner sun, his brain,
    And set afar the years of Death,
    And with exultant breath
Cry victory on matter and on pain.
Lo! in what sorrow and mysterious mirth
Do we draw up against the Night our plan!
O toil of ants, beholding the great earth!
O Titan's work, seeing how small is man!
      . . . . .
Be ye lift up, O everlasting gates
Of that far City men shall build for Man!
    O fairer Day that waits,
The splendor of whose dawn we shall not see,
When selfish bonds of family and clan
Melt in the higher love that yet shall be!
O State without a master or a slave,
    Whose law of light we crave
Ere morning widen on the world set free!
    Alas! how distant are,

To watchers of the Past,
Thy palms of peace, thy mercy and thy truth!
Yet Faith's great eyes look upward to her star,
    Strong in immortal youth:
We know the reign of Night shall end at last,
And all the ancient evil lie undone.
    O armies of the sun,
Your war is on the darkness and its tears!
    Across the gulf of years
We hear your song and see your banners shine.
Know that we too would share your toils divine,
On self and madness hastening their end.
    Lo! from our Age we send
A music brief and broken and august
    To mingle with your own—
    A strain from silence flown,
Saying we too have hungered to the sky,
And built from many tears and humble dust
A Dream that shall not altogether die—
    The vision of that day
When human strength shall serve the common good,
And man, forever loyal to the race,
Find, far beyond our seasons of dismay,
    The guerdon of its grace:
One hope, one home, one song, one brotherhood,
And in each face the best-beloved's face.

From "Ode: On the Opening of the Panama-Pacific International Exposition, San Francisco," February 1915. George Sterling (San Francisco: A. M. Robertson, 1915).

LXIX

Harriet Monroe

The Exposition drew throngs of California votaries from every corner of the United States and every corner of the world, but the great majority came also to view the sights of the state; and foremost on the list of sights was the wonderful valley called Yosemite, which in 1890 had been set aside as a National Park in response to the pleadings of John Muir. And two years before the Exposition, Muir had published his exciting volume *Yosemite Valley*.

But Muir's presence in the valley was now only spectral; he had died in 1914. In a unique way Harriet Monroe (1860–1936), founder-editor of *Poetry: A Magazine of Verse*, helped to preserve that presence by publishing in a Muir memorial issue of the *Sierra Club Bulletin* two lyrics inspired by the champion of Yosemite, with an explanation of the circumstances leading to their creation. Indeed the circumstances were perhaps of greater interest to posterity than the stanzas themselves, but the combination offered a genial annotation on the side enthusiasms of Miss Monroe, then the recognized arbiter of contemporary poetry, and the editor who introduced to American readers names like Carl Sandburg, Rupert Brooke, Vachel Lindsay, and Robert Frost. Almost a quarter of a century earlier she had won national recognition by playing the same kind of role in Illinois that George Sterling played in California, when she wrote "The Columbian Ode" for the Great Chicago Exposition of 1892.

Morning of Creation

It was on two occasions in the Yosemite that John Muir gave me perhaps the richest of my mountain days. And each day took form in a poem. . . . One morning we were climbing out of the Valley by way of Vernal and Nevada Falls. I was a poor climber, always the last on the trail, and Nevada, the dancer, held me back with her beauty.

When at last I reached the level granite above her, John Muir was there, mounted on the horse which he rode now and then when no woman would accept the loan of it. He was rapt, entranced; he threw up his arm in a grand gesture. "This is the morning of creation," he cried, "the whole thing is beginning now! The mountains are singing together"—ah, I cannot remember his dithyrambic paean of praise, which flowed on as grandly as the great white waters beside us.

Four days later I made of it this poem, which offers something of what he said, though his free biblical rhythms feel somewhat cramped in my rhymes, and it was I who dragged the human beings in:

It is creation's morning—
  Freshly the rivers run.
The cliffs, white brows adorning,
  Sing to the shining sun.

The forest, plumed and crested,
  Scales the steep granite wall.
The ranged peaks, glacier-breasted,
  March to the festival.

The mountains dance together,
  Lifting their domed heads high.
The cataract's foamy feather
  Flaunts in the streaming sky.

> Somewhere a babe is borning,
>   Somewhere a maid is won.
> It is creation's morning—
>   Now is the world begun.

A few days later we took the "long, long hike," . . . from Lake Merced to Tuolumne Meadows. Before many hours I met John Muir, who insisted on my riding his horse most of the time; and so it was in his company that I crossed the wet snows and slushy waters of Vogelsang Pass. He introduced me to that lady of the snows, the mountain hemlock, who was just then lifting her head from under the white weight of winter, and spreading her trailing garments in the sun.

He told me how she pushed out of the rock and grew, how she bowed to the wind and gently resisted the storm; how she bent under mountain loads of ice each year, and rose again to the beauty of the sun for a brief summer of joy. He described her moods, revealed her graces—gave me her individuality, her character, until I felt something of his love and intimacy. "You poet, write about that!" he commanded, and so once more—a few days later—I tried to catch the beauty of the moment:

> The mountain hemlock droops her lacy branches
>   Oh, so tenderly
>   In the summer sun!
> Yet she has power to baffle avalanches—
>   She, rising slenderly
>   Where the rivers run.
>
> So pliant yet so powerful! Oh, see her
>   Spread alluringly
>   Her thin sea-green dress!
> Now from white winters' thrall the sun would free her
>   To bloom unenduringly
>   In his glad caress.

From "An Appreciation," Harriet Monroe, *Sierra Club Bulletin*, January 1916.

LXX

Upton Sinclair

California appeared to be entering a period of relative tranquillity, free from the feverish excitement that had been agitating the state periodically ever since the gold rush, when suddenly commotion reigned again: the huge Signal Oil Field at Long Beach had been discovered. The direct effect was upon Greater Los Angeles, but repercussions from such a discovery could not be localized. The excitement swept over the state like a tidal wave. Everyone knew that millions had been made from an earlier oil strike in the heart of Los Angeles. No telling, any Californian might have an oil well hiding under the rose bushes of his front yard.

It was a situation made to order for Socialist Upton Sinclair (1878–   ), professional reformer and occasional politician, the novelist who wrote with a conscience and a compulsion to reveal the hypocrisies and social evils of the day. Already he had aroused national indignation over his exposure of the industrial shortcomings of the Chicago stockyards in *The Jungle* and the roguery of the coal barons in *King Coal*, and now he leveled his sights on California petroleum, to produce the widely popular *Oil!* Discreetly he set his fictitious strike in "Beach City," but left no doubt of the real locale he was describing. Here skullduggery was running riot. Paupers were being turned into capitalists, capitalists into paupers, and in all the excitement over the deluge of oil fly-by-night shysters and wildcat promoters were robbing average, honest citizens of their life savings.

This Land of Hope

The number of the house was 5746 Los Robles Boulevard, and you would have had to know this land of hope in order to realize that it stood in a cabbage field. Los Robles means "the oaks"; and two or three miles away, where this boulevard started in the heart of Beach City, there were four live oak trees. But out here a bare slope of hill, quite steep, yet not too steep to be plowed and trenched and covered with cabbages, with sugar beets down on the flat. The eye of hope, aided by surveyors' instruments, had determined that some day a broad boulevard would run on this line; and so there was a dirt road, and at every corner white posts set up, with a wing north and a wing east—Los Robles Blvd.—Palomitas Ave.; Los Robles Blvd.—El Centro Ave.; and so on.

Two years ago the "subdividers" had been here, with their outfit of little red and yellow flags; there had been full-page advertisements in the newspapers, and free auto rides from Beach City, and a free lunch, consisting of "hot dog" sandwiches, a slice of apple pie, and a cup of coffee. At that time the fields had been cleared of cabbages, and graded, and the lots had blossomed with little signs: "Sold." This was supposed to refer to the lot, but in time it came to refer to the purchaser.

The company had undertaken to put in curbs and sidewalks, water and gas and sewers; but somebody made off with the money, and the enterprise went into bankruptcy, and presently new signs began to appear: "For Sale, by Owner," or "Bargain: See Smith and Headmutton, Real Estate." And when these signs brought no reply, the owners sighed and reflected that someday when little Willie grew up he would make a profit out of that investment. Meantime, they would accept the proposition of Japanese truck gardeners to farm the land for one-third of the crop.

But three or four months ago something unexpected had happened. A man who owned an acre or two of land on the top of the hill had caused a couple of motor trucks to come toiling up the slope, loaded with large square timbers of Oregon pine; carpenters had begun to work on these, and the neighborhood had stared, wondering what strange kind of house it could be. Suddenly the news had spread, in an explosion of excitement: an oil derrick!

A deputation called upon the owner to find out what it meant. It was pure "wild-catting," he assured them; he happened to have a hundred thousand dollars to play with, and this was his idea of play. Nevertheless, the bargain signs came down from the cabbage fields, and were replaced by "Oil Lot for Sale." Speculators began to look up the names and addresses of owners, and offers were made—there were rumors that some had got as high as a thousand dollars, nearly twice the original price of the lots. Motor cars took to bumping out over the dirt roads, up and down the lanes; and on Saturday and Sunday afternoons there would be a crowd staring at the derrick.

The drilling began, and went on, monotonously and uneventfully. The local newspapers reported the results: the D. H. Culver Prospect No. 1 was at 1,478 feet in hard sandstone formation and no sign of oil. It was the same at 2,000 and at 3,000; and then for weeks the rig was "fishing" for a broken drill and everybody lost interest; it was nothing but a "dry hole," and people who had refused double prices for their lots began to curse themselves for fools. "Wild-catting was nothing but gambling anyhow—quite different from conservative investments in town lots. Then the papers reported that D. H. Culver Prospect No. 1 was drilling again; it was at 3,059 feet, but the owners had not yet given up hope of striking something.

Then a strange thing happened. There came trucks heavily loaded with stuff, carefully covered with canvas. Everybody connected with the enterprise had been warned or bribed to silence; but small boys peered under the canvas while the trucks were toiling up the hill with roaring motors, and they reported big sheets of curved metal, with holes along the edges for bolts. That could be only one thing, tanks. And at the same time came rumors that D. H. Culver had purchased another tract of land on the hill. The meaning of all this was obvious: Prospect No. 1 had got into oil sands!

The whole hill began to blossom with advertisements, and real estate agents swarmed to the "field." A magic word now—no longer cabbage field or sugar-beet field, but "*the* field!" Speculators set themselves up in tents, or did business from automobiles drawn up by the roadside, with canvas signs on them. There was coming and going all day long, and crowds of people gathered to stare up at the derrick, and listen to the monotonous grinding of the heavy drill that went round and round all day—Ump-um— ump-um—ump-um—ump-um—varied by the "puff-puff" of the engine. "Keep out—this means you!" declared a conspicuous sign; Mr. D. H. Culver and his employees had somehow lost all their good breeding.

But suddenly there was no possibility of secrecy; literally all the world knew—for telegraph and cable carried the news to the farthest corners of civilization. The greatest oil strike in the history of Southern California, the Prospect Hill field! The inside of the earth seemed to burst out through that hole; a roaring and rushing, as Niagara, and a black column shot up into the air, two hundred feet, two hundred and fifty—no one could say for sure— and came thundering down to earth as a mass of thick, black, slimy, slippery fluid.

It hurled tools and other heavy objects this way and that, so the men had to run for their lives. It filled the sump hole and poured over, like a sauce pan boiling too fast, and went streaming down the hillside. Carried by the wind, a curtain of black mist, it sprayed the Culver homestead, turning it black, and sending the women of the household flying across the cabbage fields. Afterward it was told with Homeric laughter how these women had been heard to lament the destruction of their clothing and window curtains by this million-dollar flood of "black gold"!

Word spread by telephone to Beach City; the newspapers bulletined it, the crowds shouted it on the street, and before long the roads leading to Prospect Hill were black with a solid line of motor cars. The news reached Angel City, the papers there put out "extras," and before nightfall the Beach City boulevard was crowded with cars, a double line, all coming one way. Fifty thousand people stood in a solid ring at what they considered a safe distance from the gusher, with emergency policemen trying to drive them further back, and shouting: "Lights out! Lights out!" All night those words were chanted in a chorus; everybody realized the danger—some one fool might forget and light a cigarette and the whole hillside would leap into flame; a nail in a shoe might do it, striking on a stone; or a motor truck with its steel-rimmed tires. Quite frequently these gushers caught fire at the first moment.

But still the crowds gathered; men put down the tops of their automobiles and stood up in the seats and conducted auction rooms by the light of the stars. Lots were offered for sale at fabulous prices, and some of them were bought; leases were offered, companies were started and shares sold—the traders would push their way out of the crowd to a safe distance on the windward side where they could strike a match and see each other's faces, and scrawl a memorandum of what they agreed. Such trading went on most of the night, and in the morning came big tents that had been built for revival meetings, and the cabbage fields became gay with red and black signs: "Beach Co-operative No. 1," "Skite Syndicate, No. 1, ten thousand units, $10."

Meantime the workmen were toiling like mad to stop the flow of the well; they staggered here and there, half blinded by the black spray—and with no place to brace themselves, nothing they could hold onto because everything was greased, streaming with grease. . . . No one could figure how much wealth that monster was wasting, but it must be thousands of dollars per minute.

From *Oil!*, Upton Sinclair (Long Beach: Upton Sinclair, 1927).

LXXI

J. Smeaton Chase

Until the 1920s most of the visitors who crossed the continent to see California were *travelers*—not tourists. Travelers took their journeying in dead earnest; they set out with a well-planned itinerary, with railroad tickets, hotel reservations, prearranged banking connections, and two or three trunks. The new breed of sightseer, an orthodox tourist, was less formal, less regimented, more venturesome; he went forth boldly with a general destination in mind, a small fold of hard-earned cash, and a valise stowed in the back seat of his tin lizzie. He worked out the details of his itinerary as he went along.

California was just beginning to beckon waves of these venturesome tourists. Besides San Francisco, Los Angeles, and Yosemite, which everyone had to see, less familiar points of interest were now being starred on the maps—places like Carmel, the Russian River region, Clear Lake, Pacific Grove, Death Valley, from which some of the terror had been removed, Pismo Beach, Laguna Beach, Long Beach, Lake Arrowhead, Palm Springs.

Each of these resorts had its own self-appointed spokesman—or circle. of spokesmen—whose spare time was devoted to chanting the praises of his chosen paradise. Crowding the hideouts with newcomers was the last thing the publicists wanted, but they could not resist the temptation to boast to the world of the glories and vacation advantages. Inevitably the tourists accepted the eulogies as open invitations, thronged in, and by their collective presence sooner or later robbed the resort of the very character its spokesman had lauded.

But through the twenties there were still innumerable unspoiled and idyllic retreats scattered throughout the state—on the Pacific beaches, high in the Sierra, along the shores of inland lakes and rivers, on the edge of the desert. Palm Springs was such a place. Its self-appointed publicist was London-born J. Smeaton Chase (1864–1924). He had performed the feat of making a horseback trip all the way from Mexico to Oregon, and then had written a popular book, *California Coast Trails*. That was followed by *California Desert Trails* and a book on Yosemite.

In all his travels Chase found no spot that appealed to him quite like Palm Springs. It was a desert village far off the beaten track; it possessed few of the unnecessary refinements of civilization; it was his bit of Palestinian Arabia, his "Garden in the Sun." Never realizing that it would be a tourist come-on that would help convert a rural refuge for recluses into a resort city, he wrote a whole book about Palm Springs, *Our Araby*, a swan song for the charming, unhurried, saddle-oriented, dim-lighted town he loved.

Palm Springs—by Candlelight

Village is a pretty word, though ambitious settlements are keen to disclaim the implied rusticity and to graduate into the rank of town or city. Palm Springs has no such aims, and is well content to remain far down the list in census returns. We decline to take part in the race for Improvements. . . . Rural Free Delivery does not entice us: we prefer the daily gathering at the store at mail time, Indians and whites together, where we can count on catching Miguel or Romualda if we wish to hire a pony or to get the washing done.

Electric lights are here for those who like them, yet to some of us nothing seems so homelike for the dining table as shaded candles, or for fireside reading a good kerosene lamp, while if you want to call on a neighbor after dark, we find that a lantern sheds light where you need it, instead of illuminating mainly the upper air. Telephones? No, thanks: we are here to possess our souls and

live all day in the open. How can we do that if anybody and
everybody who so wishes can jerk us back with a telephone wire,
as if we were parrots tied to a perch with a string? Cement sidewalks would be to us a calamity: we may be dusty, but dust is
natural and we prefer it. After all, the pepper- or cottonwood-
shaded streets of our Garden of the Sun are really only country
lanes, and who wants a country lane cemented . . .

The Hot Spring is the outstanding natural feature of our
village. . . . The water, which is just comfortably hot and contains mineral elements which render it remarkably curative,
comes up mingled with quantities of very fine sand. You may bask
in the clear water of the surface of the pool or, if you want all the
fun you can get for your money, you may lower yourself into the
very mouth of the spring where the mixture comes gurgling up.
This will yield you—especially at night and by candlelight, a
novel and somewhat shuddery experience, though one absolutely
without risk; and you will come forth with a sense of fitness and
fineness all over to which only a patent medicine advertisement
writer of high attainments could possibly do justice.

Our village is bisected by the Reservation line, which thus
makes a geographical division of the population. Only geographical, though, for fortunately there has never been anything but
complete harmony between whites and Indians. . . . I for one
could not wish for better neighbors than our Indians: I should be
pleased, indeed, to feel sure that they could say as much for us.
They are but few in number, forty or fifty, for the Cahuillas are
scattered in small *rancherías* over a wide territory.

The white population is variable. In winter and spring, when
the "Standing Room Only" sign hangs out, there may be a total of
300 or more residents and visitors (the latter much the more
numerous); in the hot months residents may number a dozen or
two, and visitors there are none. In desert phrase, the whites have
"gone inside" (i.e., to the coast), an odd turn of speech, but one
quite appropriate to the point of view of the man of the Big
Spaces—"inside" where one is shut in and boxed up. . . .

Wealth and fashion, as such, are not much attracted to our
village. On the other hand, the scientists, writers, painters, musi-

cians—in fact, all kinds of people who love quiet, thoughtful things and whose work or enjoyment lies in natural instead of artificial fields, come and share with us the wholesome pleasures and interests that are inherent in a clean, new, unspoiled bit of the wonderful old world.

One little detail that really deserves to be named . . . is the delightful way the children have of everlastingly careering about on horseback. Tanned and possibly tattered, bareheaded and barelegged, eyes dancing and hair flying, all day long you will find our youngsters of four years and upward tearing about, perhaps two or three together on one good-natured mount, often without saddle or stirrup, but always on the dead run, utterly fearless and uproariously happy. . . . Circus managers would seize on Palm Springs as a perfect nursery of infant prodigies.

. . . The village itself is a place of two or three score of unpretentious cottages scattered along half a dozen palm- and pepper-shaded streets. We do not run much to lawns and formal gardens: we live in the desert because we like it, hence we don't care to shut ourselves away in little citified enclosures. But the two or three old places which formed the nucleus of the settlement are bowers of bloom and umbrageous greenery. Gray old fig trees lean out over the sidewalk, while oranges, dates, grapefruit, lemons and trees of other sorts for fruit or ornament flourish. . . . By excellent luck, the State Highway, which threatened to bring an ever-increasing roar of automobile traffic through our quiet streets, has been diverted—averted is the better word—to the north side of the valley, leaving Palm Springs with no more than its own quota of traffic racket to put up with. . . .

The time has come, too, when flying must be counted in when one thinks of ways and means of amusement or of getting about. There is not, of course, much to be said yet on this score, but it may be remarked that our Araby is not lagging behind the rest of the world, and already is critical of the pilot who fails to bring his "bus" neatly to earth regardless of cactus and creosote bush. Certainly it would seem that the spacious, level desert is the very model of a natural airdrome, and I look to see aëronauts, professional and amateur, taking Nature's hint and exploiting these advantages. . . .

We have, for those who must be up to date, "the movies"—not
the commonplace side of the great modern pastime, the sitting in
a "palace" and watching the reeling off of pictures on a screen,
but the more exciting first-hand experience of seeing them made,
the thrill of the real thing, flesh and blood—with paint and
powder thrown in. In the last few years Palm Springs has become
headquarters, so to speak, for Algeria, Egypt, Arabia, Palestine,
India, Mexico, a good deal of Turkey, Australia, South America,
and sundry other parts of the globe.

Wondrous are the sights and sounds the dwellers in Palm
Springs are privileged to see and hear when "the movies are in
town"; wondrous the "stars" that then shine in broad daylight;
wondrous the cowboys, cavalcades and caballeros, the tragedies
and feats of daring, the rescues and escapes for which our dunes
and canyons provide the setting. The quiet village becomes in
fact a movie studio for the time, and the visitor whose ideal is
"Something doing every minute" has then little reason to pine
away with ennui. . . .

Naturally radio, the newest and most "broadcast" of scientific
amusement fads, is not wanting, even in this desert community.
After all, we are but a hundred miles or so from Los Angeles,
proud exponent of "the latest" in every form of up-to-dateness. So
at Palm Springs you may "listen in" to your heart's content every
evening, and catch whatever wisdom or beauty there may be in
our modern Voices of the Night.

Following the lead of a few other communities of individuality,
such as Carmel-by-the-Sea, an annual outdoor play has been instituted. The plays are intended to be appropriate to the place,
for instance, representations of local Indian legends or the like.
They are performed on the natural stage, the desert itself. . . .
Beyond the active amusements, so to speak, there are some im-
material pleasures to be enjoyed in Our Araby which, I venture to
think, remain long in the memory of those who come here. It may
sound commonplace to talk of sunset colorings and sunrise pan-
oramas, but anyone who has watched the sunset light on the
Morongos from the rocky point that overlooks our village will
allow that it is a revelation of Nature in a mood of utmost loveliness. . . . And then there is the night. It may seem odd to speak

of sleep under the head of Amusements, but such sleep as one gets on the desert fairly ranks as enjoyment. . . . Few people know what night at its best can be: the desert is the best place to learn it. Calmness, quietude, restfulness . . . here approach the absolute. . . .

Though Palm Springs is strong for simplicity, our visitors need fear no hardships; indeed, our leading hotel is apt to prove a surprise to guests who come with the thought of "putting up with things." . . . It should be said that the best accommodation is offered by the Desert Inn, while less expensive quarters may be found at one or two other places in the village. A number of pleasant small tent houses are rented . . . and these again are supplemented by a few other houses of various sizes and rates of rental. Inquiries regarding quarters addressed to the Postmaster would be handed by him to the person most likely to be able to suit the applicant.

Condensed from *Our Araby,* J. Smeaton Chase (Palm Springs and New York: J. S. Chase, 1923).

LXXII

Robinson Jeffers

Palm Springs was a favored hideaway for artists of southern California; northerners preferred Carmel, and there in a modest stone house with a tower constructed by his own hands, Robinson Jeffers (1887–1962) established himself before the local candlelit era was entirely spent, long before neighbor coast watchers had crowded in cheek by jowl. His eyrie commanded a magnificent ocean view, Cyprus Point to the north, Point Carmel to the south, backed by the foothills of the Coast Range. Jeffers adopted it all as his poetic domain, along with the gulls, seals, sea lions, fishing craft, fog, the spring flowers that blanketed windswept promontories, screaming gales, lighthouses, dunes, stark headlands, and gnarled cypresses.

Point Pinos and Point Lobos

A lighthouse and a graveyard and gaunt pines
Not old, no tree lives long here, where the northwind
Has forgot mercy. All night the light blinks north,
The Santa Cruz mountain redwoods hate its flashing,
The night of the huge western water takes it,
The long rays drown a little off shore, hopelessly

Attempting distance, hardly entering the ocean.
The lighthouse, and the gaunt boughs of the pines,
The carved gray stones, and the people of the graves.

· · ·

Point Joe

Point Joe has teeth and has torn ships; it has fierce and
    solitary beauty;
Walk there all day you will see nothing that will not make
    part of a poem.

I saw the spars and planks of shipwreck on the rocks, and
    beyond the desolate
Sea-meadows rose the warped wind-bitten van of the pines,
    a fog-bank vaulted

Forest and all, the flat sea-meadows at the time of year
    were plated
Golden with the low flower called footsteps of the spring,
    millions of florets,

Whose light suffused upward into the fog, flooded its vault,
    we wandered
Through a weird country where the light beat up from earth-
    ward, and was golden.

One other moved there, an old Chinaman gathering seaweed
    from the sea-rocks,
He brought it in his basket and spread it flat to dry on the
    edge of the meadow.

Permanent things are what is needful in a poem, things
    temporally
Of great dimension, things continually renewed or always
    present.

Grass that is made each year equals the mountains in her
      past and future;
Fashionable and momentary things we need not see nor
      speak of.

Man gleaning food between the solemn presences of land and
      ocean,
On shores where better men have shipwrecked, under fog
      and among flowers,

Equals the mountains in his past and future; that glow
      from the earth was only
A trick of nature's, one must forgive nature a thousand
      graceful subtleties.

Carmel Point

The extraordinary patience of things!
This beautiful place defaced with a crop of suburban houses—
How beautiful when we first beheld it,
Unbroken field of poppy and lupin walled with clean cliffs;
No intrusion but two or three horses pasturing,
Or a few milch cows rubbing their flanks on the outcrop rock-
      heads—
Now the spoiler has come: does it care?
Not faintly. It has all time. It knows the people are a tide
That swells and in time will ebb, and all
Their works dissolve. Meanwhile the image of the pristine beauty
Lives in the very grain of the granite,
Safe as the endless ocean that climbs our cliff.—As for us:
We must uncenter our minds from ourselves:
We must unhumanize our views a little, and become confident
As the rock and ocean that we were made from.

"Point Pinos and Point Lobos" and "Point Joe" from *Roan Stallion and Other Poems* (New York: Boni and Liveright, 1925); "Carmel Point" from *Hungerfield and Other Poems,* Robinson Jeffers (New York: Random House, 1951).

LXXIII

William Saroyan

For two hundred years men with an eye to the future had been bring-ing into California from far-off places new plants to test in the produc-tive soil of the Golden West. The mission padres and the Spaniards started it; philanthropic explorers and traders, overlanders from the East, immigrants from Europe and the Orient, farmers with wide vision like John Bidwell and John Frémont had all added to the cul-ture; and latter-day scientists from colleges and experiment stations had joined in the cause, to cross, graft, hybridize, and perfect, until California was producing some of the most famous yields of fruits, grains, nuts, and vegetables anywhere in the world. Around Fresno the specialty was raisin grapes, and the only trouble there was that the farmers were drying more grapes than anyone would buy.

California's wittiest of yarn spinners, William Saroyan (1908–   ), born and brought up in Fresno, explained how that predicament was at least temporarily surmounted; it was from the author of *The Daring Young Man on the Flying Trapeze*—and from the advertisements of Sun-Maid raisins—that the American public first learned about Fresno.

A Raisin in Every Pot

A man could walk four or five miles in any direction from the heart of our city and see our streets dwindle to land and weeds. In many places the land would be vineyard and orchard land, but in most places it would be desert land, and weeds would be the strong dry weeds of desert. In this land there would be the living things that had had their being in the quietness of deserts for centuries. There would be snakes and horned-toads, prairie-dogs and jack rabbits. In the sky over this land would be buzzards and hawks, and the hot sun. And everywhere in the desert would be the marks of wagons that had made lonely roads.

Two miles from the heart of our city a man could come to the desert and feel the loneliness of a desolate area, a place lost in the earth, far from the solace of human thought. Standing at the edge of our city, a man could feel that we had made this place of streets and dwellings in the stillness and loneliness of the desert, and that we had done a brave thing. We had come to this dry area that was without history and we had paused in it and built our houses and we were slowly creating the legend of our life. We were digging for water and we were leading streams through the dry land. We were planting and ploughing and standing in the midst of the garden we were making.

Our trees were not yet tall enough to make much shade, and we had planted a number of kinds of trees we ought not to have planted because they were of weak stuff and would never live a century, but we had made a pretty good beginning. Our cemeteries were few and the graves in them were few. We had buried no great men because we hadn't had time to produce any great men. We had been too busy to get water into the desert. The shadow of no great mind was over our city. But we had a playground called Cosmos Playground. We had public schools named after Emerson and Hawthorne and Lowell and Longfellow. Two great railways had their lines running through our city and trains were always coming to us from the great cities of America and somehow we could not feel that we were wholly lost. We had two newspapers and a Civic Auditorium and a public library two-thirds full of books. We had the Parlor Lecture Club. We had every sort of church except a Christian Science church. Every house in our city had a Bible in it, and a lot of houses had as many as four Bibles in them. A man could feel our city was beautiful.

Or a man could feel that our city was fake, that our lives were empty, and that we were the contemporaries of jack rabbits. Or a man could have one viewpoint in the morning and another in the evening. The dome of our courthouse was high, but it was ridiculous and had nothing to do with what we were trying to do in the desert. It was an imitation of something out of Rome. We had a mayor, but he wasn't a great man and he didn't look like a mayor. He looked like a farmer. He *was* a farmer, but he was elected mayor. We had no great men, but the whole bunch of us put together amounted to something that was very nearly great. . . .

Our enterprise wasn't on a vast scale. It wasn't even on a medium-sized scale. There was nothing slick about anything we were doing. Our enterprise was neither scientific nor inhuman, as the enterprise of a growing city ought to be. Nobody knew the meaning of the word efficiency, and the most frightening word ever used by our mayor in public orations was *progress*, but by *progress* he meant, and our people understood him to mean, the paving of the walk in front of the City Hall, and the purchase by our city of a Ford automobile for the mayor. . . . This sort of thing gave our city an amateur appearance, as if we were only experimenting and weren't quite sure if we had more right to be in the desert than the jack rabbits and the horned toads, as if we didn't believe we had started something that was going to be very big, something that would eventually make a tremendous change in the history of the world.

But in time a genius appeared among us and he said that we would change the history of the world. He said that we would do it with raisins. He said that we would change the eating habits of man.

Nobody thought he was crazy, because he wore spectacles and looked important. He appeared to be what our people liked to call an *educated man*. . . . What our valley needed, he said, was a system whereby the raisin would be established as a necessary part of the national diet, and he said that he had evolved this system and that it was available for our valley. He made eloquent speeches in our Civic Auditorium and in the public halls of the small towns around our city. He said after he got America accustomed to eating raisins, we would begin to teach Europe and Asia and maybe Australia to eat raisins, our valley would become the richest valley in the whole world. China! he said, . . . if we could get every living Chinaman to place one raisin, only *one*, mind you, in every pot of rice he cooked, why, then, we could dispose of all our raisins at a good price and everybody in our valley would have money in the bank, and would be able to purchase all the indispensable conveniences of modern life, bath tubs, carpet sweepers, house electricity and automobiles.

Rice, he said. That's all they eat. But we can teach them to drop one raisin in every pot of rice they cook.

Raisins had a good taste, he said. People liked to eat raisins. People were so fond of eating raisins they would be glad to pay money for them. The trouble was that people had gotten out of the habit of eating raisins. . . . The raisins hadn't been packed in attractive packages.

All we needed, he said was a raisin association with an executive department and a central packing and distributing plant. He would do the rest. He would have an attractive package designed, and he would create a patented trade name for our raisins. He would place full-page advertisements in *The Saturday Evening Post* and other national periodicals. He would organize a great sales force. He would do everything. If our farmers would join this raisin association of his, he would do everything, and our city would grow to be one of the liveliest in California. Our valley would grow to be one of the richest agricultural centers of the world.

He used big words like *co-operation, mass production, modern efficiency, modern psychology, modern advertising* and *modern distribution,* and the farmers who couldn't understand what he was talking about felt that he was very wise and that they must join the raisin association and help make raisins famous.

He was an orator. He was a statistician. He was a genius. I forget his name. Our whole valley has forgotten his name, but in his day he made something of a stir. . . . There was excitement all over our valley. Farmers from all over our valley came to town in surreys and buggies. They gathered in small and large groups in front of our public buildings, and they talked about this idea of making the raisin famous.

It *sounded* all right.

The basic purpose of the raisin association was to gather together all the raisins of our valley, and after creating a demand for them through national advertising, to offer them for sale at a price that would pay for all the operating expenses of the association and leave a small margin for the farmers themselves. Well, the association was established and it was called the Sun-Maid Raisin Association. A six-story Sun-Maid Raisin Building was erected, and an enormous packing and distributing plant was erected. It contained the finest of modern machinery. These machines cleaned the raisins and took the stems from them. The whole plant was a picture of order and efficiency.

. . . One Thursday evening I had a copy of *The Saturday Evening Post* spread before me on our living-room table. I was turning the pages and looking at the things that were being advertised. On one page I read the words, *Have you had your iron today?* It was a full-page advertisement of our Raisin Association. The advertisement explained in impeccable English that raisins contained iron and that wise people were eating a five-cent package of raisins every afternoon. Raisins banished fatigue, the advertisement said. At the bottom of the page was the name of our Association, its street address, and the name of our city. We were no longer lost in the wilderness, because the name of our city was printed in *The Saturday Evening Post*.

These advertisements began to appear regularly in *The Saturday Evening Post*. It was marvelous. People were hearing about us. It was very expensive to have a full-page advertisement in the *Post*, but people were being taught to eat raisins, and that was the important thing.

For a while people actually *did* eat raisins. Instead of spending a nickel for a bottle of Coca-Cola or for a bar of candy, people were buying small packages of raisins. The price of raisins began to move upward, and after several years, when all of America was enjoying prosperity, the price of raisins became so high that a man with ten acres of vineyard was considered a man of considerable means, and as a matter of fact he was. Some farmers who had only ten acres were buying brand-new automobiles and driving them around. Everybody in our city was proud of the Raisin Association. Everything looked fine, values were up, and a man had to pay a lot of money for a little bit of desert.

Then something happened.

It wasn't the fault of our Raisin Association. It just happened. People stopped eating raisins. Maybe it was because there was no longer as much prosperity as there had been, or maybe it was because people had simply become tired of eating raisins. There are other things that people can buy for a nickel and eat. At any rate, people stopped eating raisins. Our advertisements kept appearing in *The Saturday Evening Post* and we kept asking the people of America if they had had their iron, but it wasn't doing any good. We had more raisins in our Sun-Maid warehouse than we could ever sell, even to the Chinese, even if they were to drop *three* raisins in every pot of rice they cooked. The price of raisins began to drop. . . . It got so low it looked as if we had made a mistake by pausing in the desert and building our city in the first place.

Then we found out that it was the same all over the country. Prices were low everywhere. No matter how efficient we were, or how cleverly we wrote our advertisements, or how attractive we made our packages of raisins, we couldn't hope for anything higher than the price we were getting. The six-story building looked sad, the excitement died away, and the packing house became a useless ornament in the landscape. Its machinery became junk, and we knew a great American idea had failed. We hadn't changed the taste of man. Bread was still preferable to raisins. We hadn't taught the Chinese to drop a raisin in their pots of cooking rice. They were satisfied to have the rice without the raisin.

And so we began to eat the raisins ourselves. It was amazing how we learned to eat raisins. We had talked so much about them we had forgotten that they were good to eat. We learned to cook raisins. They were good stewed, they had a fine taste with bread. All over the valley people were eating raisins. People couldn't buy raisins because they were a luxury, and so we had to eat them ourselves, although they were no luxury to us.

From "Fresno" in *The Saroyan Special* by William Saroyan (New York: Harcourt, Brace & World, 1948).

LXXIV

John Steinbeck

A national economic crisis as well as a declining taste for raisins was responsible for Fresno's troubles, and the same kind of trouble spread rapidly over much of California during the 1930s. The searing droughts that brought disaster to many sections of the prairies in 1934, 1936, and 1937 did not extend to the West Coast, but their aftermath created chaos in the central and southern valleys of California. To escape the destitution of the dust bowls stretching intermittently from Oklahoma to the Dakotas, thousands upon thousands of farm families packed up and crowded West in an epic migration, certain that they would find relief and a bright new future on the fertile California expanses.

They were to be disappointed. The Great Depression had upset the Eastern market for Imperial Valley lettuce, Riverside oranges, Santa Clara plums, Fresno raisins, and every other kind of farm produce. While the government continued to pour funds into projects for development of more prolific fruits and vegetables, the demand for even a normal supply steadily dwindled.

The "Okies" were given a poor reception. They merely added to the armies of unemployed laborers already wandering aimlessly through the state. In squalid encampments, often surrounded by the plenty that growers could not sell, yet could not afford to give away, they were caught up in the magnificent American paradox.

In his 1939 novel, *The Grapes of Wrath,* John Steinbeck (1902–   )

sympathetically presented the tragicomedy of these migrant victims of the dust bowl. As a native of Salinas, seat of Monterey County and center of a sprawling agricultural area that grew everything from sugar beets to strawberries, artichokes to apricots, barley to Burbank potatoes, Steinbeck could draw from a wealth of experience and first-hand observation. It was at Salinas, too, that a strike of lettuce pickers in 1936 erupted into costly violence.

So immensely popular was the book that in the first six months after its publication, it went through half a dozen printings, was awarded the Pulitzer Prize in 1940, was made into a celebrated motion picture, and is still widely read as a semiclassic depicting the irony in the plight of this segment of the American proletariat.

A Great Sorrow on the Land

The spring is beautiful in California. Valleys in which the fruit blossoms are fragrant pink and white waters in a shallow sea. Then the first tendrils of the grapes, swelling from the old gnarled vines, cascade down to cover the trunks. The full green hills are round and soft as breasts. And on the level vegetable lands are the mile-long rows of pale green lettuce and the spindly little cauli-flowers, the gray-green unearthly artichoke plants.

And then the leaves break out on the trees, and the petals drop from the fruit trees and carpet the earth with pink and white. The centers of the blossoms swell and grow and color: cherries and apples, peaches and pears, figs which close the flower in the fruit. All California quickens with produce, and the fruit grows heavy, and the limbs bend gradually under the fruit so that little crutches must be placed under them to support the weight.

Behind the fruitfulness are men of understanding and knowl-edge and skill, men who experiment with seed, endlessly develop-ing the techniques for greater crops of plants whose roots will resist the million enemies of the earth: the molds, the insects, the rusts, the blights. These men work carefully and endlessly to per-fect the seed, the roots. And there are the men of chemistry who spray the trees against pests, who sulphur the grapes, who cut out disease and rots, mildews and sicknesses. Doctors of preventive medicine, men at the borders who look for fruit flies, for Japanese beetle, men who quarantine the sick trees and root them out and burn them, men of knowledge. The men who graft the young trees, the little vines, are the cleverest of all, for theirs is a surgeon's job, as tender and delicate; and these men must have surgeons' hands and surgeons' hearts to slit the bark, to place the grafts, to bind the wounds and cover them from the air. These are great men.

Along the rows, the cultivators move, tearing the spring grass and turning it under to make a fertile earth, breaking the ground to hold the water up near the surface, ridging the ground in little pools for the irrigation, destroying the weed roots that may drink the water away from the trees.

And all the time the fruit swells and the flowers break out in long clusters on the vines. And in the growing year the warmth grows and the leaves turn dark green. The prunes lengthen like little green birds' eggs, and the limbs sag down against the crutches under the weight. And the hard little pears take shape, and the beginning of the fuzz comes out on the peaches. Grape blossoms shed their tiny petals and the hard little heads become green buttons, and the buttons grow heavy.

The men who work in the fields, the owners of the little orchards, watch and calculate. The year is heavy with produce. And men are proud, for of their knowledge they can make the year heavy. They have transformed the world with their knowledge. The short, lean wheat has been made big and productive. Little sour apples have grown large and sweet, and that old grape that grew among the trees and fed the birds its tiny fruit has mothered a thousand varieties, red and black, green and pale pink, purple and yellow; and each variety with its own flavor. The men who work in the experimental farms have made new fruits: nectarines and forty kinds of plums, walnuts with paper shells. And always they work, selecting, grafting, changing, driving themselves, driving the earth to produce.

And first the cherries ripen. Cent and a half a pound. Hell, we can't pick 'em for that. Black cherries and red cherries, full and sweet, and the birds eat half of each cherry and the yellow jackets buzz into the holes the birds made. And on the ground the seeds drop and dry with black shreds hanging from them.

The purple prunes soften and sweeten. My God, we can't pick them and dry and sulphur them. We can't pay wages, no matter what wages. And the purple prunes carpet the ground. And first the skins wrinkle a little and swarms of flies come to feast, and the valley is filled with the odor of sweet decay. The meat turns dark and the crop shrivels on the ground.

And the pears grow yellow and soft. Five dollars a ton. Five dollars for forty fifty-pound boxes; trees pruned and sprayed, orchards cultivated—pick the fruit, put it in boxes, load the trucks, deliver the fruit to the cannery—forty boxes for five dollars. We can't do it. And the yellow fruit falls heavily to the ground and splashes on the ground. The yellowjackets dig into the soft meat, and there is a smell of ferment and rot.

Then the grapes—we can't make good wine. People can't buy good wine. Rip the grapes from the vines, good grapes, rotten grapes, wasp-stung grapes. Press stems, press dirt and rot.

But there's mildew and formic acid in the vats.

Add sulphur and tannic acid.

The smell from the ferment is not the rich odor of wine, but the smell of decay and chemicals.

Oh, well. It has alcohol in it anyway. They can get drunk.

The little farmers watched debt creep up on them like the tide. They sprayed the trees and sold no crop, they pruned and grafted and could not pick the crop. And the men of knowledge have worked, have considered, and the fruit is rotting on the ground, and the decaying mash in the wine vats is poisoning the air. And taste the wine—no grape flavor at all, just sulphur and tannic acid and alcohol.

This little orchard will be part of a great holding next year, for the debt will have choked the owner.

This vineyard will belong to the bank. Only the great owners can survive, for they own the canneries too. And four pears peeled and cut in half, cooked and canned, still cost fifteen cents. And the canned pears do not spoil. They will last for years.

The decay spreads over the State, and the sweet smell is a great sorrow in the land. Men who can graft the trees and make the seed fertile and big can find no way to let the hungry people eat their produce. Men who have created new fruits in the world cannot create a system whereby their fruits may be eaten. And the failure hangs over the State like a great sorrow.

The works of the roots of the vines, of the trees, must be destroyed to keep up the price, and this is the saddest, bitterest thing of all. Carloads of oranges dumped on the ground. The people came for miles to take the fruit, but this could not be. How would they buy oranges at twenty cents a dozen if they could drive out and pick them up? And men with hoses squirt kerosene on the oranges, and they are angry at the crime, angry at the people who have come to take the fruit. A million people hungry, needing the fruit—and kerosene sprayed over the golden mountains.

And the smell of rot fills the country.

Burn coffee for fuel in the ships. Burn corn to keep warm, it makes a hot fire. Dump potatoes in the rivers and place guards along the banks to keep the hungry people from fishing them out. Slaughter the pigs and bury them, and let the putrescence drip down into the earth.

There is a crime here that goes beyond denunciation. There is a sorrow here that weeping cannot symbolize. There is a failure here that topples all our success. The fertile earth, the straight tree rows, the sturdy trunks, and the ripe fruit. And children dying of pellagra must die because a profit cannot be taken from an orange. And coroners must fill in the certificates—died of malnutrition—because the food must rot, must be forced to rot.

The people come with nets to fish for potatoes in the river, and the guards hold them back; they come in rattling cars to get the dumped oranges, but the kerosene is sprayed. And they stand still and watch the potatoes float by, listen to the screaming pigs being killed in a ditch and covered with quicklime, watch the mountains of oranges slop down to a putrefying ooze; and in the eyes of the people there is the failure; and in the eyes of the hungry there is a growing wrath. In the souls of the people the grapes of wrath are filling and growing heavy, growing heavy for the vintage.

From *The Grapes of Wrath*, John Steinbeck (New York: Viking Press, 1939).

LXXV

Donald Culross Peattie

Unlike the cultivated crops of the valleys, the floral harvests of the deserts were borne without reference to the wrath, hunger, or need for beauty among mankind. As the seasons willed, the bloom was lavish whether or not a human viewer was there to witness the spectacle. It was one of the exciting excesses of nature—like rampant fire, flood, or tempest. Donald Culross Peattie (1898–1964), author of over thirty books on nature, covering various regions of the country from the Carolinas to California, arrived at his Mojave ranchhouse under cover of darkness one night, unaware of the surprise that spring had in store for him. Next morning he opened his front door to be confronted by the dazzling miracle.

The Smile of Mojave

I opened my door in early sunshine and stepped out.

The desert, I saw, was in bloom.

Not every spring does the stone roll back like this, but only when the rain and the snows and the sun combine fortuitously to decree it. I had not seen the miracle before, road-runners though we had been for years, crisscrossing the southwestern wastes in

[498]

all directions, across the Antelope Valley and down into Death Valley, beside the Salton Sea and over the Yuma dunes, across Nevada sagebrush, Arizona mesas, alkaline playas of the Amargosa Desert, spaces of the Gila Desert where solid things have the unreality of mirage.

I knew occasional flowery spots, brief blossomings licked by blast of wind and blaze of sun; I knew the secretive blooming of the desert shrubs, in flowers without petals, or lonely corollas falling beside some seepage of water in the high clefts of the hills, where even the bees, you'd think, would not thread their way to find them. Dusty, wiry, naked but for thorns, resinous, bitter, sparse, the desert brush and cacti are admirable for enduring where they do at all; they are, like the scorpions and centipedes and rattlesnakes of their environment, much to be respected. In a sort of dead and silvery and almost invisible way, they are even beautiful, as the ghosts of Tamerlane's Tartars might look, if one had an hallucination of their passing in a blur of heat and whirling dust.

But here to my feet, that April morning, swept a radiant populace of flowers, sprung overnight, it seemed to me, from what had looked barren soil. As anyone will cry out involuntarily at an unexpected sharp pain, so there was no stopping the laughter that rose in the throat at the sight.

The desert flora at all ordinary times is grandly, confidently monotonous, made up of certain hardy species little varied over an area as great as the two Virginias plus the two Carolinas. That is the norm, the always present uncompromising reality, in season or out. But this other, this dazzling profusion of color and dancing shapes, this unexpected smile breaking over the Mojave's stern face, was all herbaceous, made of delicate annuals. The sea of bloom was only ankle-deep; many species were not an inch tall, though with flowers sometimes two inches across. In this fashion the beautiful little rose namas, the desert stars like English daisies, desert-gold, tiny-tim, and humble gilia with its petals the color of moonlight on frost made a dense carpet that it seemed heartless to tread upon.

Above this close undermat danced a second tier of flowers,

goldenglow and white tidy-tips and desert dandelions with heads
of canary yellow. And, pervading the sunny waste with fragrance,
rose sprawling sand-verbenas, lavender as they are pink. There
was a lupine blazing here and there throughout, a taper of royal
purple. There were the scabiosa sages, salvias really, that the
Spanish settlers called *chia*, whose brilliant blue two-lipped flowers leap out of a tiny spiny sphere of bracts. There were desert
mallows, with their crumpled dusty leaves and flowers varying
from vivid apricot to deep grenadine.

But most profuse, most constantly in motion on their hair-fine
stems, most innocently frail, were the blue gilias. Some were clear
white, some lilac, some true blue, some with yellow eyes, some
tall, some dwarf; what looked like many species was only one variable kind, *Gilia Davyi*. When the wind blew, and these children
of the desert danced, their fragrance was blown quite away;
when the sun baked perfume from the sand-verbena, the gilias'
odor was smothered. But when I brought them inside the cool
adobe room, I became aware of a tender perfume stealing into my
thoughts, getting into my dreams at night.

Every day, every hour, you saw the gilias, but you never got
used to the sheer improbability that anything so dainty could be
put forth from the Mojave. Indestructible, thorny, bare, the
creosote bush and salt bush, the burro bush and rabbit bush are
the natural sons of the desert, warrior sons, like Homeric soldiers
naked but for spear and shield, thorns and bitterness. But just as a
savage old man might beget gentle daughters too, so the Mojave
sends forth blue gilias, once in many years a million of them, like
this.

Above the two tiers of flowers there rose spindling examples of
a third. Here and there, for instance, a slim wand of lilac larkspur.
Or thistle sage, kingly tufts of cottony silver thick with long
mauve salvia flowers the longer for their orange anthers. And an
aster with lavender heads in bold clumps of twenty blooms and
more.

In all, those April days yielded to my vasculum some seventy-
five species. Large as this number sounds, it is not a greater
variety than would be found at a corresponding stage of seasonal

development anywhere else; what brought delight was the sheer abundance of the bloom, the feeling that we were besieged by an army of little flowers.

The bees were drunk with them; they came in thousands from only the Mojave knew where. I saw the hummingbirds flash by in such a state of excitement that they looked as if they had been shot sideways out of a cannon with a twisted bore. They seemed unable to settle their scattered brains on anything; they went so fast I couldn't follow them with my glasses to identify which of California's many kinds of hummer they were.

We used to wonder, at the ranch, how far this flood of rare flowering washed across the desert floor. You couldn't tell; you only knew it went to the rim of the horizon. And you knew it was brief. It must be loved while you had it, like the song of the thrush in the southern states. Something that each morning you dread to find gone at last, whelmed by the advance of summer heat.

Resting from the sweat and blindness of collecting in full sunlight at noon, I would lie on my back in the adobe room, on the cool of the tiles, and let the flowers dance before my closed eyes. And their biologic meaning was borne in upon me. Desert plants do not follow what we consider a normal cycle—green in summer, and dying back to some perennial root in winter. For when it is calendar summer here it is biologic winter; the leaves drop and everything dies or wears the look of death.

It is also, biologically, winter in autumn as well as in winter when snow lies on the desert. But spring is not only spring but summer and autumn in swift succession. And of all desert plants the best equipped to deal with this climatic extravagance are these little annuals, these fragile exquisites so prodigal of their scant waters. Swiftly indeed do they wilt. They not only wilt, they die, completely, the entire crop—only to survive as seeds. As seeds, a year later or, if conditions oblige, ten years later, they will sprout again, and in from two to six weeks rush to full flower, become pollinated, set seed, distribute seed, and die again. Such is the life of an annual, and of all forms of life history the annual is the best for desert life.

. . . The swift vanishing spring desert flora passes the greater part of its time as dormant seeds. Only irregularly and most briefly does it escape as a flower, before the continuous stream of life is caught inside a seed again, indefinitely to wait. So the champion desert plant is not the tough creosote, the malicious cholla, not the Joshua tree or the sage, but seed as tiny as gilia's. For a seed is not just part of a plant; detached it is a complete plant, with a plantlet folded inside, a supply of food, and an infinitesimal supply of moisture. Boxed in its shell, it defies drought, heat, cold, poisonous alkaline soils. Only water has the password to open its prison.

Now I began to notice seeds everywhere. The deliberate big harvester ants, who can both bite and sting so fiercely, were bearing away seeds of all sorts of plants, as fast as they fell, in industrious braided lines. I saw chaff outside the untidy nests of pack rats, and I presume that all of the desert's tremendous rodent population of gophers and kangaroo rats, ground squirrels and field mice are in part dependent on seeds; birds too devour them. As they are the secret and triumphant desert flora, so they are the hidden larder, the basic food supply.

The heat, and still more the light, were often insupportable as the days crawled lizardlike across the desert. . . . The rim of snow on the San Gabriel Range looked mockingly cool, and distant as the moon. Finally I cowered under the redwood beams . . . and only went out at dusk.

It was then that I discovered that the desert dandelions and Mojave asters and many other flowers close up at night. And another flora, nocturnal, steals into bloom. All day long one lax and weedy plant had looked dead, its flowers withered. But by twilight this wild four-o'clock secretly opened its rose-pink calyces and emitted a faint odor. Where I had tramped the burning blossoming swells and hollows at four and seen nothing of it, a flower called evening-snow suddenly appeared at dusk. Leaf and stem are mere sand-colored threads; flowers are twirled up by day into a pointed bud absolutely invisible in the glare. But fifteen minutes after twilight's fall, millions of them open, with a soundless silken uncurling of their petals, and lo, they are white gilias, the color of starshine. As they expand, a delicate fragrance takes the air.

The West is a kingdom of evening primroses; though I knew many species, still I was unprepared for the dune primrose I found in the desert dusks. . . . They are white, but as soon as you pick them they turn pink, and in ten minutes they are faded and cannot be revived. They seem to have just the turgor in their gleaming cells requisite to sustain life only if they are not sun-smitten or touched by human hands. They are so secret that they cannot survive the appreciation of a fingertip, and they hold their sweet breath until the approach of darkness.

In mid-April I had left the ranch, wanting not to see this rainbow fade. Early in May a friend wrote: "Come back; there is another flora on the way." It was easy to quit my desk at that, and make the four-hour motor journey to the desert. Gone was the first candor of the early flowers, and in their place had come a gaudier, coarser, stronger flora, corresponding, I suppose, to that of eastern summers.

Yellow buckwheat was everywhere, and another flower, called alkali goldfields, had replaced the coreopsis. A ranker, branching dandelion took over from the desert dandelions; the weedy rock pink was in bloom, and the desert trumpet too; deep rose cups glowed on the beaver-tail cactus. . . . And where the sunlight blazed the fiercest, where the hard sands reflected its intolerable glare, there burnt up from the ground an almost stemless chalice of fiery orange. It is something to look a desert mariposa in the eye. You find mariposas all over the West . . . but nothing you ever saw of them prepares you for the desert's one species, for that intense cup of flame holding in reserved candor the geometrically elegant display of its organs. . . .

In the innocent phase of spring there had bloomed an astragalus, very like a lupine, but straggling, crazy, clouded, its pea flowers sickly pink. This is the locoweed of the cowboys. Now its bloated pods, that popped between my fingers, were blotched and scrawled in madder with a meaningless alphabet; in this could be read only madness and death for the horses that crop it and fall victim to its deadly chemical, selenium.

The paper-bag bush, too, had gone to pod, just a few of its purple mint flowers left, where it had seen the hummingbirds at pollination. The hop-sage was turning red, as if with autumn tints; the color of the fruits upon the Mormon tea was trembling between purple and pink; bronze was overcasting the salt bush foliage. . . . The desert at last had bloomed itself out; it had exhausted the gamut of beauty and, like a decadent, found beauty in the repulsive.

Now I had come again, when by the calendar it was June. In Illinois the prairies of my childhood would be flowing under a fresh wind, timothy and daisies and foxtail grass blowing all one way in long rooted ripples. In Maryland the Queen Anne's lace was dancing under apple trees that make wide pools of shadow. In Cambridge the old lawns would be green. Mid-June, the day after school closes—youth's moment. But the desert and I were past that. . . . Life was going off the land; even the meagre foliage of the shrubs was dropping, leaving naked thorns. . . .

There was nothing anywhere, from the foot of the San Bernardinos to and beyond the Colorado River, but heat and wind, and sand upon the wind, and blinding light. The color had seeped out of the world, the laughing tints, the fiery hues that followed; now there were the enduring ochres and grays, the washed-out rusts, the silvered stalks, the horizons dancing with heat waves.

The desert had forgotten its one relenting tenderness; it had gone back to the vast inertia of being desert, as dryly and sternly itself as an old squaw. Even at ten thousand feet the snows of the San Gabriels were going; they too were for winter's intercession. They were not eternal. The dew was going from the mornings, each day a little less, until at last there was no sip for the linnet; the song of the orioles was silenced in the Joshua trees, the birds were hatched; the brown pouch hung empty.

From *The Road of a Naturalist*, Donald Culross Peattie (Boston: Houghton Mifflin Company, 1941).

LXXVI

George R. Stewart

Not infrequently the glory and the great bounty of California were balanced almost proportionately by great catastrophe: appalling floods, widespread searing drought, calamitous earthquakes, sweeping conflagrations. Forest fires were the recurrent disaster. Regularly every year thousands of acres of mountain timberland were devastated. The fires seemed to blaze up inevitably during long periods of summer heat and dry wind.

It had always been so. Early discoverers and traders reported seeing from their ships enormous clouds of smoke billowing over valleys and mountain ranges, and emigrants told of crossing blackened miles of fire-ravaged country. Lightning started fires; Indians started them; and white men started more. For generations, once a mighty forest fire swept out of control, it was allowed to burn on until a change in weather or some natural barrier halted it. Woods were expendable: if the source of lumber disappeared on one mountain slope, there was an ample supply on another.

Then early in the century conservationists began to speak up and be listened to: forests were no longer expendable; the state could not afford- the loss of such wealth. In the next three of four decades seasonal lookouts, linked by telephone, were posted all through the mountains, and armies of fire fighters were recruited, trained, and placed on call to battle a blaze as soon as it was reported.

In 1948 George R. Stewart (1895–   ), revered professor of English at the University of California, dramatized these Sierra and Coast Range fires as no one before had ever succeeded in dramatizing any forest conflagration. To assemble and authenticate his material, he worked for two summers with the United States Forest Service, served as a lookout, flew with parachutists, labored on the fire lines, and then produced his classic *Fire*. It was a novel, but the fire he created was as credible as any real fire that ever ran rampant in the Sierra.

Toward the end of a long period of drought, the fire started as a mere smudge from a stroke of lightning in a remote canyon between Reverse Ridge and Howell Mountain and smoldered for days before it actually took hold. By the morning of the sixth day it had spread along the canyon slope for several hundred yards to send up a thin column of smoke that was spotted by an alert lookout some ten miles distant. Within minutes crews were on their way to battle the "Spitcat Fire." With the same attention to meticulous detail and with the same sustained suspense found in his other books, like *Storm* and *Ordeal by Hunger*, Professor Stewart narrated the story of the Spitcat through nine exciting days, starting with the spark that gave it birth.

The Spitcat

As late as 5:53 a single active man with a shovel could have scraped away the duff from the front of the fire, and gradually extending his line could have contained the flames and let them burn themselves out. . . . At that minute, however, one chance out of the millions possible continued to change the situation considerably.

In its diagonal upslope advance before the down-canyon wind, the fire had at last reached the pine-cone which rested against a dead twig. Both cone and branch were soon blazing, and after a few minutes the twig, nearly burned through, broke at the point where the cone rested against it.

The cone toppled downhill, rolled two feet, wobbled—hesitated. (If it had been a long sugar-pine cone, it would have rolled uncertainly and have come to rest; if it had been the tiny cone of a Douglas fir, it would have lodged in some little roughness of the ground; but it was the almost spherical cone of a Jeffrey pine, eight inches through its shortest diameter.) It toppled again with the thrust of gravity and momentum, rolled a foot, then picking up speed, went rolling and bouncing and leaping erratically downward. The wind of its own movement made it blaze more fiercely. A flying ball of fire, it catapulted down the canyon-side, leaving a trail of sparks and burning scales behind. It struck a tree-trunk, ricocheted, rolled on again, caromed off a rock, and finally came to rest against a log, a good hundred yards from where it had started.

Many of the sparks and even some of the burning scales smouldered for a moment and then went out. But many others ignited the tinder-like needles. A hundred-yard-long trail of smoke puffs began to rise. In thickly littered places the dry twigs soon blazed up. The tiny isolated fires reached out and joined. The log where the cone had come to rest began to smoke vigorously. Here and there a seedling flared up; underbrush began to crackle. All the heat combined to form an up-draft, and the air flowing in from below blew up the flames.

In an inconsiderable time the fire had thus become several times more dangerous. . . .

Sixth Day

With the wind as it was, all the little fires blew toward the line, but moving only a few feet they had no chance to get big, and when they came to the cleared line they died. But on the other side, eating backward into the wind, the back-fires moved slowly. Still they moved, and . . . spread sideways and gradually joined into a solid front. Then as the main fire grew closer, the back-fires caught the suck of the draft which the main fire pulled in toward itself against the light wind.

Suddenly the back-fires sprang to life, and went roaring through the underbrush toward the main fire. The two met. . . . As in the head-on dash of two waves, the fires piled up. A clump of underbrush suddenly disappeared in white-yellow flames. Close by, a seventy-foot fir tree, its resins vaporized by the heat, exploded into a flame that towered a hundred feet upward. There was a long-drawn hiss that was almost a roar. For twenty seconds the dying tree stood out in the twilight, a white-hot torch of flaming gas. As it burned out, the tips of the level branches glowed red for a moment, and then the tall tree was nothing but a dark silhouette of branches against the fire-lit sky. . . .

Eighth Day

By mid-morning the fire was rolling, pressed forward by a gusty northeast wind, on an unbroken front of more than a mile.

On the right flank it had entered that part of the brushfield where many tall snags (killed by some old fire) still towered gauntly above the manzanita. As the fire came to each of the dead trunks, it ran quickly up the dry moss-grown surface until the snag flared clear to the top. Then, as the wind dislodged bits of burning bark and wood, the blazing fragments sailed forward on the wind, and in their slanting fall reached far ahead. The fire thus raced along rapidly.

The snag-patch itself was an inferno. From the ground-level the flames rose white-hot from the thick manzanita. Flames licked up along the towering dead tree-trunks; a hundred feet and more in the air the tips of the dry snags blazed in the wind, smoke and flames streaming off like flags. Through the thickly drifting smoke you looked up to see the dull red disk of the sun, and through smoke-eddies the tips of the snags like torches blazing wildly in the sky.

On its left flank the fire was also entering a new phase. So far it had burned mostly along the level and downhill, but now it was beginning to breast the slope leading up to Reverse Ridge. Cut steeply into the ridge, facing almost north, the canyon of little Waupomsy Creek, funnel-like, scooped up the wind. The rising heat also swept up along the canyon. With this new aid of terrain, the fire burned more intensely among the undergrowth and small trees, although it seldom crowned in the taller trees. Gigantic, the column of gray smoke sloped off toward the southwest, spreading out as it rose, until above twenty thousand feet it felt the westerly drift of the upper air and spiraled off eastward.

In spite of all the labor and energy expended against it, the fire had grown steadily larger. . . .

Ninth Day

The fire, entering the thicker forest about mid-morning . . . roared fiercely in the thick mat of dry fern. The criss-crossed fallen tree-trunks smoked, ignited, then burned hotly. The fire ran up the dried bark of the snags. By then, no one could have complained of any lack of light in the forest.

At the same time the thick-spread canopy of foliage prevented the easy escape of heat. As in a furnace with its outlets clogged, the temperature soared. The needles withered and shriveled as their water was driven off; they began to smoke. Then suddenly, not in a single tree but over an acre at once, the tree-tops burst into fire. With a deep roar, flames and dark smoke rose some hundreds of feet, whirling upward the blazing twigs and needles and strips of bark. Tree-tops rocked and swayed in the blast of hot air. A rot-weakened snag tottered, cracked resoundingly, and went down with an echoing crash.

When the piling-up of heat was thus relieved, the fire died down somewhat. Once it was established as a crown-fire, however, it remained so. The dry wind still blew into the funnel-like mouths of the three canyons which seamed the north slope of Reverse Ridge. Terrain, dryness, wind, and the thick forest thus combined to make the fire more intense.

The ground-fire and the crown-fire advanced together. The one burned close to the ground; the other, high in the air. . . . Between the two no living tree or bush or fern or herb was left. . . . The towering line of flame appeared massive and heavy, rolling onward by the power of its own momentum. Ahead lay the upward slope and the thick forest; from behind the dry wind pressed steadily. . . .

Eleventh Day

There were no stars that night, but the men on the lines knew that cloud, not smoke, stretched across the sky. From the southeast, veering toward the south, a moist wind blew steadily. In the dark of early morning the rain began—a drifting mist at first, and then a steady drizzle, and sometimes a gentle shower. . . .

The rain fell upon the red embers and the little flames. Where each drop struck, a sudden spot of blackness showed in the red glow, or the flame fluttered. As thousands of drops fell, the blackness grew and encroached upon the red, and the flames wavered and winked out. Only here and there, deeply hidden where the drops could not reach, a few glowing points still shone through the darkness and a few flames licked up. . . .

Ten Thousand Acres Destroyed

It was as if some running conflagration had swept from Spuyten Duyvil to the Battery, leaving two-thirds of Manhattan Island in a blackened swath behind it. Yet the Spitcat Fire would not be very memorable. . . . Any old-timer could recall a score of greater ones. In comparison with the Tillamook, which in eleven flaming days had wiped out 311,000 acres of the best forest in Oregon, the Spitcat was a mere waste-basket blaze.

Even so, the costs of suppression alone would run well over a hundred thousand dollars. Two men had been killed, and a score of others had suffered injury. The value of the burned trees would pass a million dollars, figured at current prices and with no allowance for timber famines of the future.

Yet the damage could not with justice be calculated merely in terms of the present. Already the turbid streams showed that even the light rain was washing away the earth. Where previously pines had just been able to find root on the thin-soiled ridges, now half-bare rocks might be left, where only gnarled junipers would cling.

Though the Spitcat had burned for only a few days, yet its effects could be reckoned ahead in centuries. . . . Everywhere the small trees had been wiped out. . . . Where the crown-fires had raged, no trees were left to spread seed, and brush would spring up faster than forest. . . . Indeed, some said pessimistically that the forests of California had established themselves in some wetter cycle of centuries and that the brush, once rooted, would remain until some wetter cycle returned.

The flaming disaster of those few days would not be undone in a hundred years. Even after five hundred, a skilled forester might still be able to trace the scar of that old burn.

More also had vanished than any man could assay in dollars. There had been a green and gracious forest, full of the rustle and movement of life, beneficent to men. Now there was only blackness and ugliness and desolation, and over it all a heavy and terrible silence.

From *Fire*, George R. Stewart (New York: Random House, 1948).

LXXVII

Max Miller

Forest pyrotechnics or any other natural extravaganza did not provide sufficient entertainment to satisfy the strangest tribe of latter-day emigrants yet to invade California. Intent on creating a new form of extravaganza, they had been filtering into the south in ever increasing numbers since the first decade of the century, and had succeeded in those few years in establishing an entirely different trade mark for the state, superseding gold, oil, oranges, redwoods, Spanish missions, the Carmel coastline, and the Golden Gate as popular symbols. People anywhere in the world who knew nothing else about California now knew that Hollywood was the motion picture capital of the world and the films produced there the greatest achievement in theatrics since Shakespeare. To millions Hollywood was California.

Hollywood became the film capital by accident. At the turn of the century the principal fame attached to the place came from its melon patches: it grew wondrously big, sweet, succulent watermelons. The population was four hundred. It was a rural, conservative, church-oriented little town, originally established in 1887 by the pious Horace Wilcox family as a "temperance colony," appropriately named in honor of Father Junípero Serra, who, according to tradition, had once celebrated a mass there to the Holly Wood of the Cross. The Wilcoxes insisted on keeping the settlement strictly residential; intrusion of industry of any sort was summarily discouraged.

On location

But Hollywood kept growing despite the enforced climate of sobriety. By 1910 the population had jumped to four thousand, and like
other communities in the area, was running out of water. After heated
debate, the town fathers concluded that its very survival depended on
trading civic independence for a share of the Los Angeles water
supply. Inevitably it began to lose character and identity after that,
but it was still quiet enough to serve as an ideal refuge for little groups
of outlaws from Chicago, New York, and Philadelphia who were trying
to make movies in defiance of court orders and the attorneys of
Thomas A. Edison, sole owner of the patent rights to movie cameras
and projectors.

Eventually the refugees made their peace with Edison and film-
maker George Eastman, the movie clan took over what had been a
watermelon patch only a few years before, and Hollywood had the
industry it did not want. From that inauspicious beginning, it grew
into the world mecca of make-believe. Max Miller (1899–1967), often
employed there as a writer, author of *I Cover the Waterfront, Second
House from the Corner,* and a variety of books on regions from Mexico
to the Mediterranean and the Bering Sea, gave his view of Hollywood
as he saw it at its heyday in the early 1940s.

I Like Hollywood

This is Hollywood. Or at least this is that side of Hollywood
which makes young men old, and which makes old men have
ulcers.

It is not the work which is hard. It is the waiting. It is the
waiting for somebody's approval of what one has done. It is the
waiting for phone calls. It is the waiting for jobs. It is the waiting
for somebody's "definite maybe."

I am not one to sympathize with Hollywood writers. They ask
for what they get. They cry for cake. Their writing is done, not
so much on a typewriter, as on the keys of a cash register. Yet
they always are ready to yell about finding no satisfaction. They
always are eager to kick Hollywood in the teeth, then to turn
right around and fawn on Hollywood for another assignment. . . .

Writers hug the studios merely because five hundred dollars a week looks bigger than fifty. Writers hug the studios merely because, after a year of it, five hundred dollars a week becomes "necessary for bare living expenses." Writers hug the studios because in time they may get a thousand "and then maybe can save something." Writers hug the studios because, after a time, they have lost both the nerve and the ability to live on the arrangements of their own thoughts. . . .

I have seen some terrible dramas in Hollywood. But strangely, for the writers my sympathy remains as cold as it would be for a flagpole sitter. Too many of them have gotten in, not because they ever wrote, but because they "knew somebody." They are willing to parade as writers, to attend so-called "writers' meetings," and to claim on their citizenship papers: "Writer." . . . They are the ones who do most of the crying about receiving no publicized recognition "outside of Hollywood"; that the recognition all goes to the actors or producers or directors. . . .

It all adds up into making Hollywood what it is: the earth's most puzzling big-time factory. I like Hollywood. . . .

What I have said about writers "going Hollywood," then staying in Hollywood, then yapping about the mistreatment of staying in Hollywood—little of this applies to actors or producers or directors. Their story is a different story, and Hollywood more or less always has been their business, and has had to be their business. Any alternative for an actor today is a slight one. So, too, is any alternative for a man who has spent twenty years making pictures, or who has devoted his life to pictures. . . .

Obviously there are three ways of looking at Hollywood: one as an outsider familiar only with the fringe; one as a worker in the heart of the whole thing; and the third is in detached retrospect. . . . I have looked in all three ways. The result is I do not laugh at Hollywood.

I like a lot of people there. . . . They can be as much fun as a boatload of irresponsible kids. But also, in a sharpshooting way, they are so much smarter than most of us that it is better not to take seriously their flattery or their promises or to allow one's own reception to be taken too much to heart. Today with them is a different day, and yesterday was another, and tomorrow is 'way off in the distance somewhere. Their type of business is such that each person, of necessity, must think of himself first. This is essential for each individual's survival, nor should he or she be blamed for it. They are not farmers.

Nor, fundamentally, do the Hollywood workers (the directors, the actors, the writers, the producers) ever really have a good time. So much is at stake that they constantly are worried, even at play. And they work constantly, even when at play. They constantly are trying to put jigsaw pieces together, to make them match, for their own betterment, for their own next job.

Few of them, despite what they say, can ever really get used to the phraseology of such big money. Their previous backgrounds have not allowed them to swing into the surprise riches gracefully. Nor are the actual riches as rich as the figures promise. Too much has to be taken out of each check before they can see any of the money; government taxes, state taxes, agents' fees, managers' fees, labor pensions and security fees—with all of these automatically subtracted from each check, the left-over often is far less than half the original. Sometimes only a quarter.

And this is the left-over which must buy the clothes, must pay the hair dressers, must meet the rents, must settle the entertainment bills, must be spectacularly generous to all charities, and finally must keep all the dependents. . . .

I have gone through the experiment, in company with Hollywood people, of trying to have a good time in Hollywood. They are, naturally, as desperate for happiness as anybody else. They are more desperate, actually, and for this reason try harder. . . . Unaccustomed to moderation in anything, they reach for the extremes, as if by mere mass pressure they can force happiness to come their way. When they gamble they gamble bigger and harder and longer. When they play the races they really play them. When they have a big party it is a big party. Yet here is the catch: I have seen some of them, when down at my home on the ocean, literally beam with ecstasy over what to me is the commonplace, the moon over a quiet sea and a simple bonfire to cook my meal. . . .

But if we look further we will find that the initial spark behind almost any of these things, or the zest, or the initiative, was the product of outside minds on first coming here, or before coming here, or even of minds which have not come here at all. Those minds were of the lands where winters are winters, where competition is competition, where a man has to do something, and do it fast, if he is to create a name, or even if he is to survive.

. . . The huge motion picture industry . . . does continue to remain the most talked-about example of "what is being done here." But in talking about it we do prefer to forget that it was nurtured in New York by competitive little fellows who would stop at nothing in the race of outdoing others in that big town's battle for survival of the fittest—and the fastest.

There in New York the smart ones seized on Edison's flicker peepshow, as we know. They pirated his work, stole his patents outright, until finally the whole fight became such a free-for-all tangle of suits, injunctions, and raids that the companies fled New York lawyers and New York courts. The smartest, to avoid more trouble, fled as far as they could flee. They fled to California. Because of this, we of California pride ourselves on being the pioneers of the motion picture. . . .

We like to say, too, that because of the big names the industry brings here that Los Angeles today, with its Beverly Hills, its Culver City, its Hollywood, is now the cultural center of the United States.

Certainly the big names are here today, and we can brag about them. But so far as reproducing any awesome intelligence the owners of these names have promptly become eunuchs. . . . Once they establish themselves figuratively alongside their swimming pools, they seem utterly content to have the works of others washed ashore to drain for plot, for title, or to steal outright. For their own works, once they have tampered a year with Hollywood technique, have become—well, we all know what they have become. . . .

What's the answer to my state? There must be an answer to everything but for California I can reach no conclusion. Statisticians have tried. Even the Heaven on Earth Club has tried. But California continues to erupt.

If one section becomes dormant or stabilized, another section will mix up the whole pattern by bringing in something unexpected. It has been so through the years. Hides and tallow. Then gold. Then farming. Then fruit. Oil. Motion pictures. . . . Building airplanes.

California is not Wisconsin. It is not Vermont. It is . . . an heterogeneity. The state will continue to be an heterogeneity; it will continue to be a grab-box, a blind man's buff.

From *It Must Be the Climate,* Max Miller (New York: Robert M. McBride and Company, 1941).

LXXVIII

Stanton A. Coblentz

Although mercenary interests like those of the moviemakers, airplane manufacturers, real estate developers, fruit and vegetable packers, petroleum prospectors, and heavy industrialists were steadily increasing their authority in California affairs, there was still chance for the authoritative voice of a poet to be heard. The native San Franciscan, Stanton A. Coblentz (1896–   ) is such a voice. For over thirty years he published slender but richly impressive books of poetry: *Songs of the Redwoods, Songs of the Wayside, The Pageant of Man, Green Vistas, From a Western Hilltop,* and *Out of Many Songs.*

He is a poet of stature, but also proficient as a naturalist, sociologist, editor, critic, and biographer. Few California lyrists demonstrated a broader range of creativity. His stanzas are as graphic as the design of an etching, and his feeling for local settings is conveyed with similar precision. The quality of his verse is finely illustrated in lines about such special California features as redwood canyons, the cypresses of Monterey, giant sequoias, and the surf and cliffs of the seacoast.

Land's End
(Point Lobos, California)

Here range the furies that have shaped the world,
Here where a beaked old headland splits the sea
And white Niagaras of the surf are hurled

In crashing enmity
Against the rocks' worn giant filigree.
Above the thunder where the wave and shore
Merge and re-merge in fountain-bursts of spray,
The weird continual half-yelping roar
Of congregated seals rings out all day
From islets wet and gray.
And pelicans in heavy lines flap by,
And gulls skim low beneath the precipice,
And hunchback cypresses, limb-twisted, lie
On the blunt slopes and in the hoarse abyss,
And here and there a skeleton tree that stares,
Like agony petrified, with ashen bole
And boughs where life with all her struggles and cares
Incarnates her writhing soul.

Step to the gnarled cliff-edge; some Siren power
Will urge you, pull you doomward . . . down and down
There where in turquoise pools the kelp lies brown,
And where tall rollers charge in shower on shower
Of fierce erupting white, and the salt cascade
Drenching the misty shoals, and waterfalls
Replenished with every breaker, look on walls
Of inlets paved with jade.

Wild as the earth's beginning! Lone and grand
This universe of reef and cave and foam
As when scale-armored dragons clawed the sand
And the fish-lizard made the brine its home!
Hear! In each billow clamoring at the rock
Voices of masters throned aloof from man,
Lords of the deep for whom the great world-clock
Ticks not in years, but by a Cyclops' span
Of epochs and of eons. Hear the moan
Of time that stretches out to timelessness,
And power that trumpets of the shock and stress
Of planets forged in wars of storm and stone!

Ranging the headland's verge,
For but an hour I come, a transient thing,
Yet from this tumult and this beat and surge
Of elemental frenzies I shall bring
Back to the soberer world a brooding sense
Of some fresh wonder and magnificence,
The overtones of some age-hallowed glory,
When on this furrowed cypress promontory
Gods speak from the torn waves' droning eloquence.

A Mountain Is My Altar

A mountain is my altar; my temple is the sky,
And none has ever worshipped more ardently than I;
Worshipped the peace of hilltops, and blue-green shining miles,
With the ridges many-billowed, and the redwood canyon aisles.

Held in that vast cathedral whose organ is the breeze,
I have no need of praying with psalms and litanies,
For all the cliffs and valleys, the woods and gnarled old domes
Join in a prayer of gladness wherever the watcher roams.

Strangely, like shadows drifting, the peaks and cloud-land fuse.
I am timeless part of the ranges; of the crags and streams; and
     lose
The oneness of self and of passion to merge with a greater one
That embraces the gorges and summits, the groves and the rivers
     and sun.

Monterey Cypresses

Like weird fantastic wrestlers, petrified
In witches' writhings, with contorted limbs

Twisted as though in tune to wild men's hymns,
They sprawl along the surf-edged mountainside.
And timeless agony and tortured pride
Shriek from the green of each wind-ravelled tress,
Where, persecuted by the gale, they press
With seamed, dark boles the centuries gnarled and tried.

If I could watch a hundred years drive past,
Shrunk to a moment, every bough and root,
In mad encounter, would grapple, toss and fly
Like sea-waves weltering in the squally vast;
Each torn old pillar, like a scarred recruit,
Daring the arrowy Huns of earth and sky.

Sequoias

They seek no victory but the sun's embrace,
Dim tranquil years, and fog-blown hills to climb.
Yet with their cloistered green they conquer space,
And by their dateless age they vanquish time.

From *Redwood Poems,* Stanton A. Coblentz (Healdsburg, California: Nature-graph Company, 1961).

LXXIX

Eugene Burdick

From the Olympian vantage point of the University of California, where he was a professor of political theory, Eugene Burdick (1918–1965), author or co-author of half a dozen widely read and warmly disputed books, including *The Ugly American* and *Fail-Safe*, scanned the horizons of the state shortly before his death and saw not one but three Californias, which he dissected in a racy article for the magazine *Holiday*. No two Californians—no two critics or commentators on California—would accept without qualification Professor Burdick's pat geographic divisions, his categorical social assessments, even his generalizations on regional endowments. Yet the state had gathered unto itself so much antithesis that any other summary of its intrinsic character would be equally controversial.

Three Californias

The feeling of rootlessness, of obscure origin, of not knowing where one came from or where one is going, is typical of California. . . . Like people are attracted to like places, and after centuries there develops a kind of homogeneity about fellow citizens. . . . History, intermarriage, selective migration, the old

[523]

Darwinian processes usually create a people who look enough alike to be a nation of sisters and brothers. California has not had the time. Everything happened so fast. California has had to make a merit of the novel, the unique, the *sui generis*, the new, the rejected, the unarticulated, the emerging, the unformed, the rebellious. . . .

On most outsiders, the state makes a surrealistic and conflicting impression that hazes wildly different things together: Disneyland, sport shirts, sun, oranges, religious cults, Hollywood, white beaches, women in bathing suits wearing high heels and mink stoles; college kids with beards, college kids with surf boards, old people—many old people—sin, everyone tanned, everyone in cars roaring down insane freeways. . . . When pressed, the outsider will confess that he thinks the place is not quite real, but if it is real it is childish, and below the childishness there is a smell of evil. . . . It lacks authority, civility, tradition. It is a sensual paradise where practical things cannot be done. Serious people cannot abide it. The place is lush and wanton. It is—well it is like Disneyland. Not real. . . .

The vision of the outsider is true—in part. The vision is based on the South of California, which is the most publicized, visible and colorful part of the state. But it is not the character of the whole state. . . .

The North is north of San Francisco. . . . There is a staidness to the North. People walk slower, the accents are a mixture of Nebraska, Iowa and an undertone of New England. . . . The houses have a sturdy look to them. The people in the North use the word "uppity" more often. . . . The term is used to describe a man who drinks Martinis, or gets his suits in San Francisco, or gets a new car every year, or buys his wife a full-length mink. . . .

The North is not seductive. The people who went to the North were not looking for a bonanza, the soft life or excitement. They came with a thirst for land, a low, steady metabolic rate and a very high sense of what is practical. . . . The North is inhabited by country people frightened by the intimacy of city life, high on self-confidence, low on "showing off," with a reverence for courage and respect for the slow-speaking person who bulls ahead and wins out. *Work* is the word that describes good character in the North. . . .

In the South—south of the Tehachapi Mountains, that is—the immigrants are different. First of all, more of them are fresh first-generation immigrants. They come from Texas and New Orleans and Alabama and New York City. More of them are Negroes. The sounds of jazz are louder in the night, and wailing out of the cheap apartments of North Hollywood and San Diego, day and night. . . . Cool, hip and classical music are big in the South. . . . Rumor is a principal means of communication. Rumor about movie stars, the path of the newest freeway, the "inside" of the latest property development or divorce case; about stocks, . . . the horsepower of the new Mustang, . . . why Bing Crosby moved away, IBM's future. . . . On and on it goes.

They are a febrile, anxious, high-metabolic-rate, anxiety-ridden sort. . . . More of them are Jews, and they either come with the wealth to afford a superior education for their children or they work and sacrifice to get it. Anti-Semitism is there, and not just casually. . . . Mexican influence is there—real and not just an invention of Alvarado Street, which is a gimcrack and cleansed version of Tijuana. . . . Southern California is the most ghettoized part of the state. There are districts in Los Angeles where most of the neon signs are in Japanese or Spanish or Yiddish or Russian. They end precisely at one street. . . . The ghetto aspect is not merely ethnic; it is also economic and social. . . .

Beverly Hills is the home of the rich, restless and aggressive. It maintains a nervous stability, a sophisticated provincialism. It puts a great premium on ritualism; the Oscar awards are a serious matter, and so is the seating of people at formal dinners. The Hollywood people . . . are as proper and traditional as Samoans. . . . Beverly Hills' high school is so fiercely competitive that numbers of teachers and students are driven to the psychoanalyst's couch. . . . Many of the families of Beverly Hills live with their heads on the guillotines of Nielsen ratings or the vagaries of studio politics, but the worst happens when the breadwinner gets a job in New York doing the same thing he did in Hollywood. . . .

The rest of the South, the area from San Diego to the Tehach-apis, is occupied by a rootless, happy, very transient and roiling mob of people. They are exuberant rustic Jacobins, suddenly turned loose in Utopia. There is a strain of anarchy in the South that assures one thing: whatever kind of revolution occurs in America, political, social or artistic, will first occur in the South of California. The place is yeasty with promise, disaster, zest, cults, brave new thinking, LSD eaters, superior painting, unworkable freeways, yoga schools and surfers. Yet there is much more to it than that. The South is held together by bulwarks of funda-mentalism in both religion and secular affairs. Beneath the froth it is concrete-hard. But the fundamentalists seldom know one another. . . .

One of the least publicized statistics of California is that for every two migrants who come in to stay, someone *leaves*. Who stays? And why? When asked, most of them say "health" or "sun-shine" or "a healthy place for the kids to grow up," and right behind this, "better chance to get ahead—better luck out here." *Luck*. There is no word you hear more often in the South. In the South people came with a hard drive and a sense that their luck would turn. They are the optimists of the United States, the ad-vocates of causes, the believers in faiths, the youngest sons who rebelled, the visionaries, the discontented. All of them with the hope of "lucking out" under the sun and beside the sea. . . .

If the mystique word that drew them to the South is "luck," the object that enthralls the Southerner is that seductive possession, "the car." The South depends on the car, and not just in some dim Freudian sense. The South is the only place in the world so geared to the automobile that if it were eliminated the whole region would collapse. Outsiders stare with a barely disguised horror at the white, wormlike freeways of the South. . . . The freeways are expensive, hideous, congested and self-defeating. They are obsolete the day they are finished. But the Southerner cares little. He plans his life so that he can roar to work on the freeway in off-hours. . . . It is not uncommon for the Southerner to drive sixty miles to work; 120 miles on a date; and fifty miles to shop for loss leaders at the colossal supermarkets. . . .

The City is the central part of California. It takes in everything from the Tehachapis in the South, to a line somewhere in Marin County, just across the Golden Gate Bridge. Above that is the North. The City, San Francisco, is a living fiction. It is an invention, a manufactured thing, contrived and not wholly true. Everyone within the pull of the City "lives" there. People from Palo Alto, San Jose, Santa Cruz, Berkeley, Orinda, Piedmont, Atherton and Oakland always say to an outsider that they are "from the City—I mean San Francisco."

. . . The City is unlike anything else in America. . . . There are two causes for the City's feeling of uniqueness: the Bay and the Great Fire. . . . People of the City never grow tired of the Bay. Apartments that have a view of the Bay command approximately twice the rent of viewless apartments. Even those that have no view but are in earshot of a foghorn fetch relatively higher prices. People who have lived in the City all their lives still fall silent when the fog comes rolling in through the great arches of the Golden Gate Bridge.

The Great Earthquake and Fire gave the City a shared catastrophe, something that not only bound immigrants to citizens but also marked a point of time when chaos was destroyed and a culture emerged. Each detail of the Fire is perfectly remembered, sharply etched but softened in some golden way. . . . The City emerged from the Fire like a place cleansed. It now had a history; a grinding, searing history, but a history. . . . The City had another great advantage: it is a snug little community. There is no way for the City to expand except upward. . . . The suburbs that grew down the Peninsula and into Marin County adopted the City's manners.

Just as the City influences the thinking of millions of Californians who live outside its physical boundaries, it also works a strong magnetism on the rest of the country. Untold millions have tried to push into the gleaming, fog-washed, tight little city by the Bay. Most return whence they came, but some wriggle in— and often they are miserable. . . .

But the City has begun to lose its grip on its chunk of California. It has, most significantly, become narcissistic—which is the first step toward decay. . . . The South grows strong and powerful. It is designed for the mass man and there is no hiding the fact. But along with the mass man it also has gathered most of the writers, sculptors, painters, designers, dancers, actors and artists in California. If culture follows the dollar, the South is going to get the culture. The North finds the South lascivious and wanton. The City has few attractions for the Northerner. He is self-contained, remote, certain and insular, and wants to remain that way. . . .

. . . There are three Californias—the North, the South and the City. Each is made up of immigrants from other states. But the immigrants do not just come to California; they come to one of the three Californias.

Condensed from "Three Californias," Eugene Burdick, *Holiday Magazine*, October 1965.

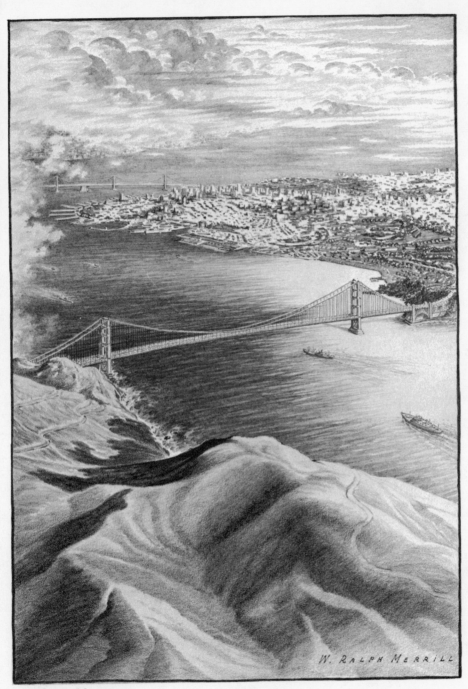

The Golden Gate

LXXX

Remi A. Nadeau

For all its contradictions, weaknesses, and immaturity, California came to be looked upon as a utopia by millions of malcontents, opportunists, unemployed persons, and ordinary seekers of ease and sunshine from less temperate, more austere states. They poured into California every year by the hundreds of thousands to sightsee, to sample the life, to stay. And for every hundred thousand that found their way there, there were two hundred thousand more who would join them, had they the courage to break with a past that bound them to another locale.

Remi A. Nadeau (1920–), fifth-generation descendant of a Los Angeles pioneer, professional writer for the North American Aviation Company, a scholarly observer who had demonstrated his understanding of California history and his ability to narrate it with wit and insight in brilliant studies like *The Water-Seekers* and *California: The New Society*, analyzes the effect that the invasion has had upon the state and confronts himself with the challenging question: "Who is a Californian?" His startling conclusions are acceptable, even self-evident, to all except those who still prefer to *utopianize* the Golden State.

American in the Making

California, perhaps more than any other state, is really a fulfillment of the American dream. Except for some areas of blight,
here is the good life—considerable comfort, escape from drudgery and hardship, reasonable leisure time, and the environment to
make the most of it. Is this not the American promise—freedom
to enjoy life as the fruit of honest labor? Following the American
tradition to its ultimate, California is really a sort of secular
Kingdom Come.

. . . If the Californians did not invent togetherness, they are at
least the first to make it a religion. Moreover, tolerance for others
is a natural corollary to the Californian's preoccupation with self.
One has difficulty doing as one pleases in a society of busybodies
or bigots.

California's individuality has therefore worked against conformity. Long before Los Angeles became noted for its crackpots,
San Franciscans were humoring the boulevard eccentric, treasur-
ing him for his contribution to local color, taking pride in him as
evidence of their cosmopolitan bigness of heart. . . . It is this
very tolerance, in fact, that explains California's tradition of
health faddists, faith healers, occultists, political quacks, and
economic medicine men. Open minds are not always intellectual.
They will give a hearing to gimcrackery as well as to logic.

This form of credulity finds vindication in the Califonia environment. It is a state of extremes, superlatives, and near miracles. The classic postcard showing palm and orange trees against
a background of snowy mountains is no curiosity, but a California
commonplace. The climate varies from the arid Mojave Desert to
the rain forest of the Redwood coast. Scenery ranges from the
rugged, wave-splashed cliffs of the coastline to some of the jag-
gedest mountains of the world.

As if nature itself did not stretch one's credulity enough, the
state's dynamic growth has been equally unbelievable. Its Amer-

ican history began with the greatest rush of people, migrating as individuals, ever recorded up to that time. The coming of the railroads and the automobile kept the human tide running high until California became the most populous state in the Union. Colossal fortunes were made in gold mining, railroads, petroleum, the movies. Spurred by the energy of real estate promoters, whole towns (today, whole cities) have sprung up virtually overnight. Water to serve these new millions was brought over mountains and plains in several of the longest aqueducts on the globe. Hydroelectric power was transmitted over longer distances than anywhere in the world. No engineering challenge—railroads over the Sierra, bridges over San Francisco Bay—was avoided.

One could not be in California long without catching this fever. Nothing is impossible. Someone claims a new revelation from God? Maybe so. Beat the Depression by giving money to the old folks? Tell us more. Invent a new idea and make a million? Many have done it in California's dynamic economy. A few are still doing it.

All of this spurs the Californian's inclination to gimmick solutions. California itself, as a lure to the dissatisfied of other states, is a gimmick. Many Americans consider California the easy answer to their problems. Are they in ill health? They come to California. Are they unhappy in their jobs? Come to California. Is their marriage in trouble? A change in environment, a new start in California. . . .

All of this is a glimpse of what is known as "California Living." . . . What has been called the "fun morality" is the dominant mode in California and has been pushed to a farther extreme than in almost any society of comparable size in the world.

Is all this very important? California has always been a renegade among states, populated by renegades among people. But it is now the most populous in the Union. It has more inhabitants than Canada and more than the whole population of the United States as late as 1840. It is still growing at a headlong pace— 17,000,000 in 1963, an estimated 25,000,000 in 1975. This is more than the individual populations of some ninety foreign countries.

California has also been a pacesetter and an exporter of culture. The tract home, the backyard barbecue, the private swimming pool, the drive-in, the supermarket, the house trailer, the sports car, the suntan, the bare midriff, the get-rich-quick scheme, the get-with-God scheme—all these either originated in, or were converted into a craze by, California.

In the past, these were considered quaint customs brought back from the American frontier. California was out in the provinces; she was absorbed in winning an empire; and she had little of enduring substance to say to the rest of the world.

Today California has become big time . . . [and] may soon be not the outpost but the wellspring of American culture. So if the Californians are developing a new society—some might call it an antisociety—the effect on the nation may be more than incidental.

Generalizations about California are always risky. For at least five generations it has been in continual change, and the rate of change is, if anything, accelerating. It exhibits a variety of climate, geography, and peoples that is unequaled by any other state (and that make it a true microcosm of the nation). Few statements about California are completely true, or are even approximately true for very long.

But it must also be said that California, through this very change and diversity, is a forcing house of national character. Having left behind the social inhibitions of his old home town, the Californian is a sort of American in the making. What the American is becoming, the Californian is already.

From *California: The New Society*, Remi A. Nadeau (New York: David McKay Company, Inc., 1963).

KEY DATES IN CALIFORNIA ANNALS

1540 Discovery of Colorado River by Hernando de Alarcón, first white man known to have reached Alta California.

1542 Coastal survey made by Juan Rodríguez Cabrillo.

1579 "Nova Albion" claimed for England by Sir Francis Drake.

1602 Exploration of coast by Sebastían Vizcáino.

1697 Permanent colony established by Jesuits on Baja California.

1701 Father Kino crosses Colorado River into Alta California.

1768 Jesuit missionaries replaced by Franciscans.

1769 Mission established at San Diego. First overland expedition to San Francisco Bay, led by Gaspar de Portolá.

1770 Presidio and mission established at Monterey.

1775 Monterey declared capital of California.

1776 Mexican colonists led overland to San Francisco by Juan Bautista de Anza.

1781 Los Angeles founded.

1804 Demarcation of Alta and Baja California.

1810 Mexican revolt against Spain.

1812 Fortified Russian trading post established at Fort Ross.

1822 Mexican separation from Spain. California proclaimed province of the Empire of Mexico.

1823 San Francisco Solano, last of twenty-one missions, founded.

1825 California proclaimed territory of new Republic of Mexico.

1826 American fur trappers, led by Jedediah S. Smith, made first overland trip to California.

1833 Secularization of missions decreed by Mexican Congress.

1840 Sutter's Fort established.

1841   Russian colonization in California terminated by purchase of Fort Ross by John A. Sutter. Bidwell-Bartleson overland party reach California.

1843   Lumber mill opened at Bodega.

1845   Last Mexican governor of California deposed. Immigration of Americans into California prohibited by Mexican government.

1846   May 13. War between Mexico and United States declared. June 14. Bear Flag Revolt. July 7. California formally declared possession of United States.

1848   January 24. Discovery of gold by James W. Marshall. February 2. War with Mexico terminated by Treaty of Guadalupe Hidalgo. California ceded to United States.

1849   November 13. State constitution ratified.

1850   September 9. California admitted to Union (Population 92,-597).

1854   Capital established at Sacramento.

1856   First wagon road over Sierra opened.

1857   First overland stage reaches San Diego.

1861   Transcontinental telegraph line completed.

1868   University of California chartered.

1869   Central Pacific–Union Pacific Railroad completed.

1885   Real estate boom in south promoted by "Railroad-Rate War."

1891   Oil discovered at Los Angeles.

1900   Reclamation of Imperial Valley started.

1905   Salton Sea created by Colorado River flood.

1906   April 18. San Francisco destroyed by earthquake and Great Fire.

1911   First motion picture studio opened in Hollywood.

1915   Panama Pacific International Exposition at San Francisco.

1920   Great real estate boom in south inaugurated.

1921   Discovery of Signal Oil Field at Long Beach.

1930   Population 5,677,251.

1935   Hoover Dam completed.

1936   San Francisco–Oakland Bridge opened.

1937   Golden Gate Bridge opened.

1938   "Dust Bowl" immigration—10,000 persons per month.

1939   Golden Gate International Exposition.

1940   All-American Canal for irrigation of Imperial Valley completed.

1945   United Nations formed at San Francisco.

1948   Coachella Main Canal completed.

1957 State-wide Water Plan adopted. Oroville Dam started.

1963 California acknowledged as the most populous state (17,300,-000).

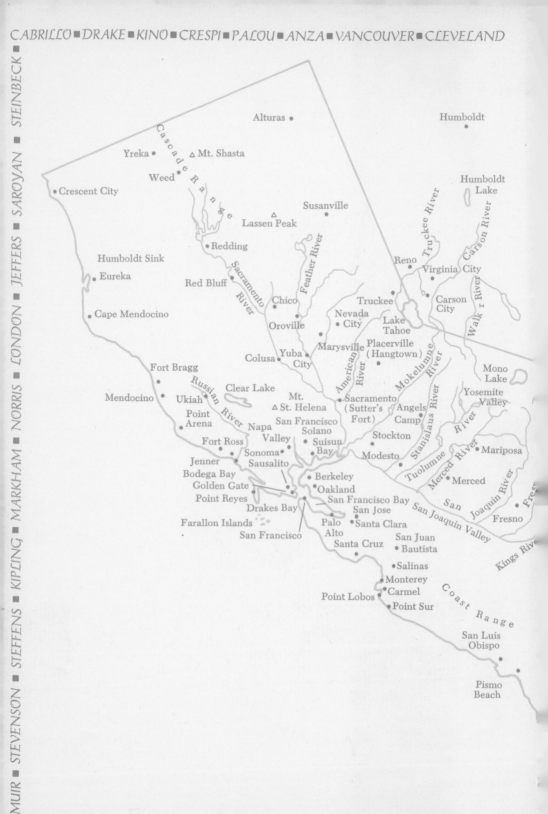